Globe Law and Business

Beneficial Ownership Registers

The STEP Handbook for Advisers

Consulting Editor **Paolo Panico**

Consulting editor
Paolo Panico

Managing director
Sian O'Neill

Beneficial Ownership Registers: The STEP Handbook for Advisers
is published by

Globe Law and Business Ltd
3 Mylor Close
Horsell
Woking
Surrey GU21 4DD
United Kingdom
Tel: +44 20 3745 4770
www.globelawandbusiness.com

Printed and bound by CPI Group (UK) Ltd, Croydon CR0 4YY, United Kingdom

Beneficial Ownership Registers: The STEP Handbook for Advisers

ISBN 9781787424142
EPUB ISBN 9781787424159
Adobe PDF ISBN 9781787424166

Table of contents

Beneficial ownership registers in Europe under the Fourth and Fifth AML Directives

Paolo Panico
Paolo Panico's Law Chambers; Private Trustees SA

1. Introduction

Since 2015 a growing political pressure has been mounting in Europe for the creation of public beneficial ownership registers of companies and trusts.

The United Kingdom was the first country in the world (or at least in the G20) to enact a public register of the 'Persons with Significant Control' (PSC) over UK corporate entities (the PSC Register). The Small Business Enterprise and Employment Act 2015 was granted Royal Assent on 26 March 2015 and provided for the creation of the PSC register in 2016.

At the same time, the legislative and regulatory production in relation to the fight against money laundering and terrorist financing significantly intensified in the European Union. Directive (EU) 2015/849 (the Fourth Anti-Money Laundering Directive – 4AMLD) was published in the *Official Journal* on 5 June 2015.[1] Prior to its coming into force in most EU member states, the European Commission proposed some relevant amendments which became Directive (EU) 2018/843 (the Fifth Anti-Money Laundering Directive – 5AMLD), which was published in the *Official Journal* on 19 June 2018[2] and should have come into force all over the European Union by January 2020.

These far-reaching legislative exercises commenced 10 years after the coming into force of Directive 2005/60/EC (the Third Anti-Money Laundering Directive – 3AMLD), which had significantly expanded the range of measures available to law enforcement agencies against money laundering and terrorist financing.

The massive publication of purloined information from offshore law firms, known as the 'Panama Papers' in 2016 and the 'Paradise Papers' in 2017, contributed to the political discussion that gave rise to 4AMLD and 5AMLD. In particular, a political position prevailed which would command full disclosure of the ultimate beneficial owners of corporate entities and trusts. As a result, 4AMLD imposed an obligation on all EU member states to create central

1 OJ L 141/73.
2 OJ L 156 /43.

registers of the beneficial owners of companies and trusts. 5AMLD expanded the access to these registers by the general public.

Articles 30 and 31 of 4AMLD deal with the creation, update and maintenance of beneficial ownership registers. Those provisions were significantly amended under 5AMLD, especially in respect of the public access to such registers.

This chapter reviews the main principles underlying the central registers of beneficial owners under 4AMLD and 5AMLD. Some elements of confidentiality are preserved in relation to trusts (but not in relation to companies) due to an important ruling by the French Constitutional Court of 2016,[3] which is also discussed in some detail.

The specific implementation of these principles in individual EU countries will be dealt with in detail in the following chapters of this book. To the extent that such national legislation is meant to implement the relevant EU directives, it will be interesting to assess to what extent some EU member states have just enacted the EU principles and in which cases they have overstepped the directives.

2. 4AMLD and the idea of beneficial ownership registers

4AMLD introduced an obligation for all EU member states to create a central register of the beneficial owners of companies and trusts.

2.1 The beneficial ownership register of companies under 4AMLD

Article 30(1) of 4AMLD reads as follows:

> *(1) Member States shall ensure that corporate and other legal entities incorporated within their territory are required to obtain and hold adequate, accurate and current information on their beneficial ownership, including the details of the beneficial interests held.*

Some EU jurisdictions have enforced this provision by obliging all corporate entities to create and maintain an internal 'register of beneficial owners'. It must be noted that the obligation to duly identify the beneficial owners was already in existence under 3AMLD for all professionally managed companies.

In addition to that, Article 30(3) of 4AMLD provides for the creation of a central register of beneficial owners:

> *(3) Member States shall ensure that the information referred to in paragraph 1 is held in a central register in each Member State, for example a commercial register, companies register [...], or a public register. Member States shall notify to the Commission the characteristics of those national mechanisms. The information on beneficial ownership in that data base may be collected in accordance with national systems.*

The access to such a central register was determined under Article 30(5) of 4AMLD:

---

3 France, Constitutional Court, Decision 2016-591 QPC of 21 October 2016, "Miss Helen S".

(5) Member States shall ensure that the information on the beneficial ownership is accessible in all cases:

(a) to competent authorities and FIUs, without any restriction;

(b) to obliged entities, within the framework of customer due diligence in accordance with Chapter II;

(c) to any person or organisation that can demonstrate a legitimate interest.

The persons and organisations referred to in point (c) shall access at least the name, the month and year of birth, the nationality and the country of residence of the beneficial owner as well as the nature and extent of the beneficial interest held.

For the purposes of this paragraph access to the information on beneficial ownership shall be in accordance with data protection rules and may be subject to online registration and to the payment of a fee. The fees charged for obtaining the information shall not exceed the administrative costs thereof.

Unrestricted access to the beneficial ownership register of companies would therefore be granted under 4AMLD to the authorities in charge of fighting against money laundering and to law enforcement agencies. An actual list of the 'competent authorities' would be drawn up in the implementing legislation of each individual member state. Unrestricted access was also granted to 'obliged entities' (ie, financial intermediaries, accountants and auditors, as well as legal professionals) when conducting customer due diligence (the activity regulated in Chapter II of the directive).[4] Finally, any natural or legal person could inspect the contents of the beneficial ownership register in relation to a specific entity provided that a 'legitimate interest test' would be passed. The directive does not specify the nature of such 'legitimate interest', but the implementing legislation of several member states introduced a fairly narrow test which specifically links 'legitimate interest' to the fight against money laundering.[5]

---

4 The definition of 'obliged entities' can be found at Article 2(1) of 4AMLD, which covers the following professionals:
(1) credit institutions;
(2) financial institutions;
(3) the following natural or legal persons acting in the exercise of their professional activities:
(a) auditors, external accountants and tax advisors;
(b) notaries and other independent legal professionals, where they participate, whether by acting on behalf of and for their client in any financial or real estate transaction, or by assisting in the planning or carrying out of transactions for their client concerning the:
(i) buying and selling of real property or business entities;
(ii) managing of client money, securities or other assets;
(iii) opening or management of bank, savings or securities accounts;
(iv) organisation of contributions necessary for the creation, operation or management of companies;
(v) creation, operation or management of trusts, companies, foundations, or similar structures;
(c) trust or company service providers not already covered under point (a) or (b);
(d) estate agents;
(e) other persons trading in goods to the extent that payments are made or received in cash in an amount of EUR 10 000 or more, whether the transaction is carried out in a single operation or in several operations which appear to be linked;
(f) providers of gambling services.

5 An example was the original Section 15 of the Austrian Beneficial Ownership Register Law (*Wirtschaftliche Eigentümer Registergesetz*), which was repealed in favour of unrestricted public access in 2020.

2.2 The beneficial ownership register of trusts under 4AMLD

Article 31 of 4AMLD introduced the obligation on all EU member states to create a beneficial ownership register of trusts.

Similar to the case of companies, the first obligation is for trustees to acquire and update adequate information on the 'beneficial owners' of their trust. More precisely:

> *(1) Member States shall require that trustees of any express trust governed under their law obtain and hold adequate, accurate and up-to-date information on beneficial ownership regarding the trust. That information shall include the identity of:*
>
> *(a) the settlor;*
>
> *(b) the trustee(s);*
>
> *(c) the protector (if any);*
>
> *(d) the beneficiaries or class of beneficiaries; and*
>
> *(e) any other natural person exercising effective control over the trust.*

This obligation was already in place under 3AMLD, which had expressly introduced it for professional trustees. Thus, 4AMLD extended it to all trustees (not only professional ones qualifying as 'obliged entities' for the purposes of the directive) of express trusts. The wording was perhaps infelicitous as it referred to express trusts "governed by the laws" of the member state. The only EU member states that had a domestic law governing trusts at the time were the United Kingdom, Ireland, Malta and Cyprus (ie, the common law jurisdictions), as well as Hungary and the Czech Republic due to recent legislative developments. For all the other EU member states a beneficial ownership register for trusts would not have been mandatory, even though Article 31(8) of 4AMLD provided for an extension of the obligation to similar arrangements:

> *(8) Member States shall ensure that the measures provided for in this Article apply to other types of legal arrangements having a structure or functions similar to trusts.*

Some of these loopholes would be closed under 5AMLD, which extended significantly the reach of a beneficial ownership register for trusts and similar arrangements, as is discussed in section 3 below.

Another condition for trusts to be the subject matter of a beneficial ownership register was that they "generate tax consequences". The wording of Article 31(4) is as follows:

> *(4) Member States shall require that the information referred to in paragraph 1 is held in a central register when the trust generates tax consequences. The central register shall ensure timely and unrestricted access by competent authorities and FIUs, without alerting the parties to the trust concerned. It may also allow timely access by obliged entities, within the framework of customer due diligence in accordance with Chapter II. Member States shall notify to the Commission the characteristics of those national mechanisms.*

'Tax consequences' are not defined in the directive and only the United Kingdom and Malta articulated a definition to this effect. No other jurisdiction legislated along this line, however, as 5AMLD radically amended Article 31 so that the current condition for a trust to be entered into the beneficial ownership register of a member state is that it is managed by a trustee in that member state, not that it is governed by the law of that member state and produces tax consequences there.

Access to the beneficial ownership register of trusts under 4AMLD was not open to the public. Only the 'competent authorities' and 'obliged entities' performing customer due diligence could access its information.

3. 5AMLD and the extension of public access

4AMLD was due to come into force by 26 June 2017, but less than half of the 28 EU member states had passed the required implementing legislation on the due date.

One of the reasons for this significant delay in a majority of EU member states was the human rights issues raised by the creation of central registers of beneficial owners which would be partially available to the general public. Articles 7 and 8 of the EU Charter of Fundamental Rights protect the fundamental right to privacy, both in relation to private and family life, and to personal data.[6] Public access to the beneficial ownership information of companies may represent a breach to such fundamental right.

Nevertheless, the EU Commission pushed through a series of amendments to 4AMLD, which substantially increased the opportunities for the public to access beneficial ownership information. The European Data Protection Supervisor had expressed some serious concerns about the extension of public access to beneficial ownership information,[7] but the European Parliament overwhelmingly voted for the amendments which led to 5AMLD.[8]

---

6 EU Charter of Fundamental Rights:
Article 7 – *Respect for private and family life*
Everyone has the right to respect for his or her private and family life, home and communications.
Article 8 – *Respect of personal data*
Everyone has the right of protection of personal data concerning him or her.
Such data must be processed fairly for specified purposes and on the basis of the consent of the person concerned or some legitimate basis laid down by law. Everyone has the right of access to data which has been collected concerning him or her, and the right to have it rectified.
Compliance with these rules shall be subject to control by an independent authority.

7 European Data Protection Supervisor, "Opinion 1/2017 on a Commission Proposal amending Directive (EU) 2015/849 and Directive 2009/101/EC. Access to beneficial ownership information and data protection implications" of 2 February 2017.

8 On 27 February 2017 the Economic and Monetary Affairs and Civil Liberties Committee of the European Parliament voted by 89 to 1 (and 4 abstentions) in favour of unrestricted public access to the beneficial ownership information of companies and trusts with no need to demonstrate a 'legitimate interest'. A different treatment was eventually granted to trusts where the 'legitimate interest' requirement has remained in place, as is discussed in section 3.2.

3.1 The beneficial ownership register of companies under 5AMLD

The new Article 30(5), as amended under 5AMLD, reads as follows:

(5) Member States shall ensure that the information on the beneficial ownership is accessible in all cases:

(a) to competent authorities and FIUs, without any restriction;

(b) to obliged entities, within the framework of customer due diligence in accordance with Chapter II;

(c) any member of the general public.

The persons and organisations referred to in point (c) shall be permitted to access at least the name, the month and year of birth, the nationality and the country of residence of the beneficial owner as well as the nature and extent of the beneficial interest held.

Member States may, under conditions to be determined in national law, provide for access of additional information enabling the identification of the beneficial owner. That additional information shall include at least the date of birth or contact details in accordance with data protection rules.

The main difference between this version and the original one under 4AMLD is paragraph (c): the register is no longer reserved to "any person or organisation that can demonstrate a legitimate interest", but is accessible to "any member of the general public".

It is legitimate to question whether indiscriminate, unrestricted access to the beneficial ownership information of companies is in fact a breach of the fundamental right to privacy under Articles 7 and 8 of the EU Charter of Fundamental Rights. It is difficult to seriously believe that this publicity will make an effective contribution to the fight against money laundering which justifies this interference with such a fundamental human right. At the same time, fully public beneficial ownership registers represent an intrusion into the private lives of hundreds of thousands, if not millions, of law abiding citizens whose personal information may be accessed not only by law enforcement agencies or 'obliged entities' performing customer due diligence, but also by people furthering dishonest purposes and relying on anonymous access to such information.[9]

It may be useful to quote here some relevant sections of the Opinion 1/2017 issued by the European Data Protection Supervisor (EDPS) in relation to the EU Commission's Proposal to amend 4AMLD and make beneficial ownership information available to the general public.

The EDPS noted in the first place that a fundamental principle of data protection, that of purpose limitation, was expressly infringed by the European Commission. In other words:

9 It must be noted that the beneficial ownership registers of some EU member states may be accessed without being identified. For example, the Luxembourg register of beneficial owners of companies (*Registre des Bénéficiaires Effectifs*) can be freely accessed by an 'anonymous user' simply by replying to a query such as 'what is half of 8?'.

65 The Commission is proposing new amendments to the AML Directive in order to put it up to speed with technical and financial innovation and new means to perform money laundering and terrorist financing. At the same time the Proposal aims at improving the transparency of financial markets for a number of purposes that we identify, among others, in the fight against tax evasion, protection of investors and fight against abuses of the financial system.

This led to the following conclusion in the Executive Summary to the Opinion:

Processing personal data collected for one purpose for another, completely unrelated purpose infringes the data protection principle of purpose limitation and threatens the implementation of the principle of proportionality. The amendments, in particular, raise questions as to why certain forms of invasive personal data processing, acceptable in relation to anti-money laundering and the fight against terrorism, are necessary out of those contexts and on whether they are proportionate.

[..]

Last, and most importantly, the amendments significantly broaden access to beneficial ownership information by both competent authorities and the public, as a policy tool to facilitate and optimise enforcement of tax obligations. We see, in the way such solution is implemented, a lack of proportionality, with significant and unnecessary risk for the individual rights to privacy and data protection.

The EDPS made express reference to the European Court of Justice (ECJ) decision in *Österreichischer Rundfunk*,[10] where it was discussed whether the policy objective "could not have been attained equally effectively by transmitting the information as to names to the monitoring bodies alone". 4AMLD already provided for unrestricted access to beneficial ownership information by the "competent authorities". It remains to be seen whether its extension to the general public respects the principle of proportionality. A judicial review to this effect was triggered in the last quarter of 2020 by the Luxembourg district court, which referred a case to the ECJ.

It is hoped that the ECJ decision on this matter will bring back a reasonable balance between the two equally deserving purposes of increased transparency in the financial market and the protection of the fundamental right to privacy of individual beneficial owners.

The EDPS drafted its Opinion at the beginning of 2017 when the EU Commission's Proposal essentially provided for unrestricted public access to the beneficial ownership information of both companies and trusts. However, the final version of 5AMLD maintains a "legitimate interest test" in relation to trusts. The French Constitutional Court decision of 21 October 2016[11] played an important role in this respect.

---

10 ECJ, Judgment of 20 May 2003, joint cases C 465/00, C 138/01 and C 139/01.

11 Quoted *supra*, footnote 3.

3.2 Public access to the beneficial ownership information of trusts: the French Constitutional Court decision

French residents who are settlors or beneficiaries of foreign trusts, as well as foreign trustees of such trusts and of trusts that include French property, have been subject to a reporting obligation to the French tax authorities since 2011. The Law 2011-900 of 29 July 2011 rectifying the Budget Law of 2011[12] introduced this obligation for the first time.

The French Law 2013-1117 of 6 December 2013 against tax fraud and serious economic and financial crime[13] provided for the creation of a register within the Ministry of Finance based on the information supplied by French taxpayers (and possibly foreign trustees) in compliance with the obligation introduced in 2011. The register was created under a new Article 1649 AB of the French General Tax Code.

4AMLD was published in the *Official Journal* on 5 June 2015, as we have seen, and in its original redaction did not directly apply to France as far as trusts are concerned. The original Article 31, as we have seen, provided for the creation of a register of beneficial owners of trusts governed by the law of each member state. France has no domestic trust law apart from the *'fiducie'* introduced into the Civil Code under the Law 2007-211 of 19 February 2007,[14] which has its own express system of publicity.

Independently of the debates which led to 5AMLD, on 10 May 2016 the French minister of finance issued Decree 2016-567, which provided for the trust register to be freely searchable online by the name of the trust or by the name of an individual.[15] It must be noted that this register had been created in 2013 based on information that the French Ministry of Finance had received from complying French taxpayers. In a sense, the decree opened up a section of those taxpayers' tax returns to public inspection.

Ms Helen S, an American lady who lived in France and had organised her succession by way of various trusts, took issue at this indiscriminate publicity and petitioned the French Constitutional Court (*Conseil Constitutionnel*) on the compatibility of the decree creating a public register of trusts with the French Constitution. A first result was obtained on 22 July 2016, when public access to the register was blocked pending the determination of the issue.[16]

The decision of 21 October 2016 definitively held that a public register of trusts is unconstitutional and even contrary to the Declaration of the Rights of Man and the Citizen of 1789. More precisely:

(3) The freedom proclaimed by Article 2 of the 1789 Declaration of the Rights of

---

12 *France, Loi 2011-900 du 29 juillet 2011 de finances rectificative pour 2011.*

13 *France, Loi 2013-1117 du 6 décembre 2013 relative à la lutte contre la fraude fiscale et la grande délinquance économique et financière.*

14 *France, Loi 2007-211 du 19 février 2007 instituant la fiducie.*

15 *France, Décret 2016-567 du 10 mai 2016 relatif au registre public des trusts.*

16 France, Constitutional Court, Decision 2016-555 QPC of 22 July 2016.

Man and the Citizen implies the right to respect for private life; Owing to this, collecting, recording, keeping, consulting and communicating information of a personal nature shall be justified by general interest and implemented in an adequate and proportional manner.

[...]

(6) Listing, in a registry accessible to the public, the names of the settlor, the beneficiaries and the administrator of a trust provides information on the manner in which a person intends to manage his or her estate. The result is an infringement on the right of respect for private life. However, the legislature, which did not specify the quality nor the motives that justify consulting the registry, did not limit the people that have access to the information in this registry, placed under the responsibility of the tax administration. Therefore, these disputed provisions have a clearly disproportionate effect on the right of respect for private life in regard to the objectives sought. As a result, without reviewing other grievances, the second paragraph of Article 1649 AB of the General Tax Code should be declared counter to the Constitution.

To the extent that the Declaration of the Rights of Man and the Citizen is at the basis of most modern European legal systems, the French constitutional court judgment had a very significant bearing on the shaping of 5AMLD. As a result, under the far-reaching amendments which were brought about by the new directive, an element of confidentiality was preserved in relation to trusts. Only persons demonstrating a legitimate interest, and not the general public indiscriminately, will be allowed to access the beneficial ownership register of trusts.

3.3 The beneficial ownership register of trusts under 5AMLD

Article 31 of 4AMLD was significantly amended under 5AMLD. The amendments encompassed the definition of trusts and other legal arrangements which must be entered into the beneficial ownership register, as well as the conditions to access such register.

The new Article 31(1) reads as follows:

(1) Member States shall ensure that this Article applies to trusts and other types of legal arrangements, such as, inter alia, fiducie, *certain types of* Treuhand *or* fideicomiso *where such arrangements have a structure or functions similar to trusts. Member states shall identify the characteristics to determine where legal arrangements have a structure or functions similar to trusts with regard to such legal arrangements governed under their law.*

Each Member State shall require that trustees of any express trust administered in that Member State obtain and hold adequate, accurate and up-to-date information on beneficial ownership regarding the trust. That information shall include the identity of:

(a) the settlor(s);

(b) the trustee(s);

(c) the protector (if any);

(d) the beneficiaries or class of beneficiaries; and

(e) any other natural person exercising effective control over the trust.

Member States shall ensure that breaches of this Article are subject to effective, proportionate and dissuasive measures or sanctions.

Express trusts 'administered' in an EU member state, as opposed to 'governed under its law', are now the subject matter of the beneficial ownership register under 5AMLD. This expands the application of Article 31 to virtually all EU member states, including those which do not have a domestic trust law. Some civil law member states recognise trusts under the Hague Convention of 1 July 1985 on the Law Applicable to Trusts and on their Recognition (the Hague Trusts Convention): Italy, the Netherlands and Luxembourg.[17] Other member states recognise trusts under express provisions in their private international law, such as Belgium,[18] Romania[19] and the Czech Republic.[20] In any case, a trust may be administered in an EU member state even though its domestic law does not recognise it as a legal arrangement, provided that a trustee is based in that jurisdiction or the trust fund includes property situated there.[21]

Furthermore, all EU member states have in their domestic legal systems "other types of legal arrangements, such as, *inter alia, fiducie,* certain types of *Treuhand* or *fideicomiso* where such arrangements have a structure or functions similar to trusts". Each member state should therefore determine which of its domestic legal arrangements are 'similar' to trusts for the purposes of creating a register of their beneficial owners. It must be noted that private foundations, which are a substitute for trusts under the laws of several EU member states (Austria, Belgium, the Czech Republic, Estonia, Germany, Hungary, Malta and the Netherlands), tend to be treated in some cases as companies (with a publicly accessible beneficial ownership register) and in some other member states as trusts (where access to the register is subject to a 'legitimate interest test').

The international experience of trusts shows that a majority of trustees are based outside of the European Union. A new Article 31(3a) deals with this case and extends the obligation to register the beneficial owners of trusts administered outside the European Union but having certain connections to a member state:

(3a) Member States shall require that the beneficial ownership information of express trusts and similar legal arrangements as referred to in paragraph 1

---

17 The United Kingdom, Malta and Cyprus have also ratified the Hague Trusts Convention, but in their case a trust register would also have been a requirement under 4AMLD by virtue of their domestic trust law.

18 Belgium, Code of Private International Law of 16 July 2004, Chapter XII (Articles 122–124).

19 Romania, New Civil Code (in force since 1 October 2011), Articles 2659–2662.

20 Czech Republic, Law 91/2012 on Private International Law (in force since 1 January 2014), Section 73.

21 The UK Supreme Court confirmed this principle in *Akers v Samba Financial Group* [2017] UKS 6, in the case of a trust of shares in a Saudi Arabian company.

shall be held in a central beneficial ownership register set up by the Member State where the trustee of the trust or person holding an equivalent position in a similar legal arrangement is established or resides.

Where the place of establishment or residence of the trustee or the trust or person holding an equivalent position in similar legal arrangement is outside the Union, the information referred to in paragraph 1 shall be held in a central register set up by the Member State where the trustee of the trust or person holding an equivalent position in a similar legal arrangement enters into a business relationship or acquires real estate in the name of the trust or similar legal arrangement.

Where the trustees of a trust or persons holding equivalent positions in a similar legal arrangement are established or reside in different Member States, or where the trustee of the trust or person holding an equivalent position in a similar legal arrangement enters into multiple business relationships in the name of the trust or similar legal arrangement in different Member States, a certificate of proof of registration or an excerpt of the beneficial ownership information held in a register by one Member State may be considered as sufficient to consider the registration obligation fulfilled.

In other words:

- a trust with a single trustee based in an EU member state will have to publish the information of its beneficial owners (as defined under 5AMLD) in the trust register created in that member state;[22]
- a trust with more than one trustee, based in different EU member states, may register in the trust register of one member state only;
- a trust with a trustee based outside of the European Union will have to be entered into the trust register of the EU member state where the trust "enters into a business relationship or acquires real estate".

While the acquisition of real estate in an EU member state creates a clear condition for a trust to publish its beneficial ownership information in the trust register of that member state, the directive does not define the concept of a 'business relationship' for these specific purposes. Various interpretations have been advanced, but it is up to the implementing legislation of each EU member state to specify the circumstances under which a trust administered by a non-EU trustee will have to be entered into the local trust register.

Not only has the definition of 'trusts' been significantly expanded by a shift from the governing law to the place of administration, but access to the beneficial ownership information of trusts is now determined by the new Article 31(5) of 5AMLD:

22 Although trusts have no legal personality, some short-cut expressions are used in this chapter, as they appear to be easier than sentences referring to the fact that the trustee has to perform the corresponding actions in the name of the trust.

(4) Member States shall ensure that the information on the beneficial ownership of a trust or a similar legal arrangement is accessible in all cases to:

(a) competent authorities and FIUs, without any restriction;

(b) obliged entities, within the framework of customer due diligence in accordance with Chapter II;

(c) any natural or legal person that can demonstrate a legitimate interest;

(d) any natural or legal person that files a written request in relation to a trust or similar legal arrangement which holds or owns a controlling interest in any corporate or other legal entity other than those referred to in Article 30(1), through direct or indirect ownership, including through bearer shareholdings, or through control via other means.

The information accessible to natural or legal persons referred to in points (c) and (d) of the first subparagraph shall consist of the name, the month and year of birth and the country of residence and nationality of the beneficial owner, as well as the nature and extent of beneficial interest held.

Trust registers remain fully accessible with no restrictions to the 'competent authorities', as well as to financial intermediaries and other regulated professionals performing customer due diligence, as was the case under 4AMLD. In addition to that, the new paragraph (c) extends access to "any natural or legal person that can demonstrate a legitimate interest". This was originally the condition for access to the beneficial ownership register of companies under 4AMLD and is now extended to trusts. 'Legitimate interest' is still not defined under 5AMLD and the same criteria that were worked out for companies in the legislation of the EU member states that have enacted 4AMLD are therefore extended to trusts.

The new paragraph (d), which was inserted under 5AMLD, is more puzzling. It provides for unrestricted public access (the only condition is a written request) to the beneficial ownership information of trusts which hold a controlling interest in a company outside of the European Union. It is difficult to understand the rationale for this provision. A literal construction appears to lead to the following cases.

- A trust administered by a trustee in an EU member state with no shareholdings in any companies will have its beneficial ownership information accessible only to people who can demonstrate a legitimate interest.
- A trust administered by a trustee in an EU member state with a shareholding in an EU company will have its beneficial ownership information accessible only to people who can demonstrate a legitimate interest. In addition to that, the information of the persons who qualify as 'beneficial owners' of the underlying EU company will be accessible to the general public in the corresponding beneficial ownership register of companies (the determination of these persons may vary from one EU member state to another).

- A trust administered by a trustee in an EU member state with a controlling interest in a company outside the European Union will have its beneficial ownership information accessible to any member of the general public who makes a written request.
- A trust administered by a trustee outside the European Union with a shareholding in an EU company may have its beneficial ownership information published in the trust register of the EU jurisdiction where the underlying company has its registered office, if such a shareholding qualifies as a 'business relationship' under the legislation of that member state. The beneficial ownership information of that trust will be accessible only to people who can demonstrate a legitimate interest. In addition to that, the information of the persons qualifying as 'beneficial owners' of the underlying EU company will be accessible in the corresponding beneficial ownership register of companies.
- A trust administered by a trustee outside of the European Union with shareholdings in one or more companies outside the European Union is outside the scope of the EU directives.

Of course, the beneficial ownership information of all these types of trust (except the one which is outside the scope of the EU directives) will also be available to the competent authorities, as well as to financial intermediaries performing customer due diligence.

It is difficult to understand the rationale for this difference of treatment, particularly in relation to a trust holding a controlling interest in a non-EU company. Unrestricted public access to the beneficial ownership information of trusts is an infringement of the fundamental right to the respect of private life under the Declaration of the Rights of Man and the Citizen of 1789 (as discussed in section 3.2 above). It appears unlikely that a trust holding a controlling interest in a company outside the European Union represents an inherently higher money laundering risk justifying such an infringement than a trust holding a corresponding shareholding in an EU company or not holding any shares in any company. The United Kingdom is a clear example to this effect: it has been a 'third country' outside of the European Union since 1 January 2021, but it is the first European nation to introduce a publicly accessible beneficial ownership register of companies.

The implementing legislation of some EU member states has clarified some of these contradictory aspects in 5AMLD. However, different approaches in different EU member states increase the overall confusion in the bloc and may lend itself to arbitration between jurisdictions following different standards for their beneficial ownership registers. The ECJ decisions on the cases referred by Luxembourg will certainly bring some additional clarity. An EU Regulation streamlining some of these issues would also be a welcome development.

The origins of beneficial ownership registers in the European Union

John Riches
RMW Law LLP; Withers LLP
Eleanor Riches-Lenaghan
RMW Law LLP

1. Anti-money laundering policy: a history

The previous decade has seen the international transparency agenda develop significantly. In 2010, a year into Barack Obama's presidency, the cross-border corporate and trusts world was bounded by some light regulation, but the horizon appeared to be clear of substantial disclosure. Jurisdictions were competing with each other, eager to attract business by demonstrating high standards, good infrastructure, a fair legal system and reliable service providers, rather than joining together in a cohesive front against a tsunami of measures and regulation.

The biggest changes in regulation in the last decade have been driven by the anti-money laundering (AML) agenda, and the automatic exchange of (tax) information. The timeline below sets out the development of the European Union's AML policy over the last 30 years and its inter-relationship with the Financial Action Task Force's (FATF) initiatives.

2. Timeline of AML policy

- 1990: FATF 40 Recommendations
- 1991: First Anti-Money Laundering Directive
- 2001: Second Anti-Money Laundering Directive
- 2002: UK Proceeds of Crime Act
- 2003: Revised FATF 40 Recommendations
- 2005: Third Anti-Money Laundering Directive
- 2008: FATF Risk-Based Approach Guidelines
- 2012: FATF Recommendations
- 2013: G8 Lough Erne Summit
- 2015: Fourth Anti-Money Laundering Directive
- 2018: Fifth Anti-Money Laundering Directive
- 2018: Revised FATF Risk-Based Approach Guidelines
- 2019: FATF Guidance to Trust and Corporate Service Providers

In the 1990s, the European Commission's schema for regulatory reporting was in its infancy. Until 2005, reporting requirements applied only to financial institutions, such as banks, insurance companies and investment firms. Professional firms such as lawyers and accountants were not required to collect and retain significant client information until circa 2007–2008, when the Third Anti-Money Laundering Directive (3AMLD) came into force. Furthermore, the timeline reveals a rapid acceleration in the rate of development in AML legislation over the last 10 years.

3. A turning point: the FATF 2012 Recommendations and Lough Erne

However, it is the FATF 2012 Recommendations (the 2012 Recommendations) that lay out the seminal architecture for beneficial ownership disclosure, particularly in Recommendations 10, 24 and 25. Yet if the 2012 Recommendations set out guidance on how to implement this concept of transparency, it was at the G8 Lough Erne Summit in 2013 that governments publicly pledged to implement the transparency agenda. The first paragraph of the Lough Erne Declaration reads as follows:

> *Private enterprise drives growth, reduces poverty, and creates jobs and prosperity for people around the world. Governments have a special responsibility to make proper rules and promote good governance. Fair taxes, increased transparency and open trade are vital drivers of this.*[1]

The governments of eight countries – of Canada, France, Germany, Italy, Japan, Russia, the United Kingdom and the United States – and the European Union are declaring that their responsibility is to uphold and promote the equitable and lawful growth of private enterprise by way of increased transparency. The first three specified action points in the Declaration encapsulate the essence of the transparency agenda in the private enterprise sector during the last decade:

1. *Tax authorities across the world should automatically share information to fight the scourge of tax evasion.*
2. *Countries should change rules that let companies shift their profits across borders to avoid taxes, and multinationals should report to tax authorities what tax they pay where.*
3. *Companies should know who really owns them and tax collectors and law enforcers should be able to obtain this information easily.*[2]

In relation to point 1 above, in 2010, the idea of the easy flow of information cross-border between tax authorities was new, and soon developed rapidly through the automatic exchange of information introduced by the US

---

1 G8 Lough Erne Declaration, 18 June 2013, www.bundesregierung.de/resource/blob/975254/388930/6098f70212e30e5b0dccedf36a70dea9/g8-lough-erne-erklaerung-en-data.pdf?download=1.

2 G8 Lough Erne Declaration.

Foreign Tax Account Compliance Act (FATCA) in 2010 and the Common Reporting Standard (CRS) introduced by the Organisation for Economic Cooperation and Development (OECD) in 2014. Point 2 is the origin of the subsequent measures to tackle 'base erosion and profit shifting', as proposed by the OECD. However, it is point 3 that sets in motion the idea that beneficial ownership information should be available to tax collectors and law enforcers. It is interesting to note that there is no reference to public access to such information, but this is perhaps the first time that the governments of eight major private enterprise countries publicly declared their commitment to scrutinising the beneficial ownership of private structures.

4. What is a 'beneficial owner'?

The text of the 2012 Recommendations sets out the basis for beneficial ownership disclosure under subsequent regulations, such as the Fourth and Fifth Anti-Money Laundering Directives (4AMLD and 5AMLD). Given how widespread beneficial ownership reporting is now, it is easy to forget that in 2012 this was a relatively novel concept. Recommendation 10 concerns customer due diligence, which at first instance involves:

> ***(b) Identifying the beneficial owner, and taking reasonable measures to verify the identity of the beneficial owner, such that the financial institution is satisfied that it knows who the beneficial owner is. For legal persons and arrangements this should include financial institutions understanding the ownership and control structure of the customer.*** [emphasis added][3]

Specifically, the Interpretive Note to Recommendation 10[4] stated the requirement to:

> *b) Identify the beneficial owners of the customer and take reasonable measures to verify the identity of such persons, through the following information:*
>
> *(i) For legal persons:*[5]
>
> *(i.i) The identity of the natural persons (if any – as ownership interests can be so diversified that there are no natural persons (whether acting alone or together) exercising control of the legal person or arrangement through ownership) who ultimately have a controlling ownership interest in a legal person; and*
>
> *(i.ii) to the extent that there is doubt under (i.i) as to whether the person(s) with the controlling ownership interest*[6] *are the beneficial owner(s) or*

3 FATF (2012–2020), *International Standards on Combating Money Laundering and the Financing of Terrorism & Proliferation*, Paris, France, www.fatf-gafi.org/recommendations.html, p14.

4 FATF International Standards, pp65–66.

5 Measures (i.i) to (i.iii) are not alternative options, but are cascading measures, with each to be used where the previous measure has been applied and has not identified a beneficial owner.

6 A controlling ownership interest depends on the ownership structure of the company. It may be based on a threshold, eg, any person owning more than a certain percentage of the company (eg, 25%).

where no natural person exerts control through ownership interests, the identity of the natural persons (if any) exercising control of the legal person or arrangement through other means.

(i.iii) Where no natural person is identified under (i.i) or (i.ii) above, financial institutions should identify and take reasonable measures to verify the identity of the relevant natural person who holds the position of senior managing official.

(ii) For legal arrangements:

(ii.i) Trusts – the identity of the settlor, the trustee(s), the protector (if any), the beneficiaries or class of beneficiaries,[7] *and any other natural person exercising ultimate effective control over the trust (including through a chain of control/ownership);*

(ii.ii) Other types of legal arrangements – the identity of persons in equivalent or similar positions.

However, while both the recommendation and its corresponding interpretive note use the headline definition of 'beneficial owner', there is, in reality, a second and distinct concept in operation: that of 'the natural person exercising effective control' (defined in this chapter as a 'controller'). The 'beneficial owner' is the person who enjoys 'the benefit of property of which another is the legal owner'.[8] A 'controller' is an individual who is not required to have a proprietary interest in, or title to, the property being reported on. While these definitions may seem self-evident, it is important to note that this is why, when applying the relevant jurisdiction's legislation, one may not end up disclosing the literal 'beneficial owner' on the beneficial ownership register at all. Of course, the purpose of these definitions within the 2012 Recommendations is to comprehend the 'ownership and control structure' of legal persons and arrangements. In some instances, this can result in the 'true' beneficial owners remaining anonymous.

5. Interaction between AML and automatic exchange of information policy

While AML policy initially dictated the scope of the transparency agenda, in recent years there has been significant cross-fertilisation between the AML agenda and the automatic exchange of taxation information, most notably the CRS. The CRS was adopted by the European Union on 1 January 2016, and in 2017 and 2018 multiple jurisdictions commenced reporting. The CRS involves the cross-border disclosure of beneficial ownership, and, once again, the issue

7 For beneficiary(ies) of trusts that are designated by characteristics or by class, financial institutions should obtain sufficient information concerning the beneficiary to satisfy the financial institution that it will be able to establish the identity of the beneficiary at the time of the payout or when the beneficiary intends to exercise vested rights.

8 'Beneficial owner', *Merriam-Webster.com Dictionary*, Merriam-Webster, www.merriam-webster.com/dictionary/owner.

of how to define a 'beneficial owner' arises. The CRS's solution is to borrow from the 2012 Recommendations. The CRS handbook states that:

> *the definition of Controlling Persons is an important additional detail [...] It must be construed in such a manner to correspond to the definition of the term "beneficial owner" as described in the Financial Action Task Force ("FATF") Recommendation 10 and the accompanying Interpretative Note as adopted in February 2012.*[9]

The policy objectives adopted by tax authorities seeking information about trusts are markedly different from those of law enforcement agencies charged with combatting organised crime in AML policy. The objectives differ, but the starting point for the relevant controlling authority is to seek to identify the key actions involved in trusts and companies, looking for the 'ultimate beneficial owner'. For companies, as set out in 2012 Recommendation 24, this usually revolves around a percentage of beneficial ownership of the company share capital, such as 25% for normal risk or 10% where there is potential for enhanced risk.

According to Recommendation 24 'Transparency and beneficial ownership of legal persons':

> *Countries should ensure that there is adequate, accurate and timely information on the beneficial ownership and control of legal persons that can be obtained or accessed in a timely fashion by competent authorities. In particular, countries that have legal persons that are able to issue bearer shares or bearer share warrants, or which allow nominee shareholders or nominee directors, should take effective measures to ensure that they are not misused for money laundering or terrorist financing.*[10]

The Interpretive Note to Recommendation 24 expands on this:

> *Controlling shareholders as referred to in paragraph 5(b)(i) of the interpretive note to Recommendation 10 may be based on a threshold, eg, any persons owning more than a certain percentage of the company (eg, 25%).*[11] [...]
>
> 3. *In order to determine who the beneficial owners of a company are, competent authorities will require certain basic information about the company, which, at a minimum, would include information about the legal ownership and control structure of the company. This would include information about the status and powers of the company, its shareholders and its directors.*[12]

These rules cast a wide net in the context of whom should be identified as a beneficial owner. When the 2012 Recommendations were published, it was only necessary for a company to disclose a person (legal or individual) who owned a

---

9 OECD (2018), *Standard for Automatic Exchange of Financial Information in Tax Matters – Implementation Handbook*, Second Edition, OECD, Paris, p21.

10 FATF (2012–2020), *International Standards on Combating Money Laundering and the Financing of Terrorism & Proliferation*, FATF, Paris, France, www.fatf-gafi.org/recommendations.html, p22.

11 FATF International Standards, p91, footnote 46.

12 *Ibid*, p91.

25% interest, or a 10% interest if enhanced due diligence was required. However, for trusts, one always had to identify the settlor, the beneficiaries, the protector and the person exercising effective control, as set out in Recommendation 25.

Recommendation 25 'Transparency and beneficial ownership of legal arrangements' reads as follows:

Countries should ensure that there is adequate, accurate and timely information on express trusts, including information on the settlor, trustee and beneficiaries, that can be obtained or accessed in a timely fashion by competent authorities.[13]

The Interpretive Note to Recommendation 25[14] then expands on this, setting out that:

1. *Countries should require trustees of any express trust governed under their law to obtain and hold adequate, accurate, and current beneficial ownership information regarding the trust. This should include information on the identity of the settlor, the trustee(s), the protector (if any), the beneficiaries or class of beneficiaries, and any other natural person exercising ultimate effective control over the trust. Countries should also require trustees of any trust governed under their law to hold basic information on other regulated agents of, and service providers to, the trust, including investment advisors or managers, accountants, and tax advisors.*
2. *All countries should take measures to ensure that trustees disclose their status to financial institutions and Designated Non-Financial Businesses and Professions (DNFBPs) when, as a trustee, forming a business relationship or carrying out an occasional transaction above the threshold. Trustees should not be prevented by law or enforceable means from providing competent authorities with any information relating to the trusts; or from providing financial institutions and DNFBPs, upon request, with information on the beneficial ownership and the assets of the trust to be held or managed under the terms of the business relationship.*
3. *Countries are encouraged to ensure that other relevant authorities, persons and entities hold information on all trusts with which they have a relationship. Potential sources of information on trusts, trustees, and trust assets are:*
   (a) Registries (eg, a central registry of trusts or trust assets), or asset registries for land, property, vehicles, shares or other assets.
   (b) Other competent authorities that hold information on trusts and trustees (eg, tax authorities which collect information on assets and income relating to trusts).
   (c) Other agents and service providers to the trust, including investment advisors or managers, lawyers, or trust and company service providers.

13 FATF International Standards, p22.
14 FATF International Standards, pp96–97.

4. *Competent authorities, and in particular law enforcement authorities, should have all the powers necessary to obtain timely access to the information held by trustees and other parties, in particular information held by financial institutions and DNFBPs on: (a) the beneficial ownership; (b) the residence of the trustee; and (c) any assets held or managed by the financial institution or DNFBP, in relation to any trustees with which they have a business relationship, or for which they undertake an occasional transaction.*

6. Definition of 'beneficial ownership' in relation to trusts

In the case of trusts, from inception a markedly different approach was adopted. As with Recommendation 10 noted above, Recommendation 25 seeks to identify all beneficial owners for a trust without reference to a materiality or percentage test. The common list is:

- settlors;
- trustees;
- beneficiaries;
- protectors (if any); and
- any other natural person exercising effective control ('controllers').

The policy rationale for setting a lower effective threshold for trusts, in defining the 'beneficial owner', as compared with companies and comparable legal persons, is based on the perception from policy makers that the more fluid nature of a trust and the division between legal and beneficial ownership inherent in such an arrangement means, in the absence of identifying all actors, there could be scope for improper manipulation that would assist the aim of – in the relevant context – tax evaders, criminals or terrorists.

However, there is also wide consensus among policy makers that whatever the theoretical risks that may exist through such manipulation, practical experience suggests that trusts are not commonly used as direct vehicles for money laundering or terrorist financing. This is because their creation and ongoing administration inevitably require the assistance of regulated parties such as trust and corporate service providers, lawyers and accountants who will scrutinise the trust and its usage to an extent that is not required in the context of corporate entities. It is far simpler to put the legal ownership of shares into the name of a third-party nominee who can, more easily, act as a 'front' for hidden third parties.

This is a central point that the advocates of centralised beneficial ownership registers sometimes fail to acknowledge. Those whose intentions are to commit crime or finance terrorism do so by concealing their identity and lying to achieve that goal. The effectiveness of central registers that record the names of registered owners may, in certain circumstances, be of limited utility in actually achieving the registers' goals, especially if those filing the information are disposed to conceal their identity.

In relation to disclosing beneficiaries on the register, the United Kingdom's HM Revenue and Customs, for example, has provided guidance that where beneficiaries are identified generally by reference to a class rather than by naming specific individuals, it is sufficient to record the class as a whole in the register unless and until one reaches the position where a specific member of that class receives an actual distribution. This is considered to be a sensible and practical approach. It is interesting to note that the response to these developments from those advising families establishing new trusts are actively considering a more subtle approach to beneficial classes; settlors are favouring more generic descriptions among younger beneficiaries who are not expected to benefit until a later point. Alternatively, the trust may be established with a relatively narrow class of beneficiaries but with a power to add that could be used at the relevant time to add beneficiaries to the class prior to a distribution.

7. Characterisation of 'control' under the 2012 Recommendations

In relation to protectors and other controllers, the characterisation of 'control' for the purpose of the 2012 Recommendations appears to have a commonplace approach to individuals who may, while not being trustees, have some practical influence over certain aspects of the trust. It is unfortunate and, in many senses, unhelpful that the policy language has fixed on the word 'control' to characterise the control of such power holders. In many cases, the role concerned is intended to act as a form of check or balance over the unlimited discretion of the trustees. While there may be instances where reserve powers exist such that a power holder does exercise a degree of 'control' over some aspect of trust operation, this is very much the exception rather than the rule. That being said, unfortunately, we are not in a position to wind back the clock and persuade policy makers to use a more accurate and descriptive phrase to cover such actors as an umbrella term.

One has some sympathy with policy makers in this context. There may be instances where protectors will have vastly different powers from one trust to another. Equally, there are circumstances in which an individual who is given key powers in relation to a trust (eg, an enforcer of a purpose trust) is not a protector but has powers that might be seen as commensurate – for example, the power to enforce the purposes established by the trust or indeed a power to appoint and remove trustees. It is hardly surprising, in this context, that inconsistencies have emerged in the way in which power holders are characterised when different definitions are adopted for the purposes of identifying beneficial owners.

In light of this 'cross-over' of FATF concepts into the CRS, it is therefore noteworthy to turn to the 2019 guidance issued by FATF to trust and corporate service providers.

8. Updates to FATF Guidance – 2019 Guidance to trust and company service providers

In updating its risk-based guidance to trust and company service providers (TCSPs) in 2019, FATF rectified the absence of a formal definition, since 2012, of 'a natural person exercising effective control'. While for certain purposes policy makers may have found it helpful to adopt an open definition without clear parameters, it was clear to many that the absence of any guidance in this area was deeply unhelpful, particularly in circumstances where different service providers, such as banks, were taking an inconsistent position on this definition.

In this context, it is interesting to note that the model that FATF adopted in the Annex to its 2019 Guidance was, perhaps unsurprisingly, to adopt an expansive definition of who might be regarded as a controller in relation to a trust. The language has been taken (with some significant amendments) from the definition of 'control' used by the United Kingdom in its transposition of 4AMLD into its domestic law. It reads as follows:

Natural person exercising effective control

b) For these purposes "control" means a power (whether exercisable alone or jointly with another person or with the consent of another person) under the trust instrument or by law to:

i. dispose of or invest (other than as an investment manager or adviser) trust property;

ii. direct, make or approve trust distributions;

iii. vary or terminate the trust;

iv. add or remove a person as a beneficiary or to or from a class of beneficiaries and or;

v. appoint or remove trustees.

c) TCSPs who administer the trust or otherwise act as trustee must, in addition, also obtain information to satisfy itself that it knows the identity of any other individual who has power to give another individual "control" over the trust; by conferring on such individual powers as described in paragraph (b) above.[15]

Notably, while this definition references the exercise of effective control, the definitions focus on the mere capacity to exercise that control without any factual tests as to whether the powers are actually being exercised in that way. It is also clear, for these purposes, that where more than one individual has the capacity to exercise a power, he or she is attributed with the power of others. Thirdly, it is not possible to argue that the individual lacks control merely because another person needs to consent to the exercise of that power. If one turns to the five instances of power that are equated with control, it can be

15 FATF (2019), *Guidance for a Risk-Based Approach for Trust & Company Service Providers (TSCPs)*, FATF, Paris, www.fatf-gafi.org/media/fatf/documents/reports/RBA-Trust-Company-Service-Providers.pdf, p56, Annex 1.

acknowledged that these do focus on key administrative or dispositive provisions in a trust. Finally, it is apparent from the concluding part of the definition that the indirect ability to confer a power on others will also be equated with control for these purposes.

If one looks at the equivalent definition of 'control' used for the purpose of the UK Trust Register, there is an important and material difference. Specifically, the UK Trust Register definition of 'control' goes wider in its final paragraph 2(e) to include in the category of controllers the individuals who might "direct, withhold consent to or veto the exercise of a power".[16] The material difference here is that while the individual who has a power cannot reference the existence of a third-party veto as negative in control, the UK regulations see the person who holds the veto as also having control. This is obviously a subtle point, but one that could have an important outcome in terms of identifying controllers in different contexts.

9. Origins of 4AMLD and 5AMLD found in the FATF 2012 Recommendations

A closer analysis of the Interpretative Notes to 2012 Recommendations 24 and 25 reveals the seeds that germinated into 4AMLD and 5AMLD. Paragraphs 7 to 11 of the Interpretative Note to Recommendation 24 is the starting point for company registers:

> *(7) Countries should ensure that either: (a) information on the beneficial ownership of a company is obtained by that company and available at a specified location in their country; or (b) there are mechanisms in place so that the beneficial ownership of a company can be determined in a timely manner by a competent authority.*
>
> *(8) In order to meet the requirements in paragraph 7, countries should use one or more of the following mechanisms:*
>
> *(a) Requiring companies or company registries to obtain and hold up-to-date information on the companies' beneficial ownership;*
>
> *(b) Requiring companies to take reasonable measures to obtain and hold up-to-date information on the companies' beneficial ownership;*
>
> *(c) Using existing information, including: (i) information obtained by financial institutions and/or DNFBPs, in accordance with Recommendations 10 and 22; (ii) information held by other competent authorities on the legal and beneficial ownership of companies (eg, company registries, tax authorities or financial or other regulators); (iii) information held by the company as required above in Section A; and (iv) available information on companies listed on a stock exchange, where disclosure requirements (either by stock*

16 UK – Section 6(2)(e) of *The Money Laundering, Terrorist Financing and Transfer of Funds (Information on the Payer) Regulations 2017.*

> *exchange rules or through law or enforceable means) impose requirements to ensure adequate transparency of beneficial ownership.*[17]

In paragraph 8, FATF sets out the options for mechanisms to gather and make use of beneficial ownership information. With the lens of hindsight, we can see that it is option 8(a) that was implemented through 4AMLD and 5AMLD – for "companies and company registries to obtain and hold up-to-date information on the companies' beneficial ownership".

Similarly, in paragraph 3 to the Interpretative Note to Recommendation 25, FATF recommended that:

> *(3) Potential sources of information on trusts, trustees, and trust assets are:*
> *(a) Registries (eg, a central registry of trusts or trust assets), or asset registries for land, property, vehicles, shares or other assets.*
> *(b) Other competent authorities that hold information on trusts and trustees (eg, tax authorities which collect information on assets and income relating to trusts).*
> *(c) Other agents and service providers to the trust, including investment advisors or managers, lawyers, or trust and company service providers.*[18]

This is similar, although perhaps less prescriptive, than Recommendation 24 in relation to companies. Again, at paragraph 3(a), FATF introduces the concept of a central registry of trusts. However, while in 2012 the concept of central registers was a specialist tool propounded in a 136-page booklet, it was in 2013, at the Lough Erne 2013 G8 summit, that they gained political traction. In 4AMLD, which entered into force in June 2015, corporate registries were introduced in the European Union, but they were not fully public registers. Interestingly, the 2012 Recommendations do not mention that the registers should be available to the public. Under 4AMLD, the corporate registers were required to be available to competent authorities and those who could demonstrate a legitimate interest. Trust registers were introduced, although these were completely private. The United Kingdom voluntarily elected that its beneficial ownership register (known as the Persons with Significant Control or PSC register) for companies be publicly available from April 2016. However, it was not until 5AMLD came into force, in January 2020, that corporate registers were required to be public on an EU-wide basis, and trust registers were opened up to those who could demonstrate a legitimate interest. As is normal, each EU/EEA jurisdiction is at liberty to decide how to transpose the directives into their national law.

---

17 FATF International Standards, pp92–93.
18 FATF International Standards, p96.

10. Different approaches across jurisdictions implementing trust registers

It is interesting to compare the differing approaches that have been taken by the examples of four jurisdictions' approach to implementing 4AMLD and 5AMLD. The United Kingdom's amended regulations that implement 5AMLD do not contain any material changes to the concepts of 'beneficial ownership' or 'control'. Taking the United Kingdom, Malta, Ireland and Cyprus, one can note different approaches being taken by the two former and the two latter. In the case of Ireland and Cyprus, the approach is simply to repeat the list of beneficial owners of a trust as set out at Article 1(2)(b) of 5AMLD.[19] In this context, therefore, neither Ireland by its statutory instrument nor Cyprus in its primary legislation that transposes 4AMLD have attempted to put any 'gloss' on the expressions within the directive and, in particular, that relating to the definition of 'controller'.

One further interesting point to note about the United Kingdom, in an uncanny replication of the CRS rules for equity interest holders for a trust which qualifies as a financial institution, has omitted all references to protectors, presumably on the assumption that a person with protector powers that are material will be deemed to be a controller given the wide definition involved. This may, however, generate a situation where a person who is a protector but lacks one of the relevant powers listed in the UK regulations would not be obliged to be included on the UK trust register even though they would be identifiable for AML purposes as a protector so named.

Turning to Malta, rather than use the concept of 'control', the draftsman has referenced the concept of 'material action'.[20] The Maltese draftsman has, to a certain extent, gone further than the UK draftsman in the expanded definition of 'control', in particular by referencing the ability to agree to a change in the proper law of a trust or an acceptance of an additional settlor. Furthermore, the concept is wider in terms of anyone who has to agree to an amendment of the trust instrument. Intriguingly, in its definition of 'beneficial owner' in the regulations implementing 4AMLD, the Maltese legislation includes protectors expressly and under its final Category B references persons 'other than those already referred to in paragraphs A to D'. This appears to be a clearer approach and one that is more consistent with the approach being taken in the CRS context defining 'controllers', which is less likely to lead to confusion.

To summarise, therefore, there is some concern that is apparent from the different approaches being taken by these four jurisdictions. Specifically, there is an important change set out in 5AMLD, adding a new paragraph 3a to Article 31 of 4AMLD, that where a trust is obliged to be registered within the European

19 Directive (EU) 2018/843 Of The European Parliament And Of The Council, 30 May 2018, Article 1(2)(b).
20 Malta – Trusts and Trustees Act (Register of Beneficial Owners) Regulations 2017.

Union for a particular reason, that registration suffices for the rest of the European Union/European Economic Area.[21] It is apparent that, in circumstances where definitions in relation to protectors and controllers are not consistent, the registers in these different jurisdictions will vary and it will therefore be a somewhat arbitrary outcome to consider who needs to be properly registered depending on which jurisdiction the trust is obliged to register with first.

It seems that there is a desirable need here for these jurisdictions to come together and to seek to employ a more harmonised approach to avoid future confusion for all. Recent developments in terms of the FATF 2019 Guidance are helpful in terms of giving more granularity as to how to identify the residual category of potential 'controllers' of a trust (using the language of FATF rather than one based on the actual exercise of powers). It is to be hoped that as EU jurisdictions do consider matters in this area, they harmonise their approach to avoid unnecessary confusion, which will only frustrate the purposes for which trust registers were intended by their policy makers.

11. Future developments

It seems likely that the trend towards public registers for companies will increase internationally. The United Kingdom is encouraging the British Crown Dependencies and Overseas Territories to move towards the 'global standard' of open public registers for companies by 2023; at the time of writing, US Congress had passed the Corporate Transparency Act, which requires both US and US-registered foreign companies to report on beneficial ownership. Many people also believe that 5AMLD creates the potential for quasi-public information about trusts. Commentators in the United States have indicated that there is no strong support for public beneficial ownership registers of companies and no support for any sort of centralised trust register. It will be interesting to see in future years whether the rest of the world will follow the approach taken by the United States, or the approach taken by the European Union.

21 Directive (EU) 2018/843 Article 1(16)(c).

Austria

Christiane Edelhauser
Michael Petritz
KPMG Austria

1. Background and legal status based on the Fourth and Fifth EU Anti-Money Laundering Directives[1,2]

Designed and intended as significant contributions to the international combat for preventing the financial system from being abused for the purposes of money laundering and terrorist financing, the Fourth EU Anti-Money Laundering Directive (4AMLD) and the Fifth EU Anti-Money Laundering Directive (5AMLD) require member states to establish central registers that hold adequate, accurate and current information on beneficial owners of corporate and other legal entities incorporated within their territory, as well as of trusts and trust-like arrangements governed under their law, which ensure timely and unrestricted access by competent authorities and financial intelligence units.[3]

In order to implement the requirements of 4AMLD, Austria enacted the Beneficial Owners Register Act (BORA) (*Wirtschaftliche Eigentümer Registergesetz – WiEReG*)[4] in 2017, which became effective in its entirety on 15 January 2018. Based on this implementation act, corporate and a wide range of other listed entities[5] seated (managed) in Austria were obliged to register their ultimate beneficial owners (UBOs) with the newly established Austrian UBO Registry.

In 2019 the EU *Finanz-Anpassungsgesetz – EUFinAnpG* 2019[6] was passed in Austria to implement the UBO requirements of 5AMLD by amending the Austrian BORA. The amendments to the Austrian BORA mainly became effective on 10 January 2020 and a new section regarding the so-called 'BORA Compliance Package'[7] was enforced on 10 November 2020.

---

1 See Directive (EU) 2015/849 on the prevention of the use of the financial system for the purposes of money laundering or terrorist financing, amending RL (EU) No 648/2012 and repealing Directive 2005/60/EC Directive 2006/70/EC, *Official Journal* of the EU No L 141, dated 5 June 2015, p73.

2 See Directive (EU) 2018/843 amending Directive (EU) 2015/849 on the prevention of the use of the financial system for the purposes of money laundering or terrorist financing and amending Directives 2009/138/EC and 2013/36/EU, *Official Journal* of the EU No L 156, dated 19 June 2018, p43.

3 See Article 30 and Article 31 of RL (EU) 2015/849.

4 See *Wirtschaftliche Eigentümer Registergesetz – WiEReG*, BGBl. I Nr 136/2017 idF BGBl. I Nr 23/2020 and the English translation of *WiEReG*/BORA issued by the Austrian Regulator (Financial Market Authority (FMA)) following this link: www.fma.gv.at/en/national/supervisory-laws/.

5 See Section 1 para 2 BORA.

6 See Austrian EU *Finanz-Anpassungsgesetzes – EU-FinAnpG* 2019, BGBl. I Nr 62/2019.

7 See Section 5a BORA.

1.1 Annual identification, verification and documentation duties

All entities subject to BORA are obliged to apply 'appropriate measures' in order to analyse and understand the ownership and control structure throughout all ownership levels of their (corporate) entity group in order to gain firm opinion and understanding of who their UBOs are.

This means they have the obligation annually to obtain, review, verify and document adequate, conclusive and current information and documentary evidence regarding their UBOs, including information on type and size of the beneficial interest held (shares/ownership interest, voting rights, ultimate effective control by other means) in order to ensure that their registered UBOs are correct, complete and up to date.[8]

The mandatory UBO registration requires the prior identification and verification of UBOs (only natural persons) based on valid UBO-relevant information and documentary evidence that must be obtained and duly analysed upfront. This review may be completed no sooner than when the 'whole picture' of the ownership and control structure and the identified UBOs becomes clear in effect. Entities are also advised to document their mandatory annual UBO review procedure in order to be able to prove having applied 'appropriate measures' towards the registration authority (Ministry of Finance (BMF)) and/or the tax authorities subsequently.

Compliance with these due diligence obligations means the following:

- all entities subject to BORA are required to obtain customary documentary evidence regarding their UBOs and their ownership and control structures. Adequate sources of evidence in particular are:
  - excerpts of public registers (eg, excerpts of commercial registers or similar registers, such as the Austrian or the German Commercial Register, or UBO and trust registers according to Articles 30 and 31 of 4AMLD and 5AMLD), in order to prove the existence and/or the ownership structure of an entity; and
  - non-public documents (eg, articles of association, company/partnership agreements, voting agreements, fiduciary relationship agreements, deeds of trusts), in order to prove the ownership and/or differing voting and control structures of an entity.

If there is no customary evidence (available or detectable) for certain countries, other types of evidence from impartial and reliable sources must be obtained (eg, annual financial statements, database queries, internet research etc). Subject to the place of incorporation/organisation/management and the legal type of the entity, customary documentary evidence required may vary among jurisdictions.

8 See Section 3 paras 1 and 3 BORA.

As effective of 10 November 2020, BORA[9] was amended outlining in detail the type of information and documentary evidence considered adequate for the identification and verification of UBOs for different types of local and foreign entity as legal 'minimum standard'. Recently, the much-anticipated revised BORA Directive[10] was issued by the BMF as of 23 October 2020, specifying, among other things, customary documentary evidence adequate and required for certain legal types of foreign entity as well as for certain foreign jurisdictions.

If an entity is unable to obtain (preferably certified) copies of the required (original) documents, a 'qualified third party'[11] may instead, under certain circumstances, create an adequate note summarising all UBO-relevant parts contained in the document. Such suitable notes must contain at least the following: date and place of the review of the original document; signature and personal data of the reviewer; precise denomination of the document; name and function of the person/s who issued and/or signed it; content and purpose of the document; and, most importantly, all UBO-relevant parts of the documentary evidence in question. Nonetheless, such notes *in lieu* of the entire documents must not be created by the obliged entity nor its legal or beneficial owners. The provision of notes instead of original documents is prohibited for documents relating to 'AML high-risk countries' by all means.[12]

In general, the following review steps are required pursuant to Austrian BORA:

- provision and review of commercial or similar registers and articles of association, company/partnership agreements, certificates of good standing;
- provision and review of deeds of trust and accompanying relevant agreements of a foundation (*Stiftung*), a similar legal person, a trust or a trust-like arrangement;
- provision and review of passport copies or copies of other official photo IDs of foreign UBOs without registered permanent address in Austria; and
- provision and review of information and documentary evidence (or certified copies or notes thereof) regarding voting and other control structures differing from identified ownership structures (eg, for legal, factual or joint ultimate effective control of a group of shareholders or partners, such as voting agreements, fiduciary relationship agreements etc).

---

9 See Section 5a para 1 BORA idF EU *Finanz-Anpassungsgesetzes – EU-FinAnpG* 2019, BGBl. I Nr 62/2019.

10 See revised Austrian BORA Directive, BMF-AV Nr 171/2020, issued 23 October 2020, following this link: https://findok.bmf.gv.at/findok?execution=e1s1.

11 See Section 5a para 3 BORA.

12 See Section 2 subpara 16 of the Austrian *Bundesgesetz zur Verhinderung der Geldwäscherei und Terrorismusfinanzierung im Finanzmarkt (Finanzmarkt-Geldwäschegesetz – FM-GwG)*, BGBl I Nr 118/2016 idF BGBl I Nr 62/2019.

For complex ownership and control structures of (corporate) entity groups, an organisational chart (organigram) is required, displaying all layers of the ownership structure as well as all differing voting and control rights.

- All entities subject to BORA are also obliged to review the registered data of their UBOs at least once a year in order to ensure that this data is valid, complete and up to date based on conclusive documentary evidence. The established annual review process, the applied compliance procedures and the results gained must be duly documented by all obliged entities.

1.2 Disclosure of UBOs and archiving obligations

Furthermore, all entities are obliged to retain the information and documentary evidence obtained, which is adequate and required for the identification and verification of their UBOs, depending on the complexity of the ownership and control structure and the types of entity involved. They are required to retain these records locally themselves for at least five years after the end of beneficial ownership of the respective UBOs.[13] However, these archiving obligations are fulfilled as soon as a 'compliance package' is electronically filed by Austrian obliged entities (see section 2 below).

Alternatively, they may also outsource the retention of all UBO-relevant documentation to a 'qualified third party',[14] which in most cases will be a professional counsel (eg, an attorney, notary, tax counsel or auditor), as long as they are able to ensure that the records stored on their behalf will be provided to them in a timely manner. Nonetheless, the liability for their archiving obligations always remains with the obliged entities themselves.

Starting 10 January 2020, the so-far-established penal provisions in BORA were expanded;[15] thus, intentional or grossly negligent violations of said archiving obligations will also be prosecuted by tax authorities imposing penalties up to €75,000.

Entities subject to BORA are also obliged to disclose their UBOs and to provide conclusive documentary evidence to all 'obligated parties' (eg, banks, legal and tax counsels),[16] whose customers they are. Moreover, the registration authority (BMF) may request – and enforce, if necessary – the disclosure of all UBO-relevant information and documentation from the entity, as well as from its legal and beneficial owners at any time.[17]

---

13 See Section 3 para 1 and 2 BORA.
14 See Section 5a para 3 BORA.
15 See Section 15 para 2 BORA.
16 See Section 9 para 1 BORA.
17 See Section 14 para 4 and 5 BORA.

1.3 Duties of legal and beneficial owners to cooperate

Local as well as foreign legal and beneficial owners are obligated to support actively 'their' Austrian entities in respect of their due diligence obligations of identifying, reviewing and documenting all relevant UBOs. Hence, they themselves may also be held accountable for intentional or grossly negligent violation of their duties to cooperate and to support UBO identification, verification and registration in Austria.[18]

In cases where legal or beneficial owners of an entity do not comply with these mandatory BORA requirements, obliged entities must evidently point out to them (in writing) their duties pursuant to Section 4 as well as the impending sanctions applicable to them pursuant to Section 15, in order to prove having fulfilled their due diligence duties towards competent authorities and thus to mitigate the risk of being held accountable for their legal representatives as well as for themselves.

1.4 Mandatory reporting requirements

The initial registration of UBOs in Austria was due no later than 1 June 2018; however, this deadline was extended to 15 August 2018.

Since then, newly established entities are obliged to register their UBOs within four weeks following incorporation. In cases where relevant changes of circumstances occur regarding reportable data, entities are obliged to amend their UBO registration accordingly within four weeks, the earlier these changes become known or effective.[19]

For entities exempt from UBO reporting[20] (the direct UBOs of which can be identified automatically as natural persons filed as direct shareholders or partners with the general registers), all relevant changes in their ownership and control structure must be amended in these general registers (eg, commercial register) within four weeks.

Starting 10 January 2020, all entities obliged to report their UBOs must actively confirm or amend their registration in 2020 and hereinafter annually, even though no changes may have occurred since the initial registration.

Due to this new reporting requirement, obliged entities must confirm formally that based on the results of their annual review for identifying and verifying their UBOs, all reported data is valid, complete and up to date – if this is the case – by filing a so called 'confirmation report' each year. The deadline for these reports ends no later than the date of the last (manual) report plus 12 months plus four weeks.

This new reporting requirement also applies to 'subsidiary reporting' with or without automatic transfer of reportable UBO-data (see section 1.6(h) below).

---

18 See Section 4 BORA and Sections 11 FinStrG, 15 BORA; see also *Edelhauser, Beteiligung am finanzstrafrechtlichen Sonderdelikt*, SWK 9/2020, 487f.

19 See Section 5 para 1 BORA.

20 See Section 6 BORA.

This means that respective corporate entities must also confirm once a year that the legal requirements for applying the 'subsidiary rule' are still fulfilled by filing a (manual) confirmation report. This new duty was established to reduce or disclose the number of subsidiary UBO registrations in cases where subsidiary reporting was merely applied in case of doubt, since UBO-relevant documentation was or could not be obtained.

In this regard it is important to understand that 'obligated parties' (eg, banks, legal or tax counsels) are legally prohibited from entering into a new business relationship, or obliged to terminate it, in case the UBOs of their (prospective) entity-client may not be duly identified and verified by them.[21]

Entities required to register their UBOs with the Austrian UBO Registry may technically only do so by using the federal electronic online portal (Business Service Portal) on their own or through a professional party representative (eg, authorised attorney, notary, tax adviser or certified public accountant).

In order to recognise a UBO-relevant change in circumstances that occurred in respect of registered entities, a new 'change management service' is implemented in the electronic registration system, which may be used by all companies, as well as by obligated parties, as soon as they establish a web service account (free of charge) in the Business Service Portal.

This way, the web service will provide the registration numbers (master numbers) of all entities for which relevant changes occurred (eg, a new report was filed; new UBOs were registered; new documents were added to a compliance package (see section 2 below); the due date for filing the annual UBO report for an entity subject to reporting or the fact that an entity exempt from reporting becomes subject to reporting will be indicated in good time in advance).

Moreover, obligated parties will be enabled to call up the Register of Beneficial Owners directly from their customer management programmes, either manually or semi-automatically. Thus, professional party representatives may submit reports for specific clients directly from their management software, retrieve excerpts and import data from the register into their own system semi-automatically.

1.5 Violation of registration requirements – administrative penalties and penal provisions

If registration obligations are deliberately or negligently violated 'by omitting the disclosure of UBOs', representatives of obliged entities and the entities themselves face harsh penalties.[22]

As stated before, the disregard of an entity's obligation to retain all UBO-relevant documentation may be severely fined too.

---

21 See AML provisions, eg, in FM-GwG, RAO, NO, WTBG 2017.
22 See Section 15 BORA.

In case of non-compliance with registration requirements, Austrian tax authorities impose administrative penalties of up to €5,000 by default, regardless of culpability. These administrative penalties may be imposed twice (with increasing penalties) for as long as registration duties are not met; subsequently, a penal offence may be established.

For deliberate violations of BORA-reporting obligations, penal sentences (passed by the tax authorities) may range up to €200,000. In case of gross negligence, sentences of up to €100,000 may be imposed. These penalties are primarily addressing entity representatives, yet entities themselves may also be punished under certain circumstances (in case the requirements of the Austrian *Verbandsverantwortlichkeitsgesetzt – VbVG*[23] are met). Moreover, UBOs may also face legal prosecution as remote parties in case of intentional or gross negligent non-compliance with their duties to cooperate and to support their entities in respect of their due diligence and reporting obligations.[24]

1.6 Identification of UBOs

(a) Beneficial ownership in corporate entities

Beneficial ownership in corporate entities (eg, stock corporations, limited liability companies, general and limited partnerships etc)[25] is generally based on legal ownership. For corporate entities, three different, equally valid types of beneficial ownership exist:

- ultimate beneficial ownership due to a sufficient percentage of shares or ownership interest;
- ultimate beneficial ownership due to sufficient voting rights; and
- ultimate beneficial ownership due to ultimate effective control by other means.

Depending on the levels of the ownership structure in respect of the entity subject to UBO reporting, one primarily may distinguish between two different types of shareholding/ownership interest that establish beneficial ownership according to Austrian BORA: direct beneficial ownership and indirect beneficial ownership.

(b) Direct beneficial ownership

A direct beneficial owner is a natural person that is a shareholder of 25% plus one share or holds an ownership interest or voting rights of more than 25% in the entity (personally or through a fiduciary relationship) or directly controls

23 See Austrian *Verbandverantwortlichkeitsgesetz – VbVG*, BGBl I Nr 151/2005 idF BGBl. I Nr 26/2016.
24 See Sections 4, 15 BORA and Section 11 FinStrG.
25 See Section 1 para 2 subpara 1-11, 13 and 14 BORA.

the entity personally or jointly with other natural persons. Here, it is important to understand that in case the shareholding/ownership interest or the voting rights reach exactly 25%, the respective natural person/s must not be identified as UBO/s of the entity according to Austrian BORA.

(c) ***Indirect beneficial ownership***

Indirect beneficial ownership means a shareholding of 25% plus one share or an ownership interest or voting rights of more than 25% in the obliged entity held by another (corporate) entity, which is:

- under direct or indirect control of (a) natural person(s); or
- held by multiple corporate entities, which are under common control of the same natural person(s).

For both types of indirect beneficial ownership, a shareholding/ownership interest or voting rights in the obliged entity, on the first level of the ownership structure, is only sufficient in case it exceeds 25%; yet for all higher levels of ownership within an ownership structure of a corporate group, ultimate effective control over the entity is required, which is assumed for a shareholding/ownership interest or voting rights of more than 50% or by exercising ultimate effective control over the entity by other means. The relevant thresholds for beneficial ownership must always be calculated separately for each level of the ownership and control structure (not applying a summarised 'through' calculation for the entire structure).

Thus, upwards, starting from second level of participation/ownership, the relevant criteria for the identification of beneficial ownership is whether or not a respective natural person exercises directly or indirectly ultimate effective control over the obliged entity.

Whenever an indirect beneficial ownership of a natural person is identified, the UBO-relevant 'ultimate legal entity' (see section 1.6(f) below) that is directly or indirectly controlled by the UBO must also be registered with the UBO Registry in Austria.

This rather unique registration requirement of the Austrian BORA was implemented for excerpts of the UBO Registry to provide a clear picture of the entire UBO-relevant ownership and control structure of an obliged entity to 'obligated parties' and all other parties with granted access.

(d) ***Ultimate effective control***

The term 'ultimate effective control' applies to direct as well as to indirect control throughout all levels of the ownership and control structure of (corporate) entity groups according to BORA.[26]

26 See Section 2 subpara 1 BORA.

This means that 'ultimate effective control' may only be identified:

- in case of direct or indirect shareholding/ownership interest of more than 50%;
- in case one of the following criteria laid down in Section 244(2) of the *Unternehmensgesetzbuch – UGB*[27] applies between related entities (control scenarios):
  - majority of voting rights;
  - right to appoint/recall the majority of legal representatives of the entity;
  - right to exercise commanding influence over the entity; or
  - relevant voting agreements (providing majority of voting rights for involved parties);
- in case a natural person holds a UBO-relevant function at an 'ultimate legal entity' (eg, as settlor, trustee(s), beneficiary/ies of a foundation (Austrian *Privatstiftung*), a similar legal person, a trust, or a trust-like arrangement that is identified as 'ultimate legal entity'); or
- in case of a fiduciary relationship or similar legal arrangement, where the trustor exercises direct or indirect ultimate effective control over the shareholding/ownership interest held by the trustee on his/her behalf, the trustor (natural person) must be identified as UBO of the entity.

In case the trustor him/herself also holds a percentage of shares or ownership interest in the entity on his/her own behalf, his/her shareholding/ownership interest must be added to the shareholding/ownership interest held through means of the fiduciary relationship.

The trustee (as legal owner) must also be identified as UBO when holding sufficient ownership interest on behalf of the trustor and/or additionally perhaps on his/her own behalf.

In this regard it is important to recognise that significant fiduciary relationships, relevant for UBO registration, must always be disclosed and registered. Disregard of these reporting requirements will result in severe penalties.

Furthermore, any natural person that ultimately controls an entity in effect 'by other means' must be identified as UBO of the entity too. This type of ultimate effective (factual) control, not necessarily based on granted legal rights (eg, vote or value), may be assumed if relevant business decisions are made according to the 'effectively controlling person' (eg, based on kinship ties with senior managing officials or to legal owners). However, beneficial ownership based on factual effective control 'by other means'– beyond legal rights – may be assumed only if it may be identified based on unambiguous facts that must

27 See Austrian *Bundesgesetz über besondere zivilrechtliche Vorschriften für Unternehmen (Unternehmensgesetzbuch – UGB)*, dRGBl. S 219/1897 idF BGBl. I Nr 63/2019.

also be documented accordingly. This, finally, means that rumours or assumptions shall not suffice for determining this (factual control) type of beneficial ownership in Austria.

(e) ***'Common control' exercised by a group of people***[28]

Moreover, according to BORA – and in compliance with EU requirements – ultimate effective control over corporate entities may also be established based on 'common control' jointly exercised by a group of people.

Ultimate effective control may thus also be exercised mutually by a group of natural persons, but only if this type of control is based on relevant legal agreements such as voting agreements (eg, syndicates). Thus, ultimate effective control may be jointly exercised by the group acting like one consistently aligned body towards (external) third parties, given that resolutions within the aligned body are passed unanimously.

In this case natural persons that are members of such a group of shareholders/partners are considered joint UBOs of the obliged entity, based on the percentage of shares, ownership interest or voting rights they jointly control. Consequently, the beneficial interest for each member of the aligned group is not allocated *pro rata*.

Figure 1. Joint ultimate effective control based on a voting agreement

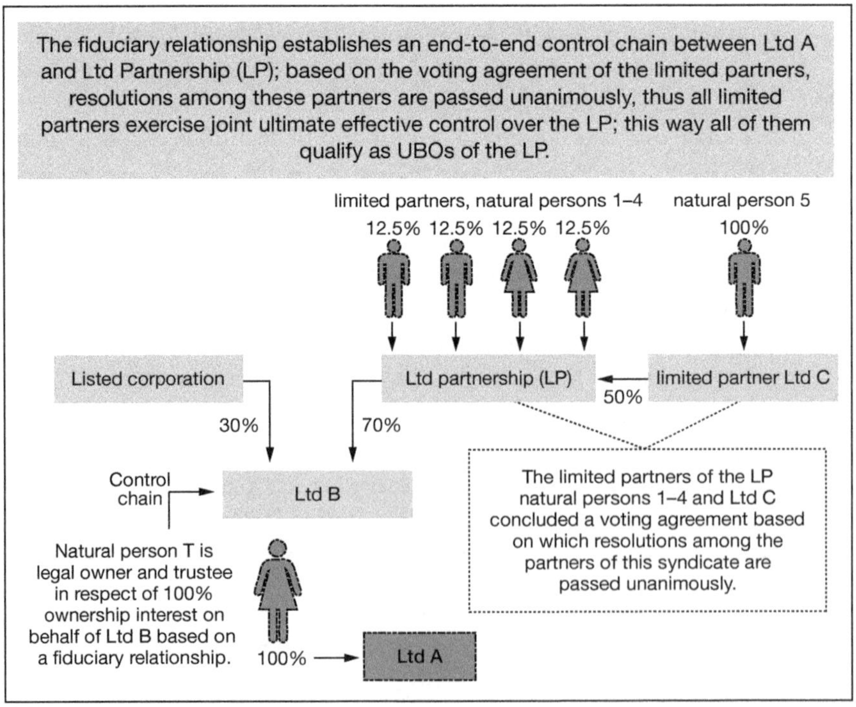

Description/solution to Figure 1: In this ownership and control structure the following natural persons must be disclosed as indirect UBOs of the obliged Ltd A, based on the established 'unanimity-syndicate' in this structure: natural persons 1–4 as direct limited partners of the LP as well as natural person 5 that directly controls Ltd C, which in turn is another limited partner of the LP. All these limited partners of the LP are jointly associated by an established voting agreement based on which resolutions of the partners are passed unanimously. Moreover, natural person T holding the position of a trustee/nominee, that legally owns the entire shares of Ltd A in its own name, yet on behalf of Ltd B, must also be identified as direct UBO of Ltd A. The trustee/nominee at the same time establishes a UBO-relevant control relationship (control chain) for and on behalf of Ltd B, based on the established nominee agreement.

Alternatively, in cases where due to a shareholder/partner agreement, resolutions within the aligned body (eg, a group of shareholders aligned by the voting agreement) are passed based on majority vote, beneficial ownership is only established for (the) natural person/s that hold/s the majority of voting rights within the aligned group (syndicate, consortium).[29]

Starting 10 January 2020, also the percentage of shareholding/ownership interest controlled by UBOs must be reported to the Austrian UBO Registry, in case the respective beneficial ownership was based on 'ultimate effective control' and the respective percentage of the controlled beneficial interest may be identified.[30]

(f) *'Ultimate legal entity': a unique Austrian registration requirement*

The term 'ultimate legal entity'[31] is relevant for UBO registration in case of indirect beneficial ownership (see section 1.6(c) above) according to BORA. This rather unique registration requirement of the Austrian BORA was implemented for excerpts of the UBO Registry to provide a clear picture of the entire UBO-relevant ownership and control structure in order to disclose the end-to-end control chain of an obliged entity.

An 'ultimate legal entity' is an entity within an ownership structure or corporate group that is:

- controlled by an indirect beneficial owner;
- an entity, where indirect beneficial owners directly hold shares, ownership interest or voting rights that establish beneficial ownership together with the controlled entity(ies) mentioned above; or

---

28 See Section 2 subpara 1 lit a BORA.

29 See Directive of BMF, dated 26 April 2018, BMF-460000/0007-III/6/2018, BMF-AV Nr 60/2018, Sec 2.3.2, S. 15.

30 See Section 5 para 1 subpara 3 lit a BORA.

31 See Section 2 subpara 1 lit a sublit bb BORA (*'oberster Rechtsträger'*).

- an entity, where the beneficial owner holds one of the UBO-relevant functions[32] with a foundation (Austrian *Privatstiftung*), a similar legal person, a trust or a trust-like arrangement – for example, as settlors, trustee(s), beneficiaries of a foundation (Austrian *Privatstiftung*), a trust or a trust-like arrangement.

However, a statutory corporation/public body may never be identified as 'ultimate legal entity'.

It is important to point out that in case a foundation (Austrian *Privatstiftung*), a similar legal person, a trust or a trust-like arrangement seated/managed in Austria is identified as 'ultimate legal entity', only the relevant data of this ultimate legal entity must be reported individually by subordinate entities. Natural persons holding UBO-relevant functions in such Austrian 'ultimate legal entity', however, do not have to be reported; instead, their UBO-relevant data will be sourced and transferred automatically to the UBO registration of all subordinate entities (this technical relief was implemented into the electronic Austrian UBO Registration System).

(g) ***BORA also applies to (inter)national listed companies***

Another unique characteristic of the Austrian BORA for corporate entities must be emphasised since companies listed on a regulated stock market are also included in the definition of 'corporate entities' obligated to identify, verify and report their UBOs, which clearly exceeds the relevant definition of 'beneficial ownership' for corporate entities according to Article 3(6)(a)(i) of 4AMLD.

Thus, it is essential to recognise that listed companies incorporated in Austria – but also related entities (Austrian subsidiaries) of listed international companies incorporated in member states or third countries – must comply with Austrian BORA requirements and thus are obliged to disclose and document their UBOs and ultimate legal entities pursuant to BORA provisions.

(h) ***Subsidiary reporting of senior managing officials***

If, in applying the identification and verification rules for corporate entities[33] for determining direct and/or indirect UBOs, after having exhausted all possible means and provided there are no grounds for suspicion, no natural person may be identified as UBO for a corporate entity – or if there is doubt about the identified beneficial owner(s) – the natural person(s) holding the position(s) of senior managing official(s) must be considered direct UBOs of the obliged entity.

In case legal and/or beneficial owners refuse to cooperate and provide the required information and documentary evidence for the identification and

32 See Section 2 subparas 2 and 3 BORA.
33 See Section 2 subpara 1 BORA.

verification of UBOs, the obliged entity must still attempt to obtain this data without the help of its owners. Then, the obliged entity must emphasise towards its owners their legal obligation to cooperate and support pursuant to Section 4 BORA and must also stress the impending sanctions as laid down in Section 15 BORA; such warning information must be properly documented by the obliged entity.

As a result, the obliged entity must duly document, end to end, all steps and actions taken in its attempt to obtain valid and complete documentary evidence for the identification and verification of its UBOs.

This requirement particularly applies to cases in which the entity has reasons to believe that specific natural persons or groups (most likely may) qualify as its UBOs (eg, based on effective factual control established within a corporate entity group, or based on respective information published on the homepage or in annual reports of the ultimate legal entity, or based on reliable publicly available (media) information on a corporate group effectively controlled by a group or a pool of (family) shareholders). Thus, in such cases it may also be necessary to obtain reliable documentary evidence that no UBOs exist in effect for the obliged entity, if this is the case, in order to prove conclusively the lack of 'real' UBOs despite prior assumptions.

Only if the entity is unable to determine its UBOs most certainly, after having exhausted all possible means (including the meticulous documentation of all its efforts made), must it report all its senior managing officials as its (subsidiary) direct UBOs instead.

Therefore, the 'subsidiary rule'[34] only applies for corporate entities if no direct nor indirect beneficial ownership can be identified after having exhausted all possible means, or no UBOs exist for this entity in effect – for instance, for an entity that does not have any legal owners or does not have owners with sufficient shareholding/ownership interest or voting rights (eg, associations[35] or companies listed on a regulated stock market with widely held stock).

Starting 10 January 2020, subsidiary UBO reporting of senior managing officials additionally requires the indication of the precise reason for this type of reporting (ie, whether no UBOs could be identified and verified by the obliged entity, or whether no UBOs exist for the respective entity in effect).

Effective as of 29 January 2019, a relevant technical relief for reporting senior managing officials of corporate entities was established; hence, subsidiary reporting must only be checked on the first screen of the electronic registration tool. The reporting of relevant personal data of all senior managing officials is no longer required. Instead, the required UBO data is directly sourced from the commercial register (and the central register of residents in case of a registered

34 See Section 2 subpara 1 lit b BORA.
35 See Section 1 Austrian *Vereinsgesetz – VerG*, BGBl I Nr 66/2002 idF BGBl I Nr 32/2018.

permanent residence in Austria) and fed automatically and on an ongoing basis to the UBO Registry.[36]

However, in case a change in circumstances regarding the relevant ownership and control structure occurs, the obliged entity is required to file an amended report within four weeks, if it was able to identify and verify its 'real' UBOs based on adequate documentation. Otherwise, if no changes occurred since the last UBO reporting of senior managing officials, the obliged entity must still file a 'confirmation report' once a year (see section 1.4 above).

(i) ***Beneficial ownership in foundations, trusts and trust-like arrangements***

Beneficial ownership in foundations (*Stiftungen*), similar legal persons, trusts and trust-like arrangements is always established by holding a special position (function) with these entities, such as:

- grantor, trustor, settlor;
- beneficiary (sufficiently determined, actual and not contingent beneficiary, one-time beneficiary or ultimate beneficiary);
- trustee or persons holding a similar function;
- protector (if any); or
- by a person that exercises ultimate effective control over the entity by other means.

The following are classed as UBOs of an Austrian private foundation (Austrian *Privatstiftung*):[37]

- the grantor;
- the beneficiaries (quoted by name or may be identified by other means, independent of receipt of donation; contingent beneficiaries are not yet UBOs and do not have to be registered in Austria);
- among a clearly assigned class of beneficiaries, those natural persons that have been determined to receive donations of more than €2,000 per calendar year (one-time beneficiaries);
- the class/es of beneficiaries (if any);
- the trustee(s); and
- any other natural person that exercises ultimate effective control over the entity by means of direct or indirect ownership or by other means. This may, for instance, be the case if one of the UBO-relevant functions is held by a legal entity (eg, a limited company). In such a case the natural person/s effectively controlling the legal entity that holds the function must be identified as UBOs of the Austrian *Privatstiftung* based on ultimate, effective control 'by other means'.

---

36 See Section 5 para 5 BORA.
37 See Section 1 Austrian *Privatstiftungsgesetz – PSG*, BGBl. Nr 694/1993 idF BGBl. I Nr 104/2019.

Auditors of the private foundation (*Stiftungsprüfer*), members of a supervisory or an advisory board (*Mitglieder des Aufsichtsrats oder Beirats der Privatstiftung*) must not be identified as UBOs, unless these natural persons have been granted specific rights to exercise ultimate effective control over the private foundation.

The following are classed as UBOs of a trust or a trust-like arrangement:[38]

- the settlor/trustor;
- the trustee(s);
- the protector (if any);
- the beneficiaries (quoted by name or may be identified by other means, independent of receipt of donation; contingent beneficiaries are not yet UBOs and do not have to be registered in Austria);
- a defined class/es of beneficiaries; and
- any other natural person that exercises ultimate effective control over the trust or the trust-like arrangement by means of direct or indirect ownership or by other means.

The provisions of the Austrian BORA generally apply to a trust or a trust-like arrangement if this entity is managed in Austria (eg, the permanent residence of the trustee(s) is in Austria) and furthermore – starting 10 January 2020 – in case the (foreign) trust or trust-like arrangement is not registered in the trust registry of another member state and a business relationship is started (eg, a bank account is opened) or property is acquired on its behalf in Austria. However, there is an exemption for trusts and trust-like arrangements already registered in the European Union but managed in a third-country jurisdiction for which property is acquired in Austria, since these entities are obliged in turn to register their UBOs (also) in Austria.

It is important to recognise that reportable trusts and trust-like arrangements must first be registered with a special Austrian register – the so-called 'supplementary register for other parties'[39] – before their UBOs may duly be reported to the Austrian UBO Registry.

For the identification of UBOs of a foundation (Austrian *Privatstiftung*), of a similar legal person, a trust or a trust-like arrangement, based on holding one of the said UBO-relevant functions, it is not relevant whether these natural persons have been granted specific rights to effectively control these entities too; instead they always must be identified as UBOs since they hold one of the UBO-relevant functions laid down in BORA,[40] even though an/other person/s may exercise ultimate effective control over the entity.

In case a certain class of beneficiaries has been assigned for such entity, this

---

38 See Section 1 para 2 subparas 17 and 18 BORA.
39 See '*Ergänzungsregister für sonstige Betroffene*' that is established with the Austrian Ministry of Economics.
40 See Section 2 subparas 2 and 3 BORA.

class of beneficiaries must also be registered by reporting the abstract specification of the defined class.

For the identification of a natural person as beneficiary of an Austrian private foundation (Austrian *Privatstiftung*), this person must be sufficiently determined as beneficiary based on the documentation, deed of the foundation, accompanying documents or based on a respective decision of the trustee/s or any other representative or board entitled to make such decisions. This means that the beneficiaries of an Austrian *Privatstiftung* must be legally entitled to this position according to Austrian *Privatstiftungsgesetz – PSG*.[41]

In case a natural person holds one of the said UBO-relevant functions with an entity (foundation, similar legal person, trust or trust-like arrangement), which in turn holds a sufficient ownership interest in a subordinate obliged entity within an entity group, the superior entity always qualifies as 'ultimate legal entity' (see section 1.6(f) above). All function holders (eg, settlors, trustees, beneficiaries) of the ultimate legal entity this way qualify as indirect UBOs of the subordinate obliged entity too, because they all exercise ultimate effective control over this entity through an end-to-end control chain.

In case natural persons hold at the same time such UBO-relevant functions with two or more foundations/trusts that once again hold ownership interests in the same subordinate obliged entity within an ownership structure of an entity group, the ownership interests of respective foundations/trusts must be added on behalf of their multi-function holders, which again may establish beneficial ownership of said multi-function holders based on control 'by other means'. This rule applies, if the total amount of ownership interests of such multi-function holders sufficiently exceeds the relevant threshold, even though this may not be true for the individual ownership interest held by each of the foundations/trusts respectively.

Description/solution to Figure 2: In this ownership and control structure the direct ownership interests held by foundations PS 1, PS 2 and PS 3 in the limited partnership (KG) must be added with respect to multi-function-holders, natural persons 1 and 2, as these persons are considered indirectly controlling the KG as well as the subordinate obliged Ltd A, based on their added and thus sufficient total indirect ownership interests (above 50% in total, respectively). The direct beneficial interest of the General Partner (Ltd) of the KG must be included in the calculation too, as the Ltd in turn is controlled by natural person 1 based on the majority of shares (80%). This means that natural persons 1 and 2 are UBOs to be disclosed for the KG as well as for the subordinate obliged Ltd A. Thus, for persons 1 and 2 the beneficial interests in the KG must be added as follows:

41 See Sections 5, 6 PSG.

Figure 2. Adding ownership interests of multi-function-holders

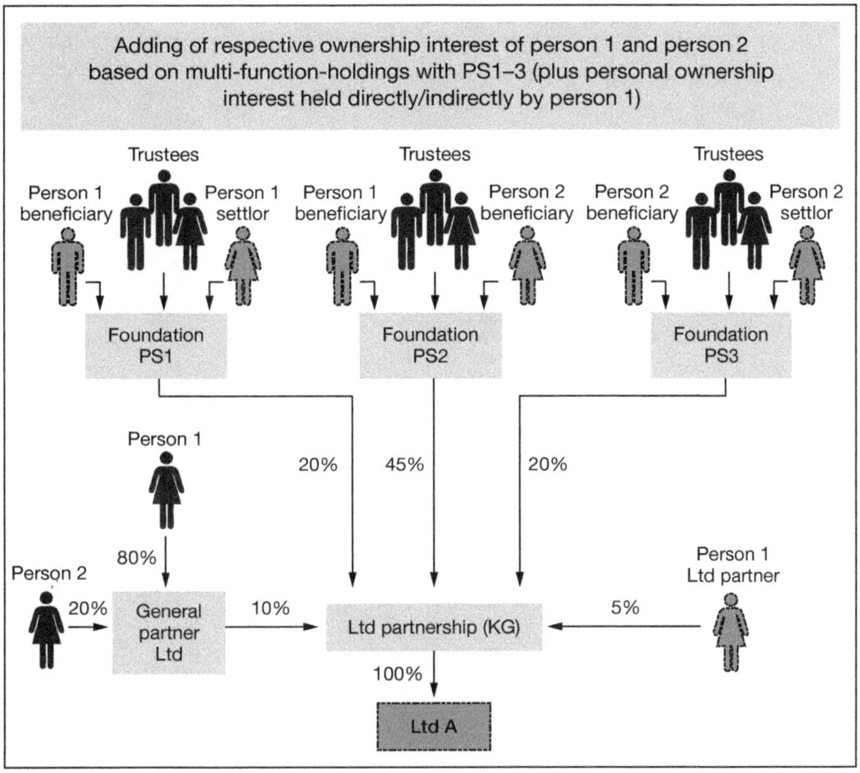

For person 1: 10% + 20% + 45% + 5% = 80%
For person 2: 45% + 20% = 65%

The same calculation (summation) is mandatory for a natural person personally holding an ownership interest in a subordinate entity and at the same time holding a UBO-relevant function with a superior foundation/trust. Also in this scenario the (direct or indirect) ownership interest in the subordinate entity held personally by the natural person on his/her own behalf and the ownership interest of the foundation/trust (where the person holds a UBO-relevant function) in the same subordinate entity have to be added in order to determine whether the total ownership interests of this natural person exceed the relevant threshold for beneficial ownership in the subordinate entity (more than 25% on the first level and more than 50% at all higher levels of the ownership and control structure).

Figure 3. Adding ownership interests held personally and indirectly by means of function-holding

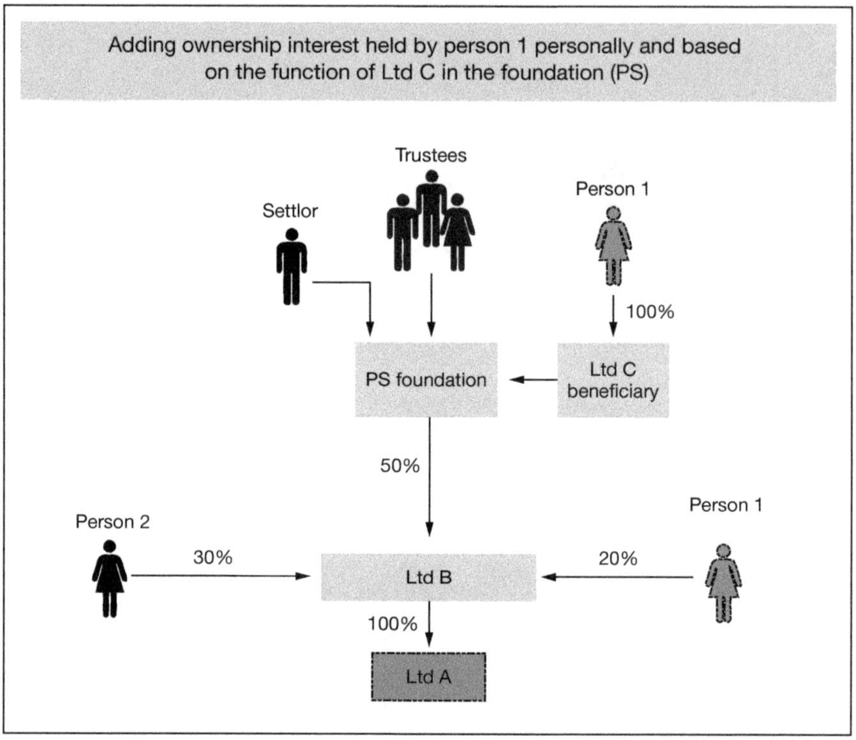

Description/solution to Figure 3: In this ownership and control structure the direct ownership interest in Ltd B held personally by natural person 1 (20%) must be added to the direct ownership interest in Ltd B held by foundation PS (50%), because natural person 1 is fully controlling one of the UBO-relevant function-holders of the PS, Ltd C (the beneficiary of PS), based on 100% of shares, and must thus be considered also controlling the PS indirectly. Therefore, the direct ownership interest of natural person 1 in Ltd B must be added to the beneficial interest ('ultimate effective control') held indirectly by natural person 1 via Ltd C and PS. This means, natural person 1 holds/controls (directly and indirectly) a total of 70% of the ownership interest in Ltd B, which in turn requires the disclosure of (only) natural person 1 as indirect UBO of the subordinate obliged entity Ltd A.

In these last two scenarios (Figures 2 and 3) all other (single-) function holders of the involved foundations/trusts do not qualify as UBOs of the subordinate entity, in case each of their superior entities does not hold a sufficiently high ownership interest on its own.

In case a UBO-relevant function with a foundation/trust is held by a legal person (eg, a limited company), the UBO review must be extended to this legal function-holding entity. Only in cases where this legal entity is also effectively controlled by a natural person/s, will these persons qualify as UBOs of the foundation/trust based on control 'by other means'.

1.7 New obligation of all 'obligated parties' to mark discrepancies in UBO Registry

Based on the requirements of 5AMLD, all obligated parties[42] (eg, banks, attorneys, notaries, tax consultants, chartered public accountants) are legally bound to mark discrepancies among UBO data which they recognise in the electronic UBO Registry during their customer review, in case they are convinced that the registered data is incorrect or incomplete; thus, a (mere) suspicion is not sufficient in this context. To our understanding, the obligation to mark an entity in the UBO Registry applies only as soon as the obligated party has obtained all UBO-relevant documentary evidence that is required for proper identification and verification of the UBOs of its prospective or existing entity-client.

When an entity is 'marked', obligated parties must provide standardised reasons for this action; the respective information is also provided to the affected entity. The 'flagging' of an entity will be displayed in excerpts of the UBO Registry to all other obligated parties, as well as to all authorities, yet the obligated party that flagged the entity remains anonymous.

Obligated parties may only refrain from 'marking' an entity for which they detected discrepancies among registered data if this entity amends its registration in a timely manner (within a maximum of four weeks) after having been informed by the obligated party about identified divergences in its registered UBO data.

The BMF is obliged to review randomly all 'marked' entities whose registration has not been amended within six weeks after the respective entity was 'marked'. These entities will be requested to provide all relevant UBO documentation and further information to the BMF when it performs a regular review of the UBOs of the 'marked' entity subsequently.

In order to ensure that the UBO Registry holds adequate, accurate and up-to-date information on beneficial owners, the BMF was granted extended rights to extract, compare and analyse UBO-relevant data; thus, the BMF is obliged to monitor these data and to perform regular entity reviews on UBOs in case it identifies discrepancies or peculiarities that need to be clarified and/or based on random sampling, which has intensified lately.

---

42 See Section 9 para 1 BORA.

1.8 Public access to UBO Registry for trusts and trust-like arrangements

Starting 10 January 2020, public access to UBO data was granted in Austria to the extent required by 5AMLD (eg, no residence address and no place of birth of UBOs is displayed in public UBO Registry excerpts). Excerpts of the UBO Registry are now available to everyone, with proof of legal interest no longer required. Through a link[43] on the Homepage of the BMF, anyone may now obtain a public excerpt of the UBO Registry for a given entity for a small fee (€3.00).

Thus, Austria did not take advantage of the option of 5AMLD[44] to restrict access to information on the beneficial ownership of trusts and trust-like arrangements only to natural and legal persons that can demonstrate a legitimate interest.

1.9 Application for restriction of access to the UBO Registry

In compliance with EU requirements, UBOs may apply for a restriction of access in respect of their registered data according to BORA, in cases where they can substantiate firm reasons to be considered significantly worthy of data protection due to severe personal endangerment (eg, in case of excessive risk of falling victim to certain listed crimes or in case of minors or legally incompetent persons). If the requested restriction of access rights is granted by the BMF (initially for a period of five years), no UBO data of the applicant will be displayed in excerpts of the UBO Registry with respect to all entities listed in the UBO's application.

Within 14 days of the application, the BMF must grant an interim restriction of access to all registered UBO data of the applicant, unless the application proves immediately unreasonable. Hence, the BMF issues a final decision in respect of the application for restriction of access within 12 months. The applicant may file a complaint against the BMF's administrative notice, at which point the federal administrative court (*Bundesverwaltungsgericht*) is bound to give its (final) court ruling.[45]

2. Austrian innovation: optional 'compliance package' for valid UBO documentation

All entities subject to BORA are obliged to identify and verify their UBOs annually. This annual review must be based on conclusive UBO documentation. Each entity is required to obtain, review and retain all UBO-relevant documentation annually and must be able to provide the relevant documentary evidence to obligated parties as well as to the registration authority (BMF) any

43 https://wieregms.bmf.gv.at/at.gv.bmf.wiereg-p/wiereg?execution=e1s1.
44 See Art 31 para 4 lit d RL (EU) 2018/843.
45 See Section 10a BORA.

time on request. For foreign ownership and control structures, Austrian banks generally accept only current documentary evidence no older than six weeks (eg, excerpts of foreign public registers), according to guidance of the Austrian Regulator (FMA), which are often difficult to obtain in time.

Starting 10 November 2020, obliged entities may voluntarily file and store their valid, complete and up-to-date UBO documentation on a newly established data platform linked to the UBO Registry. Such centrally and securely stored 'compliance package' may only be accessed by obligated parties (eg, banks, legal and tax counsels) depending on the decision of the entity that filed it. However, BORA compliance packages may never be accessed by the general public.

The validity of such compliance package is extended by law to 12 months and may also be extended further under certain circumstances. Obliged entities may manage and steer the access to all UBO-relevant documentation and thus keep control over their UBO documents in a time- and cost-efficient way.

Sensitive documents such as trust deeds or articles of incorporation must not necessarily be disclosed in full. Instead, based on reasonable considerations, all UBO-relevant parts of the original document may be summarised in a note by a professional counsel to be filed as an appropriate substitute.

In case of local and/or cross-border ownership and control structures, subordinate entities may refer to already stored compliance packages of their Austrian superior/ultimate legal entity/ies without having to review and provide the documents contained therein themselves. In fact, they neither have responsibility nor liability for the correctness and completeness of the compliance package they refer to, which remain solely with the superior/ultimate legal entity that filed it.

All entities using (referencing) a centrally stored compliance package hereby also comply with their obligation to retain their UBO-relevant documentation, which otherwise must be fulfilled individually and on an ongoing basis by every member of a (corporate) entity group. All compliance packages that are filed and stored centrally with the UBO Registry must have been reviewed and explicitly confirmed by a professional counsel (eg, a public auditor, attorney or notary) as conclusive, complete and up-to-date evidence for the mandatory UBO registration that must be filed together with the compliance package.

In our opinion, the detailed list of types of document required for filing a valid compliance package according to the new BORA provision,[46] effective since 10 November 2020, should generally be applied by obliged entities as welcome guidance for all required UBO reviews in order to be confident having applied 'appropriate measures' to comply with their due diligence obligations under BORA.

46 See Section 5a para 1 BORA.

As a result, adequate documentary evidence for the identification and verification of UBOs that needs to be obtained for the mandatory UBO registration fully corresponds to the explicitly listed documents that are required for filing a valid voluntary compliance package, which may be distinguished by way of required proof depending on:

- the type of ownership and control structure of the obliged entity;
- the place of incorporation of the involved entities inside and/or outside of Austria;
- the involved types and legal forms of entity;
- the type of adequate proof for the existence of an entity;
- the type of adequate proof for the ownership structure of an entity; and
- the type of adequate proof for voting or other control structures that differ from the identified shareholding/ownership structures of an entity.

Finally, further clarification and specification in respect of required UBO documentation was published in Austria recently as part of the revised BORA Directive issued by the BMF as of 23 October 2020, as well as additional information that the BMF progressively publishes on its BORA Homepage since January 2021, providing guidance for customary documentary evidence required for different types of legal forms of entity in different member states and third-country jurisdictions.

Belgium

Saskia Lust
Stephanie van Gils
Loyens & Loeff

1. Belgian legal and administrative framework

The Belgian Law of 18 September 2017 on the prevention of money laundering and terrorist financing and on the limitation of cash payments (AML law) implemented the Fourth Anti-Money Laundering Directive of 20 May 2015 (4AMLD) in Belgium and introduced the Belgian ultimate beneficial owner (UBO) register. The AML law includes the framework for the Belgian UBO register. The incorporation and practical implementation of the UBO register is laid down in the Royal Decree of 30 July 2018 (Royal Decree). A ministerial order on the further practical implementation of the Belgian UBO register has been announced; however, it has not been published to date.

The General Administration of the Treasury within the Federal Public Service Finance (Administration of the Treasury) has published Frequently Asked Questions (FAQs), most recently amended on 21 April 2021.

On 1 October 2020 the Royal Decree of 23 September 2020 (New Royal Decree) was published, amending the Royal Decree of 2018. In addition to textual adjustments and technical corrections, the New Royal Decree introduced new (disclosure) obligations. The accuracy of the submitted information must be demonstrated with supporting documents.

2. Entry into force

The Royal Decree entered into force on 31 October 2018. The deadline for the reporting of the information was, in principle, 30 November 2018 (ie, one month after the entry into force of the Royal Decree). The deadline was postponed several times by the Federal Public Service Finance, finally until 30 September 2019. An administrative tolerance period was installed until 31 December 2019, during which no sanctions for non-compliance were imposed.

The New Royal Decree entered into force on 11 October 2020. The Administration of the Treasury has installed an administrative tolerance period until 31 August 2021 for registration of the supporting documents.

3. Targeted entities

3.1 Legal entities incorporated in Belgium: companies, foundations and (international) non-profit organisations

The Belgian UBO register collects the information of all UBOs of legal entities incorporated in Belgium, irrespective of the legal form of the Belgian entity and regardless of whether or not the entity has legal personality. The concerned legal entities incorporated in Belgium are companies (including partnerships), foundations and (international) non-profit organisations ((I)NPOs).

All UBOs of civil law partnerships (*maatschap/société simple*) (partnership) must be reported in the UBO register of companies.

Branches of foreign companies are (generally) not incorporated in Belgium and therefore do not need to report their UBOs to the Belgian UBO register.

3.2 Exception: FAQs – listed companies and 100% subsidiaries

The 4AMLD provides for an exemption for companies:

> *listed on a regulated market that [are] subject to disclosure requirements consistent with Union law or subject to equivalent international standards which ensure adequate transparency of ownership information (ie, listed companies).*

The Belgian AML law (or the Royal Decree) does not provide for an exemption for listed companies.

However, the Administration of the Treasury FAQs state that companies listed on a regulated market that are subject to disclosure requirements consistent with EU law or equivalent international standards, and that guarantee adequate transparency of ownership information are exempted from registering their UBOs in the Belgian UBO register. The regulated markets that are deemed to be subject to disclosure requirements consistent with EU law are the regulated markets listed in the European Commission's implementing acts as far as they are still in force. In the most recent FAQs, reference is made to a list of Equivalence Decisions taken by the European Commission. These listed companies are entirely exempted from registration in the UBO register, pursuant to the FAQs.

According to the FAQs, the exemption equally applies to subsidiaries that are directly or indirectly 100% owned by such a listed company.[1] In order to be identified as 100% (directly or indirectly) owned by such a listed company, the subsidiaries must sign up to the UBO register and register their ownership structure, including the listed company and all intermediate entities. Other than 100% owned subsidiaries of listed companies have the obligation to identify and register their UBOs.

---

1 The most recent FAQs state that, pending further clarification from the European Commission on the equivalence of the United Kingdom – which has not been established since the end of the transitional period on 31 December 2020 – the exception for the UBO register also applies to subsidiaries of UK listed companies.

As the Administration of the Treasury FAQs are 'for information purposes only' and despite the fact that the exception is in accordance with the 4AMLD, the exception for listed companies and their 100% subsidiaries has no legal basis in Belgium.

3.3 Trusts, fiduciaries and similar entities

Trustees are required to collect and keep adequate, accurate and current information on all UBOs of trusts, fiduciaries or similar legal entities – incorporated outside Belgium – if these trusts, fiduciaries and similar entities are administered in Belgium.

Belgian domestic law does not provide for the legal form of a trust. The AML law refers to the Belgian Code of Private International Law for the definition of a trust. According to the code, a trust is:

> *a legal relationship created by an act of the settlor or by a judicial decision, by which assets are placed under the control of a trustee in order to be administrated in the interest of the beneficiary or for a certain purpose.*[2]

Characteristics are that: (i) the assets of the trust form a separate estate and are not part of the estate of the trustee; (ii) the title to the assets of the trust is drafted in the name of the trustee or the name of another person on behalf of the trustee; and (iii) the trustee has the authority and the duty, in respect of which he/she is accountable, to manage, administer or dispose of the assets in accordance with the provisions of the trust and the special duties imposed by law on the trustee. The AML law confirms that in the context of the obligations of the Belgian UBO register, the 'express trust' is relevant (ie, the legal relationship created by a legal act of the settlor).

Trustees must register the information in the Belgian UBO register when:

- the trustee is established, domiciled or resides in Belgium;
- the registered office, the main office, the place of management of the trustee is located in Belgium; or
- the trustee established a business relationship or acquires real estate in Belgium in the name of the trust.

If the above-mentioned criteria are fulfilled in several EU member states including Belgium, trustees responsible for providing information are considered as having fulfilled their reporting obligation by transmitting an excerpt of the information on the UBOs registered in a similar register of another EU member state to the Administration of the Treasury.

---

2 Article 122 of the Law of 16 July 2004 holding the Belgian Code of Private International Law.

4. UBOs of Belgian legal entities

4.1 General rule

As a rule, UBOs who must be reported in the Belgian UBO register are the individuals – irrespective of their state of residency and/or nationality – who ultimately own or control the Belgian legal entity, and/or on whose behalf a transaction is executed or a business relationship is entered into.

Individuals who hold the Belgian legal entity through one or more (Belgian and/or foreign) intermediaries also count as UBOs of the Belgian legal entity. They are broadly defined as individuals who benefit, or will benefit, from a transaction or business relationship and who, *de jure* or *de facto*, directly or indirectly, have the power to decide on the execution of the transaction or the business relationship and/or to determine or agree to the modalities involved.

The definition of a UBO depends on the type of legal entity.

4.2 UBOs of Belgian companies

(a) Definitions – AML law

The AML law introduced the following definitions of UBOs of Belgian companies:

- **Category 1:** The UBOs of a company are the individuals who directly or indirectly own a sufficient percentage of voting rights or a sufficient ownership interest in a company. The following shareholdings are deemed to be an indication of a sufficient percentage of voting rights or a sufficient ownership interest:
  - the individuals who directly hold more than 25% of the voting rights, the shares or the share capital of a Belgian company (ie, a direct shareholding); and
  - the individuals who control the holding company or companies, in cases where the Belgian company is indirectly held through one or more holding companies, who hold more than 25% of the shares or the share capital of the Belgian company (ie, an indirect shareholding).
- **Category 2:** The individuals who control the company by other means. Control by other means may be assessed on the basis of the notion of 'control' specified in Article 1:14 of the Belgian Code on Companies and Associations, such as holding the majority of the voting rights, holding the right to appoint or dismiss the majority of the directors of the company, holding veto rights, having concluded a shareholders' agreement and joint control (ie, the control a select number of shareholders exercise together, when they have agreed that decisions regarding the orientation of the management cannot be taken without their mutual consent – eg, through a shareholders' agreement).

The aforesaid categories of UBOs are cumulative – that is, all individuals who can be identified based on these definitions must be reported to the UBO register.

- **Category 3:** In the event that no individual can be identified on the basis of the aforesaid definitions, or if there is doubt that the identified persons are the ultimate beneficiaries, the individual(s) who hold(s) the position of senior managing official need(s) to be reported to the UBO register. According to the explanatory memorandum, the senior managing official(s) is/are the leader(s) of the company who, in practice, exercise(s) the most decisive influence on the management of the company. In most cases, according to the explanatory memorandum, this will be the chief executive officer (CEO) or the chair of the executive committee. The Administration of the Treasury FAQs add that – in the absence of the CEO or the chair of the executive committee – the director, the manager, the representative of the executive committee and a member of the board of directors can be considered as senior managing official(s).

(b) 'Indirect shareholding' – FAQs

According to the Administration of the Treasury FAQs, an indirect UBO can be determined as follows:

- if an individual holds more than 50% of the voting rights, the shares or the share capital in an intermediary company ('control'), that holds more than 25% of the voting rights or shares of the Belgian company, the individual is deemed to be an indirect UBO; or
- if an individual holds a weighted percentage of more than 25% of the shares or voting rights through intermediary companies in an ownership chain, the individual is deemed to be an indirect UBO. This method is an extension of the definition in the AML law and therefore seems to have no legal basis.

We illustrate the difference between the definitions in the AML law and the Administration of the Treasury FAQs by way of examples on the next page.

Example 1: Notion of 'indirect control' – weighted percentages

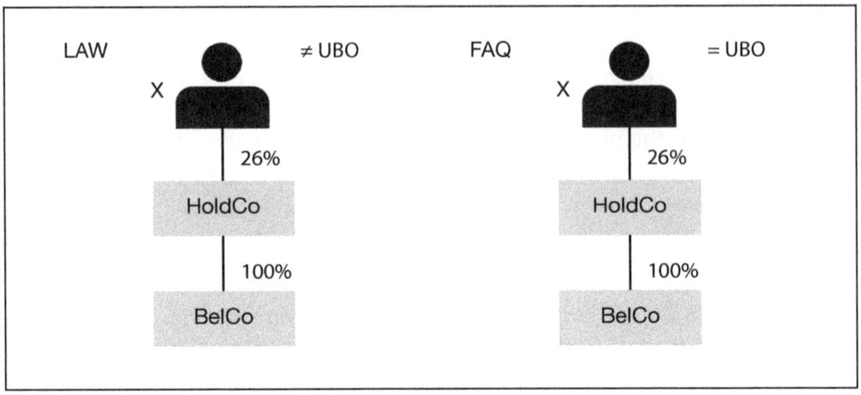

Individual X holds 26% of the shares of a holding company (HoldCo). HoldCo holds 100% of the shares of a Belgian company (BelCo). X does not control HoldCo (eg, by having the majority of the voting rights and/or by having a veto right).

According to the AML law, X is not deemed to be an indirect UBO of BelCo, as X does not control HoldCo.

According to the Administration of the Treasury FAQs, X is deemed to be an indirect UBO, as X holds a weighted percentage of more than 25% of the shares of BelCo.

Example 2: Notion of 'indirect control' – veto rights

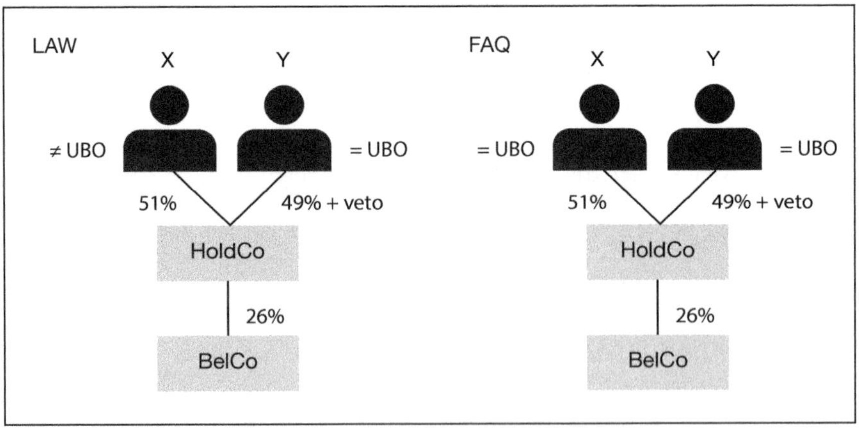

Individual X holds 51% of the shares of a holding company (HoldCo). Individual Y holds 49% of the shares of HoldCo. Y holds a veto right in HoldCo. HoldCo holds 26% of the shares of a Belgian company (BelCo).

According to the AML law, X is not deemed to be a UBO of BelCo, as Y holds a veto right in HoldCo and therefore X does not control HoldCo. Y is deemed to be a UBO of BelCo, as Y controls HoldCo and HoldCo holds more than 25% of the shares of BelCo.

According to the Administration of the Treasury FAQs, X and Y are both deemed to be UBOs of BelCo. X holds more than 50% of the shares of BelCo. Y holds more than 50% of the voting rights (veto right).

(c) Usufruct and bare ownership

If a bare owner holds more than 25% of the shares, the bare owner must be registered as the UBO who holds a sufficient ownership interest. If the usufructuary holds more than 25% of the shares and is entitled to the voting rights attached to these shares, the usufructuary must be registered as the UBO who holds a sufficient percentage of voting rights. This standpoint is taken in the (general) Administration of the Treasury FAQs and is not incorporated in the AML law or the Royal Decree.

(d) Partnerships

Partnerships are very often used as an estate-planning tool in Belgium. A partnership is a legal entity without legal personality. The UBOs must be reported in the UBO register of companies, on the basis of the definitions of UBOs of companies (see section 4.2(a) above).

Example: Notion of control 'by other means'

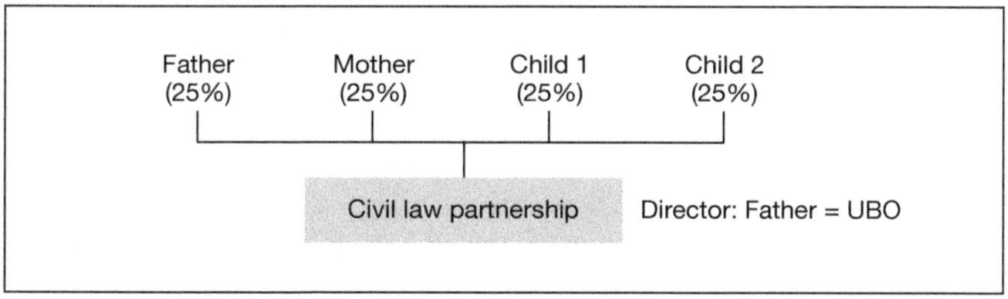

A mother, a father and their two children each hold a 25% interest (*delen/parts*) in a partnership. The father is the director of the partnership.

None of the family members qualifies as UBO of the 'first category', given a 25% shareholding. The father qualifies as UBO of the 'second category' (see section 4.2(a) above).

4.3 UBOs of Belgian foundations and (I)NPOs

The following individuals qualify as the UBOs of foundations and (I)NPOs:

- the members of the board of directors of the foundation and the (I)NPO;

- individuals who are entitled to represent the (I)NPO;
- individuals in charge of the daily management of the foundation and the (I)NPO;
- founders of the foundation;
- either the individuals, or the category of individuals when these have not yet been appointed, in whose interest the foundation or the (I)NPO has been established (ie, the beneficiaries); and
- any other individual who controls the foundation or the (I)NPO by other means.

The categories of UBOs mentioned above are cumulative. All individuals of these categories must be registered.

For the first three categories of UBOs of (I)NPOs, the information included in the Crossroads Bank for Enterprises, which is already publicly available, can be adopted and confirmed in the UBO register.

4.4 UBOs of trusts, fiduciaries and similar entities

The following individuals are considered as the UBOs of trusts, fiduciaries and similar entities:

- the founder(s);
- the fiduciary/fiduciaries or trustee(s);
- the protector(s) (if any);
- either the individuals, or the category of individuals when these have not yet been appointed, in whose interest the trust or fiduciary has been established or operates (ie, the beneficiaries); and
- any other individual who, by reason of his/her direct or indirect ownership or by other means, ultimately controls the fiduciary or trust.

The categories of UBOs mentioned above are cumulative. All individuals of these categories must be registered. If an individual qualifies as UBO according to more than one of the above-mentioned categories, the individual must be registered as UBO of each category separately.

5. Information to be reported

5.1 Electronic submission of information and term for submission

Adequate, accurate and current information on the UBO must be reported. The information that needs to be reported depends on the type of legal entity.

The reporting task rests with the members of the administrative body, the directors or legal representatives of the legal entity (see section 7.1 below).

The information on the UBOs needs to be submitted electronically via the website *MyMinFin* of the Federal Public Service Finance. The information must be reported within one month (after it becomes known). The accuracy of the information needs to be confirmed annually (see section 7.1 below).

Belgian legal entities (including partnerships and trusts) are registered in the UBO register on the basis of their enterprise number.

5.2 UBOs of companies

For UBOs of companies, the information that needs to be registered in the UBO register is as follows:

- the name of the UBO;
- the first name of the UBO;
- the day of birth of the UBO;
- the month of birth of the UBO;
- the year of birth of the UBO;
- the nationality of the UBO;
- the country of residence of the UBO;
- the full address of the UBO;
- the starting date of UBO-ship;
- the (Belgian or foreign) identification number of the UBO;
- the categor(y)(ies) of UBO-ship (see section 4.2(a) above);
- whether the UBO is a sole UBO or part of a group of UBOs;
- whether the UBO is a direct or an indirect UBO;
- in case of an indirect UBO, the number of the intermediate entities and details on the intermediate entities (including at least the name, date of incorporation, trade name, legal form, address and company number), irrespective of their state of establishment;
- the extent of the interest held. In case of a direct UBO holding shares or voting rights, it concerns the percentage of shares or voting rights. In case of an indirect UBO (indirectly) holding shares or voting rights, it concerns the weighted percentages of shares or voting rights in the Belgian company. The New Royal Decree introduces the obligation to also report the (weighted) percentage of shares or voting rights held in each intermediate entity. For UBOs who control a company 'by other means', it must be specified by which other means the Belgian company is controlled; and
- every document demonstrating that the information regarding the UBO is adequate, accurate and current (ie, the supporting documents, according to the New Royal Decree).

5.3 UBOs of foundations and (I)NPOs

For UBOs of foundations and (I)NPOs, the information that needs to be registered in the UBO register is as follows:

- the name of the UBO;
- the first name of the UBO;

- the day of birth of the UBO;
- the month of birth of the UBO;
- the year of birth of the UBO;
- the nationality of the UBO;
- the country of residence of the UBO;
- the full address of the UBO;
- the starting date of UBO-ship;
- the (Belgian or foreign) identification number of the UBO;
- the categor(y)(ies) of UBO-ship (see section 4.3 above);
- whether the UBO is a sole UBO or part of a group of UBOs; and
- every document demonstrating that the information regarding the UBO is adequate, accurate and current (ie, the supporting documents, according to the New Royal Decree).

5.4 UBOs of trusts, fiduciaries and similar entities

For UBOs of trusts, fiduciaries and similar entities, the information that needs to be registered in the UBO register is as follows:

- the name of the UBO;
- the first name of the UBO;
- the day of birth of the UBO;
- the month of birth of the UBO;
- the year of birth of the UBO;
- the nationality of the UBO;
- the country of residence of the UBO;
- the full address of the UBO;
- the (Belgian or foreign) identification number of the UBO;
- the categor(y)(ies) of UBO-ship (see section 4.4 above);
- the starting date of UBO-ship; and
- every document demonstrating that the information regarding the UBO is adequate, accurate and current (ie, supporting documents, according to the New Royal Decree).

To enable the registration of their UBOs in the Belgian UBO register, trusts, fiduciaries and similar entities must register in the Belgian Crossroads Bank for Enterprises to obtain an enterprise number.

5.5 Informing of the UBO

Belgian legal entities must inform the UBOs about the obligation to report information on the UBOs to the Belgian UBO register. They are also obliged to inform their UBOs of the following:

- the registration, the processing and the keeping of the information in the UBO register;

- the name and the address of the Administration of the Treasury, charged with the management of the Belgian UBO register;
- the access modalities for competent authorities, obliged entities and members of the public;
- the rights of the UBO according to Articles 12–22 and 34 of the European General Data Protection Regulation 2016/679 (GDPR); and
- the term during which the information is kept in the UBO register.

The Administration of the Treasury notifies the UBOs about the registration in the UBO register and informs them about the registered information.

5.6 Storage of information

The information registered in the UBO register will be stored for 10 years from the day of the loss of legal personality or the permanent liquidation of (the business of) the entity.

6. Access to the information

6.1 Two separate, online UBO registers

In Belgium, separate registers are established online for the UBOs of companies and for the UBOs of trusts. Foundations and (I)NPOs are treated like trusts for this purpose.

Access is granted to current information and the history of the changes made in the UBO register. The information can be consulted only on the basis of the enterprise number and/or the name of the Belgian legal entity.

6.2 Access to UBO register of companies

(a) Entities/persons with access

The following entities/persons have access to the UBO register of Belgian companies:

- the competent authorities;
- the obliged entities within the framework of their client identification obligations (eg, banks, notaries, lawyers etc); and
- any member of the public (with or without legitimate interest).

(b) Restrictions

Any member of the public has, in principle, access to the information listed in the first, fourth, fifth, sixth, seventh, ninth, eleventh, twelfth, thirteenth, fourteenth and fifteenth bullet points in section 5.2 above. Members of the public will have no access to:

- the first name of the UBO (second bullet point);

- the day of birth of the UBO (third bullet point);
- the full address of the UBO (eighth bullet point);
- the identification number of the UBO (tenth bullet point); and
- the supporting documents (sixteenth bullet point).

The obliged entities will have no access to the supporting documents, according to the New Royal Decree.

6.3 Access to UBO register of foundations and (I)NPOs

(a) Entities/persons with access

The following entities/persons have access to the UBO register of Belgian foundations and (I)NPOs:

- the competent authorities;
- the obliged entities within the framework of their client identification obligations (eg, banks, notaries, lawyers etc);
- every person or organisation who can demonstrate a legitimate interest.

The legitimate interest should be linked to the fight against money laundering or the financing of terrorism. The notion of 'legitimate interest' is not specified by the AML law, the Royal Decree or the Administration of the Treasury FAQs. It remains to be seen how this concept will be implemented in practice.

If a legitimate interest can be demonstrated, access will be granted to certain information reported on the UBOs in the six categories of foundations and (I)NPOs listed in section 4.3 above; and

- any member of the public (without legitimate interest) to the information of the UBOs in the first four categories listed in section 4.3 above, according to the New Royal Decree.

(b) Restrictions

According to the New Royal Decree, the obliged entities will have no access to the supporting documents.

Every person or organisation who can demonstrate a legitimate interest will have access to the information listed in the first, fourth, fifth, sixth, seventh, ninth, eleventh and twelfth bullet points in section 5.3 above. Persons or organisations with a legitimate interest will have no access to:

- the first name of the UBO (second bullet point);
- the day of birth of the UBO (third bullet point);
- the full address of the UBO (eighth bullet point);
- the identification number of the UBO (tenth bullet point); and
- the supporting documents (thirteenth bullet point).

The New Royal Decree introduced the access of members of the public without legitimate interest to information of the UBOs in the first four categories of foundations and (I)NPOs listed in section 4.3 above. The New Royal Decree does not provide for a limitation of access to certain information of these UBOs.

6.4 Access to UBO register of trusts, fiduciaries and similar entities

(a) Entities/persons with access

The following entities/persons have access to the UBO register of trusts, fiduciaries and similar entities:

- the competent authorities;
- the obliged entities within the framework of their client identification obligations (eg, banks, notaries, lawyers etc); and
- every person or organisation who can demonstrate a legitimate interest (see section 4.4 above).

(b) Restrictions

Every person or organisation who can demonstrate a legitimate interest will have access to the information listed in the first, fourth, fifth, sixth, seventh, tenth and eleventh bullet points listed in section 5.4 above. Persons or organisations with a legitimate interest will have no access to:

- the first name of the UBO (second bullet point);
- the day of birth of the UBO (third bullet point);
- the full address of the UBO (eighth bullet point);
- the identification number of the UBO (ninth bullet point); and
- the supporting documents (twelfth bullet point).

The obliged entities will have no access to the supporting documents, according to the New Royal Decree.

6.5 Access to UBO register of companies held via (private) foundation, (I)NPO, trust or fiduciary

The Administration of the Treasury FAQs confirm that if a company is held via a foundation, a(n) (I)NPO, a trust or a fiduciary, the information about the company's UBOs will be accessible to the public only if a legitimate interest can be demonstrated.

6.6 Request regarding limitation of access

Upon specific request of the UBO(s) or its legal representative, the Administration of the Treasury can limit access to the UBO register for (certain) obliged entities and members of the public. The access can either be fully blocked or limited to certain information about the UBO.

The Administration of the Treasury will allow the access limitation if the UBO can demonstrate that due to the exceptional circumstances of the case at hand, (unlimited) access to his/her personal information could lead to a disproportionate risk of fraud, kidnapping, blackmail, harassment, violence or intimidation. The UBO (or his/her legal representative) needs to demonstrate the disproportionate risk by evidentiary documents. The Administration of the Treasury provides the following examples of evidentiary documents in its FAQs:

- a reasoned derogation granted by another country with a similar register;
- the conclusions of a risk analysis report drawn up by an independent third party;
- a complaint to the police, a conviction or (court) decision, measures of police protection; or
- any other document demonstrating the existence of any of the risks.

The request concerns only the access to the registered information. The request for/approval of the access limitation does not exempt the entity from reporting the required information to the UBO register.

Upon registration of the required information on the UBO(s), the request can be submitted. As soon as the request has been submitted, the information will be blocked for (certain) obliged entities and members of the public (with or without a legitimate interest) until a final decision has been reached. In any case, the information regarding intermediate entities remains visible.

The limitation of access to information of minors and UBOs who are legally incapacitated is automatically granted.

The request concerns an administrative procedure. The request must be submitted to the Administration of the Treasury. According to the New Royal Decree, a second request can be submitted if the first request is unsuccessful. A (second) decision denying a limitation of access may be appealed to the Council of State (*Raad van State/Conseil d'Etat*).

The Royal Decree provides that a ministerial order can further implement the modalities of the request to limit access; however, no ministerial order has been published to date.

6.7 Consultation of the UBO register

The Royal Decree states that members of the public will be able to ask for information about UBOs only on the basis of either the enterprise number or the name of the entity, and therefore not on the basis of the name of the UBOs. A ministerial order could further implement the access for members of the public.

Every consultation of the UBO register will be registered and kept for 10 years.

Any individual or legal entity that may consult the data contained in the UBO register will pay a fee for each consultation. The fee shall not exceed the administrative costs of making the information available, including the costs of maintaining and developing the register. The fee amounts to €1.50 per consultation.

The Administration of the Treasury can conclude an agreement with the individuals or legal persons referred to above under which these individuals or legal persons pay an annual or quarterly flat-rate fee.

7. Compliance and sanctions

7.1 Reporting of information

All Belgian legal entities (companies, foundations and (I)NPOs) are required to collect and hold information on their UBO(s). The members of the administrative body of companies, foundations and (I)NPOs must report the UBO information required within one month after it becomes known or is changed. The accuracy of the information needs to be confirmed annually. The one-year term starts with the initial registration or with the most recent change. In principle, an automatic reminder will be sent by the UBO platform one month before the deadline expires. According to an administrative tolerance due to technical reasons, the first annual confirmation will have to be made in 2021.

Administrative fines between €250 and €50,000 may apply to the responsible members of the administrative body (board members/managers and, if any, one or more members of the executive committee and the individuals who, in the absence of an executive committee, participate in the effective management) for non-compliance with these obligations. The amount of the administrative fine shall be determined considering all relevant circumstances (including the severity and duration of the infringement, the degree of responsibility, the financial capacity, the degree of cooperation and/or any previous infringements of the person concerned).

Criminal fines ranging between €50 and €5,000 (to be multiplied by eight) may also apply.

7.2 Providing of information

The UBO has the obligation to provide the legal entity, of which he/she is the ultimate beneficiary, with all the information required to comply with the obligations under the UBO legislation.

Administrative fines of between €250 and €50,000 may apply to the UBO for non-compliance with this obligation. The amount of the administrative fine shall be determined considering all relevant circumstances, as described above.

7.3 GDPR compliance

As UBOs are by definition 'natural persons', the information that needs to be registered in the Belgian UBO register qualifies as personal data under the EU General Data Protection Regulation 2016/679 (GDPR).

The GDPR requires data controllers to have a valid legal ground for each type of personal data processing. In the context of the UBO register, this is the necessity for the data controller (the company) to comply with its legal obligations, which is established in the public interest (the prevention of money laundering and terrorist financing). This legal basis can also serve as justification for the collection and processing of the identification number in the National Register of the UBOs (which is as a general rule forbidden).

In addition, the GDPR contains a strict legal framework for the processing of personal data. As data controllers, companies have internal record-keeping obligations, data security obligations and an obligation to inform transparently all UBOs about the processing of their personal data, as well as an obligation to comply (under certain conditions) with requests for information, rectification, deletion etc.

The application of the GDPR also means that the personal data of UBOs may not be processed in any way that goes beyond the controller's legal obligations, that an information notice (complying with Article 13 of the GDPR and with the Royal Decree) must be presented to the UBO, that any outdated or erroneous data must be adjusted or deleted without delay, and that the UBOs personal data may not be kept for longer than 10 years.

Crown Dependencies

Paul Matthams
Stonehage Fleming; Advocate (non-practising) of the Royal Court of Jersey

1. Introduction

This chapter reviews the current 'state of play' in relation to the expressed desire of the three British Crown Dependencies of Jersey, Guernsey and the Isle of Man to:

- respond to the international initiatives towards the centralisation of beneficial ownership data in jurisdictions; and
- as part of the process of ensuring transparency concerning the ownership of legal persons, put in place processes to make relevant information publicly available.

At an international level it will be noted that the Interpretative Note issued in relation to Recommendation 24 of the Financial Action Task Force (FATF) list of Recommendations of 1990 states:

As part of the process of ensuring that there is adequate transparency regarding legal persons, countries should have mechanisms that:

(a) identify and describe the different types, forms and basic features of legal persons in the country;

(b) identify and describe the processes for: (i) the creation of those legal persons; and (ii) the obtaining and recording of basic and beneficial ownership information;

(c) make the above information publicly available; and

(d) assess the money laundering and terrorist financing risks associated with different types of legal persons created in the country.

To this initiative must of course be added the requirements set out in the Fifth Anti-Money Laundering Directive (5AMLD), which required EU member states to transpose its provisions into their domestic laws by 10 January 2020. However, before proceeding any further, it is necessary to recall the constitutional positions of the Crown Dependencies in relation to the United Kingdom and the European Union.

The Isle of Man is thought to have one of the oldest parliaments in the world, possibly dating back to the ninth century, when the Island was part of the Norwegian Kingdom of the Isles. In 1266, the Island was transferred to the

Crown of Scotland, and later to the then separate Crown of England. The Island was given its own legislature in 1765.

Jersey and Guernsey date their links to what is now the British Crown to 1066, being part of the Duchy of Normandy when Duke William became King William I at the time of the Norman conquest of England. In the early thirteenth century the English crown 'lost' most of its territories in France, including continental Normandy. However, the Channel Islands of Jersey and Guernsey remained a possession of the English Crown and with certain limitations were granted the powers to govern themselves and pass their own laws.

To this day, all three jurisdictions have their own parliaments, courts and laws. They owe allegiance to the British Queen and when passing so-called primary legislation, the equivalent to British Acts of Parliament, legislation from the three parliaments must be approved by Her Majesty's Most Honourable Privy Council, the formal body of advisers to the Sovereign, before it can become law. However, it remains the case that none of the three jurisdictions is represented in the British Parliament in London and by constitutional convention the British Parliament does not legislate directly for any of the Islands. On rare occasions UK legislation is 'extended' to the Crown Dependencies by an Order in Council of the Sovereign with their agreement. However, in relation to international matters, whilst the Crown Dependencies can and frequently do enter into bilateral agreements with other jurisdictions, they are not recognised internationally as sovereign states. Accordingly, international treaties and conventions require acceptance or ratification of such treaties and convention by the United Kingdom, such acceptance or ratification being expressly extended to them with their agreement, or they may complete specific international agreements if they have been entrusted to do so by the United Kingdom.

None of the three Islands was ever a member state of the European Union, but by what was known as Protocol 3 of the United Kingdom's Treaty of Accession to the then European Common Market of 1972 certain aspects of the United Kingdom's EU membership, particularly in relation to customs matters, applied to them. In particular, the Crown Dependencies were part of the EU Customs territory and there was free movement in agricultural goods and certain other products between the Islands and the European Union. However, they were in other respects treated as third countries by the European Union, although on occasions they would voluntarily apply EU legislation or seek to implement legislation which followed the international standards on which relevant EU legislation was based. It is in that context that the three jurisdictions are now seeking to implement legislative provisions concerning beneficial ownership registers. It should be noted that the subsequent withdrawal of the United Kingdom from the European Union in January 2020 had no direct effect on the commitments that had been given by the three jurisdictions in June 2019.

2. The joint statement

On 19 June 2019 the Crown Dependencies issued a joint statement,[1] and it is worth considering this in some detail. It followed a meeting of the chief ministers of Guernsey and the Isle of Man, and Jersey's minister for external relations, with UK parliamentarians to discuss the commitments that the three jurisdictions were prepared to make towards the implementation of laws to permit the introduction of public registers of beneficial ownership.

A register of beneficial ownership of companies had been introduced in the United Kingdom in 2015 and the British Government had then written to the Crown Dependencies encouraging them to do likewise. Bilateral agreements between the British Government and the Crown Dependencies (and others) were then signed, under which information on beneficial ownership held in the Crown Dependencies could be shared with British law enforcement agencies in certain circumstances.[2]

Not being member states of the European Union, the Crown Dependencies were not legally required to introduce the provisions of 4AMLD or 5AMLD into their domestic laws, and a commitment to extend the scope of beneficial ownership registers in the relevant jurisdictions did not at that stage extend to making such registers publicly available.

It was acknowledged in 2017 that public registers of beneficial ownership were not yet the so-called 'global standard', but the British Government indicated in the strongest terms that it would expect the adoption of public registers in the three jurisdictions when this standard was adopted as the global standard.

Matters had moved on by 19 June 2019 and, accordingly, in the joint statement it was recognised that the Crown Dependencies would implement their own publicly accessible registers of company beneficial ownership in line with what had become EU expectations, but some years after implementation in EU member states. The joint commitment by the Governments of Guernsey, Jersey and the Isle of Man pledged to "bring forward to our own parliament legislative proposals to establish public access to beneficial ownership data of companies held on a central register… within 12 months" of the publication of the EU Implementation Review of 5AMLD in January 2022.

Accordingly, whilst in the joint statement of 19 June 2019 the three governments confirmed a commitment to move towards developing

---

1 www.gov.gg/CHttpHandler.ashx?id=119716&p=0 (Government of Guernsey).

2 An example is the exchange of notes document of April 2016 between the Governments of Jersey and the United Kingdom found at www.jerseyfsc.org/media/1494/bo-exchange-of-notes-between-uk-and-jersey-sharing-of-beneficial-ownership-information.pdf.

international standards of accessibility and transparency "in the coming years", and noted that they already actively supported the development of global standards of transparency, and whilst the statement confirmed the wish of the three jurisdictions to introduce measures which were consistent with the European Union's approach to transparency of beneficial ownership data of companies under 5AMLD, they were only prepared to do so "within a deliverable timeframe" – that is, they would take their time and not be pushed into the introduction of publicly available registers before they were ready.

The commitment of the Crown Dependencies was given in order to meet the standards contained in the 4AMLD and 5AMLD provisions, and the joint announcement confirmed that there would be three clear steps to the process by which the jurisdictions would meet the developing international standards of accessibility and transparency. In summary:

- the interconnection of the Islands' registers of beneficial ownership of companies with those within the European Union for access by law enforcement authorities and financial intelligence units; then
- access for financial service businesses and certain other prescribed businesses for corporate due diligence purposes; and then
- public access aligned to the approach taken in the EU directives.[3]

Key to the proposals has always been the importance of accurate and verifiable data held on relevant files and the maintenance of a high standard of financial services regulation in each jurisdiction.

As the Guernsey chief minister stated in 2019:

The action plan also reinforces our message that it is for Guernsey to determine its own policy position. We will never compromise the high standard of our register, which is populated by verified up-to-date data, by the adoption of an inferior model. Our action plan will ensure that our register and corporate regulation continues to set a standard for larger jurisdictions to follow.[4]

While the three Crown Dependencies remain separate independent jurisdictions with their own parliaments and legislative processes, it was clear from the joint announcement that the Islands would seek to move together to introduce similar legislation in their respective territories, and to maintain the joint goals of meeting the developing international standards, in other cases without compromising the high quality of the registers and ensuring that information held was up to date and verifiable.

3. Jersey

In June 2020 the Jersey Government published draft legislation, the Financial

3 www.gov.je/News/2019/Pages/BeneficialOwnership.aspx.
4 www.gov.gg/benownership.

Services (Disclosure and Provision of Information) (Jersey) Law 2020. The law was adopted by the States of Jersey, the Island's Parliament, on 14 July 2020 received the approval of the Privy Council in accordance with the Island's constitutional arrangements with the British Crown, and came into force on 6 January 2021.

In addition to its specific aim to address requirements concerning the maintenance of registers of the beneficial ownership of legal persons, the Jersey legislation is also the vehicle by which a fully digital registry will be established in Jersey.

The law looks to the so-called 'Recommendation 24 – Beneficial ownership' contained in Recommendation 24 of the FATF list of recommendations (which in their original form date back to 1990), and introduces particular concepts and definitions to meet the particular requirements of Recommendation 24. These include statutory definitions of 'entity' and 'beneficial owner' and the adoption of the term 'significant person' to cover persons holding positions equivalent to directors and officers.

A key role in the new legislation is afforded to the local financial services regulator, the Jersey Financial Services Commission (JFSC), a department of which also acts as the Companies, Foundations and Partnerships Registry in Jersey. For many years it has been a requirement in Jersey that certain information concerning the identity of beneficial owners of companies and partnerships be provided to the JFSC on incorporation and in certain other circumstances, and this legislation subsequently extended the disclosure requirements to Jersey incorporated foundations.

Immediately following its enactment, most of the information contained in the beneficial ownership registers was confidential and there was to be further consultation with interested parties before information becomes more generally available to members of the public, this notwithstanding the commitment of the Crown Dependencies to move to publicly available beneficial ownership information by the end of 2023.

The legislation contains the concept of an 'entity', being a company, foundation or partnership, and by Article 4 of the law, on the creation of an entity, certain information must be provided to the JFSC. It must be noted that 'entity' does not include a trust and the current legislation does not anticipate the introduction of a register of trusts in Jersey. However, it should be noted that the trustee of a trust which owns or controls an 'entity' may still fall within the definition of a 'beneficial owner' in relation to an entity, and therefore its name, address and registration details may be required to be entered on the register.

The information to be provided includes the proposed entity's beneficial owner information and the proposed entity's significant person information. For these purposes, a 'beneficial owner' is defined in Article 2 of the law as follows:

'beneficial owner' of an entity means an individual who ultimately owns or controls the entity, or the individual on whose behalf a transaction is being conducted by the entity, including an individual who exercises ultimate effective control over the entity.

While it has been a requirement for beneficial owner information to be provided to the JFSC for many years (under different and earlier legislation),[5] the requirement for significant person information extends considerably the information now required to be provided to the JFSC in relation to those who will manage and control the entity. The term 'significant person' in relation to an entity includes foundation council members, company directors and secretaries, general partners of incorporated and separate limited partnerships, limited liability partners who participate in the management of the partnership and other persons purporting to act in a similar capacity to these persons in relation to another type of entity. The information to be provided will be prescribed in secondary legislation enacted pursuant to powers contained in the law.

Once information has been provided, any change must be notified to the JFSC within 21 days after the entity becomes aware of the change unless the entity is listed on a regulated market.

By Article 5 of the law, each entity must provide an annual confirmation statement verifying the accuracy of the beneficial owner information, the significant person information and any other prescribed information as at 1 January each year. The annual confirmation statement must be provided by the end of the following month (ie, by the end of February each year).

The Jersey legislation also introduces the concept of a 'nominated person' for each entity and it is the nominated person who will be responsible for the provision of the required information under Articles 4 and 5 of the law. The nominated person must fall within one of the categories listed in Article 6 of the law. These are a local regulated trust company business, funds services business or a lawyer or accountant who is ordinarily resident in Jersey and regulated under the local proceeds of crime anti-money laundering legislation, or a significant person of the entity who is ordinarily resident in Jersey.

By Article 8 of the Jersey law, the JFSC must maintain a register to hold the beneficial owner and significant person information and the information contained in the annual confirmation statements, and it must be assumed that it will be the information from this register which will become publicly available.

The law also introduces the concepts of a local competent authority and a foreign competent authority. The local competent authority means the JFSC,

5 Principally pursuant to provisions contained in the Control of Borrowing (Jersey) Order, 1958 as amended.

the local joint financial crimes unit, the attorney general of Jersey, the minister for external relations, and "any other person, organisation or office holder prescribed by Regulations". A foreign competent authority is an authority that, broadly speaking, exercises functions in relation to anti-money laundering and terrorist financing activities, and also functions relating to the failure to comply with international sanctions and certain other matters.

As far as local competent authorities are concerned, Article 9 gives them the power to seek to obtain information and documents and to answer questions in relation to an entity from a nominated person for the entity, a significant person of the entity, or the entity itself. When one remembers that a significant person of an entity includes its directors, foundation council members etc, it will be seen that the scope of persons who may potentially be served with a notice under Article 9 is very wide.

Article 10 places certain limits on the onward disclosure of information, but by Article 10(4) the JFSC may "enter into agreements and other arrangements for the sharing and exchange of information as permitted by this Article", and it is expected that it is under this article that legal authority may in due course be found for the wider disclosure of information.

As far as foreign competent authorities are concerned, they must request a local competent authority to assist them to obtain access to such information as the foreign competent authority requires, and by Article 11(4)(c) this can include beneficial ownership information which the local competent authority can obtain on behalf of the foreign competent authority. It should be noted that these provisions will come into force before beneficial ownership information becomes publicly available.

Part 4 of the law includes provisions dealing with fees and charges, gives the States of Jersey the power to make regulations and gives the JFSC the power to prepare and issue a code of practice "setting out the principles and detailed requirements that must be complied with in carrying out any requirement under this Law".

Transitional provisions contained in a schedule to the law required existing entities to notify the JFSC of the appointment of a nominated person and the information to be contained in an annual statement within three months of the law coming into force.[6]

I turn later to the proposed secondary legislation which will deal with the making of information concerning Jersey entities publicly available; but first let us look briefly at proposals in the other Crown Dependencies.

4. Guernsey

In Guernsey, a centralised register of beneficial ownership of 'legal persons' was

---

6 Time limit for filing extended to 30 September 2021.

introduced on 15 August 2017 when the Beneficial Ownership of Legal Persons (Guernsey) Law, 2017 came into force. It established a centralised non-public register of beneficial ownership of Guernsey legal persons to be maintained by the Office of the Registrar of Beneficial Ownership of Legal Persons, an office physically located within Guernsey's Financial Intelligence Service (FIS) premises.

The register can be accessed only by specified individuals from the Guernsey Financial Services Commission (GFSC), the FIS and the registry for the purposes of discharging their statutory duties.

The law requires resident agents in Guernsey to identify and collect specified information about the beneficial owners of entities that fall within the scope of the law for which they act as resident agent, and to submit the information to the registry. It also imposes duties on beneficial owners to supply information to resident agents and to update them of any changes.

It applies to Guernsey companies, limited liability partnerships and foundations, but not trusts. However, it is important to note that while a trust itself is not an entity whose 'beneficial owners' are required to be identified, in all three jurisdictions the legislation provides for cases where trusts hold stakes in entities whose beneficial owners are required to be identified. Broadly speaking, where a trust holds more than 25% of the shares or other interest in a relevant entity, the trustee must be treated and identified as the beneficial owner of that entity.[7] Where the trustee is itself a regulated entity in the relevant jurisdiction, no further information is required to be provided concerning the trustee beyond the name of the trustee and its registration number. At present the information on the register is not publicly available but is disclosable to tax authorities and regulatory and law enforcement authorities in appropriate cases. Unlike Jersey, which had maintained a centralised register of company beneficial ownership information since the 1980s, in Guernsey the 2017 legislation introduced a centralised register for the first time.

In June 2020 the Guernsey Parliament approved amendments to the 2017 legislation to extend the information-gathering powers of the Guernsey authorities and to support the Island's commitment to comply with 5AMLD.[8] However, in terms of timing, it is presently not expected that the central register will be available to businesses for due diligence purposes until 2022, and only in 2023 will proposals be brought forward to make beneficial ownership information available to the general public; although one would not be surprised to see pressure being brought to bear for that timescale to be accelerated.

7 In regulations made pursuant to the Beneficial Ownership of Legal Persons (Guernsey) Law, 2017.
8 Beneficial Ownership of Legal Persons (Guernsey) Law, 2017, as amended.

5. Isle of Man

In the Isle of Man the Beneficial Ownership Act came into force in June 2017, and in common with the other Crown Dependencies it also applies to companies, limited partnerships with corporate personality and foundations. Again, it does not apply directly to trusts. In the Isle of Man it is a requirement that each 'relevant entity' appoints a 'nominated officer' and it is that individual who is responsible for providing the information to the centralised database and for keeping it up to date. A nominated officer must either be an individual resident in the Isle of Man or a local licensed corporate services provider.

The act requires the identification of 'natural persons' – that is, individuals who own or control a relevant entity and the wording of the legislation is deliberately broad to encompass all individuals holding a relevant interest in the entity concerned or who are in a position to exercise control over it. In the case of a company that is owned by a corporate trustee, it may well be the shareholders of that corporate trustee who are the beneficial owners of the underlying company, together with beneficiaries of the relevant trust with fixed interests, but not discretionary beneficiaries.[9] It is even thought that a protector with a power to change the trustees of a trust may fall within the definition of a 'beneficial owner' of the underlying company. However, in the Isle of Man, not all beneficial owners are 'registrable' and will therefore appear on the database, and it is for the nominated officer to decide whether or not an individual meets the criteria to be 'registrable' – broadly speaking, whether or not the individual owns or controls more than 25% of a registrable entity. Legislation to amend the Isle of Man's Beneficial Ownership Act 2017 to confirm the accuracy of data, to meet international standards on timeliness for submission of information, and to permit the extraction of data to assist with international reporting obligations was passed by the local parliament in March 2021. However, separate or further revised legislation will be required before beneficial ownership information will become publicly available.

As in the case of other Crown Dependencies, the Isle of Man Government has committed to a staged process, which can be summarised as follows:

- during 2021 to develop the ability for the Island's central registers of beneficial ownership to become interconnected with central registers held in the EU member states to enable legal and beneficial ownership information to be shared with specific designated competent authorities and financial intelligence units;
- during 2022 to enable access to the central registers to be made available for due diligence purposes; and

---

9 See Guidance issued by the Isle of Man Financial Services Authority available at www.gov.im/media/1357278/beneficial-ownership-act-2017-guidance-june-2017-gc-no-2017-0003.pdf.

- by the end of 2023 to bring forward proposals to establish public access to the beneficial ownership registers in line with the principles of 5AMLD.

6. Summary

It will be seen from the above that the three Crown Dependencies of Jersey, Guernsey and the Isle of Man are on a slower track than many other jurisdictions, particularly EU member states, towards the introduction of publicly accessible registers of beneficial ownership of relevant entities. In line with the joint commitment from the governments of the three jurisdictions in June 2019, all are in the process of amending their legislation to ensure that the information held or capable of being held on the registers in each jurisdiction is accurate and verifiable and will be capable of being made publicly available when further legislation in each jurisdiction is enacted.

The legislation takes account of the principles underlying 4AMLD and 5AMLD without necessarily blindly following the specific provisions.

In Jersey, secondary legislation has now been enacted,[10] specifying:

- the information which must be provided to the JFSC;
- the information that is in due course but not immediately to be made available for public inspection; and
- the circumstances in which an application may be made for certain information not to be made available for public inspection and the procedure for making such an application.

The information required to be produced for beneficial owners and significant persons is likely to be broadly similar in the three jurisdictions.

For beneficial owners:

- the name and any former name or other names by which the individual is or was known;
- an address for correspondence to the individual;
- the residential address of the individual;
- the individual's nationality;
- the individual's occupation;
- the individual's gender;
- the individual's date of birth; and
- the individual's place and country of birth.

For significant persons:

- the name of the person;

---

10 Financial Services (Disclosure and Provision of Information) (Jersey) Order 2020 and Financial Services (Disclosure and Provision of Information) (Jersey) Regulations 2020.

- the month and year of the person's date of birth;
- an address for correspondence to the person;
- the person's nationality; and
- the person's occupation.

The regulation will not apply to information in relation to persons who are under 18 years old.

Considering again the Jersey legislation, it is intended that the significant person information (but not (yet) beneficial ownership information unless beneficial owners are also significant persons) listed above will in general be publicly available, together with, in relation to a company, the name and address of each member of the company and the class and number of shares that are held by each member. It will be possible for a significant person to apply to the JFSC to stop information in relation to the individual being publicly available on the following grounds:

- if the applicant considers that there is a serious risk that the applicant, or a person who lives with the applicant, will be subjected to violence or intimidation as a result of the information being made available for public inspection;
- if the applicant considers that there is a serious risk of damage or threat to property as a result of the information being made available for public inspection; or
- if there are exceptional circumstances that justify the making of the application.

It is expected that guidance will be issued on what does or does not constitute exceptional circumstances.

The legislation also contains an appeals process. Appeals are made to the Royal Court of Jersey against the decision on the ground that the decision was unreasonable having regard to all the circumstances of the case. On hearing an appeal the court may: (i) confirm, reverse or vary a decision of the JFSC; and (ii) make such order as to the costs of the appeal as it thinks appropriate.

So, to summarise the current 'state of play' in the Crown Dependencies of Jersey, Guernsey and the Isle of Man, one can say:

- in line with the joint statement of June 2019, all are in the process of amending their legislation to enhance the information held in their respective central registries in relation to companies and other corporate vehicles;
- that amending legislation does not at present envisage the introduction of registers of trusts;
- it is anticipated that individuals whose information may become publicly available may be able to avail themselves of a process by which

they apply for certain information not to be publicly available, but probably only on limited grounds;

- foundations are incorporated legal entities in all three jurisdictions and therefore will fall within the ambit of the amending legislation. Trusts are not legal entities for these purposes, but the trustees of trusts may still be beneficial owners of such entities; and
- the timescale is such that it is not intended that information on relevant registers concerning beneficial ownership will generally become publicly available before late 2023.

Cyprus

George Economides
E&G Economides LLC

1. Introduction and Cyprus transposing legislation

As a member state of the European Union, the Republic of Cyprus always aims to be in full compliance with all applicable EU laws, directives and guidelines. Cyprus has now fully transposed the Fourth EU Anti-Money Laundering Directive (4AMLD) and the Fifth EU Anti-Money Laundering Directive (5AMLD) into domestic legislation.

One of the main aims highlighted by 4AMLD is the creation and retention of centralised ultimate beneficial owner registers for companies and trusts. In general, through such central registers, the various competent authorities of member states shall have timely and unrestricted access in their effort to better tackle the combating of money laundering, terrorist financing and related predicate offences.

Furthermore, the most significant change brought by 5AMLD is that the general public shall be granted certain access to beneficial owner registers of EU-based companies.

1.1 Prior to the introduction of beneficial owner registers

Up until the transposition of 4AMLD into the relevant national Cyprus law, Cyprus did not have any public registers nor was there any obligation to submit or disclose to the Cyprus Registrar of Companies or to any other official authority details of beneficial or ultimate beneficial ownership without a court or other related order.

(a) Cyprus companies

The only requirement of public disclosure to the Registrar of Companies has been in relation to the registered shareholder of each Cyprus company, often being nominee shareholders. The beneficial owner information or other sensitive information relating to either companies or trusts was collected, assessed and kept as part of the needed compliance and due diligence by professionals (eg, corporate or trust professionals, lawyers, accountants, auditors) or even by banks. They would only disclose such information to a Cyprus competent authority following a specific official request and/or a Cyprus court order.

(b) Cyprus Trust Registers

In relation to trusts, as from September 2013, an amendment to the Law Regulating Companies providing Administrative Services and Related Matters 196(I)/2012 (the so-called Cyprus Fiduciaries Law), through Section 25, introduced the obligation for the establishment and keeping of registration of trusts (Trust Registers). These Trust Registers continue to be in place and are not public. In brief, each trust regulated by Cyprus laws which has at least one Cyprus resident trustee must, within 15 days of its establishment, disclose the following information: (i) the name of the trust; (ii) the name and full address of every trustee at all relevant times; (iii) the date of establishment of the trust; (iv) if applicable, the date of any change in the law governing the trust to or from Cyprus laws; and (v) where applicable, the date of termination of the trust. Other sensitive and/or confidential information such as the identity of the settlor, beneficiaries, protector or even the trust deed itself are not requested to be disclosed. The aforementioned information that needs to be disclosed is entered into the relevant Trust Register at the level of one of the three competent authorities/regulators of the fiduciary industry (depending on which regulator the professional trustee is regulated by), as follows:

- the Cyprus Bar Association (CYBAR);
- the Institute of Certified Public Accountants of Cyprus (ICPAC); or
- the Cyprus Securities and Exchange Commission (CYSEC) in all other cases in which the Cyprus resident trustee is not regulated by CYBAR or ICPAC.

It is further provided that these competent authorities may exchange information with each other for the purposes of carrying out their duties under the Fiduciaries Law and the Prevention and Suppression of Money Laundering and Terrorist Financing Law.

1.2 Implementation of the EU Anti-Money Laundering Directives

The 4AMLD was implemented in national legislation on 3 April 2018, being the date that it was published in the official newspaper (the *Gazette*) of the Republic of Cyprus. Further, most recently, on 18 February 2021 and as published in the *Gazette* on 23 February 2021, there were various additional amendments, effectively also transposing 5AMLD into national legislation.

More specifically, the Prevention and Suppression of Money Laundering and Terrorist Financing Law 188(I)/2017, which was first implemented on 31 December 2007, has been amended through the amending laws 13(I)/2018 and 13(I)/2021, thus effectively becoming the transposing legislation of 4AMLD and 5AMLD (AML Law).

Amongst various other amendments introduced in the AML Law, there came the requirement for the establishment of the relevant Cyprus beneficial ownership registers, namely through the insertion of Sections 61A and 61C. Specifically, Section 61A of the AML Law relates to the creation of a beneficial ownership register for companies and other legal entities, whereas Section 61C of the AML Law relates to the creation of a beneficial ownership register for trusts and other legal arrangements with a structure or functions similar to trusts.

Other central beneficial owner-related registers provided within the AML Law, and which are not covered within this chapter, are for:

- clubs, unions, federations and organisations (as per Section 61B of the AML Law);
- bank accounts, payment accounts and safe-deposit boxes (as per Section 61D of the AML Law); and
- providers of cryptocurrency-related services (as per Section 61E of the AML Law).

The 6AMLD, which is already published in the official journal of the European Union, provides that member states must implement it in their national legislation by 3 December 2020.

2. Definitions as per the AML Law

2.1 Definition of a 'beneficial owner'

As per Section 2 of the AML Law, a 'beneficial owner' is defined as any natural person who ultimately owns or controls the customer and/or the natural person on whose behalf a transaction or activity is being conducted, and includes at least the following.

(a) In the case of companies

Any natural person who ultimately owns or controls a company through direct or indirect ownership of the shares or voting rights or through bearer shares or ownership interest or through other means, an interest of 25% plus one share.

An indication of indirect ownership shall be an effective shareholding or ownership interest (as aforementioned) of more than 25% in the customer held by a company, which is under the control of a natural person, or by multiple companies, which are under the control of the same natural person or persons.

It is further provided that the control by other means can be verified, amongst others, based on the criteria provided for in Sections 142(1)(b) and 148 of the Companies Law. In brief, Section 148 sets out various criteria through which a company can be deemed subsidiary of another and in turn that other company being deemed as the holding company of that subsidiary; whereas Section 142(1)(b) refers to the need for consolidated accounts as per the relevant provisions of international accounting standards.

(b) ***In the case of trusts***

In the case of trusts, the following are considered beneficial owners:

- the settlors;
- the trustees or commissioners;
- the protectors, if any;
- the beneficiaries, or where the individual benefiting from the legal arrangement or legal entity has yet to be determined, the class of persons in whose main interest the legal arrangement or entity is set up or operates; and
- any other natural person exercising ultimate/effective control over the trust by means of direct or indirect ownership or by other means.

2.2 Definition of 'obliged entities'

As per Section 2A of the AML Law, 'obliged entities' include, amongst others, credit and financial institutions (banks), auditors, external accountants, tax advisers, independent legal professionals, corporate service providers, and those offering fiduciary and director services as well as trustee services.

2.3 Definition of 'competent authorities'

'Competent authorities' are defined as the Supervising Authority, the Unit for Combating Money Laundering Offences, the Inland Revenue, the Customs and Excise, and the Police.

3. Central beneficial owner register for companies

Section 61A of the AML Law governs the creation, maintenance and operation of the central beneficial owner register for companies and other legal entities (the Register).

The competent authority for the maintenance of the Register is the Registrar of Companies and Official Receiver, thereafter referred to as 'the Supervising Authority'.

The Supervising Authority issued its related Regulations on 12 March 2021, and these are covered in section 3.1 below.

Every company and other legal entity incorporated in the Republic of Cyprus is required to obtain and maintain adequate, accurate and current information on its beneficial ownership, as defined in section 2.1(a) above, including details of the beneficial interests held. The beneficial owners, other related beneficiaries and controlling persons must provide to the companies and other legal entities all necessary information so as to be compliant with the relevant provisions of the AML Law.

Companies and legal entities must provide all such information to obliged entities as part of their customer due diligence measures in accordance with the AML Law.

Further, such information must be made accessible in a timely manner to competent authorities within the framework of exercising their competencies.

The Registrar of Companies and Official Receiver is the competent Supervising Authority of the Register, and is responsible for its creation, keeping and handling. The creation, operation, right and legalisation of access and related matters of the Register shall be determined in the Regulations issued by the Supervising Authority pursuant to the provisions of the AML Law. Such Regulations shall be binding and obligatory as to their implementation by the relevant persons.

Any differences in relation to beneficial ownership information contained in the Register, which may be detected by the obliged entities or by competent authorities, shall be communicated to the Supervising Authority of the Register accordingly. Further, the Supervising Authority shall ensure prompt resolution of any resulting dispute and if considered necessary, until such resolution is achieved, to include an appropriate reference within the Register about such possible difference.

Access to beneficial ownership information contained in the Register is available to the following:

- the competent authorities, which shall have timely and unrestricted access to all information contained within the Register, and without alerting the relevant companies and other legal entities about such access. In turn, the competent authorities can provide such information to the respective competent authorities of other member states free of charge;
- the obligated entities in the framework of their customer due diligence work and beneficial ownership identification. It is further provided that obligated entities are not permitted to rely exclusively on information contained within the Register for the purposes of their due diligence related obligations as prescribed in the AML Law; and
- members of the wider public, who shall have access to the name, month, year of birth, nationality and country of residence of beneficial owners, as well as to the nature and extent of rights that they have.

Access to the Register by obligated entities and by members of the wider public must be made via electronic registration and is subject to an administrative fee to be determined in the Regulations.

In exceptional circumstances, to be determined in the Regulations, there may be full or partial access prevention on the beneficial ownership information, where such access could expose the beneficial owner to risk of fraud, kidnapping, blackmail, violence or intimidation, or where the beneficial owner is a minor or otherwise incapable. Such access prevention shall not apply to credit and financial institutions.

Persons may apply to the Supervising Authority for exclusion of making publicly available beneficial ownership information. The Regulations will provide the necessary guidelines thereon. The decision of the Supervising Authority on each such case may be challenged in the courts.

The Supervising Authority shall keep all the information on the actual beneficial owners for companies and legal entities incorporated or having their corporate seat in the Republic of Cyprus.

The procedure and timeframes for such companies and legal entities to provide or make updates/changes on the relevant ultimate beneficial owner information shall be governed by the relevant regulations.

A person who refuses or omits or neglects to fulfil the aforementioned obligations of this law in relation to the provision of relevant beneficial owner information of companies and other legal entities is subject to a €200 fine and thereafter to an additional €100 fine for every continuing day of delay, with the maximum total fine being capped at €20,000.

In cases where a person, after receiving a relevant notification from the Supervising Authority, continues, omits or neglects to fulfil their aforementioned obligations and/or the beneficial owner-related information provided is knowingly false, incorrect or misleading, such person is guilty of a criminal offence. In case of conviction, the person could be jailed for a period not exceeding one year and/or sentenced to a fine that does not exceed €100,000. The same applies to legal persons (companies) and their physical person officials, for whom it is proven that they consented or took part in this criminal offence.

In cases of companies and other legal entities which are deregistered from the Companies Registrar, the relevant information held on the Register shall remain available for up to 10 years from deregistration date. For such cases, after the lapse of five years from deregistration, access to the relevant information on the Register shall be available only for purposes of an administrative or criminal investigation by a competent authority or for the purposes of the AML Law.

The Register shall be interconnected with the European central platform that was established pursuant to Article 22 of EU Directive 2017/1132. The Supervising Authority shall be responsible for establishing relevant mechanisms, measures and procedures for ensuring timely accuracy of the contained information.

The initial date for the commencement of collection of information has been set by the Supervising Authority as 16 March 2021, with an expected grace period of six months for existing companies to collect all the details to enter into the system.

3.1 Regulations issued by the Supervising Authority

On 12 March 2021 the Registrar of Companies and Official Receiver, as the competent Supervising Authority of the beneficial owner Register for companies and other legal entities, issued its Regulations as per Section 61(4) of the AML Law.

The main elements of the Regulations that are not specifically covered by the AML Law are set out within this section.

Definitions:

- 'Company' is defined as a company of limited liability by shares or guarantee or a European public company of limited liability that is formed or registered as per the Companies Law; and
- 'Other legal entity' is defined as any legal entity registered at the Companies Registrar.

The Regulations do not apply to companies and legal entities:

- that are listed on a regulated market subject to relevant notifications as per EU legislation;
- that are subject to equivalent international standards that secure sufficient transparency on ownership information;
- that have applied to the Companies Registrar for their deregistration prior to the commencing date of these Regulations; or
- whose liquidation has started prior to the commencing date of these Regulations.

(a) Information collected

Information to be collected and maintained by companies and other legal entities and their officials in relation to beneficial owners shall need to be complete, accurate and current, and shall include the following:

- name and surname, date of birth, nationality and residential address of each beneficial owner;
- the nature and extent of the ultimate ownership held directly or indirectly by each beneficial owner, such as through share percentage, voting rights, significant influence or through other means of exercising control;
- the number, type and issuing country of the document used to verify the identity of the natural person;
- the date at which a natural person has become an ultimate beneficiary; and
- the date at which there has been a change or ceasing of a natural person as an ultimate beneficiary.

In cases where no beneficial owner can be identified after all possible efforts and provided there are no sustainable suspicions or if there is a doubt as to whether the identified person is the beneficial owner, then it is necessary to designate a natural person holding a position of a senior executive along with all the information details mentioned in the bullet points above.

All the aforementioned information is submitted, maintained, kept and updated by the company or other legal entity and its officials at the company's or other legal entity's registered office.

(b) ***Notices sent by companies and other legal entities***

Companies and other legal entities shall send a written and signed notice to any physical person who they reasonably believe to be a beneficial owner.

Such notice shall demand from that physical person to confirm within 15 days from the date of the notice whether he/she is a beneficial owner of that company or other legal entity, and if he/she is, to provide in writing current or corrected information as prescribed in the bullet points in section 3.1(a) above.

(c) ***Obligation of beneficial owners***

A person who is a beneficial owner to a company or other legal entity must notify in writing the company or other legal entity of any change or inconsistency in the prescribed information contained in the Register relating to that person or in case that person ceases to be a beneficial owner. Such notice must be provided within 15 days from the date of the relevant change or within 15 days from the date that the person could reasonably know of such change.

This obligation does not apply if the beneficial owner relating to such change has already been contacted in writing in this respect by the company or other legal entity, in which case they must comply with that other notice.

(d) ***Due dates for submission and confirmation of information***

Companies and other legal entities formed or registered before the effective date of these Regulations, and their officials, are obliged to submit via electronic means the relevant information for the Register within six months from the date of commencement of these Regulations; whereas in the case of formation or registration after the effective date of these Regulations, the relevant information must be submitted via electronic means within 30 days from the date of their formation or registration.

Any changes to the required information for the Register must be submitted via electronic means within 14 days from the date that such change has come to the attention of a company or other legal entity and its officials.

Furthermore, a company and other legal entity and its officials must confirm, via electronic means, the accuracy of the information contained in the Register during the period of 1–31 December of each year.

(e) ***Fines***

In relation to the fines for non-compliance, it is being clarified that there shall be no fine imposed on an official of a company or other legal entity, provided that such official has shown due care for compliance with the relevant law provisions and the offence is not as a result of an action, omission or neglect from the official's side.

(f) ***Electronic access to the Register information***

Submission of and access to information on the Register shall be made only via electronic means.

A company or other legal entity and its officials should obtain access codes for the ARIADNE portal system, through which they will gain electronic access for the submission of information relevant to the Register.

Competent authorities shall, free of charge, have fast and unrestricted access via electronic means to beneficial owner-related information contained in the Register.

Obliged entities and the general public shall have access to the information as prescribed in the AML Law at a cost of €3.50 per company or other legal entity, provided such obliged entity or member of the public is registered on the electronic portal.

In cases where the beneficial owner of a company or other legal entity is underage, access to the relevant information by obliged entities (excluding credit and financial institutions) or a member of the public may only be made available following a fully justified written request to the Supervising Authority, which shall be assessed accordingly before being approved or not, and where needed the Supervising Authority shall ask for further justifications or information supporting the reasons for such request. The Supervising Authority must communicate its decision to the applicant within 30 days from the date of taking its decision. In case of rejection the applicant may challenge this in the courts.

(g) ***Exclusion from making information publicly available***

For the permitted reasons as prescribed in the AML Law for which a beneficial owner wishes to have all or part of his/her details excluded from being available to obliged entities or to members of the public upon request, then the said beneficial owner, or the company or other legal entity having the approval of the said beneficial owner, or the guardian of an incapacitated person, shall make a fully justified written request to the Supervising Authority, which shall be assessed accordingly before being approved or not, and where needed the Supervising Authority shall ask for further justifications or information supporting the reasons for such request. The Supervising Authority must communicate its decision to the applicant within 30 days from the date of taking its decision, and in case of rejection the applicant may challenge this in the courts.

During the assessment of the written request, access to the relevant beneficial ownership information covered by the written request shall not be permitted to obliged entities or to members of the public.

(h) ***Reporting and resolution of inconsistencies***

Any differences in relation to beneficial ownership information contained in the Register, which may be detected by the obliged entities or by competent authorities, shall be communicated electronically to the Supervising Authority of the Register accordingly. In the case of obliged entities, such communication must be made within 30 days of this inconsistency/difference coming to its attention along with any relevant supporting documentation.

Upon receiving such reporting, the Supervising Authority shall assess it accordingly and, if considered necessary, include an appropriate reference within the Register about such possible difference until a resolution is achieved.

In the meantime, the Supervising Authority shall send a written notice to the concerned company or other legal entity along with all relevant details of the difference, and request from that company or other legal entity and its officials a fully justified reply within 30 days. Such reply should make clear whether the detected difference is justified and, if so, provide through electronic means the revised and corrected information on the Register so that a resolution is achieved. Failure to comply with such request is a criminal offence and can carry the aforementioned fines as prescribed in the AML Law.

(i) ***Incomplete information submissions***

The Supervising Authority may reject any information submitted to the Register which is incomplete or which does not conform to the applicable provisions of the AML Law or to the related Regulations.

In case of such rejection, the Supervising Authority can ask in writing from the said company or other legal entity and its officials to fill in, amend or correct the information accordingly and where applicable to submit the necessary supporting documents, via electronic means, within 15 days from the date of the written request. Failure to comply with such request is a criminal offence and can carry the relevant fines as prescribed in the AML Law.

4. Central beneficial owner register for trusts

Section 61C of the AML Law governs the creation, maintenance and operation of the central beneficial owner register for trusts and other types of legal arrangement with a structure or functions similar to trusts (the Trust Register).

The competent authority for the maintenance of the Trust Register is the Cyprus Securities and Exchange Commission (CYSEC), thereafter referred to as 'the Supervising Authority'.

As at the time of writing, the Supervising Authority has not yet issued its regulations in relation to the central beneficial owner register for trusts.

A trustee or commissioner of an express trust which is administered in the Republic of Cyprus must obtain and hold adequate, accurate and current information on beneficial ownership regarding the trust, which shall include the identity and relevant details of all the persons stated in section 2.1(b) above.

The same aforementioned obligations also apply to any other person having a similar position to a trustee in other types of legal arrangement with a structure or functions similar to trusts.

The same obligations apply to a trustee or person having a similar position to an express trust or other similar type of legal arrangement, who is situated outside the European Union, if such person conducts a business relationship or acquires, in the name of the trust or other similar legal arrangement, an immovable property situated in the Republic of Cyprus.

Further, when a trustee or person having a similar position to an express trust or other similar type of legal arrangement establishes a business relationship or carries out an occasional transaction above the thresholds set out in the AML Law, it must disclose to the obliged entities its status and provide the information stated in section 2.1(b) above. The threshold for an occasional transaction includes, amongst others, a transaction amounting equal to or higher than €15,000 (whether carried out in a single operation or over several operations which appear to be linked), for cases when there is a suspicion of money laundering or terrorist financing regardless of the amount.

Express trusts and other similar legal arrangements are excluded from registering on the Trust Register if they provide a certificate or other document evidencing that the relevant beneficial ownership information is included in a central register of another member state which follows this EU directive. This exclusion applies to cases in which all or at least one of the trustees or persons holding a similar position to a trustee are residing or being situated in another member state or conducting business in the name of the trust or other similar legal arrangement in other member states in addition to the Republic of Cyprus.

Every trustee and person holding a similar position who fall within the provisions of this Trust Register, must apply to the Supervising Authority for registration to the Trust Register and provide all the relevant beneficial ownership information, ensuring that such information is at all times complete, accurate and current.

The characteristics, creation, operation, access rights to the Trust Register, clarifications as to what constitutes an express trust for Trust Register purposes, reporting timings as well as any other related matters shall be determined in regulations to be issued by the Supervising Authority pursuant to the provisions of the AML Law.

There shall be administrative and subscription fees for the registration, assessment of requests, related notifications, issuance of certificates, access to information held on the Trust Register and other matters, as these shall be determined by the Supervising Authority in the regulations to be issued.

The Trust Register shall be published on the website of the Supervising Authority or in any other manner that it shall decide.

Access to beneficial ownership information contained in the Trust Register is available to:

- the competent authorities, which shall have timely and unrestricted access to all information contained within the Trust Register;
- the obligated entities in the framework of their customer due diligence work and beneficial ownership identification. It is further provided that obligated entities are not permitted to rely exclusively on information contained within the Trust Register for the purposes of their due diligence related obligations as prescribed in the AML Law. The Supervising Authority shall determine via regulations the access/approval procedures as well as the type of the Trust Register information that obligated entities can have access to;
- any physical or legal person after a request to the Supervising Authority. Such request must demonstrate a legitimate interest. In brief, having a legitimate interest for this purpose applies when such person's interest exclusively relates to the fight against money laundering and terrorist financing. The Trust Register related information that such persons shall be entitled to are the name, month and year of birth, nationality and country of residence of beneficial owners, as well as the nature and extent of rights that they have; and
- any physical or legal person after a written request to the Supervising Authority in relation to an express trust or other similar legal arrangement that directly or indirectly owns, participates or controls a company or other legal entity incorporated in the Republic of Cyprus or any other member state. The Trust Register related information that such persons shall be entitled to are the name, month and year of birth, nationality and country of residence of beneficial owners as well as the nature and extent of rights that they have.

The Supervising Authority shall assess any request for access to information from the Trust Register by physical or legal persons and has the right to approve or reject such request.

Access to the Trust Register by obligated entities and by members of the public shall be subject to an administrative fee to be determined in the upcoming regulations.

In exceptional circumstances (these shall be further clarified in the regulations to be issued), access to the beneficial ownership information contained in the Trust Register may have full or partial access prevention. This will mainly apply where such access could expose the beneficial owner to disproportionate risk of fraud, kidnapping, blackmail, violence or intimidation, or in cases where the beneficial owner is a minor or otherwise legally incapable. There shall however be no access prevention to competent authorities and in certain cases to credit and financial institutions.

Persons may apply to the Supervising Authority for exclusion to make beneficial ownership information publicly available. The regulations to be issued will provide the necessary guidelines thereon. The decision of the Supervising Authority on each such case may be challenged in the courts.

Any differences in relation to beneficial ownership information contained in the Trust Register, which may be detected by the obliged entities or by competent authorities, shall be communicated to the Supervising Authority of the Trust Register accordingly. Further, the Supervising Authority shall ensure prompt resolution of any resulting dispute and, if considered necessary, until such resolution is achieved, shall include an appropriate reference within the Trust Register about such possible difference.

The Trust Register shall be interconnected with the European central platform that was established pursuant to Article 22 of EU Directive 2017/1132.

A person who does not comply in providing relevant beneficial owner information for the Trust Register as per the relevant provisions of this law and relevant regulations is subject to a €200 fine and thereafter to an additional €100 fine for every continuing day of delay, with the maximum total fine being capped at €20,000.

Further, in cases of persons not complying with the provisions of this law or with the relevant regulations, who knowingly or negligently provide false, incorrect or misleading information, there can be a fine of up to €500,000 and in case of repeating the offence a fine of up to €1 million depending on the nature and size of the offence.

In addition to the above administrative fines, non-complying persons are guilty of a criminal offence. In case of conviction a person could be jailed for a period not exceeding five years and/or sentenced to a fine that does not exceed €350,000. The same applies to legal persons (companies) and their physical person officials, for whom it is proven that they consented or took part in this criminal offence.

In cases of express trusts and other similar legal arrangements which are no longer in effect, the relevant information held on the Trust Register shall remain available for up to 10 years from deregistration. For such cases, after the lapse of five years from deregistration, access to the relevant information on the Trust Register shall be available only for purposes of an administrative or criminal investigation by a competent authority or for the purposes of the AML Law.

Czech Republic

Štěpán Holub
Holubová advokáti s.r.o.

Registration of beneficial owners has become a topical issue throughout Europe. This chapter describes the basic features of the Czech legislation and points out certain existing shortcomings.

Even though the Fifth EU Anti-Money Laundering Directive (5AMLD) should have already been implemented in all EU member states, the Czech Republic is experiencing delay in this respect. It was only on 19 January 2021 that Act No 37/2021 Coll on the registration of beneficial owners was adopted. It entered into force on 1 June 2021.

The legislative process was expected to be completed by the end of 2020; however, it has lasted longer due to its delicacy within the Czech political environment.

1. Implementing instruments in the Czech Republic

1.1 The AML Act (Act No 253/2008 Coll)[1]

The AML Act is the core anti-money laundering legislation in the Czech Republic. In 2016 the act introduced a general obligation for all legal entities to be mandatorily registered in a public register and for all trusts to have their beneficial owners registered in the register of beneficial owners. The act also contains a definition of the notion of 'beneficial owner'[2] and stipulates the obligation to register and update information on beneficial owners. As of 1 June 2021, the definition of 'beneficial owner' will be removed from this act. It will only refer to the new act on the registration of beneficial owners.

1.2 The Public Registers Act (Act No 304/2013 Coll)[3]

Since 1 January 2018, the provisions governing the registration of beneficial

1 In Czech: *Zákon č 253/2008 Sb, o některých opatřeních proti legalizaci výnosů z trestné činnosti a financování terorismu.* It was amended by the 527/2020 Coll, which came partly into force on 1 January 2021. Other provisions came into force on 1 June 2021.

2 Section 4 (4).

3 In Czech: *Zákon č 304/2013 Sb, o veřejných rejstřících právnických a fyzických osob a o evidenci svěřenských fondů.* It was amended by 527/2020 Coll, which came partly into force on 1 January 2021. Other provisions came into force on 1 June 2021.

owners have been contained primarily in the Public Registers Act, specifically in Sections 118b to 118j, which was adopted within the framework of the implementation of the Fourth EU Anti-Money Laundering Directive (4AMLD). Sections 118b to 118j were removed from this act on 1 June 2021 and will be included in the new act on the registration of beneficial owners in its new wording.

The existing process of registration of beneficial owners is based on the notification principle. The obligation to register the beneficial owner lies with the legal entity or trustee. The legal entities and trustees concerned are solely responsible for ensuring that the information is complete, accurate and up to date.

The beneficial owner cannot register him/herself, and even the court lacks competence to register a beneficial owner directly. However, no proceedings are held on the registration and the court either approves or rejects the application. Where the registration is rejected, the applicant for registration is not informed of the grounds for the rejection, which is regarded by some as a weakness of the procedure. Thus, the only option for the applicant is to submit a new application for registration of the beneficial owner, hoping that the new application is considered sufficient. In combination with the unclear definition of 'beneficial owner', this regulation leads to considerable practical difficulties.

The register of beneficial owners is completely closed to the public. Access is granted only to the governmental authorities enumerated in the Public Registers Act[4] and to certain other persons for clearly defined purposes, in particular for purposes relating to the AML Act.

The Public Registers Act, in its current wording, sets out no penalties for non-fulfilment of the registration obligation.

1.3 The Court Fees Act (Act No 549/1991)[5]

The application for registration of a beneficial owner is subject to a fee of CZK4,000 for corporations. Trustees, foundations, endowment funds and institutes pay a fee of CZK2,000. The fee for other legal persons is CZK500.[6]

1.4 The Act on Registration of Beneficial Owners (Act No 37/2021 Coll)

The 5AMLD is to be transposed into Czech law by a new Act on Registration of Beneficial Owners. This act was adopted on 28 January 2021 and entered into force on 1 June 2021.

The act is going to represent a consolidated regulation of beneficial owners.

---

4 Remote access can be provided by the Ministry of Justice to courts, law enforcement authorities, tax administrators, intelligence services, the Czech National Bank, the National Security Authority and other governmental authorities listed in Section 118g of the Public Registers Act.

5 In Czech: *Zákon č 549/1991 Sb, o soudních poplatcích.*

6 All amounts as of 1 June 2021.

It incorporates certain parts of the other existing above-mentioned acts and, among other things, harmonises the currently differing definitions of 'beneficial owner'. The act is thus to become the core legislation governing beneficial owners in the Czech Republic.

Below is a brief summary of the upcoming legislation based in particular on the aforementioned act.

2. Which entities have to register the details of their beneficial owners?

According to the new definition,[7] the obligation to keep records of and register beneficial owners applies to virtually all legal entities, and also to Czech and foreign trusts.[8] Typically, this includes – apart from corporations and the above-mentioned Czech and foreign trusts – foundations[9] and endowment funds,[10] as well as registered associations[11] and registered institutes.[12]

For trusts which are not legal entities, the obligation of registration in the register of beneficial owners lies with the trustees.[13]

The registration obligation thus applies in principle to all legal entities, and the Czech law stipulates only certain exceptions where registration is not required, which concern entities that have no beneficial owners by definition.

Primarily, the obligation to register beneficial owners does not apply to the state, municipalities, regions and voluntary associations of municipalities, and to other entities established by or derived from the above-mentioned organisations.

Exempted also are entities that have no beneficial owner given their nature and because they were established by the law, such as public research institutes, professional chambers and European groups for territorial cooperation.

Political parties and political movements are also exempted from the obligation to register their beneficial owner. Further, the registration obligation does not apply to churches and religious societies, trade unions and employers' organisations.

Finally, an exemption from the registration obligation is stipulated for associations of unit owners[14] and for hunting associations.

---

7 Section 2 (j).

8 In Czech: *svěřenský fond.*

9 In Czech: *nadace.*

10 In Czech: *nadační fond.*

11 In Czech: *zapsaný spolek.*

12 In Czech: *zapsaný ústav.*

13 In Czech: *svěřenský správce.*

14 An association of unit owners is a legal person formed for the purpose of administration of a building in case of residential co-ownership of such building.

3. How are beneficial owners defined?

3.1 The person benefiting from the activities of the legal entity

The beneficial owner is a person who ultimately benefits from the activities of a legal entity. Only a natural person can be a beneficial owner, while a legal entity can have several beneficial owners. The notion of beneficial owner is defined in substantive terms in Czech law, in accordance with the wording of the introductory phrase of Article 3(6) of 5AMLD and in the sense of Recital (4) of 4AMLD, as interpreted by FATF.[15] In cases of trusts, foundations, endowment funds and institutes, the substantive aspect is, to a certain extent, combined with a formal approach. In these cases, the beneficial owner is also defined in formal terms, as explained below.

In the Act on Registration of Beneficial Owners, the beneficial owner is defined by an active criterion (ie, as a person exerting ultimate and decisive influence (active component)), or by a passive criterion (ie, as a person who is the ultimate and decisive recipient of benefits (passive component)). The position of beneficial owner follows from both criteria simultaneously. In this respect, the actual circumstances are decisive, where the position of beneficial owner can be established both by legal facts and non-legal facts. According to the explanatory memorandum to the act, non-legal facts include, for example, the possibility to exert influence stemming from the relationship between a creditor and a debtor, or even from a love relationship.

A person holding more than 25% of the voting rights in total will, in principle, have the decisive influence. In any case, the person who ultimately controls the legal entity without following someone else's instructions is the beneficial owner. The law also stipulates that every controlling natural person[16] is the beneficial owner.

Similarly, a person entitled, directly or indirectly, to more than a 25% share of profits or the liquidation balance, as appropriate, is the beneficial owner.

3.2 A member of the senior management

If the beneficial owner cannot be determined in the manner described above, Czech law stipulates that all members of the senior management are beneficial owners.

This is typical for companies with a fragmented structure of shareholders who do not act in concert. This approach also applies to corporations owned by a legal entity having no beneficial owner,[17] such as public-benefit corporations.[18] Finally, this manner of determination is used for legal entities controlled by

---

15 FATF Guidance on Transparency and Beneficial Ownership, 2014; available at www.fatf-gafi.org/documents/news/transparency-and-beneficial-ownership.html.

16 Section 74 of the Corporations Act.

17 Section 7 of the act.

18 In Czech: *příspěvkové organizace* (eg, entity established by a municipality to administrate its certain area of activity).

foreign legal entities established in countries where registration of beneficial owners is not stipulated.

A registered member of the senior management is also considered the beneficial owner of subsidiaries, if any.

4. Formally determined beneficial owner in case of trusts, endowment funds and registered institutions

A special manner of determination of the beneficial owner is stipulated for trusts,[19] foundations,[20] endowment funds[21] and registered institutes,[22] where the substantive concept is combined with a purely formal approach. Specifically, in addition to the beneficial owners determined based on the substantive criteria, all the persons specified below are automatically considered beneficial owners.

4.1 Foundations and endowment funds

Special criteria apply to foundations, where the following persons are considered the beneficial owners in addition to the beneficial owners determined based on the above-mentioned substantive criteria:

- the founder of the foundation, if alive;
- each member of the administrative board, supervisory board or the inspector; and
- the person for whose support the endowment fund is established according to the foundation deed.

4.2 Registered institutes

The beneficial owners of an institute also include the following persons, under any circumstances:

- the founder of the institute, if alive; and
- the director or each member of the administrative board of the institute.

4.3 Trusts

All the below-specified natural persons are also considered beneficial owners of a trust, under any circumstances:

- the founder of the trust, if alive;
- the trustee;
- a protector authorised to supervise over the trust administration and vested with the competence to appoint or remove the trustee or ultimate beneficiary;

---

19 In Czech: *svěřenský fond*. It includes here even foreign trusts.

20 In Czech: *nadace*.

21 In Czech: *nadační fond*.

22 In Czech: *zapsaný ústav*. The definition of '*ústav*' is in the Czech Civil Code and is defined as a legal entity that develops activity for a public or economic benefit using its own personal and material substance while its profit can only be invested on its operation and activities.

- the ultimate beneficiary of the trust; and
- the person in whose prevailing interest the trust has been established or is administered, other than the ultimate beneficiary.

5. Register of beneficial owners and other registers

Information from two registers will be automatically inserted in the register of beneficial owners, specifically:

- from the public register of legal persons; and
- from the register of trusts, as described in more detail below.

In addition to the automatic entry, legal entities may – and are obliged to – submit a special application for registration to a court or a notary if the actual information differs from the information that was inserted automatically from other registers or if no such information has been inserted. Accordingly, where the beneficial owner of a specific legal entity, as defined in substantive terms, is different from the person entered in the register, the registration must be amended so that the records correspond to the substantive definition of the beneficial owner. Where the person registered corresponds to the beneficial owner under the substantive definition, the obliged person need take no action.

5.1 Public register

Legal entities are mandatorily registered in a public register. As a rule, the legal entity is incorporated upon its registration in a public register. While the Commercial Register is the largest of public registers, the register of foundations, the register of associations, the register of institutes, etc, also exist in the Czech Republic. The aforementioned registers are kept on the basis of the Public Registers Act, and access to the information recorded therein is available to the general public without any limitations, free of charge.[23]

5.2 Register of trusts

To understand the regulation of trusts, it should primarily be noted that trusts are registered, in one way or another, in several places in the Czech Republic, specifically:

- with tax authorities;
- in the special register of trusts, which was established additionally; and, finally,
- in the register of beneficial owners.

The concept of a trust was introduced into Czech law by the New Civil Code,[24] which came into effect on 1 January 2014. Under the New Civil Code,

---

23 At: www.justice.cz.
24 Act No 89/2012 Coll.

trusts were originally not subject to mandatory registration and the only applicable obligation was to register the trust with the competent tax authority. The first amendment to the Civil Code, effective from 1 January 2018, stipulated mandatory registration of trusts. Registration is a precondition for the actual establishment of a trust, which means that a trust cannot exist unless it is registered in the register of trusts. Similar to legal entities, the trust is assigned an identification number upon registration in the register. The newly introduced mandatory registration assimilated trusts, to a certain degree, to legal entities – for example, to endowment funds, which are legal entities and are subject to less strict regulation. The register of trusts is available online.[25]

The following information is published in the register of trusts and is available online without any limitations:

- the name of the trust;
- the date of incorporation; the date of its dissolution or termination of administration including the legal ground thereof, and the date the trust ceased to exist;
- the identification number of the trust;
- the purpose of the trust; and
- the name and mailing address of each trustee.

This information from the register of trusts will now be automatically and simultaneously inserted in the register of beneficial owners, analogously to information from a public register. The information in the two registries will thus be duplicated unless the regulation is subsequently amended.

In addition to the publicly available information, the register of trusts also includes other, non-public, data, such as the names of beneficiaries and the manner of their determination. Access to the non-public data is granted only to certain governmental authorities and specifically defined persons. Moreover, complete information is available to obliged persons in connection with the KYC ('know-your-client') procedure under the Act No 253/2008 Coll on certain measures against legalising the proceeds of crime and financing terrorism.

For the sake of completeness, legal entities and trusts alike are obliged to register with the competent tax authority, which duty follows from Section 125ff of the Tax Code or from other tax laws, as appropriate. In case of trusts, the registration duty lies with the trustee and the registration procedure is analogous to that stipulated for registration of a legal person. However, the information recorded with the tax authority is not publicly available, nor is it automatically inserted in the register of beneficial owners.

25 At: https://isesf.justice.cz/.

6. Access to information entered in the register of beneficial owners

Access to the information in the register of beneficial owners should be very similar to the access to information from a public register.[26] Access to the published information should be free of charge and provided online. An extract signed with the eIDAS electronic signature should also be available for free download. Consequently, no criteria for access to and use of the information from the register of trusts will be stipulated. In addition to the passive access, the planned 'Citizen's Portal' should enable the set up of notifications of any changes in the register of beneficial owners. The information will also be transferred to the Business Registers Interconnection System.[27]

The data available online to the general public should be limited to the name, country of residence, year and month of birth, and nationality of the beneficial owner, or the information automatically inserted from a public register. For the aforementioned natural person, the information provided will include the fact that he/she is the beneficial owner, the date when he/she became and ceased to be the beneficial owner, and his/her share in the legal entity concerned.

6.1 Access to information on trusts and foundations

A special non-public regime will apply to trusts, where only the data automatically inserted from the registry of trusts will be provided.

The possibility of restricting access to information will also be available for private foundations and endowment funds established to support the founder or his/her close relatives.[28]

For trusts and, where appropriate, foundations or endowment funds, the scope of information will thus be limited to the basic identification details. It will exclude the names and personal details of the founders and beneficiaries.

6.2 Trusts controlling non-European legal entities

A specific regime further applies to trusts that control a relevant share in legal entities established in third-country jurisdictions (ie, countries other than the EU member states and countries forming the European Economic Area).[29] In case of such trusts, anyone can request information on the beneficial owner – within the scope of the name, country of residence, year and month of birth, and nationality – without having to demonstrate legitimate interest.[30] Accordingly, the court assessing the request will verify only whether the trust can actually exercise influence over a foreign legal entity.

---

26 Available at www.justice.cz or https://isesf.justice.cz/.
27 Directive (EU) 2017/1132, Article 22(1) and Article 24.
28 Section 14(4)(b) in conjunction with the new Section 34(2) of the Public Registers Act, pursuant to the amendment to Act No 253/2008 Coll published under 527/2020 Coll.
29 Recital (28) of 5AMLD.
30 Section 15(1)(b).

For such trusts, there will be no special system or list of trusts containing publicly available information, nor will the trusts be obliged to document which legal entities established in third-country jurisdictions they control. The persons requesting the information will thus have to identify the controlled entities themselves.

The fact that the trust controls a legal entity established in a third-country jurisdiction will have to be credibly demonstrated to the court in the request. Since no specific manner as to how this is to be demonstrated is stipulated, the court will determine, according to its own discretion, whether or not the trust concerned falls within this category. No appeal will be available against the decision on a request for information concerning these entities; however, requests can be submitted repeatedly.

6.3 Access by persons demonstrating legitimate interest

The general rule is that information on the beneficial owner of a legal arrangement is non-public. However, persons who demonstrate legitimate interest shall be granted access to all information. Under 5AMLD, any person can, in principle, have a legitimate interest, which is assessed individually based on the circumstances of the specific case. According to the explanatory memorandum to the Act on Registration of Beneficial Owners, persons demonstrating legitimate interest can include: non-governmental organisations and investigative journalists engaged in the prevention of money laundering and financing of terrorism; certain contracting entities for public tenders where a risk of corruption exists; and anyone who has learned, through a legal relationship with a legal entity, about circumstances that could give rise to his/her duty to report a criminal offence.

6.4 Access to information by the beneficial owners themselves

The Act on Registration of Beneficial Owners does not contain any special provisions that would grant the registered beneficial owners the right of access to the relevant information. Accordingly, the general provisions contained in the EU General Data Protection Regulation (GDPR), and in particular Article 15, will apply in this respect. Pursuant to Article 15, the beneficial owner may request access to his/her personal data that are recorded in the register of beneficial owners. The controller has a corresponding obligation to provide the data.

Nonetheless, according to the explanatory memorandum to the Act on Registration of Beneficial Owners, the registry of beneficial owners' information system should be connected to the planned Citizen's Portal, a governmental portal administered by the Ministry of the Interior. The portal should provide easy access to the registered data and enable automatic notifications to persons registered as beneficial owners.

7. Incorrect entries in the register

The Act on Registration of Beneficial Owners introduces a special type of proceedings on remedying incorrect entries, within the framework of which the asserted inconsistencies can either be confirmed or disproved. Incorrect records can be notified by governmental authorities and obliged persons within the framework of their activities under the act on certain measures against legalising the proceeds of crime and financing terrorism. The court can also initiate the proceedings *ex officio*.

At the beneficial owner's request, it will be possible to disclose all his/her data recorded in the register. On the other hand, if the registered beneficial owner wishes to have his/her personal data recorded in the register of beneficial owners deleted or corrected, the only possibility for him/her, under the Act on Registration of Beneficial Owners, will be to ask the court to initiate the proceedings. However, the beneficial owner has no legal entitlement to have the proceedings initiated. The only other option is to proceed pursuant to Article 16 of the GDPR.

The Act on Registration of Beneficial Owners does not stipulate any mechanism allowing the restriction of public access to the beneficial owner's personal data in case disclosure of such data would entail an unjustified risk for the beneficial owner (ie, make him/her a possible victim of certain criminal offences).

Similarly, no remedies are put in place for a person who has been unlawfully registered as the beneficial owner that would allow him/her to claim damages from the State or the legal entity that unlawfully registered him/her as a beneficial owner. In such cases, the aggrieved party can claim damages only under the general provisions of the Civil Code.

8. Fines for non-compliance and other consequences

While the courts keep the registers of beneficial owners, the hearing of infractions falls within the competence of municipalities in administrative proceedings, specifically proceedings on infractions.

An infraction can be committed either by the person responsible for the registration or by the beneficial owner. The person responsible for registration commits an infraction if he/she fails to arrange for the mandatory registration of the required information in the register of beneficial owners. The beneficial owner commits an infraction if he/she fails to provide the necessary cooperation to the person responsible for the registration. Such infractions are subject to a fine of up to CZK500,000.

Indirect consequences should also be mentioned. First, these include fines imposed on the obliged persons who fail to notify the client of incorrect entries in the register of beneficial owners, which can reach up to CZK100,000.[31]

31 New Section 44a of Act No 253/2008 Coll, according to amendment published under 527/2021 Coll.

Pursuant to the same provision, a fine of up to CZK1 million may be imposed on the obliged persons for failure to notify the court of incorrect entries.

According to the Act on Registration of Beneficial Owners, the failure to indicate the beneficial owner in the register would also cause further indirect consequences as follows:[32]

- rights and obligations from juridical acts that conceal the real beneficial owner, which arose in time when the beneficial owner was not registered in the register of beneficial owners, are unenforceable. This would probably even cover situations where dividends are paid out to a shareholder who subsequently hands over the dividends to the unregistered beneficial owner;
- the unregistered beneficial owner is excluded from voting on the general meeting of the corporation. Where the voting did take place nonetheless, the invalidity of the vote can be invoked. The same applies to situations where the beneficial owner acts through another legal entity or trust; and
- further, the failure to indicate the beneficial owner in the register prohibits the corporation from paying out a share of the company's profit to the beneficial owner or to an entity with the same beneficial owner, or to other legal entities which do not have a registered beneficial owner in the register of beneficial owners.

Even though the above-mentioned consequences may have no practical effect for functional companies, they can have substantial impact on the liability of directors, against whom a claim for damages can be enforced in such cases. This remedy will probably be used in particular by minority shareholders or insolvency trustees.

Another practical consequence of a failure to indicate the beneficial owner, apart from the above, can arise in public tenders, where the contracting entity will exclude the selected bidder if its beneficial owner cannot be identified in the register of beneficial owners or, where a foreign legal entity is involved, if its beneficial owner has not been documented.[33]

9. Concluding remarks

The amendment mostly follows 5AMLD. The positive development certainly lies in the fact that the new consolidated law contains a comprehensive regulation unifying various provisions in this area and remedying certain practical shortcomings of the existing legislation. However, certain practical

---

32 Sections 52–54 of the Act on Registration of Beneficial Owners.

33 New wording of Section 122 of Act No 134/2016 Coll, on public procurement, according to the amendment to Act No 253/2008 Coll, published under 527/2021 Coll.

problems with the registration process will persist. Balancing the formal and substantive approaches will cause difficulties. Moreover, it is not clear from the wording of the Act on Registration of Beneficial Owners why the same regime does not apply, by analogy, to endowment funds established for private purposes, where similar interest in the protection of privacy should exist.

Experience will show how the different approach to publicity of information on trusts controlling legal entities established in third-country jurisdictions, on the one hand, and those that do not exercise such control, on the other hand, works in practice.

The most significant shortcoming of the Act on Registration of Beneficial Owners would appear to be the inadequate mechanisms for the beneficial owners themselves to claim correction or deletion of their personal data from the register of beneficial owners.

France

Stéphanie Auféril
Arkwood
Jérôme Barré
Barré & Associés

Ordinance no 2020-115 of 12 February 2020, strengthening the national system for combating money laundering and terrorist financing, implemented several measures of the European Parliament and of the Council Directive (EU) 2018/843 of 30 May 2018, amending Directive (EU) 2015/849 on the prevention of the use of the financial system for money laundering or terrorist financing (Fifth EU Anti-Money Laundering Directive (5AMLD)), which had a transposition deadline of January 2020.

Among these measures, the 12 February 2020 Ordinance profoundly modifies the content and conditions of access to the ultimate beneficial owners' registers of trusts and companies, and consequently the trustees' and companies' reporting obligations.

As a reminder, the purpose of 5AMLD is to facilitate the identification of beneficial owners of companies and trusts by creating central registers with wider access, as part of the fight against money laundering. These registers, therefore, have a broader purpose than enabling local authorities to check the beneficial owners of companies and trusts for tax compliance.

1. Register of beneficial owners of companies

1.1 Historical background

The concept of 'beneficial owner' first appeared in common law. For a long time, the legal owner has been distinguished from the beneficial owner (ie, the person who receives an economic benefit from the activity in question). This notion then allows an understanding of the economic reality behind potential legal arrangements intended to promote tax fraud or tax evasion.

The notion of 'beneficial owner' appears for the first time in France in tax matters, through the 1977 OECD Model Convention, used by France in numerous conventions.

This notion is useful in the fight against tax fraud, since it was used by states to ensure that the benefit of a tax credit or a reduction of withholding tax is granted to the beneficial owner of the income received, and not to an intermediary structure established solely in one of the two signatory states in order to benefit from favourable treaty provisions.

With regard to the fight against money laundering, the 2003 Financial Action Task Force (FATF) recommendations define the beneficial owner as "the natural person(s) who ultimately owns or controls the customer and/or the natural person on whose behalf a transaction or activity is being conducted".

The Third Anti-Money Laundering Directive (3AMLD) of 26 October 2005 incorporates this definition in Article 3 and, in France, led to the inclusion of this concept in the French Monetary and Financial Code following the order of 30 January 2009 (Article L561-2-2).

The 3AMLD provides several clarifications on how to identify a beneficial owner. It differentiates between the cases of companies and the cases of foundations, trusts or other legal arrangements that may manage or distribute income.

In the case of companies, the beneficial owner is identified in three ways, currently set out in Article R561-1 of the Monetary and Financial Code.

1.2 The threshold of 25% ownership in capital or voting rights

First, on the one hand, the beneficial owner is the natural person(s) who ultimately owns or controls a legal entity by virtue of owning or controlling, directly or indirectly, a sufficient percentage of shares or voting rights in that legal entity. To meet this test, the participation should be above 25%.

Some difficulties have arisen with regard to this threshold criterion. Some of them are developed below.

The first difficulty is the situation in which there is a chain of participation. In this case, in order to assess whether the 25% threshold has been crossed, it is necessary to multiply the holdings held through one or more companies in the capital of the company called upon to identify its beneficiaries.

The second difficulty is the case of indivision. First of all, all undivided co-owners should be declared as beneficial owners. Although they only hold rights in the undivided shares and none of them can exercise alone the rights attached to the shares, they can nevertheless be considered to hold the capital indirectly through undivided ownership. Next, it is necessary to consider whether a proxy has been appointed to represent the undivided shares. If his/her mandate extends to the general administration of the undivided shares or units (ie, a permanent mission), then the agent will be declared the beneficial owner because the mandate he/she has received enables him/her to exercise control over the general meeting of partners or shareholders.

A final difficulty is that of the dismemberment of property. In this situation, the usufructuary and the bare owner must be declared. Indeed, the usufructuary cannot be deprived of his/her voting rights concerning the allocation of profits.[1]

1.3 Control of the company/entity

Second, the beneficial owner may be the natural person(s) who otherwise exercises control over the management of a legal entity. Currently, this notion of control is defined by the 3° and 4 of I of Article L233-3 of the French Commercial Code. This article defines control by a person as the possibility for that person, on the one hand, to determine in fact, through the voting rights he/she has, the decisions in the general meetings of that company. On the other hand, it refers to the situation where, as a partner or shareholder of that company, he/she has the power to appoint or dismiss the majority of the members of the administrative, management or supervisory bodies of that company.

1.4 Default designation

Where no natural person has been identified according to the previous criteria provided, and there is no suspicion of money laundering or terrorist financing, the beneficial owner is the natural person or persons listed below or, if the company is not registered in France, their equivalent in foreign law which legally represents the company:

- the manager(s) of the partnerships, limited partnerships, limited liability companies, limited partnerships and civil partnerships;
- the director general of public limited companies (in French, *sociétés anonymes*) with a board of directors;
- the sole managing director or the chairman of the executive board of public limited companies with a management board and supervisory board; and
- the chairman and, if applicable, the managing director of simplified joint stock companies.

The 3AMLD also had the effect of subjecting a large number of professionals (bankers, lawyers, notaries, etc) to this identification obligation in order to prevent any money laundering transaction, to identify their client and their beneficial owner even before entering into a business relationship with them. The consequence of this identification operation may indeed lead to a denunciation to Tracfin (ie, the service in charge of collecting and analysing the suspicious transaction reports that professionals transmit).

The Fourth Anti-Money Laundering Directive (4AMLD) of 20 May 2015 also stipulates that professionals will have to enter information relating to the

---

1 The right of ownership is characterised by, on the one hand, the right to enjoy the property, which consists of the right to use it (usus) and to receive income from it (fructus), and, on the other hand, the right to dispose of it (abusus) (ie, to sell it, give it, modify it).
The right of ownership may be subject to dismemberment by dissociation of usufruct and bare ownership. The usufructuary has the right of use and fructus. The bare owner retains the right to dispose of the property, respecting the rights of the usufructuary: he/she therefore only has the right to dispose of the bare ownership of the property.

identity and control procedures of these natural persons in a central register held at the disposal of the control authorities and all interested persons.

The 5AMLD has once again strengthened the national system, and extends the scope of professionals subject to anti-money laundering obligations (eg, electronic wallet providers, virtual currency exchange service providers, art dealers etc).

The 5AMLD was transposed in France by Ordinance no 2020-115 of 12 February 2020 and Decree no 2020-118 of the same date.

The directive and its transposition did not change the definition of 'beneficial owner'. However, the obligations of professionals and the disclosure of information relating to beneficial owners have been revised.

1.5 Register of beneficial owners under French transposition of 5AMLD

Companies and entities subject to the identification and disclosure obligation are listed in Article L561-45-1 of the Monetary and Financial Code and are as follows:

- companies having their head office on French territory and having legal personality (excluding companies whose securities are admitted to trading on a regulated market, which are expressly excluded from the scheme);
- economic Interest Groups (GIEs) headquartered on French territory and that have legal personality;
- commercial (foreign) companies whose head office is located outside a French department and which have an establishment in one of these departments;
- other legal persons whose registration in the Trade and Companies Register (RCS)[2] is provided for by law or regulation;
- Undertakings for Collective Investment in Transferable Securities (UCITS); and
- associations, foundations, endowment funds, sustainability funds, collective interest groupings established on French territory, as well as fiduciaries within the meaning of Article 2011 of the Civil Code and administrators of any other comparable legal arrangement governed by foreign law.

Companies whose securities are admitted to trading on a regulated market are not subject to this obligation.

The obliged companies on the other hand have several obligations. The following three categories can be identified.

2 In France, this register is known as *le registre du commerce et des sociétés* (RCS). It is a database listing all natural and legal persons engaged in a commercial activity.

(a) *Obtain and maintain accurate and up-to-date information*

First, Article L561-45-1 of the Monetary and Financial Code provides that the companies and entities quoted above are required to obtain and maintain accurate and up-to-date information on their beneficial owners.

(b) *Communicate information on beneficial owners*

Second, under Article L561-45-1 of the Monetary and Financial Code, companies are required on request to communicate to some persons information relating to beneficial owners.

These persons are mentioned in Article L561-2 of the same code. This article covers all categories of persons who are subject to the anti-money laundering obligations provided for in the same code. The 5AMLD has broadened this list, notably by including art professionals, real estate rental activities and players in the digital assets sector.

The Ordinance of 12 February 2020 introduced a sanction, codified in Article L574-5 of the Monetary and Financial Code, for failure to disclose information, or disclosing information inaccurately or incompletely. A penalty of six months' imprisonment and a fine of €7,500 is incurred for individuals and €37,500 for legal entities.

Article L561-45-2 of the same code also states that the beneficial owner him/herself is also required to disclose any necessary information requested by the company or entity subject to the identification and disclosure obligation, so that it can in turn communicate this information to the persons mentioned in Article L561-2. The same sanction as above is applicable to reluctant beneficial owners.

(c) *Report to the clerk and control of the register*

The final obligation imposed upon companies and entities by Article L561-46 of the Monetary and Financial Code is to report information relating to the beneficial owner to the RCS.

The information concerns both the reporting company itself and the beneficial owner.

First, with regard to the company or entity, the information will include its name or corporate name, its legal form, the address of its registered office and, where applicable, its identification number completed by the RCS, followed by the name of the town where the registration office is located.

Then, concerning the beneficial owner, the information declared will include his/her surname, first name, pseudonym, name in use, date and place of birth, nationality and personal address, as well as the nature, terms and extent of the control he/she exercises over the company or entity in question.

Previously, practitioners had doubts as to whether or not the exact percentage held by the beneficial owner in the structure should be specified.

Several decisions, such as that of the Lyon Court of Appeal,[3] have specified that the indication of this percentage was necessary in order to understand better the terms of the control held by the beneficial owner.

Since 9 March 2020, the transmission to the clerk's office by companies or entities of information relating to the beneficial owners has been supported by a declaration to the RCS. The form for the declaration of beneficial owners (M'BE form, cerfa no 16062*01) has recently been modified. This form currently replaces the form DBE-S-1.

Following this filing, the clerk of the Commercial Court is required to verify that the information complies with the legal requirements (Article L561-47 of the Monetary and Financial Code).

The Ordinance of 12 February 2020 also adds a new type of control, which is to be carried out by the professionals mentioned in Article L561-2, as well as on the persons mentioned in Article L561-36 of the Monetary and Financial Code.

Indeed, under Article L561-47-1 of the Monetary and Financial Code, these persons are now in charge of checking and alerting the clerk of any difference they notice between the information contained in the register of beneficial owners and the information they hold on these same beneficial owners.

In the event of a reported difference, the clerk shall invite the relevant company to correct the information in the register within one month. Failing this, the clerk may request the president of the competent court to issue an injunction to make the amendment.

Thanks to this new obligation, the exhaustiveness and continuous updating of the register should improve.

1.6 Condition of access to the French beneficial owners of companies

Article L561-46 of the Monetary and Financial Code provides a framework for access to the register of beneficial owners. The Ordinance of 12 February 2020 also modifies the conditions of access to the register of beneficial owners.

The following two situations should be noted.

(a) Access to the full register

First, recorded companies and entities may have access to information on beneficial owners, but only to the information they have reported.

Then, the article lists the following entities that have full access to the register:

- the judicial authorities;
- the national financial intelligence unit;
- the agents of the customs administration acting on the basis of the prerogatives conferred by the Customs Code;

3 Decision no 19/02040 dated 12 September 2019.

- the authorised agents of the public finance administration responsible for control and recovery in tax matters;
- authorised officers of the judicial police, of the national police and the national gendarmerie, as well as customs and tax officers authorised to carry out judicial investigations; and
- the supervisory authorities referred to in Article L561-36 of the Monetary and Financial Code.

This register is also accessible to persons subject to the fight against money laundering and the financing of terrorism mentioned in Article L561-2 of the Monetary and Financial Code as part of at least one of their due diligence measures mentioned in Articles L561-4-1 to L561-14-2 of the Monetary and Financial Code.

(b) Partial access to the register

The public has access to certain information contained in the register.

Prior to the February 2020 ordinance, such access was subject to the demonstration of a 'legitimate interest' before the judge in charge of keeping the register. This is no longer the case.

Article L561-46 lists the information to which the public may have access: name, surname, pseudonym, first names, month, year of birth, country of residence and nationality of the beneficial owners, as well as the nature and extent of the beneficial interests they hold in the company or entity. The day of birth, place of birth and home address will therefore not be publicly accessible information.

Access to all this information will be free of charge.

The health crisis related to COVID-19 has resulted in a delay in sorting out the information contained in the register that will later be made available to the public. As of 1 March 2021, the online platform allowing the public to access this information was not yet available.

2. Register of trusts

2.1 Historical background

As part of the international movement against tax fraud and promoting tax transparency, after the 2008 financial crisis France decided to create for the first time a set of tax rules for trusts. Indeed, in France the trust is viewed as a legal instrument enabling tax evasion – at least when used by French taxpayers – on the grounds that it could hide the identification of the beneficial ownership.

The Amending Finance Act for 2011 of 29 July 2011, no 2011-900 put in place a set of tax rules for trusts with French connections. In order to ensure the transparency of trusts and allow the taxation of trust assets in the hands of beneficial owners, this law created a trust reporting obligation, under Article 1649 AB of the French Tax Code, if the settlor, one of the beneficiaries or one of the trustees is a French tax resident, or when an asset in the trust is located in France.

Anticipating the registers ruled by 5AMLD, the French Parliament adopted a law on 6 December 2013[4] in the context of the fight against tax fraud, with a view to reinforcing trust transparency by compiling, in a public register, the information gathered in the context of the trust reporting provided by the above-mentioned law of 2011.

By a decision dated 21 October 2016,[5] the French Constitutional Court (*Conseil Constitutionnel*) cancelled this public register of trusts.

Two constitutional principles had to be balanced by the Constitutional Court: the objective of fighting tax evasion; and the right to privacy protected by Article 2 of the Declaration of the Rights of Man and of the Citizen of 1789.

On the one hand, the Constitutional Court noted that the public register made it possible to reveal to the public personal information: as an instrument of estate planning, trusts may provide information on the way a person intends to dispose of his/her assets.

On the other hand, the Constitutional Court underlined the lack of supervision of access to the register, on the grounds that:

> *the Parliament, which did not specify the quality nor the motives that justify consulting the register, did not limit the people that have access to the information in this register, placed under the responsibility of the tax administration.*

In those circumstances, the court commented in this decision that "these disputed provisions have a clearly disproportionate effect on the right to respect for private life with regard to the objectives sought".

The Constitutional Court finally considered that unrestricted and unregulated access to the register of trusts was manifestly a disproportionate breach of the right to privacy.

By merely indicating that the legislator should have specified "the quality and the reasons for consulting the register", and that it should have limited "the circle of persons having access to the data in this register", the Constitutional Court does not seem to have wanted to restrict only to the tax administration and other officials involved in the fight against tax fraud access to information relating to the privacy of persons mentioned in a register.

Actually, the Constitutional Court seemed to leave the door open for the adoption of a new register of trusts or similar registers, access to which could be extended to persons other than officials of State administrations, since they

4 Law no 2013-1117 of 6 December 2013 on the fight against tax fraud and serious economic and financial crime.

5 Decision no 2016-591 QPC dated 21 October 2016.

argue a 'quality' or 'reasons for consulting the register'. However, it does not specify to what extent the circle of people having access can be expanded. In this regard, it should be noted that following the cancellation by the Constitutional Court, a new French register of trusts was created, only accessible to certain specific authorities, such as the French financial intelligence unit, the judicial authorities and the tax and custom administrations. Thus, the French legislator did not want to take new risks by widening access to the register by too much.

2.2 Register of trusts under French transposition of 5AMLD

Ordinance no 2020-115 of 12 February 2020 brings Article 1649 AB of the French Tax Code relating to trustees' reporting obligations in line with Article 31 of 5AMLD. Article 13 of the ordinance adds new cases and reporting requirements to the already existing trustees' obligations.

2.3 Content of the French register of trusts

The French register of trusts currently in force compiles the information set forth in Article 1649 AB of the Tax Code, which is reported by the trustees of trusts with French connections.

Under Section I of Article 1649 AB of the Tax Code, trustees have a duty to report to the French authorities information on the trust(s) they administer in cases where:

- the settlor or one of the beneficiaries is a tax resident of France;
- the trust assets comprise at least one French located asset;
- the trustee is a tax resident of France; or
- the trustee is a tax resident outside the European Union and acquires a French real estate asset or enters into a business relationship in France within the meaning of Article L561-2-1 of the Monetary and Financial Code. This case of reporting is an addition to the cases of trust reporting existing prior to adoption of the Ordinance of 12 February 2020 – and it aligns the trust reporting with 5AMLD.

Under Article L561-2-1 of the Monetary and Financial Code:

(...) the notion of business relationship means the professional or commercial relationship with the customer and includes the beneficial owner where applicable. For life-insurance or capitalization contracts, the business relationship includes the beneficiary of the contract or if applicable the beneficial owner of such beneficiary referred to III of Article L.561-5 of the French Monetary and Financial Code.

A business relationship is entered when a person referred in Article L.561-2 enters into a professional or commercial relationship which is deemed, at the time the contact is established, to be of a certain duration. The business relationship may be provided by a contract under which several successive operations will be carried out between the contracting parties or which creates continuing obligations for the contracting parties. A business relationship is also entered when, in absence of such a contract, a client regularly benefits from the intervention of an aforementioned person for the performance of several operations or operation of a continuous nature or, in the case of the persons mentioned in 12° and 12° bis of Article L.561-2, for the performance of a legal mission.

Under Article 1649 AB I of the Tax Code, the information that trustees need to report to the French authorities in such cases is as follows:

- the setting up, modification or extinction, as well as the terms, of the trust; and
- information relating to the names, first names, address, date and place of birth and citizenship of the beneficial owners of the trusts, that should be understood as all natural persons having the quality as trustee, settlor, beneficiary and, as the case may be, protector, but also any other natural person exercising an effective control over the trust, or exercising equivalent or similar functions.

Reporting obligations of such information has been added by the Ordinance of 12 February 2020 to align the trust reporting with provisions of 5AMLD; and

- the fair market value on 1 January of each year:
  - for French tax residents, of the assets and rights located in France or outside France; and the capitalised proceeds invested in the trust; and
  - for other persons (ie, non-French tax residents), of the only assets and rights located in France and the capitalised proceeds.

Under Article 1736, IV bis of the Tax Code, any failure to report or to properly report the information provided by Article 1649 AB is subject to a fine of €20,000, applicable per failure.

In case of a tax reassessment resulting from a failure to declare assets in a trust that was not properly reported by the trustee, a penalty of 80% of the reassessed tax is applicable. Such 80% penalty is exclusive of the €20,000 fine, but cannot be less than such amount.

To date, the new reporting obligations of the trustees have not been commented on by the French tax administration.

The transposition of 5AMLD adds reporting obligations for trustees of trusts with links to France (ie, acquisition of real estate, entering into business relationships), which are intended to ensure transparency in the fight against money laundering, and no longer merely to establish taxation. Trustees will have to be attentive to their reporting obligations in France in the case of trusts which do not necessarily involve potential present or future taxation of the settlors or beneficiaries – for example, when they acquire a business in France, whether directly or even potentially indirectly.

The information required from trustees with French connections is compiled into a register of trusts referred to in Article L167 of the French Tax Procedure Code, created by Article 14 of the Ordinance.

2.4 Conditions of access to the French trusts register

Under Article L167 of the French Procedure Code, the register of trusts referred to in Article 1649 AB of the Tax Code, as well as the register of French *fiducies* referred to in Article 2020 of the French Civil Code, can be accessed under modalities and extent that vary depending on the persons concerned.

(a) Competent authorities

The following French competent authorities can access the registers without restriction:

- judicial authorities;
- the French financial intelligence unit (ie, Tracfin);
- the agents of the French customs authorities;
- the agents of the French public finance administration in charge of audit and recovery in tax matters;
- the officers of the judicial police within the national police, tax and customs administrations; and
- the authorities of control of regulated activities as listed under Article L561.36 of the Monetary and Financial Code, including the ACPR (*Autorité de Contrôle Prudentiel et de Résolution*), the AMF (*Autorité des Marchés Financiers*) and CPA's regulating bodies (*Conseil de l'ordre des avocats, Chambre des notaires, Conseil de l'ordre des experts-comptables*).

The above French competent authorities exchange with the EU competent authorities either spontaneously or upon request all information necessary for the accomplishment of their missions.

(b) Certain persons with restrictions

The following certain persons can access the registers with restrictions:

- obliged entities (ie, persons subject to the fight against money laundering and terrorist financing) can have access only to any information relating to the beneficial owners of a trust, in the context of one of their due diligence measures;
- other persons can still obtain access to certain limited information relating to the beneficial owners of a trust (ie, identity of the beneficial owner (name, surname, given name, month and year of birth, country of residence, citizenship)), as well as the nature and extent of the beneficial owner's interests in the trust. Such information is available to:
  - any person justifying a legitimate interest in the fight against money

laundering or financing of terrorism, with respect to the purpose or nature of his/her activity.

Where 5AMLD provisions do not define the 'legitimate interest' allowing any person to obtain access to information on the beneficial owners of a trust, the French transposition of the legitimate interest should be understood in light of the purpose of the AML directives (ie, the fight against money laundering, financing of terrorism, or related offences). In other words, third parties with a legitimate interest in knowing the identity of a beneficial owner of a trust, but not acting to combat money laundering and the like, could not be authorised to access the registers. On the contrary, the French transposition should allow non-governmental organisations and investigative journalists to obtain access to relevant information on the beneficial owners of trusts, in the context of the preventive work in the field of anti-money laundering, counter terrorist financing and associate predicate offences, as recommended by 5AMLD;[6] and

- any person that files a written request on a trust or a *fiducie* which holds a controlling interest in any legal entity established in a non-EU member state, through direct or indirect ownership, notably through bearer shareholdings, or other controlling means.

Under Article L102 AH of the Tax Procedure Code, the obliged entities, as well as the authorities of control of regulated entities, must notify the French administration of any discrepancy between the information contained in the registers and the information that they have on such beneficial owners, including a lack of registration of such information. The administration then informs the trustee, and based on the information obtained from the trustee, adjusts the content of the registers. In the absence of satisfactory feedback from the trustee, the register is nevertheless adjusted and the €20,000 fine might be charged to the trustee.

Access to the register of trusts has been considerably extended since the Constitutional Court's censorship of the public register in 2016. However, it complies with the directive's requirements: beyond the judicial, tax or customs authorities whose access to the register is, as in the past, unlimited, access to the register is open, in a more limited way, to persons subject to vigilance measures concerning the fight against money laundering. Moreover, any person who can justify a legitimate interest in the fight against money laundering will be able to obtain certain information on request: the requirement of a legitimate interest echoes the above-mentioned decision of the Constitutional Court,[7] which censured the public register in 2016 for breach of privacy insofar as:

6 Recital 42 of the 5AMLD.
7 Decision no 2016-591 QPC dated 21 October 2016.

the legislator, which did ***not specify the quality or the reasons justifying the consultation of the register****, did not limit the circle of persons having access to this register, which is under the responsibility of the tax authorities* [emphasis added].

The trust register, in its new version, is therefore not public, unlike the new register of beneficial owners of companies, which must be transposed by EU member states. In the particular situation of trusts controlling companies established outside the European Union, whose beneficial owners are not subject to declaration, the identification of these beneficial owners will be done through the trust declaration: in this case, access to the trust register will be considerably extended, to any person upon written request (with no requirement of justification of a legitimate interest), probably to compensate for the lack of transparency applicable to companies established outside the European Union, which are not required to make a declaration.[8] In that case, the public could gain broader access to information on trusts that hold non-EU companies, than on trusts holding financial or real estate directly, where the information on beneficial owners would be accessible only to persons with legitimate interest.

8 In that sense, Article L167 of the French Tax Procedure Code states that *(..) Information on the identity of the beneficial owner of the trust or fiducie is relating to surname, name of general use, pseudonym, first names, month and year of birth, country of residence and nationality, as well as the nature and extent of the beneficial interests held is accessible: 1° To any person who submits a written application relating to a trust or a fiducie holding a controlling interest in a company or other legal entity established in a non-EU Member State through direct or indirect ownership, in particular by means of bearer shares or through control by other means (...).*

Germany

Susanne Stauder
Heuking Kühn Lüer Wojtek

1. Introduction

As a result of the Fourth EU Anti-Money Laundering Directive of 2015 (4AMLD), the completely revised Money Laundering Act (*Geldwäschegesetz*, hereinafter GwG) came into force in Germany on 26 June 2017. In addition to numerous regulations which are aimed only at a group of obligated parties specified in more detail in the GwG and which are intended to combat money laundering and terrorist financing, the implementation of 4AMLD has for the first time also included the establishment of a so-called transparency register (*Transparenzregister*, hereinafter UBO register) in the GwG. Companies and other associations are now obliged to provide details of the ultimate beneficial owner (UBO) behind them.

The legal provisions of Sections 18ff GwG stipulate that various pieces of information on those natural persons who are behind and control (sometimes complex) corporate structures must be entered in the UBO register. The purpose of the register is to provide information about in whose interests company transactions are ultimately conducted. In order to 'feed' the register and keep it up to date, additional information obligations are imposed on numerous associations. In Germany, since 1 October 2017 there has been an obligation to register UBOs of legal entities under private law, registered partnerships, as well as trusts, fiduciary relationships and foundations without legal capacity.[1]

In implementation of the Fifth EU Anti-Money Laundering Directive (5AMLD) the GwG was amended again as of 1 January 2020 and adjustments were also made to the related requirements. In order to meet the legislative requirement for even more transparency, access to the UBO register has been made even easier. Whereas under the legal situation until the end of 2019 only

1 A foundation without legal capacity or a dependent foundation is understood to be the transfer of assets to a natural person or legal entity with the measure of administering these assets for the promotion of a specified purpose as a special fund economically separate from the other assets of the recipient (see *Weitemeyer* in: MüKo-BGB, 8 Edition 2018, Sec 80 marginal number 260). Due to the lack of legal capacity, the foundation itself cannot be the bearer of rights and obligations and thus cannot be a party in civil proceedings. In the case of a foundation without legal capacity, the holder of rights is rather the owner of the foundation's assets (see *Grüneberg* in: Palandt, BGB, 78 Edition 2019, before Sec 1 marginal number 1, 4; *Weitemeyer* in: MüKo-BGB, 8 Edition 2018, Sec 80 marginal number 260).

public authorities, persons obliged under the GwG and persons with a legitimate interest were allowed to inspect the UBO register upon request, access has been public since 1 January 2020; in principle, anyone can inspect the UBO register upon request. In addition, those subject to money laundering obligations (see Section 2 GwG) must inspect the UBO register to verify the information they are required to collect and report any discrepancies.

In Germany the UBO transparency register is maintained by Bundesanzeiger Verlag GmbH. Legal and technical supervision of the register is the responsibility of the Federal Office of Administration (*Bundesverwaltungsamt*, hereinafter BVA).

2. In more detail

2.1 Addressee – who is subject to the notification obligation?

Although the provisions on the UBO register are contained in the GwG, the obligation to register on the UBO register applies not only to market participants who are particularly exposed to money laundering risks, but also to almost all German forms of company, irrespective of their legal form and size. Only the partnership constituted under civil law (*Gesellschaft bürgerlichen Rechts* – GbR) is not covered.

Section 20(1) GwG defines the specific group of persons covered by this provision. Other partnerships (ie, an *offene Handelsgesellschaft* (oHG) and *Kommanditgesellschaft* (KG)), corporations (*Aktiengesellschaft* (AG), *Societas Europaea* (SE), *Gesellschaft mit beschränkter Haftung* (GmbH)), registered cooperatives and associations with legal capacity, as well as partnership companies are obliged to report their UBO to the UBO register under certain conditions that are regulated in more detail by law.

In addition, the obligation to register applies to the administrators of trusts, foundations, trustees of non-legally capable foundations with a foundation purpose of their own benefit, as well as trust-like structures, provided the administrator or trustee has his/her residence or registered office in Germany (see Section 21 GwG).

In principle, the duty of notification applies exclusively to the addressees of Sections 20, 21 GwG with registered offices in Germany. However, it is not limited to UBOs who live in Germany. Insofar as there is an obligation to notify the association, foreign shareholders are also required to notify it (see Section 20(3) GwG). These must always be reported to the UBO register by the entity subject to the reporting obligation if no notification fiction applies.[2]

A new provision was also introduced at the beginning of 2020, according to which associations based abroad are also obliged to report if they undertake to

2 For more details see the explanations in section 2.3(a) below.

acquire ownership of a property located in Germany (see Section 20(1) sentence 2 GwG). The same applies under Section 21(1) sentence 2 GwG to managers of trusts who have their residence or registered office outside the European Union if they enter into a business relationship for the trust with a contracting party domiciled in Germany or undertake to acquire ownership of a property located in Germany. 'Business relationship' is legally defined in Section 1(4) GwG as any relationship which is directly maintained in connection with the business or professional activities of the entities obliged by the GwG, and which is expected, at the time when the contact is established, to have an element of duration.

2.2 Central question: what has to be communicated?

The GwG distinguishes between various entities subject to notification with regard to the addressee.

The pivotal point in connection with the reporting obligations for the UBO register is the concept of the UBO. Units subject to reporting obligations regularly ask themselves the question of what exactly is to be reported to the UBO register. Of central interest here is always – as already mentioned – the UBO(s) of the entity subject to reporting obligations.

Section 3 GwG defines the 'beneficial owner' as the natural person who ultimately owns or controls the customer (Section 3(1) No 1 GwG) or the natural person on whose behalf a transaction is ultimately conducted or a business relationship is ultimately established (see Section 3 (1) No 2 GwG). It is of fundamental importance that a UBO can only ever be a natural person.

The first and last name, date of birth, place of residence, nationality and the nature and scope of the UBO's economic interest must always be entered in the UBO register.

The nature and scope of the economic interest are of particular importance. The information provided in this regard must always indicate the concrete implications of the position as UBO. This cannot only be the participation of the UBO in the entity subject to the reporting obligation in the form of capital shares, but also such participation based on voting rights or also based on the exercise of control in any other way – for example, through pooling or voting pooling agreements that establish control.

In this regard, the legislator then distinguishes between UBOs of legal entities other than foundations with legal capacity and other companies which are not listed on a regulated market in accordance with Section 2(11) of the German Securities Trading Act (*Wertpapierhandelsgesetz*, hereinafter WpHG) and are not subject to any transparency requirements in line with Community legislation (law) with regard to voting shares or equivalent international standards (Section 20 GwG). Also such entities in the form of foundations with legal capacity and legal structures with which assets are managed or distributed in a fiduciary capacity or the management or distribution is commissioned by third parties (see Section 21 GwG).

(a) ***Legal entities with the exception of foundations and companies with legal capacity within the meaning of Section 2(11) WpHG***

If the entity subject to the disclosure requirement is a legal entity but not a foundation with legal capacity and is not listed on a regulated market within the meaning of Section 2(11) WpHG or a comparable market, the UBOs include in particular those natural persons who directly or indirectly hold more than 25% of the capital of a company (shareholders), control more than 25% of the voting rights of a company (voting right holders), or exercise control over the company in some other comparable way (eg, through a controlling influence or certain agreements (see Section 3(2) GwG)).

(b) ***Foundations and trust structures***

According to Section 3(3) GwG, any natural person acting as settlor, trustee or protector, if any, is deemed to be the UBO of a foundation with legal capacity and trust or trust-like structures. Furthermore, every natural person who is a member of the executive board of the foundation, all those who have been designated as beneficiaries or the natural persons who otherwise directly or indirectly exercise a controlling influence on the management of assets or contracts are also deemed to be UBOs. Also, the group of natural persons in whose favour the assets are to be managed or distributed, if the natural person who is to become the beneficiary of the assets under management has not yet been designated, and any natural person who may directly or indirectly exercise a dominant influence on an association, who is a member of the board of directors of the foundation or who has been designated as a beneficiary of the foundation, are also deemed to be UBOs.

Finally, Section 3(4) GwG stipulates that in the case of a transaction at the instigation of a person, the UBO includes the person at whose instigation the transaction is carried out. If the customer acts as a trustee, he/she is also deemed to act on the initiative of another person.

Specificities relating to trusts: A trust is a legal structure which is recognised abroad but does not exist in this form in Germany. The fact that trusts may not be set up in Germany is due to the fact that a trust in Germany does not correspond to the established civil law system, which is regularly aimed at protecting third parties or business transactions.[3]

Even if trusts do not have legal capacity under German law and are therefore not themselves subject to the notification obligations, these obligations affect

3 *Korte* in: BeckOK-GwG, 3 Edition 2020, Sec 20 marginal number 8.

trustees resident in Germany. In this respect, Section 21(1) sentence 1 GwG stipulates the obligations to obtain, keep, update and notify the UBOs of trusts, which are to be fulfilled by the trustee resident or domiciled in Germany. The trustee is required to obtain, retain and keep up to date information on the UBOs of the trust which he/she administers, as well as the nationality of the UBOs, and to notify Transparency Register GmbH via www.transparenzregister.de.

In addition, trustees who are domiciled or have their registered office outside the European Union are obliged to notify the Transparency Register if they enter into a business relationship in terms of Section 1(4) GwG on behalf of the trust with a contracting party domiciled in Germany or undertake to acquire ownership of a property located in Germany (see Section 21(1) sentence 2 GwG). This obligation does not apply in each case if the information pursuant to Article 1 No 15c of Directive (EU) 2018/843 and pursuant to Section 19(1) GwG has already been transmitted to another register of a member state of the European Union, Section 21(1) sentence 3 GwG.

Foundations: The foundation is the only one of the legal entities that is always (ie, with no exception) required to report to the UBO register. While numerous legal entities benefit, at least in certain cases, from the so-called notification fiction of Section 20(2) GwG, the foundation is never 'exempt' from the reporting obligation in the absence of a register with publicity effect.[4]

(c) Notional UBO

Finally, Section 3(2) sentence 5 GwG regulates the cases in which a UBO cannot be identified. These include both cases in which a UBO does not exist according to the legal definition of Section 3 GwG, but also all cases in which a UBO cannot be identified even after comprehensive checks have been carried out. If no natural person was identified even after execution of comprehensive investigations and in the absence of facts as defined in Section 43(1) GwG or the existence of doubts as to the beneficial ownership of the identified person, the legal representative, the managing shareholder or the partner of the contractual partner (so-called notional UBO) is considered the UBO. This information must then be reported for entry in the UBO register.

Only in cases where the required information on the UBO(s) is/are derived from the documents and entries listed in Section 22(1) GwG, which can be called up electronically from the registers listed in Section 20(2) sentence 1 GwG,[5] is it not necessary to enter the details in the UBO register. The fact that

4 *Schwalm*, ZStV 2020, 52 (53).

5 Mentioned here are the commercial register (Sec 8 Commercial Code), the partnership register (Sec 5 Partnership Company Act), the register of cooperative societies (Sec 10 Cooperative Societies Act), the register of associations (Sec 55 Civil Code) and the register of undertakings (Sec 8b(2) Commercial Code).

the nationality of the UBO is not apparent there is irrelevant. In such cases, the nationality need not be apparent from the registers or entries/documents.

(d) ***Multi-level participation structures***

So-called multi-level participation structures are of particular practical importance. This is the case when not only natural persons hold a direct interest in the entity subject to reporting requirements, but also (possibly several) legal entities – sometimes also at a higher level of participation – are involved in the ownership structure. In these cases, the shares of the person in question must always be added together when determining the UBO. If, for example, a natural person directly or indirectly controls capital shares or voting rights, the individual shares must be added together.

2.3 Notification fiction – any exceptions to the reporting obligation?

(a) ***In general***

In certain cases the GwG considers an entry in the UBO register not to be required. If the information required for the UBO register already results from other public and electronically accessible German registers within the meaning of Section 20(2) GwG, the transparency obligation is deemed as fulfilled. If the required information can be found in the commercial register or in the register of partnerships, cooperatives or associations, for example, notification to the UBO register can be omitted. With regard to the commercial register, it should be noted that the notification obligation only ceases to apply if the commercial register contains lists of shareholders that were filed electronically after the Law for the Modernisation of the German Limited Liability Company Law and the Prevention of Misuse (MoMiG) came into force in 2008.

The share register, on the other hand, is not one of the public registers with the consequence that every non-listed joint stock company will always have to report to the UBO register.

In case the registers listed in Section 20(2) GwG do not reveal the nature and extent of the beneficial interest of the UBO (eg, in such constellations in which control over the entity subject to the reporting obligation is based on corresponding voting pool agreements or pooling agreements which are not evident from the commercial register), this may result in an obligation to report all information required under the GwG.

Finally, separate information to the UBO register is also always required if, following notification, the UBO or the relevant details change and the changes are entered in another public register. In such cases, a separate notification to the UBO register is mandatory. This notification must show that the information on the UBO is now derived from another public register or only that these details have changed.

In view of the numerous cases and the diverse shareholding structures, particularly in corporate groups, it is necessary always to check carefully whether there is an obligation to report or whether a notification fiction exists. Furthermore, it should always be carefully checked whether the documents deposited in other registers meet the requirements of a notification fiction within the meaning of Section 20(2) GwG.

Since in this context there are many different case constellations in practice which prohibit a schematic approach, both the Federal Financial Supervisory Authority (*Bundesanstalt für Finanzdienstleistungsaufsicht* – BaFin) and the BVA have dealt with these fundamental issues and the determination of a UBO. Both institutions have laid down their administrative practice in this respect in the interpretation and application notes on the GwG[6] respectively in their catalogue of frequently asked questions.[7]

(b) Excursus: planned amendment to the law

Please note that on 10 February 2021, the Federal Government passed the draft of the Transparency Register and Financial Information Act (TraFinG). The planned innovations will bring extensive changes to the GwG, primarily affecting the regulations of the transparency register. Numerous companies will have to prepare for new reporting obligations. The law is expected to come into force on 1 August 2021. With regard to the transparency register, the following changes are planned, among others.

As mentioned, up to now the transparency register has been designed as a so-called catch-all register. This means that those legal entities whose ownership and control structure and UBOs are already evident from other publicly accessible registers no longer have to report them to the transparency register. Thus, if all relevant information results, for example, from the commercial register or the register of cooperatives or associations, and if this information can be retrieved electronically, it did not have to be reported additionally to the Federal Office of Administration, the register-keeping body of the transparency register, until now. This so-called 'notification fiction', which has so far been standardised in Section 20 paragraph 2 GwG, will cease to apply when the TraFinG comes into force.

Consequently, the transparency register will be transformed into a full register. In future, all legal persons under private law and registered partnerships will be obliged to report the UBOs they have identified to the transparency register, irrespective of whether and, if so, which information has already been

6 *Auslegungs- und Anwendungshinweise zum GwG*, status December 2018, available at: www.bafin.de/SharedDocs/Downloads/DE/Auslegungsentscheidung/dl_ae_auas_gw_2018.html.

7 *Transparenzregister* FAQ, status 19 October 2018, available at: www.bva.bund.de/SharedDocs/Downloads/DE/Aufgaben/ZMV/Transparenzregister/Transparenzregister_FAQ.pdf?__blob=publicationFile&v=23.

deposited in other registers. The abolition of Section 20 paragraph 2 GwG also removes the privileged status of listed companies. For these, the reporting obligation was previously always considered fulfilled. Now they too must report the required information on their UBOs to the transparency register.

The background to this regulation are the efforts laid down in the EU Money Laundering Directive to interconnect all transparency registers of the EU member states via a European platform by 10 March 2021. Since such interconnection requires the existence of structured data records on UBOs in a uniform data format, the legislator believes that it is necessary to transform the transparency register into a full register.

In order to give companies time to adjust to the unrestricted obligation to report to the transparency register, the draft law provides for corresponding transitional regulations. Thus, Section 59 paragraphs 8 and 9 GwG-E regulate both transitional periods and the suspension of the prosecution of administrative offences.

For all those companies that have so far not had to report to the transparency register due to the reporting fiction, extended deadlines – depending on their legal form – are to apply beyond the date of entry into force of the TraFinG on 1 August 2021 until, at the latest, 31 December 2022 for proper reporting.

In addition, the TraFinG provides for further measures, the most important of which is probably the one described above.

(c) Individual cases

Since the introduction of Sections 18ff GwG have raised numerous questions, a final presentation is not possible here in view of their scope. Nevertheless, the recurring questions in consulting practice will be dealt with briefly. In addition to notification obligations concerning the limited liability company (*Gesellschaft mit beschränkter Haftung* – GmbH) and the joint stock company (*Aktiengesellschaft* – AG), these relate in particular to the changed administrative practice of the BVA with regard to limited partnerships (*Kommanditgesellschaften* – KG) and foundations with legal capacity.

Limited liability company (GmbH): The GmbH always benefits from the notification fiction if all the necessary information can be obtained from the commercial register and the list of shareholders can be accessed electronically. If, on the other hand, the necessary information is provided only in the minutes of a shareholders' meeting or the articles of association, this does not fulfil the requirements of the notification fiction.

The same applies if the electronically retrievable list of shareholders does not cover the entire period since 1 October 2017. Finally, the definition of 'notification' does not apply if the beneficial ownership results from pool associations or voting rights ties which cannot be identified from the electronically filed documents. In these cases, the UBO(s) must be reported to the UBO register.

Joint stock company (AG): In case of companies that are listed on a regulated market as defined in Section 2(11) WpHG or subject to transparency requirements corresponding with Community legislation (law) with respect to voting rights shares or equivalent international standards, the obligation to notify to the UBO register shall always be deemed as fulfilled (see Section 20(2) sentence 2 GwG). This includes listed companies if their shares are admitted to trading on a regulated market within the meaning of Article 44(1) of Directive 2014/65/EU (MiFID 2) or if their shares are admitted to trading on an organised market in a third country that is subject to transparency requirements equivalent to those of Community law with regard to voting rights shares or equivalent international standards. The wording of this provision is limited to listed companies.

By contrast, joint stock companies that are not organised on one of the above-mentioned markets are always obliged to notify their UBO to the UBO register, as the share register in Germany is not considered a register within the meaning of Section 20(2) GwG. Consequently, the notification fiction does not apply to such companies.

For subsidiaries of listed joint stock companies, the reporting fiction applies in principle so that this is also always deemed as fulfilled in accordance with Section 20(2) sentence 2 GwG, provided that the parent company holds at least 50% of the capital shares or controls at least 50% of the voting rights and no other UBOs exist at the subsidiary. Furthermore, it is necessary that the entire chain of shareholdings from the subsidiary subject to notification to the parent joint stock company can be ascertained electronically from the documents and entries listed in Section 22(1) GwG and the registers in accordance with Section 20(2) sentence 1 GwG. If this chain is interrupted at any point – for example, by taking control of a foreign company not covered by Section 20(2) sentence 2 GwG – the notification fiction does not apply to the domestic subsidiary.[8]

Limited partnerships (KG): With regard to the notification obligations of a KG and thus also of a GmbH & Co KG, the BVA has changed its administrative practice since the introduction of the UBO register in 2017. Whereas it was initially still based on the assumption that registered partnerships – and thus also the KG – do not generally have to provide information on their UBOs in the UBO register if the notification fiction under Section 20(2) GwG applies, the BVA now takes a different view.

8 *Transparenzregister* FAQ, status 19 October 2018, p4.

This is because only the amount of liability applicable to external liability is entered in the commercial register for limited partners, and the possibly deviating compulsory contribution made by the limited partner and the amount of such contribution cannot usually be inferred from the commercial register. Since the mandatory contribution is usually decisive for voting rights, profit distribution and also the participation in company assets, the question of beneficial ownership is primarily based on the mandatory contribution and not on the amount of liability entered in the commercial register. In addition, the commercial register does not usually show what contribution the general partner has made, with the result that the percentage share of the individual shareholders in the company cannot be determined. However, this question is also decisive in determining whether individual shareholders are to be qualified as UBOs within the meaning of the GwG. This means that for KG and GmbH & Co KG they must always report their UBO to the UBO register and can no longer rely on the notification fiction of Section 20(2) GwG.

The BVA makes an exception from the obligation to report only in certain cases, including the so-called 'Einheits-GmbH & Co KG' and the 'Ein-Personen-GmbH & Co KG'.[9]

Foundation with legal capacity: As already mentioned, the foundation is subject to an obligation to report to the UBO register without exception. This applies in any case to foundations with legal capacity. In the case of non-legally capable foundations, this applies *mutatis mutandis* if the purpose of the foundation is self-interested from the point of view of the founder.[10]

The founder him/herself is deemed to be a UBO within the meaning of Section 3(3) GwG only if he/she is either a member of the executive board or exercises a direct or indirect influence on the asset management or distribution of income or is him/herself a potential beneficiary. If he/she does not fulfil any of these roles, he/she is not covered by the regulation and therefore does not have to be notified to the UBO register. Within the meaning of Section 3(3) GwG the founder is not explicitly specified as UBO.

As mentioned, foundations are in any case required to report their UBO(s) to the UBO register, as this information has not yet been obtained from public registers within the meaning of the GwG.

---

9 One-person GmbH & Co KG (GmbH & Co KG means a limited partnership with a limited liability company as general partner).

10 It has not been conclusively clarified what exactly is meant by the formulation "self-interest from the perspective of the founder". This regulation is not known to national foundation law. Taking into account Union law regulations, Section 21(2) no 1 GwG is interpreted in such a way that the wording covers, on the one hand, constellations in which the founder is also the beneficiary him/herself. On the other hand, Section 21(2) no 1 GwG should also cover the constellation that the foundation should at least also benefit other persons specifically described in the articles of association, as is regularly the case with family foundations, for example.

2.4 Duty of information – how can an association tell who its UBO is?

The corporate bodies obliged to report must collect, store and keep up to date information regarding the UBO and report it to the *Bundesanzeiger Verlag GmbH* immediately via www.transparenzregister.de. These compliance obligations apply to the management staff of the notifying association. They are therefore required to take suitable organisational measures to ensure that the legal obligations are met.

In order to ensure that the corporate bodies which are required to register actually receive information on their UBOs, the shareholders and, where appropriate, the UBOs are also subject to obligations. It follows from Section 20(3) GwG that they must communicate the information on their shareholding to the association required to report. They are also required to notify any changes to this information without delay.

The same applies to foundations. As mentioned, the duty of notification to the foundation applies to all persons named in Section 3(3) GwG. These are all those who are deemed to be the UBOs of the foundation.

If the entity subject to the reporting obligation has not received any information from the UBO, it must request from its shareholders, insofar as they are known to it, information to an appropriate extent on the UBOs of the entity subject to the reporting obligation. For their part, the shareholders are obliged to reply to the request for information within a reasonable period of time. Exceptions to the aforementioned obligation apply only if the entity subject to the reporting obligation has other means of obtaining information on its UBO or is otherwise aware of such information.

The law also explicitly stipulates a documentation obligation on the entity subject to reporting requirements: it must adequately document the request for information and the information received in response (see Section 20(3a) GwG).

The shareholder is required to notify the entity subject to reporting requirements of any changes with regard to the ultimate beneficial ownership of the association. This does not apply only if the information on the new UBO can already be seen from the UBO register or if the shareholder has positive knowledge that the entity subject to the reporting obligation already knows the new UBO.

Finally, Section 20(3b) GwG imposes corresponding recording and retention obligations on the shareholder with regard to the notification made to the entity subject to reporting requirements.

2.5 Inspection rights – who may inspect the UBO register?

(a) Principle: public access

The rights to inspect the UBO register have been considerably extended with the implementation of 5AMLD. While inspection was still reserved for a specific group of persons until the end of 2019 – authorities, obligated parties within the meaning of Section 2 GwG and persons with a legitimate interest – the UBO register is now also accessible to the public pursuant to Section 23(1) GwG. In principle, the UBO is obliged to tolerate the public inspection of the entry about him/her in the UBO register.

(b) Restriction in the case of prevailing legitimate interests worthy of protection

The far-reaching transparency is regularly achieved at the expense of the interest of the UBOs in the protection of their personal data. For this reason, the BVA has the possibility, for its part, to restrict the inspection by the public, provided that the UBO affected by the inspection demonstrates that the inspection of the UBO register conflicts with predominant legitimate interests of his/her person worthy of protection. Such a restriction of inspection can be either complete or partial. The restriction or refusal of inspection must be made by way of a weighing of interests. Particularly in the case of family businesses and foundations, the legislator has recognised the risk that inspection of the UBO register may encourage the commission of property offences and provide potential offenders with sound evidence of sources of funds. For this reason, it has attempted to strike an appropriate balance between the public interest in access on the one hand and the interest of the UBOs in the protection of their personal data on the other.[11]

For this purpose, the UBO must demonstrate that, taking into account all the circumstances of the individual case, the inspection is contrary to the prevailing interests of his/her person worthy of protection. The interests worthy of protection are laid down in Section 23(2) sentence 2 nos 1 and 2 GwG. Accordingly, interests worthy of protection exist if facts justify the assumption that the inspection would expose the UBO to the – abstract – risk of becoming the victim of various offences specified in more detail in the law. Explicitly mentioned here are fraud, hostage taking, extortion, predatory extortion, extortionate kidnapping, coercion or threat, or finally criminal acts against life or limb. Furthermore, interests worthy of protection exist if the UBO is underage or legally incompetent.

The details with regard to the application for restriction of inspection are governed by the Regulation on the inspection of the UBO register (*Transparenzregistereinsichtsnahme-verordnung* – TrEinV) of 19 December 2017. The applicant is required to present those facts which justify the assumption that the inspection by the public exposes the UBO to the risk of becoming a victim of the offences listed exhaustively in Section 23(2) sentence 2 GwG. In addition, he/she must demonstrate that these interests worthy of protection outweigh any other interests and thus prevent inspection. Exceeding the relevant danger threshold can always only be proven and verified in individual

11 BT-DRS 18/11555, p133; *Grosner*, CB 2020, 182 (183).

cases. The UBO is therefore required to explain this in as much detail as possible in order to ensure that his/her application for restriction or complete refusal of access is successful.

If a UBO submits an application for refusal or restriction of access to the UBO register and the BVA does not remedy the application legally, an administrative procedure will follow. The UBO first has the opportunity to appeal against the negative decision. If this is not accepted, a procedure before the administrative court will follow. As long as no final decision has been reached on the matter, the third party requesting access is not granted access or granted only limited access (depending on the scope of the UBO's application). There is no case law on this in practice to date.

Finally, the UBO has the possibility of obtaining information about the inspections made to the public by means of a corresponding application to the UBO register (Section 23(6) GwG).

(c) Access by obligated entities to verify the information collected

It is not only members of the public and authorities who have the possibility to inspect the UBO register, but also those who are obliged to do so under Section 2 GwG. Since the beginning of 2020, they have even been explicitly required to verify the information on the UBO received from their contractual partner by inspecting the UBO register as part of their general due diligence obligations (see Section 11(5) sentence 2 GwG).

Nevertheless – and this is a contradiction – the UBO register does not provide protection in good faith; legal transactions should not be able to rely on the information contained in the register.

If the information provided by the contracting party differs from the information stored in the UBO register, Section 23a GwG now stipulates an obligation to report, according to which the obligated parties must report such discrepancies to the UBO register without delay if they discover discrepancies between the information on the UBOs accessible in the UBO register and the information and knowledge on the UBOs available to them. The UBO register will verify the report and, if necessary, transmit it to the authority responsible for the prosecution of administrative offences for further action.

2.6 Sanctions – what could happen in the event of violations?

Section 56 GwG contains a large number of different types of fine. Among other things, these relate to the notification obligations in respect of the UBO register. Both wilful and negligent violations of these regulations will be punished. Violations can be punished with a fine of up to €150,000. If this entails serious, repeated or systematic violations of the regulations, this can result in a fine of up to €5 million or 10% of the total annual turnover achieved by the legal person or association of persons in the financial year preceding the official decision.

Furthermore, the GwG provides for disqualification from holding a managerial position. Finally, Section 57 GwG stipulates that administrative measures and verdicts regarding fines, together with the type and nature of the violation and the persons responsible for it, will be published on the website of the relevant supervisory authorities for a period of five years (so-called 'naming and shaming'). In certain cases, such publication may be postponed (see Section 57(2) GwG).

3. Practical experience

As mentioned above, since October 2017 many corporate bodies have been required to notify their UBOs to the UBO register. After a longer 'grace period' during which the BVA, which is responsible for the prosecution of administrative offences, refrained from initiating administrative offence proceedings, it began sending out hearing forms to numerous companies in Autumn 2019. In the course of this hearing, the notifiable corporate body was first given the opportunity to comment on the alleged infringement, which in most cases concerned missing or late entries of its UBO(s) in the UBO register.

Since it is often not possible for the BVA itself to check reliably whether the notification fiction of Section 20(2) GwG might apply to the specific association, the entity subject to the obligation to notify is in fact itself responsible for explaining any missing entries in the UBO register by reference to the notification fiction applicable to it.

3.1 Catalogue of fines of the BVA

In cases where the notification fiction does not apply, the BVA has subsequently sent out corresponding notices of fines and imposed fines. The amount of the fine is determined on the basis of a catalogue of fines issued by the BVA.[12] The framework of fines distinguishes between simple and serious, repeated or systematic violations. As a rule, the fine is then calculated as follows:

Standard rate according to the catalogue of fines × factor I × factor II × factor III.

The individual factors are determined by applying dutiful discretion.

Factor I thus assesses the subjective facts of the case. The BVA considers factor I to be cases of negligent action. In the case of wilful action, factor I is generally increased to two.

Factor II is determined on the basis of the economic circumstances of the person or persons concerned. If these cannot be determined, they must be estimated. The economic circumstances at the time of the decision on the fine are decisive. The BVA distinguishes between legal persons or associations of

12 Catalogue of fines BVA, status 22 October 2018, available at: www.bva.bund.de/SharedDocs/Downloads/DE/Aufgaben/ZMV/Transparenzregister/Transparenzregis-ter_Bu%C3%9Fgeldkatalog.pdf;jsessionid=902AC7610950C1580B1AAECD227F2763.intranet672?__blob=publicationFile&v=8.

persons and foundations and associations. It has set corresponding thresholds for legal persons or associations of persons, which refer to the last annual accounts carried out.[13]

For foundations and associations, the principles relating to factor II are to be applied accordingly. In the case of foundations, the income of the foundation is to be equated with the annual turnover and the assets of the foundation with the annual balance sheet total. In the case of associations, membership fees, donations and other income, as well as the association's assets shall be taken into account.

With regard to factor II, the adjusted gross annual income applies to natural persons; the factor is 0.5 for an adjusted gross annual income below €30,000 and increases in steps of 0.5 up to 3 or higher for an annual income of more than €70,000.[14]

Factor III finally describes serious, repeated or systematic violations. If it is a simple infringement, factor III is always to be assessed at 1. For serious, repeated or systematic infringements, factor III is determined according to the severity of the infringement (medium, serious, very serious, exceptionally high) and lies between 2 and 10.[15]

In addition, there is the possibility of increasing or reducing the fine calculated according to the standard rate and factors in the case of special circumstances. The BVA stipulates in this respect that an increase may be considered in particular if the person concerned is not reasonable, if he/she has already been fined or given a written warning for a similar administrative offence within the last two years, or if he/she is in extraordinarily good financial circumstances etc.[16]

On the other hand, the fine may be reduced if, for example, the person concerned is reasonable, if the specific accusation in the individual case appears to be less than the normal case for special reasons, or if the person concerned willingly cooperates with the authorities or if the economic circumstances simply do not permit a fine of the amount determined.[17]

3.2 Case study

For a better understanding and implementation of the provisions of the catalogue of fines, here is a practical example.

Two years after the existence of the obligation to report to the UBO register (ie, in October 2019), a non-listed joint stock company will notice that it has not fulfilled its reporting obligations under Sections 18ff GwG. It will make up for this failure immediately after this discovery.

---

13 See catalogue of fines BVA, status 22 October 2018, p4.
14 See catalogue of fines BVA, status 22 October 2018, p5.
15 See catalogue of fines BVA, status 22 October 2018, p6.
16 See catalogue of fines BVA, status 22 October 2018, p6.
17 See catalogue of fines BVA, status 22 October 2018, p6.

Only a few days after fulfilling the reporting obligation it receives a hearing letter from the BVA, which shows that the company's legal representatives are accused of having submitted a late notification of UBOs to the UBO register. The late notification to the UBO register constitutes an administrative offence pursuant to Section 56(1) No 55d Var 4 GwG, Section 20(1) sentence 1 Var 4 GwG. The BVA subsequently decides not to take action against the organs of the legal entity entitled to represent it, but to impose a fine solely on the company itself. The BVA then calculates the fine as follows.

The standard rate for the allegation of a negligent breach of the obligation to notify is €100. Since the obligation of transparency was only negligently breached in the underlying example, the BVA sets factor I and factor III at 1 each. With regard to factor II, the economic circumstances, the annual financial statements of the company show a balance sheet total of €11.2 million. The BVA then sets the relevant value for factor II at €11.4.

This results in the calculation €100 × 1 × 11.4 × 1 = €1,140. The BVA does not see any reasons for an increase or reduction in the above example, which is why it sets the fine at €1,140 in total.

3.3 In addition

Finally, the provision of Section 149 of the German Trade Regulations (*Gewerbeordnung* – GewO) is of considerable practical relevance for the individual units subject to reporting requirements for which fines are imposed. According to this provision, all such legally binding decisions in which the fine exceeds €200 must be entered in the central trade register.

At present, several proceedings are pending before the local court in which the units subject to reporting requirements have lodged an appeal against the fine order and which the BVA has not remedied. Published decisions in connection with violations of the provisions of Section 18ff GwG (ie, reporting obligations and corresponding entries in the transparency register), hardly exist to date.[18]

18 See Higher Regional Court of Cologne (OLG Köln), NZG 2020, 1077.

Greece

Angeliki Chimona
Petros-Fotios Chr. Fatouros
Phi Lambda Law Firm

---

1. Legal background and framework

Directive (EU) 2015/849 of the European Parliament and Council of 20 May 2015 (Fourth Anti-Money Laundering Directive – 4AMLD) on the Prevention of the Use of the Financial System for the Purposes of Money Laundering or Terrorist Financing amending Regulation (EU) No 648/2012 of the European Parliament and the Council repealing Directive 2005/60/EC of the European Parliament and the Council and Commission Directive 2006/70/EC was incorporated into Greek legislation by virtue of Law 4557/2018 (enacted in July 2018 (*Official Gazette* no 139/2018)), replacing the previous legal framework under Law 3691/2008.

Law 4557/2018 (the UBO Register Law) introduced in Greece stricter rules with reference to the prevention of the aforementioned crimes (ie, money laundering and terrorist financing) and, in particular, in relation to the obligation of specific obliged entities (eg, financial institutions, attorneys, accountants, etc) to apply customer due diligence measures, among others, with regard to the verification of their identity and the close monitoring of their transactions.

Taking into consideration the risks posed to financial stability by the illegal flow of capital into the markets of European countries, the primary aim of both the EU and national legislation is to create an adequate legal formula that would eventually prevent the abuse of corporate structures by strengthening transparency in the legal entities and enabling audit/prosecution authorities direct access to them.

The first step was the establishment of a national database for each entity's ultimate beneficial owner by virtue of Article 20-21 of Law 4557/2018 and the creation of three types of register (analysis on each type is provided under section 3.2 below):

- The Beneficial Ownership Special Register (Article 20 paragraph 1 Law 4557/2018), to be maintained within each entity's headquarters (hereinafter referred to as the Special Register);
- The Beneficial Ownership Central Register (Article 20 paragraph 4 Law 4557/2018), to be kept at a national level by the General Secretariat of

Information Systems (GSIS)[1] of the Ministry of Finance (hereinafter referred to as the Central UBO Register); and
- The Special Register of Beneficial Ownership of express trusts (Article 21 Law 4557/2018) (hereinafter referred to as the Special Register for Trusts).

Following the aforementioned registers' functional operation, the European Union's ultimate scope is the interconnection of each member state's national central UBO register and the creation of a European central platform, to become operational within 2021.

At a national level, following the enactment of Law 4557/2018 and the creation of the Central UBO Register, the Greek minister of finance published Decision No 67343 EX 2019 (GR Government Gazette B 2243/20-6-2019) regulating specific issues regarding record-keeping and the reporting procedure to the Central UBO Register, as further amended.[2]

Matters that were specified by the amended decisions included:
- the full list of persons required to register;
- the full details that should be reported; and
- the reporting deadlines.

These three amended decisions resulted in the Central UBO Register acquiring full legal effect in Greece.

The above-mentioned framework has been updated and launched via the adaptation of the Directive (EU) 2018/843 (Fifth Anti-Money Laundering Directive – 5AMLD) into the Greek legal system by virtue of Law 4734/2020, which revised Law 4557/2018.

2. Defining 'ultimate beneficial owners' and identifying direct/indirect control

According to the relevant UBO Register Law's scope, which is in line with EU guidelines, a 'beneficial owner' is:

any natural person(s) who ultimately owns or controls a legal entity, as well as, the natural person(s) on whose behalf a transaction or activity is conducted.

As such, the implementation of a substance control test is required to be performed by each underlying entity for the purpose of identifying its ultimate beneficial owners, while each entity is also obliged to proceed to a required reporting procedure before the Central UBO Register.

Indications of direct/indirect control that could potentially lead to a certain person in their capacity being considered a 'beneficial owner' are, amongst others, the following:

1 The so-called 'Γενική Γραμματεία Πληροφοριακών Συστημάτων'.
2 Decisions no 73900 ΕΞ 2019, no 121950 ΕΞ 31-10-2019 and no 24963 ΕΞ 2020/28.2.2020.

- the shareholding or ownership interest exceeding 25% held by a natural person;
- the shareholding or ownership interest exceeding 25% held by another entity whose control is exercised by one or more natural persons or by multiple corporate entities which are under the control mentioned in the bullet point above of the same natural person(s);
- the parent company holding the majority of: (i) the voting rights; (ii) the partners; and/or (iii) members of a subsidiary entity;
- the entity's control exercised through non-corporate agreements such as a shareholders' agreement;
- the exercise of dominant influence or power in the appointment of the entity's senior management; or
- the application of conditions laid out in Article 32 paragraphs 2–5 of Law 4308/2014 – applied in subsidiary companies[3] – whereby control is exercised via other means.

It should be noted that the above criteria do not apply to companies listed on a regulated market, due to the presumed transparency level of such entities.

Furthermore, persons holding influential and senior management positions should be registered as the entity's beneficial owner(s) exceptionally and on a case-by-case basis; in principle, in the absence of someone who can be identified as a beneficial owner according to the aforementioned rules (see bullet points above), only managers who are proven to have both an adequate knowledge of the entity's potential exposure to risks related to money laundering and terrorism financing activities, and at the same time enjoy sufficient seniority in order to take decisions affecting the entity's risk of exposure, can be identified as beneficial owners, while board of director positions are not considered as a prerequisite.

Despite the efforts of the Greek legislator to expand as much as possible the provisions' scope and apply the substance control test to all underlying entities, the aforementioned criteria are not applicable to certain types of legal entity, such as:

- undisclosed partnerships;
- not-for-profit organisations: in addition to the registration in the Central UBO Register of those stakeholders holding above 25%, any person holding presiding or other senior or influential management positions is

3 Such conditions are, amongst others, the following: If a parent entity: (i) has a majority of the voting rights of the shares, partners or members of another entity (subsidiary); (ii) has the right to appoint or terminate the majority of the members of the other entity's (subsidiary) governing, management or supervisory body and is – at the same time – a shareholder, partner or member of that entity; or (iii) has the right to exercise a dominant influence over the other entity (subsidiary) of which it is a shareholder, partner or member, either under a contract entered into with that entity or under a provision of its founding document or articles of association.

also required to be registered, thus presidents, secretaries, treasurers and administrators; and
- foundations: it needs to be pointed out that foundations established in Greece are exclusively of public benefit purposes, governed by the provisions of the Civil Code and, as such, a clear distinction lies between national and foreign foundations with reference to their purpose.

While national foundations are registered in the Central UBO Register, the registration and reporting obligations of foreign non-public benefit foundations in the Central UBO Register are yet to be clarified either by statutory provisions or by the competent Greek tax authorities; nevertheless, foreign (non-public benefit) foundations could be subjected to the provisions of Article 21 of Law 4557/2018 for the Special Register of Beneficial Ownership of express trusts (subject to pending relevant guidelines expected by the authorities), as laid out in section 5 below.

3. Entities required to register and report

3.1 Obliged entities

The Greek legislator's objective has been to extend the reporting obligation to the widest possible range of legal entities. As such, according to the relevant UBO Register Law provisions, all legal companies and/or entities based in Greece or those conducting taxable business activity in Greece are obliged to report to the Central UBO Register (hereinafter referred to as the 'obliged entity/ies'). Such legal entities are, amongst others, as follows:
- corporate enterprises that are not listed on a regulated market or on a multilateral trading mechanism;
- shipping and ship owning companies;
- civil law partnerships;
- not-for-profit entities;
- trusts and similar entities;
- cooperative entities; and
- companies that are in a state of bankruptcy, liquidation or special liquidation, or in similar insolvency proceedings.

The reporting rule does not apply to entities that do not meet the criteria set above regarding their established seat and their tax obligations towards the Greek State, as well as in cases where, due to the entity's special characteristics, the intended transparency criteria are already fulfilled. Such cases are, indicatively and not restrictively, the following:
- all bodies, legal companies and/or entities belonging to the Register of General Government Bodies;

- foreign entities operating in Greece (due to 'indirect taxation in the country');
- companies listed on a regulated market or on a multilateral trading mechanism operating in Greece, which are automatically reported to the Central UBO Register through the reporting line between the Central Securities Depository and the GSIS;
- legal companies and/or legal entities which, despite operating in Greece, have been released from the obligation to file an income tax return under special provisions;
- the offices or branches of foreign shipping companies that are established in Greece based on the provisions of Article 25 of Law 27/1975, which are not obliged to submit an income tax return for the income exempted according to these provisions; and
- parents' and guardians' associations.

3.2 Registers

As already analysed above, focusing on the ultimate purpose of transparency within each corporate structure, Law 4557/2018 has introduced the creation of three types of register.

(a) Special Register (Article 20 paragraph 1 Law 4557/2018)

Based on the said provisions, all corporate and related entities with registered offices in Greece, as well as those that exercise/carry out business activity taxed in Greece, are obliged to collect and keep adequate, accurate and updated information in relation to their beneficial owners. Such information shall be recorded in their Special Register incorporated in the place in which such entities are seated and shall include at least the following information: name and surname; date of birth; nationality; and country of residence of all beneficial owners; as well as the nature and extent of the rights held by them and/or any other information that could lead to the identification of the ultimate beneficiary. The Special Register should always be adequately documented and duly updated, under the responsibility of the entity's legal representative or the specially authorised person following the competent corporate body's resolution.

(b) Central UBO Register (Article 20 paragraph 4 Law 4557/2018)

In addition to the above, all data kept by each obliged entity in their Special Register shall be transferred into the Central UBO Register. This type of register is kept at a national level by the GSIS of the Ministry of Finance and is electronically linked with each entity's Tax Identification Number, obtains information collected by the authorities, and can be linked to other institutions that keep records regarding beneficial owners.

Each legal entity is obliged to report the required information to the Central UBO Register within 60 days of its establishment. The same deadline applies in regards to any amendments/updates, as of their effective date.

(c) ***Special Register for express trusts (Article 21 Law 4557/2018)***

The Greek law provisions made a distinction by creating a Special Register for Trusts, which would eventually, following its activation and efficient operation, be linked with the Central UBO Register. As such, provided that the trust is considered an obliged entity by fulfilling the conditions referred to in the said article, the information to be disclosed by the trustee shall include the identity of: (i) the settlor; (ii) the trustee(s); (iii) the protector (if any); (iv) the beneficiaries or class of beneficiaries; and (v) any other natural person exercising effective control over the trust. This data, as well as any updates thereof, should be recorded in a special section of the Central UBO Register.

It should be noted that given the lack of a statutory framework for trusts in Greece and in light of the incorporation of 5AMLD in the Greek territory by Law 4734/2020 enacted early October 2020, the operation of this register has not yet been initiated. As referred to in the explanatory memorandum of the draft law for the incorporation of 5AMLD, Greece did not share any relevant data in the list of trusts and similar legal formations governed by the law of the member states (as notified to the Commission (C360/2019), as corrected on 27 December 2019). Detailed criteria applicable to trusts' obligations in regards to the UBO registers are given below under section 5 of this chapter.

4. Registration process – provision of information – access to Central UBO Register

4.1 Registration process and provision of information

The reporting procedure to the Central UBO Register is carried out via the e-platform of the GSIS,[4] to which obliged entities have access for the data reporting, through their authorised representatives, who are liable for the data's accuracy and completeness.

The data to be disclosed and registered includes: (i) the obliged entity; (ii) their data provider; (iii) the intermediate entities; and (iv) their beneficial owners.

In particular:

- for legal entities: their Tax Identification Number, trade name, distinctive title and other information such as address, telephone, email and the legal entity identifier if the legal entity is listed;
- for the authorised representative: their Tax Identification Number,

4 See: www.gsis.gr.

name/surname, certification document, date of birth and address of the person filing the registration;

- for the ultimate beneficiary: their Tax Identification Number, name/surname, father's name, certification document, nationality, address, tax residence and ID, capacity, and type and extent of powers;
- if the company is held by another company: the trade name and distinctive title of such company, Tax Identification Number, General Commercial Registry (GEMI) number, legal form, address, tax residence and ID, and type and extent of powers; and
- for other legal entities (eg, trusts): the main data of the founder of the trust, the trustee, the beneficiary or the category of beneficiaries and any other person who exercises control on the trust.

4.2 Rights of access according to Law 4557/2018

As mentioned previously, one of the most important issues arising from both EU and national legislation on the prevention of the use of the financial system for the purposes of money laundering or terrorist financing is the right of access to the data to be kept at the Central UBO Registry and the Special Registers for expressed trusts.

To that extent, by virtue of Article 20 paragraphs 5–7 of Law 4557/2018 (in regards to 4AMLD), the access rights are as follows:

- unrestricted/unlimited access to all data registered is granted to competent prosecutorial or audit authorities, to Greek tax authorities (ie, the Anti-Money Laundering, Counter-Terrorist Financing and Source of Funds Investigation Authority) and to EU member states, following a relevant reasoned request;
- limited access to supervising competent authorities, as well as any natural person and/or entity who is considered as liable towards the Greek State for the implementation of due diligence measures against their clients in regards to certain business activities for the prevention of the use of the financial system for the purposes of money laundering or terrorist financing, according to the relevant provisions of Article 6 of Law 4557/2018 (hereinafter referred to as the 'liable persons/entities'), for the purposes of implementation of any due diligence measures, subject to the payment of an annual fee (€100); and
- public access to limited information (name, nationality, type and extent of rights held by the actual beneficiaries) is also granted to natural persons, provided that an annual fee of €20 is paid, which includes 10 searching actions.

4.3 Rights of access following enactment of 5AMLD by Law 4734/2020

Although the aforementioned access legal framework has triggered a number of objections in light of data protection issues and potential infringements, the implementation of 5AMLD into Greek legislation has further enhanced the right of access by widening the public's already established limited access rights.

In particular, the newly legislated provisions of Law 4734/2020, which entered into force in early October 2020, are introducing the following changes.

- Any member of the public can be granted access to the information registered in the Central UBO Register concerning information provided by 4AMLD, plus the ultimate beneficiaries' month and year of birth, without the annual fee obligation.
- Any persons/entities subject to statutory due diligence measures and obligations, in light of Law 4557/2018, will have immediate access to the Central UBO Register, without restrictions and without prior notice of the person concerned exclusively, within the context of their obligations arising from any applicable due diligence procedures.
- The aforementioned persons/entities (within their due diligence obligations), as well as members of the general public, following proof of special legitimate interest established following a prosecutor's order, may also have access to additional information that allows the identification of the ultimate beneficiary, such as his/her precise date of birth or contact details. A special fee is charged for the above access, which is collected by issuing an electronic administrative fee.
- Restrictions may be imposed on the access of aforementioned entities and members of the general public to all and/or part of the information concerning the beneficial owner, in cases where such access may reasonably expose the beneficial owner to a disproportionate risk of fraud, abduction, extortion, harassment, violence or intimidation, or if the beneficial owner is underage and/or otherwise incapable of legal action.

5. Special Register for trusts (Article 21 of Law 4557/2018)

5.1 Evolution of Law 4557/2018 and subsequent incorporation of 5AMLD

As already mentioned (see section 3.2(c) above), Article 21 of Law 4557/2018 enacts the creation of a Special Register for express trusts in Greece. According to the article's objective and definition introduced by the article's initial version before the enactment of Law 4734/2020:

Trustees of any express trust governed under the Greek legislation shall obtain and hold adequate, accurate and up-to-date information on beneficial ownership regarding the trust in a Special Register kept to their established seat, which shall be linked with the Central UBO Register.

The information to be disclosed by the trustee shall include the identity of: (i) the settlor; (ii) the trustee(s); (iii) the protector (if any); (iv) the beneficiaries or class of beneficiaries; and (v) any other natural person exercising effective control over the trust.

From a Greek law perspective, the aforementioned article has been criticised as a rather incomplete transfer of the relevant directive's provisions to the national legal system. The article's applicability in Greece is rather questionable in light of the lack of a statutory framework for trusts in Greece (also due to the fact that Greece is not a signatory to the international Convention of The Hague, of 1 July 1985, on the law applicable to trusts and their recognition, as developed by the Hague Conference on Private international law).

Apart from the issues arising from the article's general applicability, another issue worth exploring is that of a trust's discretionary beneficiary/ies. Considering that such persons are often unaware of their capacity as such, their assimilation with the non-discretional beneficiaries could potentially raise many hurdles in regards to the legitimacy of a legal framework based on the core principle of equal rights and obligations.

Certain of the aforementioned regulatory inconsistencies have already been restored/solved by virtue of Directive (EU) 2018/843 and the amendments of Law 4734/2020, which have fundamentally revised the provisions of Law 4557/2018.

In particular, the new law has introduced the following amendments:

- the creation of the Special Register for trusts is to be annulled. The information to be collected and kept by the trustees should be directly registered in the Central UBO Register of Article 20 paragraph 4 Law 4557/2018);
- the trustees of express trusts whose management takes place in Greece or who live in Greece and are tax liable towards the Greek State will be obliged to obtain and hold the information required on beneficial ownership regarding the trust. As such, the crucial factor for the application of the trustees' reporting responsibility is no longer the jurisdictions within which the trust is governed (taking into account the Greek statutory hurdles mentioned above) but the place where management is exercised;
- the same obligations are to be applied for those trustees whose place of establishment or residence is outside the European Union, but who enter into a business relationship or acquire real estate in the Greek territory on behalf of the trust; and
- furthermore, in cases of trustees holding multiple establishments, residences or trust-related business relationships in various EU member states, the registration obligation is fulfilled in any of the member states.

5.2 Right of access to the Special Register for trusts

In regards to the access rights to the Special Register for trusts, even if the provisions of the relevant Article 21 (of Law 4557/2018, enacting 4AMLD) were not activated in Greece, as mentioned above, it should be noted that the access rights framework (up to the enactment of 5AMLD, Law 4734/2020) had been quite restrictive with regards to the Central UBO Register, given that direct access was granted only to the Anti-Money Laundering Authority and certain competent authorities (referred to in Article 6 of Law 4557/2018).

According to the newest provisions launched by the implementation of 5AMLD (EU 2018/843) in Greece, and in line with the European Union's desire to increase transparency, the national articles are currently amended as follows:

- unrestricted/unlimited access without any restriction has been recently granted to the Anti-Money Laundering Authority and the competent authorities referred to in Article 6, as well as to the competent public prosecutor or other authorities with investigative or control powers in the field of money laundering, major offences and terrorist financing;
- limited access to any liable person/entity, exclusively within the context of the application of due diligence measures to the customer in accordance with the provisions of the said legal framework;
- limited access to data (concerning the name, month and year of birth, country of residence and nationality of the beneficial owner, as well as the type and extent of the reported person's rights) for any person demonstrating a legitimate interest and/or any person submitting a written request concerning a trust or similar legal entity that holds or owns a controlling interest in any corporate or other legal entity, other than those referred to in paragraph 1 of Article 20, by direct or indirect ownership, among others, through shares in the bearer or through control by other means. Access to additional information allowing the identification of ultimate beneficiaries, including at least the date of birth or contact details, according to the EU General Data Protection Regulation, can also be granted provided that a proof of a legal interest following a public prosecutor's order is granted; and
- it should be noted that by decision of the minister of finance, upon the recommendation of the authority, restrictions may be imposed on the access of the liable entities and the members of the general public to all or part of the information concerning the trustee, when such access may reasonably expose the trustee to a disproportionate risk of fraud, abduction, extortion, harassment, violence or intimidation, or if the trustee is a minor or otherwise incapable of legal action.

6. Penalties for non-compliance

Failure of an obliged entity to comply with the obligations outlined in Law 4557/2018 in regards to their registration in the Central UBO Register may incur the following sanctions:

- suspension of its ability to proceed to the issuance of a tax clearance certificate (a document issued by the competent tax authority stating that the entity has fulfilled its tax obligations towards the Greek State) until it registers the required information with the Central UBO Register; and
- a fine of €10,000 imposed by means of a decision of the Greek Anti-Money Laundering Authority, which could be doubled in case of subsequent non-compliance or recurrence.

7. Current Central UBO Register's operation and expected developments

Given the multiple issues that have arisen from the enforcement of Law 4557/2018 regarding the Central UBO Register's operation, affected also by the pandemic crisis, several commencing extensions have been legislated. As such, besides the fact that the official commencement of the register's operation had been set for 3 March 2020–1 May 2020, it has (as of 1 October 2020) been reactivated. The reporting deadline for obliged entities to conclude the relevant procedures ended on 31 December 2020.

Ireland

Aileen Keogan
Aileen Keogan Solicitor & Tax Consultant

1. Relevant Irish legislation

The relevant legislation in Ireland concerning anti-money laundering originated in the Criminal Justice Act 1994,[1] but when the Criminal Justice (Money Laundering and Terrorist Financing) Acts 2010 (the 2010 Act) and 2013[2] implemented the Third EU Anti-Money Laundering Directive 2005/60 (3AMLD),[3] the 2010 Act became the basis for the legislation going forward, so all later legislation amended the 2010 Act on a consolidation basis.

The European Union (Anti-Money Laundering: Beneficial Ownership of Corporate Entities) Regulations 2016 (SI No 560/2016)[4] (the 2016 Regulations) transposed the 3AMLD provisions requiring companies to have internal registers of beneficial owners.

The Criminal Justice (Money Laundering and Terrorist Financing) (Amendment) Act 2018[5] transposed the majority of the Fourth EU Anti-Money Laundering Directive 2015/849 (4AMLD)[6] into Irish law amending the 2010 Act.

The 2016 Regulations were replaced by the European Union (Anti-Money Laundering: Beneficial Ownership of Corporate Entities) Regulations 2019 SI No 110/2019[7] (the 2019 Company Regulations). The 2019 Company Regulations transposed the elements of 4AMLD and some of 5AMLD (see below) that require corporate and legal entities to maintain an internal register of their beneficial owners and to file this information with a central register by establishing the Central Register of Beneficial Ownership (RBO) on 22 March 2019.

The European Union (Anti-Money Laundering: Beneficial Ownership of Trusts) Regulations 2019 SI No 16/2019[8] (the 2019 Trust Regulations) introduced an obligation on the trustee (or manager in the case of collective investment schemes) to create and maintain an internal beneficial ownership register;

1 www.irishstatutebook.ie/1994/en/act/pub/0015/index.html.
2 www.lawreform.ie/_fileupload/RevisedActs/WithAnnotations/HTML/en_act_2010_0006.htm.
3 http://eur-lex.europa.eu/legal-content/EN/TXT/?uri=cellar:3aa3f6e7-74dd-4a02-84c7-d3af2531e10b.
4 www.irishstatutebook.ie/eli/2016/si/560/made/en/print.
5 www.irishstatutebook.ie/eli/2018/act/26/enacted/en/html?q=Criminal+Justice+Money+Laundering+and+Terrorist+FinancingAmendment+Act+2018.
6 http://eur-lex.europa.eu/legal-content/EN/TXT/?uri=celex:32015L0849.
7 www.irishstatutebook.ie/eli/2019/si/110/made/en/print.
8 www.irishstatutebook.ie/eli/2019/si/16/made/en/pdf.

however, the trustee was not required to file this data with the central RBO. These were short-lived regulations.

The European Union (Money Laundering and Terrorist Financing) Regulations 2019 SI No 578/2019[9] amended the legislation further in the context of 4AMLD regarding supervision by competent authorities and cooperation with member state competent authorities.

The Fifth Anti-Money Laundering Directive (EU) 2018/843[10] (5AMLD) entered into force on 9 July 2018, where the deadline for transposition by EU member states was 10 January 2020. The Criminal Justice (Money Laundering and Terrorist Financing) (Amendment) Act 2021[11] (the 2021 Act) was enacted on 18 March 2021 but provisions did not commence until ministerial orders were issued on 23 and 24 April 2021.

The 2019 Trust Regulations were replaced in full by the European Union (Anti-Money Laundering: Beneficial Ownership of Trusts) Regulations 2021 SI No 194/2021[12] (the 2021 Trust Regulations). The 2021 Trust Regulations came into operation on 23 April 2021[13] introducing the requirement for trustees of in scope trusts to maintain an internal register and furthermore to file with a central register of beneficial owners. Guidance Notes (in the form of Frequently Asked Questions (FAQs)) to augment the 2021 Regulations are to be published by the registrar of the Central Register of Ownership of Trusts (the Guidance Notes) setting out the mechanism of registration. It is anticipated that these will be published on 30 June 2021.

For the sake of completeness in the context of anti-money laundering in the European Union, while not relevant for beneficial ownership registers, it should be noted that the Sixth Anti-Money Laundering Directive (EU) 2018/1673[14] (6AMLD) deadline for transposition into national law was 3 December 2020. No Irish legislation has yet been published to transpose this directive into Irish law; the current legislation only deals with the giving effect to 5AMLD.

2. The Company Register

2.1 The Register of Beneficial Ownership (RBO)

Under the 2019 Company Regulations, the function of managing the register is given to the Companies Registration Office (CRO). The new register is a stand-alone register (ie, stand-alone from the normal register of companies) known as the Register of Beneficial Ownership (the RBO). The filing of beneficial

9 www.irishstatutebook.ie/eli/2019/si/578/made/en/print?q=money+laundering&years=2019.
10 https://eur-lex.europa.eu/legal-content/EN/TXT/?qid=1597662379360&uri=CELEX:32018L0843.
11 www.irishstatutebook.ie/eli/2021/act/3/enacted/en/html.
12 www.irishstatutebook.ie/eli/2019/si/16/made/en/pdf.
13 Apart from Section 8 of the 2021 Act relating to checking the register on entering into a business relationship which came into effect the following day, 24 April 2021, SI 188 of 2021.
14 https://eur-lex.europa.eu/legal-content/EN/TXT/?uri=celex:32018L1673.

ownership data must be done through the online portal on the RBO website,[15] and is therefore a process separate to the registration of information/forms under the Companies Acts etc.

All corporate and legal entities, other than companies listed on a regulated market, including all companies/industrial provident societies/Irish collective asset-management vehicles (ICAVs) (but not trusts), must identify their beneficial owners and register these details with the RBO within five months of their date of incorporation.[16] This is in addition to meeting their existing statutory filing obligations with the CRO under the Companies Acts in relation to directors, shareholders, etc or in relation to other non-company legislation (eg, industrial and provident societies). Any changes to the list of beneficial owners must be notified to the RBO within 14 days of the change.

In addition, companies/societies/ICAVs are obliged to maintain their own internal register in accordance with the 2019 Company Regulations,[17] keeping the details of the beneficial owners on their own internal register. Regulation 5(6) of the 2019 Company Regulations states that the company/society's internal register of beneficial owners must be available for inspection by any member of the Garda Síochána (the Irish police force), the Revenue Commissioners, a competent authority, the Criminal Assets Bureau, or an inspector appointed under Section 764(1) of the Companies Act 2014 (the inspector appointed through the Office of the Director of Corporate Enforcement).

The company/society's officers (director(s) and company/society secretary) are the persons responsible to obtain and confirm beneficial ownership information, to keep the company/society's own beneficial ownership register current and accurate, and to deliver the required beneficial ownership information to the RBO within the prescribed timeframes. Their duty is to maintain "adequate, accurate and current information in respect of its beneficial owners". Failure to comply with these requirements is a breach of statutory duties and a criminal offence which is subject to sanctions.

2.2 Who is a beneficial owner?

The 2019 Company Regulations apply the same definition of 'beneficial owner' as set out in Article 30, 4AMLD. A beneficial owner is defined in Article 3(6),

---

15 https://rbo.gov.ie.

16 In relation to companies incorporated on or after 22 June 2019. For companies incorporated before that date, the deadline for registration was 22 November 2019.

17 But not a company listed on a regulated market that is subject to disclosure requirements consistent with EU law or subject to equivalent international standards which ensure adequate transparency of ownership information – Paragraph 4. A branch is not an entity incorporated in Ireland and so is not required to file beneficial ownership details with the RBO. This includes charities that are companies. Investment funds and trusts are also required to keep an internal register under the 2019 Trust Regulation and not under the 2019 Company Regulation. Foundations as not an entity registered in Ireland as a corporate or trust would not be included as a legal entity incorporated in Ireland.

4AMLD as any natural person(s) who ultimately owns or controls a legal entity, either through direct or indirect ownership of a sufficient percentage of the shares or voting rights or ownership interest in the entity, including through bearer shareholdings, or through control via other means. These include:

- ownership (directly or indirectly) of more than 25% of the company/society's shares;
- controlling (directly or indirectly) more than 25% of the company/society's voting rights; or
- control via other means which is explained in Recital 13 of 4AMLD as follows:

  Control through other means may, inter alia, include the criteria of control used for the purpose of preparing consolidated financial statements, such as
  - *through a shareholders' agreement,*
  - *the exercise of dominant influence or*
  - *the power to appoint senior management.*

If a company/society is a subsidiary owned by another corporate entity, any natural person(s) who holds or controls a shareholding of 25% plus one share, or an ownership interest of more than 25% in the parent corporate entity, is a beneficial owner(s) of the subsidiary.

If a company/society is a subsidiary owned by multiple corporate entities, Article 3(6), 4AMLD states that a shareholding of 25% plus one share or an ownership interest of more than 25% in a subsidiary held by multiple corporate entities which are under the control of the same natural person(s) shall be an indication of indirect beneficial ownership.

Ultimately, it is a natural person(s) who must be identified and entered on the RBO as the beneficial owner(s) of the company/society, irrespective of how many layers of ownership there are in the company/society's structure. The name of another company/society cannot be entered on the RBO.

If, after having exhausted all possible means and provided there are no grounds for suspicion, no natural person is identified as a beneficial owner, or if there is any doubt that the person(s) identified is/are the beneficial owner(s), Regulation 5(4) of the 2019 Company Regulations provides that the natural person(s) who holds the position of senior managing official(s) of the company/society shall be recorded on the RBO as the beneficial owner. Relevant entities are required to keep records of the actions taken to identify their beneficial owners in accordance with Regulation 5(5) of the 2019 Company Regulations.

For instance, in the case of charities, if a charity has three or fewer members, the beneficial ownership will be treated as those members; if a charity has more than three members, those who have control by any other means must be identified; and, if not identifiable, the chief executive officer (CEO) and directors should be registered.

If the beneficial owners do not identify themselves to the company/society, then the company/society must give notice to each person that it reasonably believes to be a beneficial owner requesting them to confirm if they are and their details, and give notice to any person or entity that it has reasonable cause to believe knows the identity of the beneficial owner and ask them whether they have such knowledge.

2.3 Information for the RBO

The following information is required for each beneficial owner for filing in the RBO:

- company/society name;
- company/society number;
- surname;[18]
- forename;
- date of birth;
- PPS Number (the Irish tax registration number);[19]
- nationality;
- country of residence;
- statement of the nature and extent of interest held;
- statement of the nature and extent of control exercised;
- residential address;
- eircode/postcode (optional);
- date of entry as beneficial owner;
- date of cessation as beneficial owner; and
- if either:
  - after having exhausted all possible means and provided that there are no grounds for suspicion, no natural person is identified; or
  - if there is any doubt that any natural person so identified is a beneficial owner of the company/society,

  the names and details of the one or more natural person(s) who holds the position(s) of senior managing official(s) of the company/society must be entered in the company/society's internal register as its beneficial owners.

---

18 The forename and surname entered in the RBO portal must match the legally registered name of the natural person (ie, the name as registered on his/her PPSN with the Department of Employment Affairs and Social Protection).

19 The registrar of beneficial ownership is obliged by law to verify the identity of every beneficial owner and for beneficial owners who have a PPSN the RBO will verify their identity against data already verified by the Irish Department of Social Protection (DEASP) in respect of that person. For beneficial owners who do not have a PPSN, the Form BEN2 – Declaration as to Verification of Identity – is the method to be used by the registrar to verify the person's identity. Only one BEN2 will be required in respect of each beneficial owner and once this has been processed successfully and an RBO Number issued by the registrar, that RBO Number can be used for making future beneficial ownership filings for that person. Note the PPSN is not disclosable by the registrar and the registrar can only store a version (a 'hashed version') of the number from which it is not possible to determine the actual PPS number.

All the same details must be entered in the internal register and in the RBO as for any other beneficial owner. The company/society must keep records of the actions taken to identify its beneficial owners. (Regulations 5(4) and (5) of the 2019 Companies Regulations.)

The 2019 Company Regulations provide that the company/society will provide such other information as the registrar of the RBO may determine. Further, additional information may be required depending upon whether the beneficial ownership information is delivered to the registrar by the company/society, acting through its officer or employee, or by a person acting on behalf of the company/society (the presenter), such as:

- presenter details;
- name of presenter;
- address of presenter;
- phone number of presenter;
- email address of presenter;
- capacity in which the presenter is acting (eg, officer/employee of company/society, person acting on behalf of the company/society etc); and
- if the presenter is not a natural person, the name, address, phone number and email address of a natural person for correspondence purposes.

The regulations impose an obligation on the company/society to keep the information in its beneficial ownership register aligned with the information that the relevant entity has filed with the registrar in the RBO. The company/society must deliver any changes in the company/society's beneficial ownership information to the registrar so as to allow the central register to be amended with the corresponding changes. The regulations refer to this as the "follow up obligation" and prescribe the process and requirements for compliance with it.

2.4 Access to the RBO

(a) Unrestricted access

The RBO can be inspected by certain members of the Garda Síochána, the Revenue Commissioners, Financial Intelligence Unit (FIU) Ireland, the Criminal Assets Bureau and members of staff of a competent authority engaged in the prevention, detection or investigation of possible money laundering or terrorist financing. The ranking and authorisation requirements of those who can inspect the central register are prescribed in detail in the regulations (Regulation 5(7) of the 2019 Companies Regulations).

The 2010 Act establishes the following number of competent authorities that monitor designated persons and secure compliance with the requirements of the act:

- the Central Bank of Ireland for credit institutions or financial institutions;
- the designated accountancy bodies for auditors, external accountants or tax advisers;
- the Law Society of Ireland for solicitors;
- the General Council of the Bar of Ireland for barristers; and
- the minister for justice and equality for any other designated person under the act, administered by the Anti-Money Laundering Compliance Unit.

These bodies are entitled to all the information (save for PPS numbers) on the register, subject to certain safeguards (ie, the request must come from an individual of or above a specified position or rank, acting on the authority of an individual of or above a specified higher rank).

Any such authority (save for the FIU) may disclose the information it receives from the central register to a corresponding authority in any EU member state.

Regulation SI No 578/2019 provides, among other things, that the competent authority must adopt a risk-based approach to the exercise of its supervisory functions, base the frequency and intensity of on-site and off-site supervision on the risk profile of the designated persons and take into account the degree of discretion allowed to the designated person, and appropriately review the risk assessments underlying this discretion and the adequacy and implementation of its internal policies, controls and procedures.

(b) Restricted access

A designated person[20] has a right of access to some information in the central register when the company/society enters into an occasional transaction (a transaction in relation to which the designated person is required to apply customer due diligence measures) or forms a business relationship with a designated person. A designated person for this purpose is an organisation which is required to carry out anti-money laundering due diligence on its customers or clients, such as credit institutions, banks, accountants, solicitors etc. An occasional transaction is a transaction for which a designated person must apply customer due diligence.

In such a case, the designated person can access each beneficial owner's name, month and year of birth, country of residence and nationality, and a

20 As defined in Section 25 Criminal Justice (Money Laundering and Terrorist Financing) Act 2010 as amended, as set out in the Annex at the end of this chapter.

statement of the nature and extent of the interest held, or the nature and extent of control exercised of each such beneficial owner (Regulation 5(8) of the 2019 Companies Regulations).

A member of the public may also inspect similar information as the designated person (above) may inspect.

The right of access of both designated persons and the public is restricted where a beneficial owner is a minor. In such a case the designated person or member of the public must demonstrate to the registrar's satisfaction that there are substantial grounds for the contention of the applicant that it is in the public interest in them having the requested information.[21]

In addition, the registrar may require the person to pay a fee[22] in respect of the access provided.

The Data Protection Act 2018 applies to the access that the registrar affords to the designated person and any member of the public in respect of the information in the RBO.

2.5 Further obligations relating to access to company internal register and information on identity of beneficial owners

In addition to its obligations as set out in the 2016 Company Regulations, the company/society is obliged, on request, to provide Garda Síochána, the Criminal Assets Bureau, the Revenue Commissioners and any other 'competent authority' (eg, the Central Bank, the Financial Services Authority, the Law Society etc) with timely access to its internal register.

The 2019 Company Regulations permit competent authorities to disclose any information on a company/society's internal register to any corresponding competent authority of another requesting member state.

If a company/society enters into an 'occasional transaction' with a 'designated person' or forms a business relationship with a designated person, then the company/society must provide the designated person with:

- details of its beneficial ownership as well as legal ownership; and
- on request, the information identifying all the beneficial owners of the company/society.

Having done so, they are then under an obligation to notify the designated person of any changes to the beneficial owners of the company/society within 14 days from the date on which the relevant entity became aware of any change.

21 Regulation 25(5) 2019 Company Regulations. This only applies for minors (under age 18) and not for those beneficiaries who may be vulnerable by reason of mental incapacity or those who might be able to demonstrate that for security purposes their assets should not be made public. There are no known cases on this aspect as yet.

22 Currently a beneficial ownership report for a company is available online for €2.50.

2.6 Remedies and sanctions

As under the 2016 Regulations, if:

- any details are entered incorrectly in or omitted from the RBO; or
- a default is made or unnecessary delay takes place in updating the RBO to reflect that a person has ceased to be a beneficial owner,

then the aggrieved person or any other interested person may apply to the High Court for the RBO to be amended.[23] The High Court may refuse the application or it can order for the RBO to be amended or require the company/society to compensate the aggrieved person for any loss sustained.[24]

The 2019 Company Regulations confirm that 'any other interested party' means any other person who is a member or other beneficial owner of the relevant entity.

A relevant entity who breaches the 2019 Company Regulations may be liable on summary conviction to a fine[25] or, on indictment, to a fine not exceeding €500,000. In addition to these fines, custodial sentences of up to 12 months can be imposed on any person who makes a statement to the registrar which is false in a material particular, and does so knowingly or recklessly.

Where an offence is found to have been committed by a relevant entity under the 2019 Company Regulations, and is proved to have been committed with the consent or connivance of any of its officers, those officers will also be guilty of an offence.

2.7 Sanctions

For the purpose of EU sanctions regulations, the following have been designated as Ireland's 'competent authorities':

- **Department of Foreign Affairs and Trade:** The Department of Foreign Affairs and Trade is responsible for foreign policy and representing Ireland internationally. In the context of sanctions, this involves engagement with the relevant bodies at the United Nations and the European Union, and ensuring information is shared with the appropriate government departments and agencies in Ireland. The department's officials represent Ireland at EU working groups where sanctions measures are negotiated and this participation is underpinned by input as appropriate from other departments. The department is also responsible for considering any requests for humanitarian exemptions pursuant to a sanctions regime.

---

23 Regulation 15, 2019 Company Regulations.

24 Regulations 6–9 of the 2019 Company Regulations sets out notices to be given to persons believed to be beneficial owners and other steps and notices to be given to establish beneficial ownership and duties of a natural person to notify the company/society in relation to his/her status as beneficial owner.

25 Class A fine currently between €4,000 and €5,000.

- **Department of Business, Enterprise and Innovation:** The Department of Business, Enterprise and Innovation is responsible for enforcing trade-related sanctions. Such sanctions may include restrictions or complete embargos on certain exports (eg, dual-use items and military equipment) to designated entities or regions. Sanctions may also apply to associated support services such as maintenance and repair. In some instances, exporters may be required to obtain prior authorisation from the department for exports of certain items.
- **Central Bank of Ireland:** The Central Bank of Ireland is responsible for the administration, supervision and enforcement of relevant aspects of financial sanctions in Ireland. Financial sanctions are primarily concerned with curtailing the movement of payments and capital.

3. The Trust Registers

Previously under the 2019 Trust Regulations, between 29 January 2019 and 23 April 2021 trustees were required to establish and maintain a beneficial ownership register as an internal register for each trust known as a beneficial ownership register. This register must still be maintained by the trustees[26] but, in addition, with effect from 23 April 2021, on the revocation of the 2019 Regulations, the 2021 Trust Regulations repeated much of the previous obligations concerning the internal register to be maintained, but also required trustees of relevant trusts to report beneficial ownership information from that internal beneficial ownership register to the Central Register of Ownership of Trusts ('the Central Register').

All trusts must register the necessary information on the Central Register within six months of 23 April 2021 or six months from the trust's coming into existence.

3.1 Territoriality considerations

The requirement for both registers applies to all in scope trusts and not just those with Irish tax consequences, as had been the case under 4AMLD. The 2021 Trust Regulations impose requirements on a trustee of a relevant trust where:

- the trustee is resident in Ireland; or
- where the trust is otherwise administered in Ireland.[27]

Where no trustees are resident in the European Union and the trust is not administered in the European Union, then the requirements of the 2021 Trust Regulations apply where:

---

26 Regulation 7 and 17, SI 194 of 2021. There are rights for persons named or who ought to be named on this internal register to seek rectification of the register if sufficient cause is shown to the High Court.

27 Regulation 6, SI 194 of 2021.

- a trustee of the relevant trust, when acting as trustee, enters into a business relationship in Ireland; or
- a trustee of the relevant trust, when acting as trustee, acquires land or other real property in Ireland in the name of the trust.[28]

The residence of a trustee is not defined in either the legislation or regulations. While it may be considered that this is residence in the ordinary meaning of the word (living in Ireland) and not tax residence under Irish tax legislation, nevertheless it is likely that the legislature did mean tax residence for these purposes. It is hoped that there may be more clarity provided for this in practice, particularly in Guidance Notes.

The administration of a trust is also not defined. It is unclear as to whether all or the majority of the trustees must carry out administrative duties in Ireland to constitute the trust being treated as administered here.[29] It is assumed that the trustees need to carry out particular acts over the greater part of the trust fund while in Ireland (eg, hold regular meetings or sign documents while present in Ireland) for the trust to be considered to be administered in Ireland. It would seem likely that merely holding some, but not all, of the trust assets in Ireland will not of itself mean the trust is administered in Ireland. Activities around the holding of a minor number of trust assets in Ireland in comparison to the greater number of trust assets being held abroad and the trustees being resident and carrying out their activities on those assets from abroad would not appear to be considered to be administration of the trust in Ireland. This is on the basis the initial acquisition of an asset or dealing with such an asset in Ireland after 27 April 2021 is anyhow likely to trigger a reporting requirement of beneficial ownership details to a designated person as an 'occasional transaction' or on the basis a business relationship has been formed.[30] Again, clarity in Guidance Notes or indeed by amending legislation would be welcome on this point.

For the purposes of the Central Register, where a relevant trust is administered in more than one member state or two or more of the trustees of a relevant trust reside in different member states or the trustees have already entered into a business relationship or acquired land/real property in another member state, then proof of registration of the relevant trust in the other member state is regarded as compliance with the 2021 Trust Regulations.[31]

28 Regulation 6 2021 Trust Regulations.
29 The rules for income tax and capital gains tax for trusts differ in such cases.
30 See further below as to occasional transaction.
31 Regulation 18(2) 2021 Trust Regulations.

3.2 Relevant trust

A 'relevant trust' means an express trust established by deed or other declaration in writing and any other arrangement or class of arrangement prescribed.[32]

The regulations do not define an 'express trust', but generally under trust law an express trust arises where:

- the subject matter is certain;
- the objects are certain;
- the words relied on to create the trust are imperative; and
- any formalities specific to the type of trust are complied with.

If the trust is an 'excluded arrangement' as listed, it is not a relevant trust. The 2021 Trust Regulations impose the obligations only on relevant trusts as defined and so any trust that is not a relevant trust is not in scope of the 2021 Trust Regulations.

A relevant trust includes a trust established under a will. In private family contexts, discretionary trusts, limited or interest in possession trusts and bare trusts are all express trusts. While statutory trusts, such as those arising for minor children on intestacy, are express trusts, nevertheless they are not established by "deed or other declaration in writing and any other arrangement or class of arrangement prescribed" and so they are not in scope as relevant trusts requiring registration in the Central Register.

There is uncertainty as to whether the trust under which a personal representative (executor or administrator) of an estate during the course of administration of the estate holds the deceased's assets is a relevant trust requiring registration in the Central Register. The estate itself is certainly not established by "deed or other declaration in writing" in the case of an intestacy. The trust under which either an executor (in the case of a testate succession) or an administrator (generally in the case of an intestate succession) holds the estate for the benefit of the beneficiaries of a will is set out under the Succession Act 1965 and so would be considered to be a statutory trust and therefore also not in scope. However, the AML legislation[33] provides that in the case of an estate of a deceased person in the course of administration and in relation to which there is a provision for a relevant trust, the executor or administrator of the estate, and no other person, is deemed to be the beneficial owner of the trust for the period in which the estate is being administered for AML purposes.[34] This is useful in ensuring that designated persons dealing with the personal representatives, such as when opening an estate bank account or paying assets of a deceased person to the estate, can rely on the grant of representation and

---

32 Section 106ZC (1) 2010 Act as inserted by Section 26 2021 Act.
33 Both the 2021 Trust Regulations and the 2021 Act.
34 Section 106ZD(7) 2010 Act inserted by Section 26 2021 Act and Regulation 3(8) 2021 Trust Regulations.

do not have to identify or verify who are the beneficial owners of the estate and so do not need to have sight of the will or understand the family tree in terms of identifying who might be ultimate beneficial owners after the administration of the estate has ended. However, as it appears that no relevant trust arises in the estate itself, there seems no reason for the personal representative to register the estate in the Central Register. Whether there is an obligation to register the personal representative in the Central Register and then update the Central Register on the completion of the administration is therefore questionable. Particularly given the burdensome nature of this and the low risk of money laundering arising in such instances, it is hoped that more clarity would be given around this, for instance that the Guidance Notes would confirm that the reference in the legislation to the personal representative being a beneficial owner is for the purposes of the information passing to the designated persons only and that there is no obligation for the personal representatives to register.

Where property is bought and sold in Ireland, express trusts can arise during the transaction; however, again it would be considered that these arise by operation of law and so are not express trusts. They are not declarations in writing and so are out of scope of the legislation on the basis that they are not relevant trusts. Thus the myriad of trusts that would be considered incidental in the course of a single normal conveyance, while directly dealt with in enabling legislation in similar situations in the United Kingdom, ought to be managed in Ireland by falling out of scope in the first place because the definition of the relevant trust is confined to an express trust established by deed or declaration in writing.

The use of express trusts is a relatively common feature of certain commercial or financing transactions – for example, security trusts are often used for multi-lender loan transactions, custodian and pension trusts, and funds. Trusts encountered in employee share schemes and employee benefits trusts are express trusts. However, these are specifically excluded from being in scope as will be seen below.

Where business arrangements are based on contractual relationships or are established in accordance with legal principles other than trusts, each of these ought to fall out of scope of the definition of relevant trusts as again they are not set out as declarations of trusts expressly (other than incidentally in default situations under the terms of the contract). It is hoped that the Guidance Notes might confirm that default trusts such as these are not in scope.

Charitable trusts are express trusts and are required to register. Private or public foundations, while not legal entities in Ireland,[35] would only be treated as relevant trusts if they fall under the definition of an express trust under general trust law. However, to the extent that a foundation is administered in

35 In Ireland, philanthropic or family foundations are set up as either trusts or corporate entities.

Ireland and they are not considered express trusts, it appears that these regulations do not apply to foundations. It is likely, however, that they will already have been registered as akin to a trust in the member state in which they were set up under the local AML legislation there.

There is also room for particular arrangements to be prescribed as express trusts (none yet so prescribed) and trusts and arrangements can be specifically excluded from the definition of express trusts with provision to add to that list of excluded arrangements.

The current listed excluded arrangements are as follows:

- an occupational pension scheme that is an approved scheme pursuant to specific taxing legislation;
- an approved retirement fund within the meaning of specific taxing legislation;
- a profit sharing scheme or employee share ownership trust approved pursuant to specific taxing legislation;
- a trust for restricted shares within the meaning of specific taxing legislation;
- the Haemophilia HIV Trust, a specific trust established by the State in 1989; and
- a unit trust within the meaning of the European Union (Modifications of Statutory Instrument No 110 of 2019) (Registration of Beneficial Ownership of Certain Financial Vehicles) Regulations 2020 (SI No 233 of 2020), the beneficial ownership of which, by virtue of the European Union (Anti-Money Laundering: Beneficial Ownership of Corporate Entities) Regulations 2019 (SI No 110 of 2019), is required to be registered in the Central Register of Beneficial Ownership of Irish Collective Asset-management Vehicles, Credit Unions and Unit Trusts.

3.3 Who is a beneficial owner?

'Beneficial owner', in relation to a relevant trust, is defined as being any of the following:[36]

- any individual who is entitled to a vested interest in possession, remainder or reversion, whether or not the interest is defeasible, in the capital of the relevant trust property;
- in the case of a relevant trust other than one that is set up or operates entirely for the benefit of individuals referred to in the bullet point above, the class of individuals in whose interest the trust is set up or operates;[37]
- any individual who has control over the relevant trust;

---

36 Differing from the 4AMLD definition where it refers to 'natural persons' rather than 'individuals'.

37 In effect a discretionary trust.

- the settlor;
- the trustee; and
- the protector.

'Control' in relation to a relevant trust means a power (whether exercisable alone, jointly with another person or with the consent of another person) under the trust instrument concerned or by law to do any of the following:

(a) dispose of, advance, lend, invest, pay or apply the trust property;
(b) vary the relevant trust;
(c) add or remove a person as a beneficiary or to or from a class of beneficiaries;
(d) appoint or remove trustees; or
(e) direct, withhold consent to or veto the exercise of any power referred to at (a) to (d) above.

For instance to the extent that a typical life interest trust in Ireland might provide a veto for the life tenant over the power of the trustees to advance capital to the remaindermen, the life tenant will be treated as having control, but in any event that life tenant would be a beneficial owner anyhow by virtue of holding an interest in possession. The use of protectors in trusts is not common in Ireland as trustees of the typical private family trust are predominantly family or friends, not professionals; however, depending on the nature of the powers attached to a protector under the trust deed, such a protector might be treated as holding control and so be a beneficial owner for AML purposes.

For the purposes of the definition of 'control' in the definition of beneficial owner, an individual does not have control solely as a result of the power exercisable collectively at common law to vary or extinguish a trust where the beneficiaries under the trust are at least 18 years of age, have full capacity and (taken together) are absolutely entitled to the property to which the trust applies.[38]

As mentioned above, the legislation provides that in the case of an estate of a deceased person in the course of administration and in relation to which there is a provision for a relevant trust, the executor (in the case of a testate succession) or administrator (generally in the case of an intestate succession) of the estate, and no other person, is deemed to be the beneficial owner of the trust for the period in which the estate is being administered for AML purposes.[39] As mentioned, charitable trusts are express trusts and required to register. In the case of a relevant trust that is a charitable trust within the meaning of Section 2 of

38 The application of the rule in *Saunders v Vautier,* [1841] EWHC J82.
39 Section 106ZD(7) 2010 Act inserted by Section 6 2021 Act and Regulation 3(8) 2021 Trust Regulations.

the Charities Act 2009, the legislation provides that the trustees and the committee or other governing body of the charitable trust and any other individual who has control over the charitable trust is deemed to be the beneficial owner.[40]

There is special mention of typical sporting structures in Ireland. In the case of a relevant trust established for holding assets of an approved body of persons established for or existing for the sole purpose of promoting amateur games or amateur sports, the trustees and the committee or other governing body of the club or association and any other individual who has control over the relevant trust are deemed to be the beneficial owner.[41] Insofar as certain sporting bodies do not designate control to a committee but rely on instructions through the entire membership, the practicalities of this will need to be considered. Also the limitation of this to only amateur games leaves many other unincorporated associations for other causes (whether or not charitable) excluded from this special provision. For instance, concern has already been raised by student bodies that each student of a university who is a member of a student's union currently must be registered as a beneficial owner on entering university and deregistered once they finish university, which is very burdensome and yet low risk in money laundering terms.

There is facility in 5AMLD for consideration to be given to the burden of administration of registration in situations where there is low risk for money laundering. While this is also available in the 2021 Act,[42] to date there has been no listing of prescribed arrangements that are to be treated as low risk, despite the issues raised above.

3.4 Information on the internal beneficial ownership register and on the Central Register

The information to be gathered by trustees on beneficial owners is two-fold. All information gathered must be kept in the internal register of the trust (the beneficial ownership register) and some of this is then used to register the beneficial owners in the Central Register.

Under the 2021 Trust Regulations,[43] a trustee of a trust which is within scope must take all reasonable steps to obtain and hold adequate, accurate and current information in respect of each of the trust's beneficial owners, as follows:

- name;
- date of birth;

---

40 Section 106ZD(6) 2010 Act inserted by Section 6 2021 Act and Regulation 3(8) 2021 Trust Regulations.

41 Section 106ZD(5) 2010 Act inserted by Section 6 2021 Act and Regulation 3(8) 2021 Trust Regulations. This is a specific provision to deal with the position that Ireland manages local clubs for local sports typically through such bodies as the GAA.

42 Section 106ZC(3) 2010 Act inserted by Section 6 2021 Act.

43 Regulation 7(1) 2021 Trust Regulations.

- nationality;
- residential address;
- a statement of the nature and extent of the interest held, or the nature and extent of the control exercised by that beneficial owner;
- the PPSN[44] where such a number has issued;
- in the case of a beneficial owner to whom a PPSN has not issued and who is resident in a state other than Ireland, the unique number issued to that beneficial owner for the purpose of the administration of tax in that state, by the authority of that state, or the passport number or national identity card number of the beneficial owner and, for the purpose of verification of either such number, a copy of the document, issued by the authority of the state concerned, containing such number;
- in the case where a relevant trust holds assets beneficially for a legal entity that is already recorded in the RBO or the Central Register of Beneficial Ownership of Irish Collective Asset-management Vehicles, Credit Unions and Unit Trusts or a corresponding register in another member state (existing registered entities), the trustee does not need to know the individual details of the ultimate beneficial owners constituted through that entity provided the trustee holds the name and registered address of the legal entity and a statement of the nature and extent of the interest held, or the nature and extent of the control exercised by that legal entity and the filing number of the legal entity in the relevant register;[45] and
- in the case where a relevant trust holds assets beneficially for a legal entity that is not already recorded in the RBO or the Central Register of Beneficial Ownership of Irish Collective Asset-management Vehicles, Credit Unions and Unit Trusts or corresponding register in another EU member state,[46] the trustees must obtain and hold the individual details of all beneficial owners constituted through that entity.[47]

The trustee must enter this information in its internal 'beneficial ownership register', as well as the following information other than in the case of existing registered entities:

- the date on which each individual was entered into the register as a beneficial owner of the trust; and
- the date on which each individual who has ceased to be a beneficial owner of the trust ceased to be a beneficial owner.

---

44 A Personal Public Service Number (PPSN) is a unique reference number that is needed for all dealings by an individual with Irish public service agencies, including Revenue.

45 Regulation 7(2) 2021 Trust Regulations.

46 For instance a legal entity that is registered in a similar register but in a non-EU member state or not registered in any beneficial register at all.

47 Regulation 7(3) 2021 Trust Regulations.

A trustee must also maintain this register and update it, including where a person ceases to be a beneficial owner or where there is any other change which would mean that the beneficial owner's particulars are incorrect or incomplete.[48]

The information on this internal beneficial ownership register from time to time forms the basis for the trustee identifying the beneficial owners of the trust to designated persons where the trustee enters into an occasional transaction with a designated person or forms a business relationship with such a designated person.[49]

Where previously it was confirmed that a trustee must keep records of the actions it has taken to identify the trust's beneficial owners and retain those records for a period of no less than five years after the date on which the final distribution is made under the trust,[50] the requirement to retain for five years after cessation of the trust is not reproduced in the 2021 Regulations. In contrast the registrar of the Central Register must retain its records for a 10-year period.

A trustee must notify each individual whom the trustee has reasonable cause to believe to be a beneficial owner in a formal manner unless the individual has provided the information and particulars already or these were provided with the consent of the individual.[51] The trustee can also issue notices to others seeking information if the trustee has reasonable cause to believe that the other person has the necessary details of the beneficial owner requiring this information to be furnished within one month of the date of the notice.[52] Furthermore, if the trustee knows or has reasonable cause to believe that a change to the particulars of the individual has occurred, if the individual, or someone with the individual's knowledge, has not informed the trustee already of that change, then the trustee can issue a notice requesting the changed particulars to be furnished within one month.[53]

There is an obligation on a beneficial owner of a trust to inform the trustee of the necessary particulars if he/she has received a notice that he/she is a beneficial owner within a month of that notice. Furthermore, if the trustee has not sought information from him/her, nor entered his/her details in the register and the individual is aware he/she is a beneficial owner of the trust or ought reasonably to be so aware, then the individual is under a duty to notify the trustee within one month of the time the individual is (or ought to be) aware and has not received a notice from the trustees. There is also an obligation on the beneficial owner of a relevant trust to proactively notify the trustee if he/she

48 Regulation 12 2021 Trust Regulations.

49 Regulation 7(7) 2021 Trust Regulations and see Annex for definition of designated persons (eg, bank, solicitor, property service provider).

50 Regulation 5 2019 Trust Regulations.

51 Regulations 8 and 9 2021 Trust Regulations.

52 However, such a person is not required to disclose any information in respect of which a claim to legal professional privilege could be maintained in legal proceedings. Regulation 11(4) 2021 Trust Regulations.

53 Regulation 13 2021 Trust Regulations.

ceases to be a beneficial owner, or if the information held about him/her on the beneficial ownership trust register becomes inaccurate.[54]

The 2021 Trust Regulations are different to those for corporates in some respects such as:

- there are no percentage thresholds that an individual must satisfy before being classified as a beneficial owner, once the individual is one of the list above, he/she is a beneficial owner; and
- the steps that a corporate must take to try to identify its beneficial owners are more prescriptive than the 'all reasonable steps' that the trustee must take.

3.5 The Central Register of Beneficial Ownership of Trusts

While the registrar of the Central Register has been appointed by the Revenue Commissioners and the obligation already arises on trustees to register the necessary information on the Central Register within six months of 23 April 2021 or six months from the trust's coming into existence, it is not expected that the facility to register the information will be available to trustees until after the Guidance Notes have been published. It is anticipated that the Guidance Notes will be published on 30 June 2021, with the registration portal to open for applications by 26 July 2021.

Registration is required to be made electronically[55] and it is understood that this will be a separate registration portal known as CRBOT hosted through the Revenue's existing online service ROS, albeit a stand-alone portal unconnected to Revenue registrations. There will also be facility for those who are not able to access ROS to register through the MyAccount facility and also for registration from abroad. There will also be a facility to contact the registrar through the My Enquiries facility within ROS and a dedicated customer service email for non-ROS users.

Under the 2021 Trust Regulations,[56] a trustee of a trust which is within scope must deliver the following information to the registrar in respect of each of the trust's beneficial owners, as follows:

- name;
- date of birth;
- nationality;
- residential address;
- a statement of the nature and extent of the interest held, or the nature and extent of the control exercised by that beneficial owner;
- in the case of a relevant trust not set up or operating entirely for the

54 Regulation 15 2021 Trust Regulations.
55 Regulation 22(6) and (7) 2021 Trust Regulations.
56 Regulation 23 2021 Trust Regulations.

benefit of individuals entitled to a vested interest in possession, remainder or reversion (whether or not the interest is defeasible) in the capital of the relevant trust property, the class of individuals in whose interest the trust is set up or operates;[57]

- in the case where a relevant trust holds assets beneficially for a legal entity that is already recorded in the RBO or the Central Register of Beneficial Ownership of Irish Collective Asset-management Vehicles, Credit Unions and Unit Trusts or corresponding register in another member state (existing registered entities), the name and registered address of the legal entity and a statement of the nature and extent of the interest held, or the nature and extent of the control exercised by that legal entity and the filing number of the legal entity in the relevant register;[58]
- in the case where a relevant trust holds assets beneficially for a legal entity that is not already recorded in the RBO or the Central Register of Beneficial Ownership of Irish Collective Asset-management Vehicles, Credit Unions and Unit Trusts or corresponding register in another EU member state,[59] the individual details of all beneficial owners constituted through that entity other than the respective tax identification number for such individuals;[60] and
- separately the PPSN or other tax identification number, and verifying documentation of such other number, of each individual must be filed for the purposes of verification. There are separate secure storage obligations on the registrar in relation to that tax number where the tax number must not be disclosed by the Register.

The distinction between the information on the internal beneficial ownership register and that filed in the Central Register relates to the PPSN or other tax identification number – this must be kept on the internal beneficial ownership register and must be filed in a separate manner in the Central Register.

There are requirements for presenters and officers or employees of the relevant trust who discharge filing obligations for the trust with the Central Register. Information on such persons should also be provided on registration and their capacity in filing.[61]

The information on the Central Register is retained until 10 years have

57 In effect a discretionary trust.
58 Regulation 23(1)(d) 2021 Trust Regulations.
59 For instance a legal entity that is registered in a non-EU member state or not registered in any beneficial register at all.
60 Regulation 23(1)(d) 2021 Trust Regulations.
61 Regulations 23(3) and 24 2021 Trust Regulations.

elapsed from the date on which the final distribution is made under the relevant trust or the trustees cease to be resident in Ireland or the relevant trust ceases to be administered in Ireland.[62]

There are duties on the trustees to keep the Central Register up to date, corresponding with their duties to keep the information on the internal beneficial ownership register accurate and current.[63]

3.6 Access to the beneficial ownership register

A trustee must provide the Garda Síochána, the Revenue Commissioners, the Criminal Assets Bureau or any Irish competent authority with timely access to the internal beneficial ownership register on request.

These bodies in turn may disclose the information in a beneficial ownership register to any corresponding competent authority of another member state. The 2020 Act introduced a provision that the cooperation by the Irish competent authority with the member state's competent authorities may include sharing of such information as the competent authority is not prevented from disclosing by the law of Ireland, but then provides that the provision of assistance to others is not to be refused on the following bases:[64]

- the request for the sharing of information or the provision of assistance is also considered to involve tax matters;
- the law of Ireland requires the competent authority to maintain secrecy or confidentiality, except in those cases where the relevant information that is sought is protected by legal privilege; or
- there is an inquiry, investigation or proceeding underway in Ireland unless the sharing of such information or the provision of assistance would impede the inquiry, investigation or proceeding; or the nature or status of the requesting competent authority is different from that of the competent authority of whom the request is made.

This proviso is not, however, repeated in the 2021 Regulations. It remains to be seen whether a disclosure of beneficial ownership details of trusts to a member state's competent authority under this provision would be challenged on the basis that the disclosure may breach an individual's right of privacy if the Irish competent authority knows or ought to have known that the other competent authority may under its own legislation release such information publicly or to those who are entitled under a broader interpretation of who has 'legitimate interest' under local legislation.[65] The EU General Data Protection

62 Regulation 23(4), (6) and (7) 2021 Trust Regulations.
63 Regulation 25 2021 Trust Regulations.
64 Section 63B(2A) 2010 Act inserted by Section 19 2021 Act.
65 Once Irish legislation brings in provision to allow those with legitimate interest to access a trust register.

Regulation provisions would also need to be considered in this context.[66] The Irish competent authority will therefore need to be conscious of this fundamental right of an individual and consider if it is prevented from disclosing the information on the basis of Irish law, separate to the question as to whether the reference to permission to disclose knowingly in breach of a duty to maintain secrecy or confidentiality is constitutionally sound.[67] The question of proportionality in balancing the rights of privacy and the opportunity for non-Irish competent authorities to release information about Irish trusts to the public will need to be considered.

Where the trustee of a trust enters into an occasional transaction[68] with a person who is a designated person[69] for anti-money laundering purposes, or forms a business relationship with such person,[70] the trustee must:

- inform the designated person in writing that it is acting as trustee;
- on request from the designated person, provide the designated person with information identifying all the beneficial owners of the trust in a timely manner; and
- notify the designated person of any change to the beneficial ownership that occurs which is relevant to the occasional transaction or occurs during the course of the business relationship formed within 14 days.[71]

In terms of timing around disclosure, while the 2020 Act requires designated persons to ascertain that information concerning the beneficial ownership of the customer is entered in the beneficial ownership register of the trust before entering into a business relationship with a trust, by way of derogation a financial institution is allowed to open an account ahead of obtaining the information but cannot allow any transactions on that account.

The trustee is obliged under the Regulations to inform the designated person who is on the register for the purposes of identification of the beneficial owners combined with the obligation on the trustees to provide the information in the first place. The 2020 Act requires the designated person to take steps to obtain

66 Regulation 27(7) applies the Data Protection Act 2018 to the access the registrar affords to a designated person in respect of the information in the Register that relates to a relevant trust.

67 The Irish Constitution does not specifically state a right to privacy but the courts recognise that the personal fundamental rights in the Constitution (Article 40) imply the right to privacy.

68 An occasional transaction arises where the designated person does not have a business relationship with the customer and there is a single transaction or a series of linked transactions where the money or monetary value paid from or to the designated person by or from the customer is not less than €2,000 in the case of private members' gambling clubs, €1,000 in the case of wire transfers and €10,000 in the case of goods, and otherwise €15,000.

69 Such as a bank or financial institution, auditor, accountant, tax adviser, an independent legal professional (in respect of certain services), a trust or company service provider, a property service provider or certain other persons acting in Ireland in the course of business carried on by them in Ireland.

70 A 'business relationship' is a business, professional or commercial relationship between a designated person and a customer of the person that the designated person expects to be ongoing.

71 Regulation 7(7) 2021 Trust Regulations.

the relevant information from the trustees and also if the designated person sees that this information is not consistent with that listed in the Central Register, the designated person is obliged to inform the registrar of the identified discrepancy.[72]

As the beneficial ownership register is not a public register, there are no provisions for protecting minors or other vulnerable persons provided for. However, to the extent that designated persons are entitled to information from the internal register, it is assumed that the information provided to such a designated person will be kept confidential. It would, however, be preferable to have specific protections built into the legislation to copper-fasten the protection in the case of disclosures from trustees direct to designated persons.

3.7 Access to the Central Register

Unlike some central registers in some EU member states, the Central Register is not open to inspection to the public other than on a restricted basis.

A certificate in writing signed by the registrar is admissible in legal proceedings as evidence without further proof of:

- the contents of the Central Register;
- the date the information was registered; and
- the most recent date (if any) on which a requirement under the 2021 Trust Regulations was complied with.[73]

Similar to the internal beneficial ownership register, the Garda Síochána, the Revenue Commissioners, the Criminal Assets Bureau or any Irish competent authority can access the Central Register on a relatively unrestricted basis on request.[74] In addition, this unrestricted access is available to the Financial Intelligence Unit Ireland. Only members of a specified rank or higher in these bodies are allowed access to the Register and, in the case of competent authorities, only as authorised by a specified highest level authority and on a case-by-case basis where it is engaged in the prevention, detection or investigation of possible money laundering or terrorist financing.

These bodies in turn may disclose the information in a beneficial ownership register to any corresponding competent authority of another member state.[75] Similar to the right to disclose information obtained from the internal beneficial ownership register, the 2020 Act provision concerning the cooperation by the Irish competent authority with the member state's competent authorities has not been addressed in the 2021 Regulations concerning access to the Central Register. As commented on above, it remains

72 Regulation 22(3) 2021 Trust Regulations.
73 Regulation 32 2021 Trust Regulations.
74 Regulation 26 2021 Trust Regulations.
75 Regulation 26(8) 2021 Trust Regulations.

to be seen whether a disclosure of beneficial ownership details of trusts to a member state's competent authority under this provision would be challenged, particularly to the extent the corresponding register may be fully public in that jurisdiction or more easily accessible based on a wider interpretation of legitimate interests. If, however, the disclosure to the competent authority of another member state does not involve disclosure directly or indirectly to the equivalent central register of that state, presumably the openness of that register will not affect the confidentiality of the disclosure. However, insofar as the Central Register is to be connected with the central registers of other member states as contemplated by 4AMLD, how the registrar of the Central Register will ensure there is no leakage of private information via other member states' registers through such interconnection will need to be carefully considered.

The State bodies and competent authorities accessing the Central Register are obliged to report discrepancies between the information on the Central Register and information provided to them by the trustees and the registrar is then required where appropriate to mark an entry in the Register of the notice and serve a notice on the relevant trust and in turn after considering opinions furnished make necessary amendments to the Central Register.[76]

Restricted access to some information on the Central Register is also available in specified circumstances as follows:[77]

- designated persons – where the trustee of a trust enters into an occasional transaction[78] with a person who is a designated person[79] for anti-money laundering purposes, or forms a business relationship with such person,[80] the designated person has a right to access in respect of each beneficial owner the name, month and year of birth, the country of residence and nationality and a statement of the nature and extent of the interest held, or the nature and extent of the control exercised by that beneficial owner.[81]

  There is already an obligation on the trustee to furnish this information to the designated person and that designated person is now obliged to check that the information on the Central Register corresponds correctly to what is provided to it by the trustee before establishing a business relationship or entering into an occasional

76 Regulation 28 2021 Trust Regulations.

77 It is not expected that this access will be available until after 24 October 2021, the deadline for existing trusts to register.

78 Regulation 7(7) 2021 Trust Regulations.

79 Such as a bank or financial institution, auditor, accountant, tax adviser, an independent legal professional (in respect of certain services), a trust or company service provider, a property service provider or certain other persons acting in Ireland in the course of business carried on by them in Ireland. See Annex for greater detail.

80 A 'business relationship' is a business, professional or commercial relationship between a designated person and a customer of the person that the designated person expects to be ongoing.

81 Regulation 27(1) 2021 Trust Regulations.

transaction. The designated person is obliged to notify the Register of any discrepancy.

- legitimate interest – a person who demonstrates to the satisfaction of the registrar of the Central Register that he/she has a legitimate interest to inspect the Central Register by making a submission and (if required by the registrar) the supplying of information or documents including such relating to that individual's previous activities, if any, in the prevention, detection or investigation of money laundering or terrorist financing offences:
  - that the person is engaged in the prevention, detection or investigation of money laundering or terrorist financing offences;
  - that the person is seeking to inspect the information that a designated person is entitled to inspect for the purposes of an activity in which he/she is engaged relating to the prevention, detection or investigation of money laundering or terrorist financing offences (but such activity need not necessarily relate to cases of pending administrative or legal proceedings in respect of the relevant trust concerned); and
  - the relevant trust concerned:
    - is connected with persons convicted (in Ireland or elsewhere) of an office consisting of money laundering or terrorist financing offences, or
    - holds assets in a high risk third country.
- any person who shows to the satisfaction of the registrar of the Central Register that a relevant trust holds or owns a controlling interest in a non-EU corporate or legal entity, through direct or indirect ownership (including through bearer shares) or through control by other means, can apply in writing to inspect the information that a designated person is entitled to inspect.

In all of these cases, before any information relating to a minor[82] who is a beneficial owner of a relevant trust is released, the designated person or other person must provide in writing to the registrar a summary of the grounds on which he/she considers it is in the public interest that that information is disclosed to him/her and the registrar must form the opinion that there are substantial grounds that it is in the public interest to disclose the information.[83]

Unfortunately no such protection is specifically afforded to other vulnerable beneficiaries such as wards of court or those who are beneficiaries of trusts that already have been recognised by the Revenue Commissioners as in need of

82 Individual under the age of 18.
83 Regulation 27(8) 2021 Trust Regulations.

special protection because of the disability or vulnerability of the beneficiary. However, it is understood that the registrar is reviewing this to put in place a mechanism to protect such vulnerable persons' information from being disclosed, though the mechanism of doing so has yet to be finalised.

The registrar is obliged to keep a record for five years of each instance of access to or inspection of information sought and each decision made in relation to each request sought.[84]

There is no obligation on the registrar to notify the trustees of any access request made or sanctioned.

3.8 Sanctions and remedies

While the 2021 Trust Regulations are primarily aimed at trustees of relevant trusts, the legislation also creates obligations on designated persons, beneficial owners, presenters acting for trustees, officers and employees of trusts and public authorities, and there are corresponding consequences for failure to adhere to these obligations, prosecuted by the director of public prosecutions or the registrar of the Central Register.

A beneficial owner who fails to comply with his/her obligations commits an offence punishable on summary conviction to a Class A[85] fine or imprisonment for a term not exceeding 12 months or both.

If a person's name is entered into or omitted from the beneficial ownership register without sufficient cause or default is made or unnecessary delay takes place in entering in the register the fact that a person has ceased to be a beneficial owner of the trust, the person aggrieved or any other interested party can apply to the High Court for rectification of the register.[86] The High Court has the power to refuse the application or order the rectification of the register and order payment by the trustee of compensation for any loss sustained by the aggrieved person. As the beneficial ownership register links into the Central Register based on the obligations of trustees to keep the Central Register up to date, the court order will have the effect that the Central Register will correspondingly be rectified.

A trustee or individual as officer or employee of trustees who fails to comply with his/her various obligations to keep and maintain the beneficial ownership register and fails to comply with obligations in relation to the Central Register, commits an offence punishable:

- on summary conviction to a Class A fine and, in relation to certain obligations, to imprisonment for a term not exceeding 12 months or both; or

84 Regulation 27(9) 2021 Trust Regulations.
85 www.irishstatutebook.ie/eli/2010/act/8/enacted/en/print.html not exceeding €5,000.
86 Regulation 17(5) 2021 Trust Regulations. There are to date no known cases taken under the equivalent in the 2019 Trust Regulations.

- on indictment to a fine not exceeding €500,000 and, in relation to certain obligations, to imprisonment for a term not exceeding 12 months or both.

A presenter who fails to comply with its obligations commits an offence punishable on summary conviction to a Class A fine.

A designated person who fails to comply with its obligations commits an offence punishable on summary conviction to a Class A fine.

4. Practical considerations – identifying beneficial ownership in layers of companies and trusts for registers

The legislation deals with identifying companies where such companies own trusts. However, where a trust owns shares in a company but does not control that company nor do beneficiaries own more than 25% of the company, no specific provisions apply, leading to the following positions.

4.1 An estate owning shares in a company

The beneficial owners of an estate means the executors under Section 29 of the 2010 Act.

Where company shares (less than 25% of the company) are registered in the names of the executors of the estate of a deceased person and there has as yet been no allocation of the shares between the beneficiaries on the basis that the estate is still being administered or the residue is not yet ascertained, then if no one in the estate has the power to influence in a dominant manner the running of the company and if no one in the estate has the power to appoint senior management, who are the beneficial owners whose names should be entered into the RBO?

While the legislation specifically states that the beneficial owner of an estate of a deceased person in the course of administration means the executor(s) of the estate concerned, this relates to the beneficial owner of the estate and not the beneficial owner of the company itself. Therefore, where an estate owns the company, it is my opinion that the definition in Article 3(6), 4AMLD applies[87] to establish the beneficial owner of the company for the purposes of the registration in the RBO.

In contrast, in the case of the identification of the beneficial owner of the relevant trust for the internal beneficial ownership register and the Central Register, while a beneficial owner means any individual who ultimately owns or

---

87 Ultimately providing as follows: "If, after having exhausted all possible means and provided there are no grounds for suspicion, no natural person is identified as a beneficial owner, or if there is any doubt that the person(s) identified is/are the beneficial owner(s), Regulation 5(4) of the 2019 Company Regulations provides that the natural person(s) who holds the position of senior managing official(s) of the company/society shall be recorded on the RBO as the beneficial owner. Relevant entities are required to keep records of the actions taken to identify their beneficial owners in accordance with Regulation 5(5) of the 2019 Company Regulations."

controls the customer and/or the individuals on whose behalf a transaction or activity is being conducted including the beneficiaries or class of beneficiaries in whose main interest the trust is established, the beneficial owner of the estate cannot be identified because the estate is not yet administered and so no beneficiary has the right to the share in the company (their right to inherit is a chose in action). As provided for in the legislation, the executors would then be the beneficial owner for the purposes of the identification of beneficial owners to designated persons but, as mentioned above, ought not require to be registered in the Central Register on the basis that an estate in the course of administration is not a relevant trust.

4.2 An interest in possession trust owning shares in a company

If a will of the deceased provides for the estate to pass to an individual 'A' for a period such as for life, then, as holder of the interest in possession, under trust law 'A' would not own the shares or control the voting rights of those shares, as such control rests with the trustees. A life interest is a vested interest under trust law. It is the individual 'A' who is the owner of the vested interest in the company.

While the definition of beneficial owner for a company has the meaning given to it by 4AMLD itself, which provides that an individual who is the beneficial owner of a body corporate that is entitled to a vested interest or has control over the trust "is taken to be entitled to the vested interest or to have control over the trust", this provision relates to the establishment of the owner of the company where the company has a vested interest in a trust. Even though it should seem to also apply vice versa (ie, that the trust has a vested interest in the company), the definition does not in fact apply in such a case. Therefore, this element of the legislation does not apply in establishing the beneficial owner of the company where the interest is that of shares in the company itself and not what the company owns.

The trustees of a trust are not 'natural persons' at law. Under 4AMLD, the definition of beneficial owner for a company has the meaning given to it by Article 3(6), 4AMLD itself, namely:

(i) the natural person(s) who ultimately owns or controls a legal entity through direct or indirect ownership of a sufficient percentage of the shares or voting rights or ownership interest in that entity, including through bearer shareholdings, or through control via other means, other than a company listed on a regulated market that is subject to disclosure requirements consistent with Union law or subject to equivalent international standards which ensure adequate transparency of ownership information.

A shareholding of 25% plus one share or an ownership interest of more than 25% in the customer held by a natural person shall be an indication of direct ownership. A shareholding of 25% plus one share or an ownership interest of more than 25% in the customer held by a corporate entity, which is under the control of a natural person(s), or by multiple corporate entities, which are under the control of the same natural person(s), shall be an indication of indirect ownership. This applies without prejudice to the right of Member States to decide that a lower percentage may be an indication of ownership or control. Control through other means may be determined, inter alia, in accordance with the criteria in Article 22(1) to (5) of Directive 2013/34/EU of the European Parliament and of the Council;

(ii) if, after having exhausted all possible means and provided there are no grounds for suspicion, no person under point (i) is identified, or if there is any doubt that the person(s) identified are the beneficial owner(s), the natural person(s) who hold the position of senior managing official(s), the obliged entities shall keep records of the actions taken in order to identify the beneficial ownership under point (i) and this point.

Furthermore, the regulations on this implementation of the legislation state that the senior managing officials (eg, director(s) and/or CEO) shall be deemed to be the beneficial owners. Relevant entities shall keep records of the actions taken to identify their beneficial owners.

Later, 4AMLD states that:

Control through other means may, inter alia, include the criteria of control used for the purpose of preparing consolidated financial statements, such as

- *through a shareholders' agreement,*
- *the exercise of dominant influence or*
- *the power to appoint senior management.*

Therefore, the legislation for the corporate register provides that where there is no natural person able to be identified as beneficial owner, the natural person holding the position of senior managing official (and the CRO indicates this is the director(s) and/or CEO of the company) is/are the name(s) to be registered as beneficial owner. Therefore in the case of 'A', it is my opinion that it is not 'A' who is entered in the RBO, but rather the CEO/directors who should be registered.

In contrast, once again in the case of the identification of the beneficial owner of the relevant trust for the internal beneficial ownership register and the Central Register, a beneficial owner means an individual entitled to a vested interest. As 'A' holds a vested interest, 'A' is the beneficial owner for the internal beneficial ownership register and the Central Register.

4.3 A discretionary trust owning shares in a company

If a will of the deceased[88] provides for the estate to pass to trustees to hold on discretionary trust for the benefit of a class of beneficiaries, those individuals in

88 Or indeed similarly for an *inter vivos* settlement, where the settlor would also be a beneficial owner while alive.

the class would not own the shares or control the voting rights of those shares to the extent they rest with the trustees.

Once again the definition of beneficial owner for a company relates to the owner of the company where the company may hold an interest through a trust, so this element of the legislation does not apply in establishing the beneficial owner of the company itself.

The trustees of a trust are not 'natural persons' at law. Under 4AMLD, the definition of beneficial owner for a company has the meaning given to it by 4AMLD itself as outlined above. Therefore, the legislation for the corporate register provides that where there is no natural person able to be identified as beneficial owner, the natural person holding the position of senior managing official (and the CRO indicates this is the director(s) and/or CEO of the company) is/are the name(s) to be registered as beneficial owner. Therefore, in the case of trustees of a discretionary trust holding shares in a company, it is my opinion that it is not the class of beneficiaries of the trust, nor the trustees, who are entered in the RBO, but rather the CEO/directors who should be registered.

Again, in contrast, in the case of the identification of the beneficial owner of the relevant trust for the internal beneficial ownership register and the Central Register, a beneficial owner means the class of beneficiaries which class should be identified as the beneficial owner for the internal beneficial ownership register and the Central Register.

5. Conclusion to examples

To the extent that there is a need to identify the beneficial owner of any company in the group where an estate or a trust ultimately holds more than 25% of the company directly or indirectly, the directors and/or CEO of each of the companies should be registered as the beneficial owner of each such company until the allocation of the shares absolutely to the beneficiaries of the estate or for the duration of the trust on the basis that there is no natural person identifiable as a beneficial owner.

The above illustrates the gap between the corporate and the trust registers where shares in a corporate held by a trust do not disclose who is behind that trust. The rationale behind this would include protection of the privacy rights that have also resulted in the Central Register not being publicly available. If the detail of individual beneficial owners identified in the Central Register were to be kept private but that detail had to be included on the open corporate register, then there would be a back door to obtaining private trust information whenever a trust holds a corporate interest.

Annex

Definition of a 'designated person' for Irish purposes

Ref: Section 25 Criminal Justice (Money Laundering and Terrorist Financing) Act 2010 as amended

(1) A designated person is any person, acting in the State in the course of business carried on by the person in the State, who or that is-

- *(a) a credit institution, with exceptions and clarifications,*
- *(b) a financial institution, with exceptions and clarifications,*[89]
- *(c) an auditor, external accountant or tax adviser or any other person whose principal business or professional activity is to provide, directly or by means of other persons to which that other person is related, material aid, assistance or advice on tax matters,*
- *(d) subject to subsection (1A), a relevant independent legal professional, only as respects the carrying out of the following specified services specified that is*
  - *a. the provision of assistance in the planning or execution of transactions for clients concerning any of the following*
    - *(i) buying or selling land or business entities;*
    - *(ii) managing the money, securities or other assets of clients;*
    - *(iii) opening or managing bank, savings or securities accounts;*
    - *(iv) organising contributions necessary for the creation, operation or management of companies;*
    - *(v) creating, operating or managing trusts, companies or similar structures or arrangements;*
  - *b. acting for or on behalf of clients in financial transactions or transactions relating to land*
- *(e) a trust or company service provider,*
- *(f) a property service provider including a property service provider acting as an intermediary in the letting of immovable property, but only in respect of transactions for which the monthly rent amounts to a total of at least €10,000,*
- *(g) a casino,*
- *(h) a person who effectively directs a private members' club at which gambling activities are carried on, but only in respect of those gambling activities,*
- *(i) any person trading in goods, but only in respect of transactions involving payments, to the person or by the person in cash, of a total of at least €10,000 (whether in one transaction or in a series of transactions that are or appear to be linked to each other),*
- *(ia) a virtual asset provider;*

89 Amended by Section 5 2021 Act.

(ib) a person trading or acting as an intermediary in the trade of works of art (including when carried out by an art gallery or an auction house) but only in respect of transactions of a total value of at least €10,000 (whether in one transaction or in a series of transactions that are or appear to be linked to each other);

(ic) a person storing, trading or acting as an intermediary in the trade of works of art when this is carried out in a free port but only in respect of transactions of a total value of at least €10,000 (whether in one transaction or as a series of transactions that are or appear to be linked to each other), or

(j) any other person of a prescribed class set by the Minister under certain criteria.

(1A) A relevant independent legal professional shall be a designated person only as respects the carrying out of the services specified in the definition of 'relevant independent legal professional' in section 24(1) 2010 Act

(2) The person is treated as a designated person only in respect of those activities or services that render the person a designated person.

Other exclusions specified in section 25 2010 Act.

Readers should note that the information in this chapter is correct as at 16 June 2021.

Italy

Luigi Belluzzo
Belluzzo International Partners

1. Introduction to anti-money laundering legislation in Italy

In order to provide an overview of the entire discipline, anti-money laundering legislation in Italy is regulated by Legislative Decree 231/2007, which represents the point of arrival of a long international development in the fight against the use of the financial system for the purposes of money laundering and terrorist financing.

As early as the end of the 1980s, the international community noted that the investment of proceeds from crime, encouraged by the development of the process of integration of the financial markets and the liberalisation of capital movements, had developed to such an extent that it was no longer located in certain countries only, but rather was a widespread phenomenon around the world.

It is precisely with the aim of fighting these criminal activities that over time a series of projects have been undertaken aimed at introducing safeguards both in judicial terms and in terms of protecting the financial markets.

From a criminal point of view, the crime of money laundering was extended by the national legislature, first by Law No 55 of 19 March 1990, to proceeds from crimes relating to the production or trafficking of narcotic or psychotic substances, and second by Law No 328 of 9 August 1993, to the proceeds of any non-negligent crime.

From the point of view of protecting the financial markets, with regard to the main legislation adopted by the European Union and Italy, Directive 91/308/EEC of 10 June 1991 (also known as the First Anti-Money Laundering Directive – 1AMLD) is the cornerstone of the Community legal system to oversee the criminal phenomenon. Over time the directive has been the subject of several amendments and accompanied by numerous other regulatory measures, reaching the Fifth Anti-Money Laundering Directive (EU Directive 2018/843) (5AMLD), which entered into force in Italy under Legislative Decree 125/2019 published in *The Official Journal* n 252 of 26 October 2019, and provides for a series of additions and amendments to the anti-money laundering legislation as regulated by Legislative Decree 231/2007. Legislative Decree 231/2007 had also been widely modified by Legislative Decrees 90/2017

2. and 92/2017, through which the previous Fourth Anti-Money Laundering Directive (EU Directive 2015/849) (4AMLD) took place.

The intention of the Community legislator, and the national legislator, is clearly to strengthen the apparatus of instruments for preventing money laundering and, in particular, the financing of terrorism through a system of control and exchange of information between jurisdictions that is becoming more and more widespread, thanks to the involvement of an ever-growing audience of obliged entities and an increasingly effective mechanism of national and international cooperation. The fight against money laundering and terrorist financing is being conducted through information transparency, which the Community legislator seems to put before the protection of the individual and his/her personal data.

The anti-money laundering and counter-terrorism system established by the principles of the Community Directive is characterised by the risk-based approach, according to which the person obliged to the legislation must measure the extent and intensity of the concrete anti-money laundering measures to be applied to each specific case. The regulatory framework is based on a series of obligations for a category of subjects, as identified by the legislation itself, ranging from adequate customer verification to the reporting of suspicious transactions.

As better detailed in the following paragraphs, Legislative Decree 231/2007, as amended by Legislative Decree 90/2017 (and confirmed by Legislative Decree 125/2019 implementing 5AMLD), sets forth the provisions for the establishment and operation of two beneficial ownership registers:

- the Register of Beneficial Owners of business entities; and
- the Register of Beneficial Owners of Trusts and related legal institutions.

The introduction of these registers is intended to profoundly broaden the level of knowledge of the control structures and their beneficial owners.

The Italian legislator, following the Community Directives, has proposed a draft decree in order to set up these registers. The experts were asked to propose suggestions and observations by 28 February 2020. After that deadline, the legislator should have issued, by 3 July 2020, the definitive legislation. However, taking into consideration that no definitive legislation was released within the above-mentioned deadline, the draft decree has to be considered as expired and not valid. Thus, considering what has been stated by the specialised press in the early months of 2021, the publication of a new decree that is going to set up the beneficial ownership register seems to be on the horizon.

2. Beneficial owner status

The 'beneficial owner' is defined as the individual/s to whom, ultimately, the direct or indirect ownership or control of the institution is attributable.

Article 20 of Legislative Decree 231/2007 prepares a 'guided' route for the purpose of identifying the actual owner.

In accordance with Article 20, the beneficial owner of legal entities is identified through an application path of different criteria. In the first step, the beneficial owner is made to coincide with the individual/s to whom the direct or indirect ownership of the entity is attributable: the rule specifies that the participation of more than 25% of the share capital constitutes an indication of relevant ownership; and this ownership may be either direct, if held directly by an individual, or indirect, if owned through subsidiaries, a fiduciary company, a nominee or an interposed person. If the ownership structure does not allow a clear identification of the beneficial owner, the second criterion will be applied, according to which the beneficial owner is identified by virtue of the attribution of the majority of the votes that can be exercised at the ordinary shareholders' meeting or, alternatively, sufficient votes to exercise a dominant influence, or the existence of particular contractual arrangements that allow him/her to exercise a dominant influence. If the application of the criteria of direct and indirect ownership or control of the institution does not allow the unambiguous identification of one or more beneficial owners, ultimately the operator will have to resort to the residual criterion. Therefore, in accordance with the current Article 20 of the decree, the beneficial owner in such residual cases coincides with the individual/s holding powers of legal representation, administration or management of the institution.

Once beneficial owners have been identified, the obliged parties are required to keep the documentation that has allowed them to verify their identity.

In addition, Article 20, paragraph 4 provides that in the case of associations, foundations and other legal arrangements (eg, trusts), beneficial owners are cumulatively identified in:

- founders, where alive;
- beneficiaries, when identified or easily identifiable; and
- holders of management and administration functions.

In paragraph 5 of Article 22 it is provided that the trustees of the 'express trusts' must obtain and hold adequate, accurate and up-to-date information on the identity of the beneficial owners of the trust, as well as persons exercising equivalent rights, powers and faculties in similar legal entities, and by such means the identities relating to:

- the settlor;
- the trustee;
- the protector;
- the beneficiaries (if any) or of the class of beneficiaries;
- any other individuals exercising control over the trust; and
- any other individuals who ultimately exercise control over the assets

conferred on the trust through direct or indirect ownership or by other means.

Trustees and persons exercising equivalent rights, powers and prerogatives in similar legal institutions are required to retain the information for at least five years after leaving office, making it accessible to the authorities identified in Article 21, paragraph 2 letters (a) and (b) of Legislative Decree 90/2017.

The above-mentioned set of rules have to be applied to trusts and any other institutions which, by their structure and function, have equivalent legal effects to those of the trusts, including with regard to the control of the assets by a person other than the original owner, in the interest of one or more beneficiaries, or for the pursuit of a specific purpose.

For practical purposes, 5AMLD (like 4AMLD) makes no reference to the minimum threshold for control of the trust's assets (remember the 25% threshold regulated by the previous 3AMLD), in favour instead of an indistinct identification of the subjects involved, in various ways, in the events of the trust.

In addition, while in 3AMLD the concept of beneficial owner of trusts provided for clear alternatives between them, on the contrary 4AMLD and 5AMLD open up to a concept of effective 'cumulative' ownership where all the persons identified pursuant to Article 20 paragraph 4 may be understood to be beneficial owners of the trust.

3. The Register of Beneficial Owners of companies

The beneficial ownership of companies and trusts is an issue that falls within the scope of the anti-money laundering legislation, which in Italy is represented by Legislative Decree 231/2007 as subsequently amended. On 23 December 2019 the Italian Ministry of the Economy and Finance published a draft of the ministerial decree setting forth the provisions for the establishment and operation of the Register of Beneficial Owners of business entities, non-commercial entities and trusts. The establishment of the Register of Beneficial Owners is required by Article 21 of Legislative Decree 231/2007, which contains the domestic legislation implementing the EU Anti-Money Laundering Directives into Italian law. The draft decree legislation was never published in the Italian *Official Gazette* by the legal deadline of 3 July 2020.

The draft decree consists of 11 articles concerning the scope and purpose of the legislation, terms and conditions of communication, data and information subject to communication, and how to access data.

In detail, within the Italian legislation a special section of the '*Registro delle Imprese*' (Italian Companies House) will be created. The Italian Companies House is the database that collects information on all Italian companies, foreign companies with an Italian branch and all other entities performing economic activities in Italy, excluding professionals. Therefore, the Register of Beneficial Owners is going to include all the beneficial owners of the above-mentioned entities that are obliged to be registered in the Companies Register. The same register will also include the beneficial owners of private legal persons and trusts as more fully described and specified in the following section. The entities incorporated before the entry into force of the decree, following what is stated in the draft decree, should have communicated all the information about the beneficial owner by 15 March 2021. Instead, for entities established after the decree, the communication deadline is 30 days after their incorporation.

The duty of filing with the Register of Beneficial Owners falls upon:

- the directors or managers of commercial enterprises with legal personality;
- founders, administrators and managers of private juridical persons; and
- trustees or fiduciaries of trusts and similar arrangements.

Failure to faithfully and fully report information about beneficial owners carries significant penalties under the anti-money laundering law (Legislative Decree 231/2007).

The individual liable for the filing, under Article 4 of the draft decree, is required to collect, verify and keep the following information:

- the relevant beneficial owners' information and the relevant information about the entity to which it relates, including the incorporation deed and the company statute date of constitution, registered address, Italian taxpayers' identification number, place of administration and place of business;
- furthermore, for commercial enterprises (business entities) with legal personality, the filing must include:
  - the ownership percentage of the entity's share capital, when the beneficial owner is identified through the ownership test; and
  - the source and nature of the power to control the enterprise, when the beneficial owner is identified through the control test and the source and nature of the authority to legally represent and bind the entity or the power of administration or management of the entity, when the beneficial owner is identified through the power of the administration or management test.
- for legal entities that do not carry on a business (eg, associations and foundations), the filing must include the entity's name, registered address, place of administration or principal place of business, Italian tax code number, and Italian legal certified email address.

Information on beneficial owners is acquired via self-declarations issued by companies.

The filing is carried out electronically and requires registration of the entity with the Ministry of Economic Development's electronic database. In the event of any change of the facts and information that were submitted with the initial filing that change the status of the entity and identity of its beneficial owners, an amended filing must be carried out within 30 days of the change. All information and statements due with the filing shall be submitted under penalty of perjury, and any incomplete or false submissions would be treated as a failure to file and subject to penalty.

The filing may also include a statement according to which an individual identified as beneficial owner claims the status of individual with a legitimate interest against access to the beneficial ownership information set forth in the register. This prevents general public access to that information. A legitimate interest against disclosure exists whenever the disclosure of the information on the register would expose a beneficial owner to a disproportionate risk of fraud, kidnapping, ransom, extortion, violence, harassment or threat (as defined by Article 1(b) of the draft decree).

With reference to access to the register, tax authorities, anti-money laundering officials and financial police have unlimited and unconditional authority to inspect the register and retrieve the information on beneficial owners. Similarly, any member of the public at large has access to the register to retrieve information on beneficial owners of commercial enterprises (business entities) and legal entities that do not carry on a business (eg, associations and foundations). The disclosure is limited to a beneficial owner's first and last name, month and year of birth, place of residence, citizenship, and grounds for beneficial ownership status (Article 7). The access, however, is not permitted in respect of beneficial owners with a legitimate interest against disclosure, according to Articles 1 and 3 of the draft decree.

4. The Register of Beneficial Owners of trusts and related legal institutions

As already illustrated in the preceding sections, 4AMLD and 5AMLD have established specific obligations for the identification of the beneficial owners for the subjects obligated by the anti-money laundering legislation, intended cumulatively to be:

- the settlor;
- the trustee(s);
- the protector, if any;
- the beneficiaries or the category of persons in whose main interest the legal institution or legal entity is established or acts; and
- any other natural person who ultimately exercises control over the trust through direct or indirect ownership or other means.

The trustees of trusts producing tax obligations and similar legal institutions are obliged to obtain, maintain and provide information on beneficial ownership and communicate this information to the Italian Companies Register.

The EU legislation was implemented in Article 22 of Legislative Decree 231/2007 with the provision of the obligation, exclusively borne by 'trusts producing tax consequences', according to the provisions of Article 73 of the Decree of the President of the Republic of 22 January 1986 No 917 (the Italian Income Tax Code), registration in a special section of the Companies Register, by the trustee or trustees or by another person on behalf of the trustee.

In the absence of the legislation implementing the registers, the meaning of 'trusts producing tax consequences' is discussed.

Furthermore, to guarantee legal certainty and conditions of substantial equality, 5AMLD has also included among the subjects obliged to communicate those legal institutions which, due to their structure and functions, appear similar to the trust (expressed and voluntary), regardless of the *nomen juris* used.

The expansion of the group of obliged parties has been incorporated into Italian legislation through the introduction of paragraph 5-bis of Article 22 of Legislative Decree 231/2007, according to which entities and institutions which, due to their structure and functions, determine legal effects equivalent to those of the expressed trusts, also having regard to the destination of the assets to a purpose and control by a person other than the owner, in the interest of one or more beneficiaries or for the pursuit of a specific purpose.

At the same time, the subjects who exercise rights, powers and prerogatives equivalent to those of the trustee of an expressed trust have the obligation, on the one hand, to acquire and keep data and information on beneficial ownership and, on the other, to proceed with the registration in the special section of the Companies Register.

When fully operational, the special section of the register will host the information and identification data of natural persons who hold the status of beneficial owners in trusts or similar legal institutions, producing legal effects relevant for tax purposes and similar, established or resident in the territory of the Italian Republic.

Article 4 of the draft decree contains the list of data and information to be communicated, which includes:

- the identification data of the beneficial owner(s) of the express trust and of the related obliged legal institutions;
- the taxpayer's identification number of the institution;
- the name as well as date, place and details of the trust deed or similar legal institution;
- any indication of the status of a 'counter-interested party' (as better defined in section 5 below) to access the natural person indicated as

beneficial owner and the reasons why access would expose the beneficial owner to a disproportionate risk of fraud, kidnapping, blackmail, extortion, harassment, violence or intimidation (if applicable); and
- the declaration, pursuant to the Decree of the President of the Republic of 28 December 2000, No 445, of responsibility and awareness of the sanctions provided for by the criminal legislation and by the special laws on falsification of documents and declarations made.

The draft decree provides that with specific reference to trusts and similar institutions, the trustee will have until 15 March 2021 to communicate the data on the beneficial ownership previously acquired, as well as the related changes to be sent within 30 days of them taking place.

Section II of the draft decree contains all the information on how to access and consult the data and information communicated by the persons required to register.

Access to the data contained in the special section is allowed, subject to accreditation with the following:
- the Ministry of Economy and Finance, the Supervisory Authorities of the sector, the Financial Intelligence Unit, the Anti-Mafia Investigation Department and the Financial Police as the Currency Police, without any restrictions;
- the National Anti-Mafia and Counter-Terrorism Directorate and the judicial authority, in accordance with their institutional powers;
- the authorities responsible for combating tax evasion, exclusively within the limits of this purpose;
- the subjects obligated by the anti-money laundering legislation indicated in Article 3 of Legislative Decree 231/2007, upon payment of administrative fees; and
- the public with the payment of duties unless they are not interested in access.

Unlike what happens for the Register of Beneficial Owners of companies, access to the Register of Beneficial Owners of trusts and related legal institutions is more protected by the need for the applicant to obtain accreditation.

Private individuals, including those with 'widespread interests', who are interested in being accredited, must submit a specific application to the Ministry of Economy and Finance containing, under penalty of inadmissibility, the self-certification of the following data:
- the identification data of the applicant, the legal representative of the firm with 'widespread interests' and the indication of a certified email address for communications;
- for the firms, bearers of 'widespread interests':

  - the indication of the details of the instrument and articles of incorporation and the deed of incorporation, as well as the institutionally pursued purpose;
  - in the case of entities with legal personality, the details of the registration in the register of private legal persons referred to in Presidential Decree No 361/2000; and
  - in the case of entities without legal personality, the elements from which the relative degree of representativeness and territorial diffusion can be inferred unequivocally;
- an indication of the factual elements that are valid to qualify the interest in accessing information on beneficial ownership, such as:
  - relevant and differentiated, if the information is such as to found, integrate, strengthen or harm or otherwise reduce the effects of the legally protected situation;
  - direct, concrete and current, as instrumental to the establishment or continuation of a judicial proceeding and directly productive of effects on the legally protected situation;
- for exponential entities, bearers of 'widespread interests', in addition the affiliation of the interest to the statutory purpose pursued; and
- the circumstances that lead the applicant to doubt the coincidence between legal ownership and beneficial ownership.

The Ministry of Economy and Finance shall verify the regularity and completeness of the application and the existence of interest in access.

5. Causes of exclusion

An important and controversial update introduced by 5AMLD concerns access to the information contained in the registers of beneficial owners. If, on the one hand, in fact Legislative Decree 90/2017 limited access to the register of legal persons and trusts to a defined group of subjects, Legislative Decree No 125 of 4 October 2019 gives the possibility of access to the register to any member of the public.

However, the legislator seems to combine disclosure standards needed in order to counteract the money laundering and terrorist financing with the need to protect the confidentiality of the individual. Accordingly, the legislator recognises the possibility for certain subjects not to be disclosed as beneficial owner, in case the revelation of the data to the public may cause serious hazard to his/her safety.

Pursuant to Article 21, paragraph 2 of Legislative Decree No 231/2007, as amended by Legislative Decree No 125/2019, in fact, the disclosure of the information contained in the register of beneficial owners of a legal person can be excluded, in whole or in part, if the beneficial owner is an incapable person or a minor, or if the access exposes the beneficial owner to a disproportionate risk of fraud, kidnapping, blackmail, extortion, harassment, violence or intimidation, according to a case-by-case approach and after detailed assessment of the exceptional nature of the circumstances.

This is the case where there are subjects who are so-called 'access counter-interested parties' (*'controinteressati all'accesso'*) and consultation will not be allowed for the same reason, even to private individuals in the case of information regarding the beneficial ownership of trusts and related legal institutions. As no further details and possible criteria have been published, the meaning of "according to a case-by-case approach and previous detailed assessment of the exceptional nature of the circumstances" is still not completely clear.

While on the one hand it could be easier to identify cases in which the beneficial owner is exposed to an actual and current disproportionate risk, on the other hand the demonstration to which the access counter-interested party is required in cases of potential and future risk derived from publication of the name in the beneficial owner register could be extremely difficult and sometimes almost impossible.

In addition, the draft decree does not provide that beneficial owners are notified in case of access to their information by a third party, putting all subjects at actual or potential risk due to the impossibility of being able to promptly protect themselves.

The statistical data relating to the number of deliberate exclusions and the related reasons must be published and communicated to the European Commission.

6. Conclusion

Therefore, as long as the definitive decree has not been released, there is only the above-mentioned draft decree. Moreover, on 14 January 2021 the Italian Data Protection Authority gave, in general terms, its favourable opinion on the draft decree, pointing out the importance of protecting the privacy of the individuals that could have some relevant weakness in the case of disclosure. The deadline for sending observations, within the framework of the public consultation launched by the Treasury Department, expired on 28 February 2021.

The following points in the draft decree are worth underlining.

- Ultimate beneficial owners of companies: since the early years of the 2010s, there has been debate in the specialised press and among experts about how to determine who is the ultimate beneficial owner of a company when there is a complex participative chain of companies. There are three major theories: the first theory suggests that the ultimate beneficial owner is the person who owns more than 25% of the share capital of the company; the second theory instead wants to look at the 25% of control of every company in the chain, and the third theory follows the gear down principle (thus if Mr A owns 50% of company X, which owns 60% of company Y, Mr A, for the purposes of the Register of Beneficial Owners, owns 30% of company Y and therefore is an ultimate beneficial owner). The official organisation of Italian tax accountants (CNDCEC), as stated in a document issued in May 2019, clarified that it prefers the second theory. Banca d'Italia at first also preferred the second theory, but in July 2019 declared itself as not competent. Therefore, it is unclear how to individuate the ultimate beneficial owner when there is a series of companies owned by several other companies.

- Express trusts able to produce tax obligations: in Article 1, letter (g) of the draft decree considering what is stated by Article 21, clause 3 of Legislative Decree 231/2007, it is not clear whether this category includes all the Italian tax resident trusts (as defined by Article 73, clause 3 of Presidential Decree No 917 of 22 December 1986) and thus all the trusts obliged to have a tax code as Italian residents, that are able to be liable to income tax, or only the trusts that *de facto* produce income (liable as Italian residents to income tax following the worldwide principle).
- Access by individuals to the special register section for trusts and similar arrangements: in Article 8 of the draft decree it is not totally clarified (taking into consideration what is stated in Article 21, clause 4, letter (d)*bis*), what kind of individuals with what type of legitimate interest could have access to the register's section, after the appropriate accreditation. Therefore, it is unclear whether, for instance, every private individual obligated by anti-money laundering law (eg, lawyers, tax accountants, public notaries etc) could have access to the register or instead only individuals who have a signed professional engagement letter with a trust. So, in order to protect privacy and not to disclose more information than is necessary, in compliance with the privacy law and thus with the EU General Data Protection Regulation, it is necessary to understand what kind of hypothesis applies in the accepted cases and thus who can have the right to access and when.
- Arrangements similar to a trust: in Article 1, clause 2, letter (p) of Legislative Decree 231/2007, as modified over the course of time, as well as in Article 1, letter (i) of the draft decree, those entities fall under the same special section of the trust's register. Therefore, the Italian legislator wanted to give more privacy to the ultimate beneficial owner of those arrangements than other EU legislations that instead decided to put those entities in the companies' section register (ie, Austria and Germany).

- Causes of exclusion: in the draft decree there is no specification about who must communicate the will of exclusion (the person him/herself or instead the company/trust/entity that has to register all the data). Moreover, it is important to have a more specific description of the hypothesis of restriction to public access.
- Communication protocol: following publication of the draft decree, the protocol (eg, the software) for communicating the data to the company register is still unknown.

In conclusion, the Data Protection Authority has given its favourable opinion but the Council of State, with Measure No 458 of 19 March 2021, has suspended the adoption of the opinion concerning the draft decree. Furthermore, the Council of State asked the Ministry of Economy and Finance to provide some clarifications regarding the draft decree.

Taking into consideration the above-mentioned issues and the importance of having beneficial ownership registers that are compliant with innovative EU legislation, it is desirable that in the short term the Italian legislator defines the legislation, listening to the needs of those professionals who collect and organise all the anti-money laundering data day to day.

Liechtenstein

Johanna Niegel
Allgemeines Treuunternehmen (ATU)

1. Implementation of the EU Anti-Money Laundering Directives in Liechtenstein

1.1 Liechtenstein – a member of the European Economic Area

The Principality of Liechtenstein, just like Iceland and Norway, is a member of the European Economic Area, which constitutes a free trade zone between the European Union and the European Free Trade Association member states based upon the four fundamental pillars of the European Union. Relevant EU legislation that is covered by the EEA Agreement is taken over into the European Economic Area by a decision of the EEA Joint Committee, and Liechtenstein is thus required to implement and apply EU law (*acquis communautaire*).

1.2 Reception and implementation of the EU Anti-Money Laundering Directives

Liechtenstein implemented the provisions of the Fourth EU Anti-Money Laundering Directive 2015/849 (4AMLD) relating to the beneficial owner registers by enacting the Act on the Register of Beneficial Owners of Domestic Legal Entities of 6 December 2018 (*Gesetz über das Verzeichnis wirtschaftlicher Eigentümer inländischer Rechtsträger* – VwEG),[1] which entered into force on 1 August 2019. The VwEG was complemented by the Ordinance on the Register of Beneficial Owners of Domestic Legal Entities of 28 January 2020 (*Verordnung über das Verzeichnis wirtschaftlicher Eigentümer inländischer Rechtsträger* – VwEV).[2] As of 1 February 2020, the Beneficial Owner Register (BO Register) has been kept by the Liechtenstein Office of Justice. Shortly after having implemented Articles 30 and 31 of 4AMLD by enacting the VwEG in December 2018, Liechtenstein needed to implement the standards of the Fifth EU Anti-Money Laundering Directive 2018/843 (5AMLD) relating to Articles 30 and 31, which stipulate widened obligations with a view to contents and transparency of the BO Register.

---

1 *Liechtenstein Law Gazette* 2019.008, available in German at: www.gesetze.li/konso/2019008000?search_text=vweg&search_loc=text&lrnr=&lgblid_von=&observe_date=08.09.2020.

2 *Liechtenstein Law Gazette* 2020.36, available in German at: www.gesetze.li/konso/2020036000?search_text=vweg&search_loc=text&lrnr=&lgblid_von=&observe_date=08.09.2020.

On 26 January 2021 the Act on the Register of Beneficial Owners of Legal Entities (*Gesetz über das Verzeichnis der wirtschaftlich berechtigten Personen von Rechtsträgern* – VwbPG)[3] was enacted in implementation of the requirements of 5AMLD with regard to the beneficial owner registers.

The VwbPG entered into force on 1 April 2021, thereby repealing the VwEG in its entirety. On 23 March 2021 the Liechtenstein Government enacted the Ordinance on the Register of Beneficial Owners of Legal Entities (*Verordnung über das Verzeichnis der wirtschaftlich berechtigten Personen von Rechtsträgern* – VwbPV Ordinance),[4] which likewise entered into force on 1 April 2021. In implementation[5] of the VwbPG, the VwbPV Ordinance contains the definition of the term 'beneficial owner' and regulates the following:

- the details on proof of entry of beneficial owners in foreign registers;
- the obligation of legal entities to collect and report data of the beneficial owners;
- the maintenance and contents of the BO Register pursuant to Article 6 VwbPG;
- the issuance of extracts and certificates;
- the reporting of discrepancies;
- Data protection with a view to the processing and security of data;
- Disclosure of data to domestic authorities, banks and financial institutions, domestic and third parties;
- the decision making and organisation of the VwbP Commission; and
- the applicable fees.

In the following sections the main provisions of the VwbPG shall be summarised. For ease of reference the discussion[6] will follow the structure of the VwbPG, referring to the VwbPV Ordinance where appropriate. In any case, the VwbPG and the VwbPV Ordinance always must be read in conjunction.

2. The Act on the Register of Beneficial Owners of Legal Entities (VwbPG)

2.1 Purpose

Article 1 paragraph 2 VwbPG, just like the VwbPV Ordinance, contains a clear reference to the implementation of Articles 30 and 31 of 4AMLD in the version of 5AMLD. With a view to the prevention of money laundering as well as of

3 *Liechtenstein Law Gazette* 2021.33, available in German at: www.gesetze.li/chrono/pdf/2021033000.

4 *Liechtenstein Law Gazette* 2021.123, available in German: at www.gesetze.li/chrono/pdf/2021123000.

5 Articles 2 paragraph 1 lit a and c, 3 paragraph 4, 4 paragraph 7, 6 paragraph 3, 7 paragraph 2, 8 paragraph 4, 9 paragraph 4, 12 paragraph 8, 13 paragraph 4, 15 paragraph 6, 16 paragraph 7, 17 paragraph 14, 23 paragraph 1, 27 paragraph 5, 28 paragraph 2 and 33 of the VwbPG contain an explicit reference to the Implementation Ordinance.

6 The author wishes to thank Roland Altmann and Ivo Elkuch of The Liechtenstein Institute of Professional Trustees and Fiduciaries for their valuable input.

predicate offences to money laundering and terrorist financing, the VwbPG regulates the duties of both legal entities and their beneficial owners, the keeping of the BO Register, the processing and disclosure of data, the supervision over the BO Register, and penal provisions for offences.

2.2 Definition of 'beneficial owners' under the VwbPG

Article 2 paragraph 1 lit a VwbPG aligns the definition of beneficial owners with the Due Diligence Act[7] in the sense that the definition of beneficial owners under the VwbPG is identical with that contained in Article 2 paragraph 1 lit e of the Due Diligence Act. As a consequence, both acts now refer to beneficial owners as *'wirtschaftlich Berechtigte'*. Yet the VwbPG contains its own and independent definition of the term 'beneficial owner'. If in the future the provisions of the due diligence legislation are amended, this will also lead to simultaneous amendments of the VwbPG.

The term 'beneficial owner' under both acts means:

a natural person upon whose request or in whose interest a transaction or activity is carried out or a business relationship is ultimately established. In the case of legal entities a beneficial owner is also the natural person in whose ownership or control the legal entity is placed.

Article 2 paragraph 1 of the VwbPV Ordinance, aside from containing special provisions for certain legal entities (eg, for charitable legal entities), provides the actual definition of the term 'beneficial owner' for the purposes of the VwbPG:

Beneficial owners are:

a) in the case of stand-alone legal entities as defined in Schedule 1 within the meaning of Art 2 para 1 lit d of the VwbPG:

1. those natural persons who ultimately, directly or indirectly:

aa) hold or control a share or voting rights of 25% or more in these legal entities;

bb) participate with 25 % or more in the profits of these legal entities; or

cc) otherwise exercise control over such entity;

2. those natural persons who are members of the governing body, if, after exhausting all possibilities, no persons have been identified in accordance with Point 1;

b) in the case of non-stand-alone legal entities according to Schedule 1 within the meaning of Art 2 para 1 lit d of the VwbPG, unless there are additional beneficial owners under lit a):

---

7 *Liechtenstein Law Gazette* 2009.47, available in German at www.gesetze.li/konso/pdf/2009047000?version=25. The term 'professional due diligence' in Liechtenstein is understood as implementing KYC measures in combating money laundering, organised crime and terrorist financing. The Liechtenstein Due Diligence Act thus governs the application of due diligence in the professional exercise of activities covered by the act and thereby serves to combat money laundering, organised crime, and terrorist financing within the meaning of the Criminal Code.

1. *those natural persons who are the effective, non-fiduciary founders, incorporators or settlors, irrespective of whether they exercise control over the legal entity after its establishment;*
2. *those natural or legal persons who are members of the foundation board or of the board of directors or of the trustee, respectively;*
3. *any natural persons who are protectors or persons in similar or equivalent functions;*
4. *those natural persons who are beneficiaries;*
5. *if no beneficiaries have yet been designated, the group of persons in whose interest the legal entity is primarily established or operated;*
6. *in addition, the natural persons who, directly or indirectly ultimately control the entity through direct or indirect ownership or otherwise ultimately control the entity.*

According to Article 2 paragraph 3 of the VwbPV Ordinance, the following shall be deemed to be members of the governing body within the meaning of Article 2 paragraph 1: those natural persons who are members of the management, the board of directors, the supervisory board, the management board or persons in comparable functions.

According to Article 2 paragraph 2 of the VwbPV Ordinance, 'control' within the meaning of Article 2 paragraph 1 means, in particular, the possibility:

a) to dispose of the legal entity's assets;

b) to change the provisions that characterise the legal entity;

c) to change the beneficiary; or

d) to control the exercise of the control options under lit a to c.

The beneficial owners shall thus be ascertained under the VwbPG in analogy to the definition contained in the due diligence legislation and entered into the BO Register. It becomes evident from the legislative materials that for the interpretation of the terms taken over from the Due Diligence Act reference should be made to the corresponding interpretations in due diligence law.

The threshold for a beneficial ownership interest for legal entities falling under Schedule 1 to the VwbPG (ie, corporate and other legal entities) is set at 25% or more of direct or indirect participation, voting or profit rights, which corresponds to the respective Financial Action Task Force Recommendation.

Founders, settlors, foundation board members, protectors, beneficiaries and similar functions henceforth always qualify as beneficial owners regardless of whether they exert control over the entity or not, and consequently must be entered in the BO Register. In addition, the abstract description of the group of discretionary beneficiaries also needs to be entered in the BO Register, whereas the individual recipients of distributions from a discretionary entity do not.

According to Article 31 paragraph 3a of 5AMLD, the beneficial owners of foreign trusts are also entered into the BO Register under certain preconditions.

However, it is of the utmost importance to distinguish between the data that must be entered in the BO Register and which of these data must be disclosed and to whom, which will be discussed in detail in the following section.

2.3 The Liechtenstein Beneficial Owner Register of Legal Entities

The BO Register is kept by the Liechtenstein Office of Justice in electronic form. The VwbPG has again opted for one single register into which the data of legal entities falling under Schedules 1 and 2 to the VwbPG, as well as of their beneficial owners, are entered.

Schedule 1 to the VwbPG encompasses corporate and other legal entities, whereas Schedule 2 applies to trusts, foundations and establishments/trusts that are structured like a foundation and establishments whose beneficial owners are third persons.

Furthermore, any reportable discrepancies that persons subject to professional 'know your customer' (KYC) obligations,[8] and also authorities according to Article 13 paragraph 1 VwbPG, detect between the data on beneficial owners of legal entities that are already entered in the BO Register and the data that they themselves have available and report to the Office of Justice within 30 days of taking notice, are made visible in the BO Register. The BO Register is kept in German.

The Office of Justice shall, upon request and against the payment of a fee, provide to legal entities or within the framework of disclosure pursuant to Articles 15 to 17 (ie, to banks and financial institutions, domestic persons subject to professional KYC obligations, and third persons) extracts from the Register and certifications of entry in the Register.[9]

The Office of Justice thereby also verifies the identity and legitimation[10] of the applicant or of its authorised representatives. It thereby can inspect suitable documents, the Liechtenstein Commercial Register or an equivalent foreign register. The issued extracts and certifications do not enjoy public character.

The BO Register shall be electronically linked via the Central European Platform according to Article 22 Directive (EU) 2017/1132 to the central Registers of the other EEA member states.

2.4 Obligations of legal entities and beneficial owners under the VwbPG

(a) Obligations of legal entities under the VwbPG

The VwbPG obliges legal entities to determine and to verify the identity of their beneficial owners. The term 'legal entities' is defined in Article 2 paragraph 1 lit c VwbPG as follows:

8 Article 2 paragraph 1 lit b VwbPG refers to the definition contained in Article 3 of the Due Diligence Act.
9 See Article 8 of the VwbPV Ordinance with a view to their contents.
10 See Article 7 of the VwbPV Ordinance.

- domestic legal persons, companies, trusts or other entities or asset structures, according to Schedules 1 and 2, irrespective of their legal form. Trusts that are administered by persons falling under Article 3 paragraph 3 lit k of the Due Diligence Act (ie, by corporate service providers in the widest sense) are also captured, insofar as proof[11] is not provided that their beneficial owners are entered in the BO Register of another EEA member state according to Article 31 of 4AMLD (Article 2 paragraph 1 lit c Point 1 VwbPG);
- in addition, the VwbPG likewise applies to trusts or other legal arrangements that were set up abroad but are administered in Liechtenstein, insofar as proof is not provided that their beneficial owners are entered in the BO Register of another EEA member state according to Article 31 of 4AMLD (Article 2 paragraph 1 lit c Point 2 VwbPG); and
- furthermore, trusts or other legal arrangements that are administered in a third state (ie, not an EEA member state), but for which a business relationship[12] with a domestic person subject to professional KYC obligations was entered into or for which real estate was acquired also fall under the provisions of the VwbPG insofar as proof is not provided that their beneficial owners are entered in the BO Register of another EEA member state according to Article 31 of 4AMLD (Article 2 paragraph 1 lit c Point 1 VwbPG).

(b) Collection and reporting of data of beneficial owners by legal entities

The legal entities are obliged to establish the identity of their beneficiary owners. In verifying their identity, they apply adequate and risk-based measures to convince themselves that the persons they identify are the true beneficial owners. This includes risk-based and adequate measures to determine the ownership and control structure of the legal entity. It is worth mentioning in this respect that the process of establishing the identity of beneficial owners is not a one-time, but an ongoing process. Should doubts arise in the future regarding the identity of the beneficial owners, then the legal entities shall repeat the establishment and verification of the identity of the beneficial owners.

The legal entities shall collect the following data[13] about their beneficial

---

11 According to Article 3 of the VwbPV Ordinance, proof of the entry of beneficial owners in a register pursuant to Article 31 of 4AMLD can be made by an extract from such a register, an official confirmation of entry in such a register or comparable evidence.

12 According to Article 2 paragraph 1 lit g VwbPG, a 'business relationship' is defined as any business, professional or commercial relationship which is conducted in connection with the commercial activities of the legal entity and which is expected, at the time when the contact is established, to exist for a certain duration in time.

13 See Article 6 of the VwbPV Ordinance as regards the registered data of the legal entities.

owners, which they then report in electronic form to the Office of Justice using special forms.[14]

- In the case of natural persons: surname, first name, date of birth, country of residence and citizenship.
- In the case of Liechtenstein legal persons, companies, trusts or other entities or asset structures, irrespective of their legal form: company number, name or firm, legal form, seat and address, and for those that are not entered into, notified to or deposited with the commercial register, also the date of foundation.
- In the case of foreign legal persons, companies, trusts or other entities or asset structures, irrespective of their legal form: company number, name or firm, legal form, seat, address, date of formation, and place and date of entry into a foreign commercial or similar register, if applicable.
- Legal entities according to Schedule 1, apart from the data of their beneficial owners, shall also collect information on their corresponding economic interest and transmit the information to the Office of Justice in electronic form.
- Trusts or other legal arrangements that are administered in a third state (ie, non-EEA member state), but for which a business relationship with a domestic person subject to professional KYC obligations was entered into or for which real estate was acquired, insofar as proof is not provided that the beneficial owners are entered in a BO Register of another EEA member state according to Article 31 of 4AMLD, shall also notify the Office of Justice of a domestic postal address.

Legal entities must report such data to the Office of Justice within 30 days of the following:

- entry into the commercial register for legal entities according to Schedule 1;
- entry into the commercial register or of deposition with the commercial register of the notice of formation of foundations that are not entered into the commercial register or of deposition with the commercial register of the trust deed of trusts that are not entered into the commercial register for the legal entities according to Schedule 2 that either must be registered in the commercial register, or be notified to or be deposited with the commercial register;
- formation for legal entities according to Schedule 2 that are not obliged to be entered into the commercial register, nor to be notified to or deposited with the commercial register;
- commencement of their administration in Liechtenstein for trusts that

14 See Schedules 1 and 2 to the VwbPV Ordinance.

were set up abroad but are administered by persons subject to professional KYC obligations in Liechtenstein insofar as proof is not provided that their beneficial owners are entered in a BO Register of another EEA member state according to Article 31 of 4AMLD; and
- establishment of a business relationship with a person subject to Liechtenstein professional KYC obligations for trusts that are administered in a third state (ie, one that is not an EEA member state), but for which a business relationship with a domestic person subject to professional KYC obligations was entered into, or of the acquisition of the real estate.

Changes to data must also be reported within 30 days of the changes taking place. In some cases this also extends to registration requirements that have ceased to apply.

Trustees of trusts falling under Schedule 2 disclose their status with regards to persons subject to professional KYC obligations and transmit the data within the timeframe when they open a business relationship or execute an occasional transaction according to Article 2 paragraph 1 lit d of the Due Diligence Act.

(c) Obligations of beneficial owners under the VwbPG

The beneficial owners themselves are obliged to provide the respective legal entities with all the information required under the VwbPG with a view to the identification and verification of the identity of beneficial owners, as well as to collection and reporting of the data of the beneficial owners.

2.5 Data protection

(a) General

Insofar as the VwbPG does not stipulate otherwise, the data are protected by Liechtenstein data protection legislation.[15] With a view to data processing and data security, the VwbPG furthermore stipulates that the Office of Justice[16] keeps the BO Register exclusively for the purpose of fighting money laundering, predicate offences to money laundering and terrorist financing. Data must not be processed for other purposes. The Office of Justice is authorised within the scope of its duties to process the information to be entered in the BO Register as well as the corresponding personal data. The information and personal data

---

15 On 4 October 2018 Liechtenstein enacted the totally revised Data Protection Act (*Liechtenstein Law Gazette* 2018.272; www.gesetze.li/konso/pdf/2018272000?version=2) and on 11 December 2018 the Data Protection Ordinance (*Liechtenstein Law Gazette* 2018.415; www.gesetze.li/konso/pdf/2018415000?version=3), which both entered into force on 1 January 2019.

16 According to Article 11 of the VwbPV Ordinance, the Office of Justice accepts written requests for the assertion of the rights of affected persons and processes them in accordance with data protection legislation.

that are entered in the BO Register must be protected by appropriate technical and organisational measures against unauthorised and unlawful processing, accidental loss, destruction or damage.

The Office of Justice deletes personal data from the BO Register five years after the deletion of a legal entity according to Article 2 paragraph 1 lit c Point 1 VwbPG from the commercial register or its closure; if the legal entity is not registered in the commercial register, the discontinuation of the administration of a legal entity according to Article 2 paragraph 1 lit c Point 2 VwbPG in Liechtenstein or, for legal entities according to Article 2 paragraph 1 lit c Point 3 VwbPG, the discontinuation of the business relationship with a person subject to professional KYC obligations or the sale of the real estate held by such legal entity. For data protection control reasons, every processing of data must be logged in the BO Register with a view of the time of processing, the persons processing the data, and the purpose and manner of the data processing, and the log data must be transmitted to the Data Protection Authority immediately upon request. The log data are kept for a period of 10 years and are then deleted. Log data may be processed exclusively for the purposes of data protection control by the Data Protection Authority and to ensure data security. The log data may not be processed for other purposes. The government regulates by ordinance the data processing and the data security, in particular with a view to the measures guaranteeing the secure disclosure of data, the operation of the BO Register, access to the data, processing authorisations, retention, archiving and deletion of data, and the logging of requests.

(b) Data protection rights: right of information of persons affected by disclosure proceedings

Article 19 VwbPG stipulates that the right of affected persons to obtain information about personal data processed under the VwbPG is governed by Article 15 of the Regulation (EU) 2016/679. Excluded from the right to information are log data pursuant to Article 12 paragraph 6 VwbPG and data in connection with an inspection pursuant to Article 13 paragraphs 1 and 2 VwbPG (disclosure of data to domestic authorities via call procedure).

2.6 Disclosure of data

(a) Disclosure of data to domestic authorities via call procedure

The Liechtenstein Financial Intelligence Unit (FIU), the Liechtenstein Financial Market Authority (FMA), the Liechtenstein Police, the Liechtenstein Tax Authority, the Liechtenstein Public Prosecutor, the Liechtenstein Court and the Liechtenstein Chamber of Lawyers may, with a view to specific cases without limitations, inspect via call procedure the data of beneficial owners of legal entities, as long as this inspection is necessary for combating money laundering, predicate offences to money laundering and terrorist financing.[17] When inspecting data via call procedure it must be ensured that the legal entity in question is not notified about this data inquiry. Notwithstanding special legal provisions, the rights of affected persons as guaranteed by Articles 13 to 16, 18 and 21 of Regulation (EU) 2016/679 do not apply if, in fulfilment of such rights, information were to be disclosed that must be kept confidential because of prevailing legitimate interests of the Office of Justice, the FIU, the FMA, the police, the tax authority, the public prosecutor, the court, the chamber of lawyers or third persons. Article 34 paragraph 2 of the Data Protection Act[18] applies accordingly.

For each inspection, the date of inspection, the inspected or downloaded data, including the reason for inspection or download and the person requesting the data, are logged.

The Office of Justice shall inform the authorities entitled under this provision on a quarterly basis and report to the government at the end of each calendar year on the data searches that were made.

(b) Disclosure of data to foreign authorities within framework of mutual administrative assistance

The FIU, the FMA, the police, the tax authority, the public prosecutor and the court ('domestic authorities' according to Article 13 paragraph 1 VwbPG) decide on the admissibility of disclosing data in mutual administrative assistance proceedings. If applicable, they access the BO Register via call procedure and transmit the data to the requesting foreign authority.

(c) Disclosure of data to banks and financial institutions

Upon application, the Office of Justice shall disclose[19] the registered data of legal entities for purposes of fulfilling professional KYC obligations or for activities to prevent money laundering, predicate offences to money laundering and terrorist financing to:

- banks or financial institutions (ie, those according to Article 2 paragraph 2 of Regulation (EU) 2015/849, having their seat in Liechtenstein or in another EEA country); and
- banks with their seat in a third state (ie, a non-EEA member state), if, in addition to the requirements stipulated by Regulation (EU) 2015/849,

17 See Article 13 and 14 of the VwbPV Ordinance.

18 According to Article 34 paragraph 2, the reasons for the refusal to provide information shall be documented. The refusal to provide information shall be justified to affected persons, unless the communication of the factual and legal grounds on which the decision is based would jeopardise the purpose pursued by the refusal to provide information. The data stored for the purpose of providing information to the affected person and for the preparation thereof may only be processed for this as well as for data protection control purposes. For other purposes, processing shall be restricted in accordance with Article 18 of Regulation (EU) 2016/679.

19 See Articles 15 and 16 of the VwbPV Ordinance.

the requirements according to Article 45 of Regulation (EU) 2016/679 are also fulfilled.

The request shall contain very specific information on the bank or financial institution requesting the information, the firm or the name of the legal entity in question, as well as a declaration that the requested data are needed to fulfil professional KYC obligations or for activities to prevent money laundering, predicate offences to money laundering and terrorist financing. The Office of Justice shall decline the disclosure of data if the application, despite express request, does not contain the necessary information or documentation.

The legal entity in question does not enjoy standing in the disclosure proceedings to banks and financial institutions, but it must be informed about the disclosure already made.

(d) Disclosure of data to domestic persons subject to professional KYC obligations under Due Diligence Act

According to Article 16 VwbPG, the Office of Justice shall, upon application, disclose[20] the registered data of legal entities to domestic persons subject to professional KYC obligations for the purposes of fulfilling these obligations. These persons are defined in Article 3 of the Due Diligence Act and, among others, include banks and investment companies under the Banking Act, collective investment and insurance undertakings, insurance brokers, asset management companies licensed under the Asset Management Act, and professional service providers, such as trustees, lawyers and law firms authorised under the Lawyers Act and the like.

Explicit exceptions with a view to disclosure of data are foreseen for the data of settlors and protectors (ie, founders, incorporators, settlors as well as protectors and persons in similar positions) who do not exercise control over a non-stand-alone legal entity according to Schedule 1. Disclosure to banks and financial institutions according to Article 15 VwbPG is reserved. A stand-alone legal entity according to Schedule 1 is defined in Article 2 paragraph 1 lit d VwbPG as an entity in which no legal entity falling under Schedule 2 (eg, a trust or foundation) or no corresponding foreign legal entity holds or controls a share of voting rights of 25% or more, participates in the profit with 25% or more or exercises control through other means over this legal entity. This exception thus means that the corresponding data of settlors and protectors, who do not exercise control over a Schedule 1 entity that does not qualify as a stand-alone legal entity, are merely entered in the BO Register, but are not disclosed to persons subject to professional KYC obligations.

An application for disclosure under Article 16 VwbPG shall also contain

20 See Articles 15–18 of the VwbPV Ordinance.

specific information and documentation on the person subject to professional KYC obligations, the legal entity in question, as well as a declaration that the requested data from the BO Register are needed to fulfil professional KYC obligations. The Office of Justice shall upon receipt of the application also obtain a declaration from the legal entity that does not qualify as a stand-alone legal entity under Schedule 1 whether a founder or protector exercises control over the respective legal entity.

The Office of Justice shall decline the disclosure of data if the application, despite express request, does not contain the necessary information, if no founder or protector exercises control over a non-stand-alone legal entity falling under Schedule 1, or if a restriction to disclose data on account of protection of legitimate interests applies. In addition, if at the time of making the application a proceeding to restrict disclosure of data is already pending or is opened during such application for disclosure, then the application for disclosure of the data is suspended until a legally binding decision on the restriction to disclose is reached.

The legal entity in question does not enjoy standing in a disclosure proceeding to persons subject to professional KYC obligations, but it must be informed about the disclosure already made.

(e) Disclosure of data to third parties

According to Article 17 paragraph 1 VwbPG, Liechtenstein and foreign persons and organisations may, against the payment of a fee, apply to the Office of Justice for disclosure[21] of the registered data of stand-alone legal entities according to Schedule 1.

According to Article 17 paragraph 1 VwbPG, the application must be submitted to the Office of Justice and must contain detailed information about the applicant, as well as the firm or name of the stand-alone legal entity whose registered data are to be disclosed. Furthermore, it is necessary to hand in a declaration that the data requested from the BO Register are necessary to combat money laundering, predicate offences to money laundering and terrorist financing.

The Office of Justice shall decline disclosure of the corresponding beneficial owners if the application upon its express request does not contain the necessary information and documents, if the submitted declaration is not credible, or if a restriction to disclose data on account of protection of legitimate interests (Article 18 VwbPG) applies.

According to Article 17 paragraph 4 VwbPG, Liechtenstein and foreign persons as well as organisations may, against the payment of a fee, also apply to the Office of Justice for disclosure of the registered data of entities that are not

21 See Articles 15–18 of the VwbPV Ordinance.

considered stand-alone legal entities according to Schedule 1. The data of founders and protectors who do not exercise control over a non-stand-alone legal entity according to Schedule 1 do not underlie disclosure. Disclosure to domestic authorities by way of call procedure (Article 13 VwbPG), disclosure to banks and financial institutions (Article 15 VwbPG), and disclosure to persons subject to professional KYC obligations (Article 16 VwbPG) is reserved and regulated by the respective sections of the VwbPG which have been discussed previously.

The application under Article 17 paragraph 4 VwbPG must contain detailed information about the applicant, the firm or name of the legal entity whose data are to be disclosed, the use of the requested data, as well as proof of a legitimate interest (paragraph 6) or of participation that establishes control (paragraph 7).

According to Article 17 paragraph 6 VwbPG, a legitimate interest is given if the use of the requested data for the aim of combating money laundering, predicate offences of money laundering and terrorist finance can be made credible.

A participation that establishes control under Article 17 paragraph 6 VwbPG is given when a trust or a similar legal arrangement that is entered in the BO Register holds a direct or indirect participation of 25% or more in a company or legal person having its seat in a third state (ie, a state that is not a member of the European Economic Area).

Upon receipt of the application for disclosure of the registered data of legal entities that are not considered stand-alone legal entities according to Schedule 1 according to Article 17 paragraph 4 VwbPG, the Office of Justice must obtain an opinion from the legal entity affected by the disclosure whether a legitimate interest (paragraph 6) or a participation that establishes control (paragraph 7) is given, and furthermore a declaration by the affected legal entity whether there is a founder or protector exercising control over the respective legal entity.

The Office of Justice then forwards this application, according to Article 17 paragraph 4 VwbPG, including the corresponding documents to the VwbP Commission[22] (ie, the Commission on the Register of Beneficial Owners), which shall decide whether disclosure of the registered data of entities that are not considered stand-alone legal entities according to Schedule 1 shall be granted or not. The VwbP Commission shall decline the disclosure of data on the beneficial owners if the application, despite express request, does not contain the necessary information and documents, if a founder or protector does not

---

22 The VwbP Commission consists of three to five members and three deputies. The president and his/her deputy are appointed by the government; both must be legally trained. The members and deputies are recruited from the financial services and data protection sectors. They are independent in exercising their functions. The members and deputies are appointed for a period of four years; re-election is possible. The decision of the commission is taken by simple majority of the members and deputies present. In a tie the president, respectively his/her deputy, has the casting vote.

exercise control over a non-stand-alone legal entity according to Schedule 1, if a restriction for disclosure on account of protection of legitimate interests according to Article 18 VwbPG applies, if sufficient use of the data or a legitimate interest are not given, or if there is no participation according to paragraph 7 that establishes control.

If, at the time of the request, a proceeding to restrict disclosure of data due to protection of legitimate interests (Article 18 VwbPG) is already pending or is opened during such application for disclosure, then according to Article 17 paragraph 9 VwbPG, any proceeding to disclose data to third persons is suspended *ex lege* until a legally binding decision on the restriction to disclose is reached.

The disclosure of data shall be made by the Office of Justice upon the legally binding decision of the VwbP Commission on a request pursuant to paragraph 4. The affected legal entity shall not have the status of a party in proceedings for the disclosure of data to third parties.

The issuance of a statement or declaration by the legal entity pursuant to paragraph 8 is reserved. The legal entity concerned shall be informed about the disclosure made.

(f) ***Restrictions on data disclosure – protection of legitimate interests***

Article 18 VwbPG is a core provision as the Office of Justice can – upon application of a legal entity – fully or partially restrict disclosure of data to domestic persons subject to professional KYC obligations (Article 16 VwbPG), as well as to third persons (Article 17 VwbPG), if the legal entity proves that such disclosure in consideration of all circumstances of the case at hand would violate prevailing legitimate interests of its beneficial owners.

Such would be the case if, through the disclosure, a beneficial owner were exposed to a disproportionate risk of fraud, kidnapping, blackmailing, racketeering, harassment, violence or intimidation, or if the beneficial owner is a minor or otherwise incapacitated.

The restriction according to Article 18 VwbPG is granted for a period of five years; in case of minors it is granted until they become of age. If the conditions for the granting of the restriction cease to exist before this period expires, the legal entity in question must inform the Office of Justice in writing. A restriction to disclose can also be prolonged if the legal entity proves to the Office of Justice that prevailing legitimate interests of the beneficial owners continue to being opposed to the disclosure of the data.

The Office of Justice shall annually publish on its website statistical data on the number of restrictions granted and its reasons in general form, and submit these to the EFTA Surveillance Authority (ESA).

2.7 Supervision and enforcement

(a) Supervision and enforcement

Supervision and enforcement of the VwbPG are reserved to the Office of Justice, the FMA and the VwbP Commission. The Office of Justice, the FMA, the FIU, the police, the tax authorities, the public prosecutor and the court are obliged to work closely together, with a view to combating money laundering, corresponding predicate offences and terrorist financing, and to provide one another either spontaneously or upon request with all information, documentation and personal data, including personal data on criminal convictions and offences.

(b) Controls

Controls under the VwbPG are threefold. Control functions rest with the Office of Justice, the FMA and independent third persons. The enforcement of the VwbPG is subject to official secrecy, which also binds the independent third persons.

The Office of Justice keeps the BO Register according to Article 6 VwbPG and discloses the data according to Article 13 *et seq* VwbPG. It supervises the compliance with the provisions of the VwbPG and the related implementation ordinances. In particular the Office of Justice is also empowered to control the completeness as well as the plausibility of the registered data. It is equipped with all necessary powers to fulfil its functions and may obtain from the legal entities and their organs all information that is necessary for the enforcement of the VwbPG.

If the notification of data cannot be obtained, the Office of Justice may order the liquidation of a legal entity according to Schedules 1 and 2. In addition, the Office of Justice is empowered to notify the FIU, according to Article 17 of the Due Diligence Act, when a suspicion of money laundering, a predicate offence to money laundering, organised crime or terrorist financing arises.

If there is reason to believe that a legal entity has circumvented provisions of the VwbPG, the Office of Justice may itself conduct controls or empower third persons (ie, auditors) to do so. The legal entities are obliged to grant to the Office of Justice, as well as to these third persons, unlimited access to all information that is relevant with a view to the fulfilment of their obligations under the VwbPG and thus for their controls.

With a view to legal entities that are subject to professional KYC obligations or which have at least one organ that is subject to professional KYC obligations and which are placed under the supervision of the FMA, the FMA is entitled to randomly review the matching of the data collected under the VwbPG with the data collected under the Due Diligence Act. The FMA may also empower third persons to conduct these controls. Should the collected data not match, the

FMA shall file a report to the Office of Justice. If an administrative or other minor mistake has led to an incorrect or incomplete transmission of data, the Office of Justice requests the legal entity in question to repair this mistake within a certain timeframe. Penal provisions are reserved.

(c) *Legal remedies*

Complaint against decrees or decisions of the Office of Justice or the VwbPG Commission can be made within 14 days of service to the Complaint Commission for Administrative Matters. Further complaint against decisions of the Complaint Commission for Administrative Matters can be made to the Administrative Court.

2.8 Penal provisions

The penal provisions stipulate either imprisonment or financial penalties, depending on the offence. Punishable by imprisonment are the obtainment of information from the Office of Justice or the VwPG Commission under false pretences, and also the use of data received from the Office of Justice for another purpose than originally stated in an application.

The Office of Justice will punish violations that do not fall within the competence of the court with a fine of up to Sfr200,000 if a person does not comply or does not comply in a timely manner with his/her obligations under the VwbPG, respectively if a person does not fully fulfil them or fulfils them in a manner that is not correct in content, or if a person impedes the proper execution of controls or does not respond to a request of the Office of Justice to complete or rectify data or to rectify discrepancies. Negligent conduct reduces the fines by half.

If a legal entity commits violations, the penalties apply to the members of the management and other natural persons who acted or should have acted for the legal entity under joint liability of the legal entity for monetary penalties, fines and costs.

2.9 Entry into force, repeal of VwEG, amendment of Due Diligence Act

The VwbPG, as well as the VwbPV Ordinance, entered into force on 1 April 2021. The VwEG of 6 December 2018 and the VwEV of 28 January 2020 thereby were repealed in their entirety. Legal entities that were in existence on the date of the entry into force had to report the data on their beneficial owners to the Office of Justice within six months after the entry into force of the VwbPG. Persons subject to professional KYC obligations had to report any discrepancies only after the expiry of the above-mentioned six-month period. To proceedings on the disclosure of data that are pending upon entry into force of the VwbPG, the old VwEG continues to apply.

Upon entry into force of the VwbPG, the Due Diligence Act was amended in the sense that persons subject to professional KYC obligations will henceforth have to request an extract from the BO Register when entering into a business relationship with a legal entity that is obliged to report the beneficial owners to the Office of Justice, for the first time after the expiry of six months after the entry into force of the amended Due Diligence Act.

Luxembourg

Paolo Panico
Paolo Panico's Law Chambers; Private Trustees SA

1. Introduction

Ultimate beneficial ownership registers (UBO registers) of companies and trusts were established in Luxembourg pursuant to the Fifth EU Anti-Money Laundering Directive (5AMLD).[1] No enactments had taken place in relation to the corresponding provisions under the Fourth EU Anti-Money Laundering Directive (4AMLD).[2]

The UBO register of Luxembourg companies and other corporate legal entities (*Registre des Bénéficiaires Effectifs* – RBE) was created under the Law of 13 January 2019 establishing a Register of Beneficial Owners[3] (the Law of 13 January 2019). A Grand Ducal Regulation of 15 February 2019 relating to the ways to register information, to pay administrative duties, and to the access to information in the Register of Beneficial Owners[4] (the Grand Ducal Regulation of 15 February 2019) introduced the required implementing provisions. The Law of 13 January 2019 came into force on 1 March 2019 and all the Luxembourg entities that were in existence at the time had to register the personal details of their beneficial owners by 30 November 2019. The RBE has been in existence and fully accessible by the general public since the last quarter of 2019.

A UBO register of trusts and fiduciary agreements was introduced under the Law of 10 July 2020 establishing a Register of *Fiducies* and Trusts[5] (the Law of 10 July 2020). As of the time of writing[6] no Grand Ducal Regulation had been enacted to clarify a number of practical aspects for the Law of 10 July 2020 to come into force.

---

1 Directive (EU) 2018/843 of the European Parliament and of the Council of 30 May 2018 amending Directive (EU) 2015/849 on the prevention of the use of the financial system for the purposes of money laundering or terrorist financing, and amending Directives 2009/138/EC and 2013/36/EU.
2 Directive (EU) 2015/849.
3 *Loi du 13 janvier 2013 instituant un Registre des bénéficiaires effectifs.*
4 *Règlement Grand-Ducal du 15 février 2019 relatif aux modalités d'inscription, de paiement des frais administratifs ainsi qu'à l'accès aux informations inscrites au Registre des bénéficiaires effectifs.*
5 *Loi du 10 juillet 2010 instituant un Registre des fiducies et trusts.*
6 31 March 2021.

2. The UBO Register of companies

The Law of 13 January 2019 establishing a Register of Beneficial Owners created the RBE, which is maintained by Luxembourg Business Registers (LBR), the same authority in charge of the Luxembourg Register of Commerce (*Registre de Commerce et des Sociétés* – RCS) and the Electronic Journal of Companies and Associations (*Recueil Electronique des Sociétés et Associations* – RESA).

2.1 Which entities are obliged to register?

All Luxembourg corporate entities registered with the Register of Commerce have an obligation to register the details of their beneficial owners in the RBE.[7] The actual list is established by reference to Article 1, items 2 to 15, of the Law of 19 December 2002 concerning the Register of Commerce, as well as the bookkeeping and annual financial statements of companies.[8] The full list of the concerned entities is as follows:

- commercial companies (except temporary companies and silent partnerships);
- economic interest groupings;
- european economic interest groupings (*Groupements Européens d'Intérêt Economique* – GEIE);
- luxembourg branches of commercial and civil companies or of economic interest groupings governed by the law of another country;
- civil companies;
- non-profit associations (*associations sans but lucratif* – ASBL);
- foundations;
- pension savings associations (*associations d'épargne pension*);
- agricultural associations;
- public establishments of the State and the municipalities;
- mutual insurance associations;
- special limited partnerships (*sociétés en commandite spéciale* – SCSp);
- investment funds; and
- mutualities.

In practice, all corporate entities under Luxembourg law, whether or not they qualify as legal persons, must file the details of their ultimate beneficial owners in the RBE. As is common in most civil law jurisdictions, Luxembourg company law distinguishes between civil companies (*sociétés civiles*), which are governed by the Civil Code[9] and are primarily used to hold real estate, and commercial companies (*sociétés commerciales*), which are governed by the Law of

---

7 Law of 13 January 2019, Article 1(4).

8 *Loi modifiée du 19 décembre 2002 concernant le registre de commerce et des sociétés ainsi que la comptabilité et les comptes annuels des entreprises.*

9 Articles 1832–1873.

19 August 1915 concerning commercial companies, as amended.[10] Commercial companies may be incorporated in a variety of forms, some of which correspond to partnerships in the common law tradition.

All corporate entities that were in existence when the Law of 13 January 2019 came into force had to make their filings by 30 November 2019. All newly incorporated entities must make their entries in the RBE within 30 days of their incorporation or of a relevant change in their beneficial ownership structure.[11]

Fines ranging from €1,250 to €1.25 million may be meted out to companies failing to register the information of their beneficial owners with the RBE or intentionally filing inaccurate, incomplete or outdated information.[12] The same fine may be meted out to a beneficial owner who fails to provide a corporate entity with the information required to discharge its obligations in relation to the RBE.[13]

2.2 Who are the beneficial owners?

The statutory definition of 'beneficial owners' for the purposes of the Register of Beneficial Owners (RBE)[14] is made by reference to Article 1(7) of the Law of 12 November 2004 relating to the fight against money laundering and terrorist financing, as amended[15] (the AML Law).

Article 1(7)(a) of the Luxembourg AML Law is very similar to Article 3(6)(a) of 5AMLD and defines the beneficial owners of corporate entities. These fall essentially into two categories:

- individuals ultimately owning or controlling a corporate entity by their direct or indirect ownership or control of more than 25% of its shares or voting rights; and
- individuals controlling a corporate entity via other means.

Some examples of the 'other means' of control were inserted into the AML Law under an amending Law of 25 March 2020 and they encompass the following cases:

- a right to exercise a controlling influence over a corporate entity by virtue of a contractual agreement or provisions in its articles of incorporation (*statuts*);
- the circumstance that the majority of the board members of a corporate entity were appointed as a consequence of the direct or indirect exercise of the voting rights of an individual;
- the direct or indirect power to exercise a controlling influence over a

10 *Loi modifiée du 10 août 1915 concernant les sociétés commerciales.*
11 Law of 13 January 2019, Article 4(1).
12 Law of 13 January 2019, Article 20.
13 Law of 13 January 2019, Article 21(3).
14 Law of 13 January 2019, Article 1(3).
15 *Loi modifiée du 12 novembre 2004 relative à la lutte contre le blanchiment et contre le financement du terrorisme.*

corporate entity, also because it is under a common control with another entity; and
- an obligation for the parent company of a corporate entity to establish consolidated financial reports.

The default option in the event that no beneficial owner can be identified meeting the statutory definitions above is to indicate as 'beneficial owners' any natural persons holding the office of principal manager (*toute personne physique qui occupe la position de dirigeant principal*) of the concerned entity. This provision was construed under a frequently asked question (FAQ) published by the RBE as an obligation to list the entire board of directors of the concerned entity, including all the directors who hold office in a non-executive capacity, and not only the chairpersons or managing directors.

In accordance with the corresponding provision under 5AMLD, companies listed on regulated markets are exempt from the obligation to file the information of their beneficial owners in the RBE due to the transparency requirements by which they have to abide in such regulated markets.

2.3 Which information on the beneficial owners must be filed in the RBE?

Filings in the RBE are made electronically via the website of the Luxembourg Business Registers.[16]

Anybody making such filings must first confirm that they are empowered to enter the relevant information in relation to a certain company.

They must then select the case applying to the relevant entity:

- a corporate entity that is listed on a regulated market;
- a corporate entity that has no beneficial owners and, as a result, its board members are listed as such; or
- a corporate entity for which the details of one or more beneficial owners are filed.

If the corporate entity qualified in the latter category, its beneficial owners can be distinguished in two groups: (i) those who have a Luxembourg taxpayer's identification number (TIN); and (ii) those who do not.

If beneficial owners have a Luxembourg TIN, there is no requirement to upload a copy of their identity documents (IDs) to complete the filing. For beneficial owners who do not possess a Luxembourg TIN, an identification number is created on the grounds of their ID (eg, their passport number). In their case, a copy of that ID must be filed with the application.[17] No ID copy is published in the RBE, but its contents are verified to confirm the accuracy of the filing.

---

16 www.lbr.lu.
17 Law of 13 January 2019, Article 4(3); Grand Ducal Regulation of 15 February 2019, Article 5.

The following information is entered for each beneficial owner:

- name, surname;
- place and date of birth;
- nationality (or nationalities);
- residential or professional address; and
- type and extent of his/her beneficial interest.

Although this information must be filed in full, only the country of residence (and not the full address) and the place, month and year of birth (not the exact birth date) may be seen by the general public in the RBE.

2.4 Who can access the RBE?

Unrestricted access to the RBE is granted to:

- national authorities;
- professionals subject to AML obligations for the purposes of their corporate due diligence; and
- the general public.

A list of the 'national authorities' that have unlimited access to the RBE is provided under Article 1(5) of the Law of 13 January 2019:

- the attorney general and public prosecutors;
- investigating judges;
- the Financial Intelligence Unit (*Cellule de Renseignement Financier* – CRF);
- Certain judicial police officers;
- the Financial Market Supervisory Authority (*Commission de Surveillance du Secteur Financier* – CSSF);
- the Insurance Supervisory Authority (*Commissariat aux Assurances* – CAA);
- the Tax Authority in charge of stamp duties, estate tax and VAT (*Administration de l'Enregistrement, des Domaines et de la TVA* – AED);
- the Customs and excise tax authority;
- the State intelligence services (*Service de Renseignement de l'Etat* – SRE);
- the Tax Authority in charge of direct taxes (*Administration des Contributions Directes* – ACD);
- the Ministry of Foreign and European Affairs in the context of its specific competences in the fight against money laundering and terrorist financing;
- the Ministry of Finance in the context of its specific competences in the fight against money laundering and terrorist financing; and
- the Office in charge of export, import and traffic control.

Furthermore, access to the RBE is open to anybody (*à toute personne*).[18]

18 Law of 13 January 2019, Article 12.

The RBE can be freely accessed online via the website of the Luxembourg Business Registers.[19] The website cannot be searched by individual beneficial owner, but only by corporate name or registration number.[20] The fact that no search is authorised by the name of an individual, but only by the corporate name or registration number of a company was intended as a measure to maintain a limited protection of the privacy of beneficial owners.[21]

The legitimacy of the Luxembourg RBE in light of the fundamental right to privacy and the principle of proportionality, which are guaranteed under Articles 7, 8 and 52 of the EU Charter of Fundamental Rights, is the subject matter of a case which was referred to the European Court of Justice (ECJ) in the last quarter of 2020. The complaint was also framed under the contention that unrestricted public access to the information in the Register of Beneficial Owners is a breach of the EU General Data Protection Regulation (GDPR).[22] The ECJ decision on this fundamental matter will have a bearing not only on Luxembourg, but also on the beneficial ownership registers that have been put in place all over the European Union pursuant to 4AMLD and 5AMLD.

2.5 How may beneficial owners restrict public access to their personal information?

Article 15 of the Law of 13 January 2019 allows beneficial owners to request a restriction of public access to their personal information.

A corporate entity or its beneficial owners may file a motivated application to this effect if they believe that public access to the information of their beneficial owners may expose them to a disproportionate risk of fraud, kidnapping, blackmail, extortion, harassment, violence or intimidation, or where the beneficial owner is a minor or otherwise legally incapable. The text of this provision is crafted after Article 30(9) of 5AMLD and as a result is meant to apply on a case-by-case basis and in exceptional circumstances.[23]

An application under Article 15 of the Law of 13 January 2019 does not exempt a company from filing the information on its beneficial owners with the RBE. In fact, such an application can be filed only after the relevant information has been disclosed to the RBE. In the event that the required restriction is granted, the beneficial ownership information shall be accessible only to the national authorities, banking and financial institutions, and bailiffs and notaries acting in their capacity as public officials.

A restriction of public access may be granted for a maximum period of three

19 Grand Ducal Regulation of 15 February 2019, Article 7(1).
20 Grand Ducal Regulation of 15 February 2019, Article 7(2).
21 Nonetheless, it should be noted that some European daily newspapers downloaded the entire RBE with a view to making it searchable by individual names and relied on such downloads to issue a series of sensationalist articles in February 2021.
22 Regulation EU 2016/679.
23 Law of 13 January 2019, Article 15(1).

years and may be renewed on the grounds of a new motivated application filed within one month of the expiry of the restriction.[24]

In the event that the application is rejected, any interested party may file a complaint (*recours*) to the president of the district commercial court. The matter is heard and judged as a summary procedure (*procédure en référé*).[25]

Until the matter is definitively settled, the information of the beneficial owners concerned is not made available to the public.[26]

The option to file an application under Article 15 of the Law of 13 January 2019 is provided at the end of the online filing process. As a last step to a filing of beneficial ownership information in the RBE, one must confirm whether an application to restrict public access to such information will be added or not.

In 2019 all the filings to the RBE, whether or not they included an application to restrict public access, were accepted by way of a confirmation email. In the course of 2020 the RBE reviewed the applications under Article 15 of the Law of 13 January 2019 and rejected most of them. Apart from a formal point as to whether the original confirmation email should be interpreted also in respect of the filing under Article 15 of the Law (as no mention was made of a further deliberation to that effect), a more fundamental issue appears to be raised by this procedure. The authority in charge of the RBE appears to be taking the view that an application should clearly set out the actual grounds on which an individual may be directly exposed to a disproportionate risk of fraud, kidnapping, blackmail, extortion, harassment, violence or intimidation. A general inference based on the personal situation of the applicants and factors such as their wealth, country of residence, nationality, or involvement in certain industries and activities was not judged to be sufficient in the vast majority of cases.

A number of complaints were filed to this effect and one of them was deferred to the ECJ (Case C 37/20) with a view to obtaining the European Court's view on the correct interpretation of the requirements to obtain a restriction to public access of beneficial ownership information. This case will be significant for the whole of the European Union as it will provide a construction of Article 30(9) of 5AMLD, which should prompt a single and consistent handling of these cases in the entire bloc. This decision, as well as the one on the case referred to in the previous paragraph, which questions the very legitimacy of publicly accessible UBO registers, will shape the future of this area of European law and may have an impact on the international practice of this kind of register.

24 Law of 13 January 2019, Article 15(3).
25 Law of 13 January 2019, Articles 15(5) and 7(3).
26 Law of 13 January 2019, Article 15(2).

3. The UBO Register of trusts

As a civil law jurisdiction, Luxembourg does not have trusts in its domestic legal system. However, trusts have been recognised since 2004 pursuant to the Hague Convention of 1 July 1985 on the Law Applicable to Trusts and on their Recognition (the Hague Trusts Convention), which was ratified under the Law of 27 July 2003 relating to trusts and fiduciary contracts.[27] The Hague Trusts Convention allows trusts governed by a foreign law to be enforced and administered in Luxembourg in the absence of a domestic trust law, similar to the situation in other civil law countries that have ratified the convention, such as Italy and Switzerland. The Luxembourg legal system also includes a domestic trust-like contractual arrangement known as a fiduciary contract (*contrat fiduciaire*) or '*fiducie*', which is equally regulated under the Law of 27 July 2003 which ratified the Hague Trusts Convention.[28]

The Law of 10 July 2020 establishing a Register of *Fiducies* and Trusts (the Law of 10 July 2020) implemented Article 31 of 5AMLD and created the Register of *Fiducies* and Trusts (RFT). Unlike the RBE, the RFT is not maintained by the Luxembourg Business Registers and is not freely open to the public. The RFT is maintained by the Tax Authority in charge of stamp duties, estate tax and VAT (*Administration de l'Enregistrement et des Domaines* – AED).[29]

3.1 Which arrangements are obliged to register?

Fiduciary contracts and express trusts where a fiduciary or a trustee is resident or has its registered office in Luxembourg are bound to be registered in the RFT.[30]

An 'express trust' (*trust exprès*) is defined under Article 1(1)(12) of the Law of 10 July 2020 as "a trust clearly established by the settlor, usually by means of a document such as a trust instrument in writing". The statutory definition goes on to say that such a trust is different from trusts resulting from the operation of the law and not from the clear intention of a settlor to create a trust or an equivalent legal arrangement. In other words, only express trusts and not resulting or constructive trusts (which may be enforceable in Luxembourg under the Hague Trusts Convention) must register the details of their beneficial owners in the RFT.

Where the fiduciaries or the trustees of a fiduciary contract or a trust are resident in different EU member states, the proof that the fiduciary contract or the trust has been registered in the equivalent UBO register of another EU member state is sufficient to exempt it from also registering in the Luxembourg RFT.

---

27 *Loi du 27 juillet 2003 relative au trust et aux contrats fiduciaires.*

28 Additional details on trusts and fiduciary contracts in Luxembourg may be found in my 'Luxembourg' chapter in A Kaplan (ed), *Trusts in Prime Jurisdictions, Fifth Edition* (Globe Law and Business, 2019).

29 Law of 10 July 2020, Article 12.

30 Law of 10 July 2020, Article 13(1).

Where the fiduciaries or the trustees of a fiduciary contract or a trust are all resident outside the European Union, the fiduciary contract or the trust must be registered in the Luxembourg RFT if the fiduciary or the trustee:

- enters into a business relationship with a Luxembourg 'professional' on behalf of that fiduciary contract or trust; or
- acquires a piece of real estate in Luxembourg.[31]

The notion of 'professional' is expressly defined by reference to Article 2 of the Luxembourg AML Law, which lists all the professionals subject to AML obligations.

The extraterritorial extension of the obligation to register in the Luxembourg RFT to a trust administered outside the European Union if the conditions above are met is consistent with Article 31(3a) of 5AMLD.

Article 1(2) of the Law of 10 July 2020 further expands the scope of the law by extending the obligation to register with the RFT to all legal arrangements that have a structure or functions similar to trusts. Such equivalent legal arrangements are defined along the same lines of Article 2 of the Hague Trusts Convention, which defines a legal arrangement that can be recognised as a 'trust' in the ratifying states.

The information of the beneficial owners of express trusts and fiduciary contracts must be filed with the RFT within one month of the event determining a change.[32] It is expected that a Grand Ducal Regulation will indicate a term within which all the existing trusts and fiduciary contracts will have to be registered.

Fines of a maximum of twice the financial advantage derived from non-compliance with the obligation to register with the RFT and in any case no more than €1.25 million may be meted out by the AED to non-compliant trustees and fiduciaries.[33]

3.2 Who are the beneficial owners?

Similar to the corresponding definition for the purposes of the RBE, the beneficial owners of fiduciary contracts and trusts are defined with reference to Article 1(7) of the AML Law.[34]

In particular, Article 1(7)(b) of the AML Law lists all the following persons as beneficial owners of a trust:

- the settlor(s);
- the trustee(s) or fiduciarie(s);
- the protector(s) if any;

31 Law of 10 July 2020, Article 13(2).
32 Law of 10 July 2020, Article 15.
33 Law of 10 July 2020, Article 22(2)(4).
34 Law of 10 July 2020, Article 1(1)(3).

- the beneficiaries, or where the individuals benefiting from the trust have yet to be determined, the class of persons in whose main interest the trust is set up or operates; and
- any other natural person exercising ultimate control over the trust by means of direct or indirect ownership or by other means.

This definition, which attempts to catch all the individuals who have any relationship to a trust, is consistent with the approach promoted under Recommendation 25 of the Financial Action Task Force (FATF) and with the corresponding definition under Article 3(6)(b) of 5AMLD.

Article 1(7)(c) of the AML Law provides that the natural persons holding equivalent or similar positions to those listed above shall be identified as the beneficial owners of legal arrangements similar to trusts and legal entities such as foundations.

Private foundations are unknown to Luxembourg law.[35] Charitable foundations are governed under the Law of 21 April 1928 on non-profit associations and foundations, as amended.[36] Circular LBR 19/03 was issued by the authority in charge of the RBE to specify that foundations must file the details of their beneficial owners with the RBE, and that in their case the beneficial owners are the founder(s) and the member(s) of the board of directors. Foundations are registered in the RBE not in the RFT because of their nature as incorporated legal entities. Due to their charitable nature and the relatively complex authorisation process by which they come into being, unrestricted public access to the personal details of their founders and directors is much less harmful than it would be if they could be used for private estate planning purposes.

3.3 Who can have access to the RFT?

The national authorities, which are defined under Article 1(1)(1) of the Law of 10 July 2020 in an identical way to Article 1(5) of the Law of 13 January 2019 for the purposes of the RBE, have unrestricted access to the information in the RFT.[37]

The professionals subject to AML obligations can access the RFT for the purposes of their customer due diligence.[38]

In addition to that, the information in the RFT may be accessed by anybody who demonstrates a legitimate interest in the context of the fight against

35 Bill 6595 was filed with the Luxembourg Parliament on 22 July 2013 with a view to establishing "patrimonial foundations", but was unfortunately never voted.

36 *Loi modifiée du 21 avril 1928 sur les associations et les fondations sans but lucratif.*

37 Law of 10 July 2020, Article 25.

38 Law of 10 July 2020, Article 26(2).

money laundering and terrorist financing.[39] Access is granted on a case-by-case basis pursuant to a decision by the director of the AED.

A written and motivated application must be filed to that effect in relation to one single trust or fiduciary contract, which may be identified by its registration number (issued on its registration with the RFT), its name, its date of creation, or the name and surname of its settlor(s).[40] The application must include the following information on pain of being considered void:

- the personal details of the applicants (whether they are individuals or organisations);
- the identification details of the trust or fiduciary contract; and
- the grounds for the application and the purposes for which the information is requested.

The director of the AED considers all the relevant circumstances that may indicate whether the information is being requested in the context of the fight against money laundering and terrorist financing. It is expressly provided that the director of the AED, in reaching a decision to this effect, must take into account the protection of the fundamental rights of individuals – in particular, the right to private life and to the protection of personal data.

The decision of the director of the AED is notified within one month to the applicant, as well as to the concerned beneficial owners.[41]

A complaint (*recours*) against the decision may be filed with the Luxembourg administrative court (*Tribunal Administratif*) within one month of the decision.[42] The information of the beneficial owners of the concerned trust or fiduciary contract is not made available to the applicant until a final decision is made. It must be noted that unlike the procedure relating to the request of a restriction of public access to the RBE,[43] which allows summary proceedings by way of urgency, in the case of the RFT it is an ordinary administrative procedure which may be further appealed to the administrative court of appeal (*Cour Administrative*). A significant period of time may therefore elapse between the filing of a written application and the actual access to the requested information. This approach appears to strike an appropriate balance between the objective of increased transparency in relation to trusts and fiduciary contracts on the one hand, and the protection of the fundamental right to privacy of the concerned individuals on the other. It must not be forgotten that Luxembourg shares the same civil code as France, the '*Code Napoléon*', and as a result the French Constitutional Court Decision 2016-591 QPC of 21 October 2016 "Miss Helen S",

39 Law of 10 July 2020, Article 27(1).
40 Law of 10 July 2020, Article 27(2).
41 Law of 10 July 2020, Article 27(4).
42 Law of 10 July 2020, Article 27(5).
43 Law of 13 January 2019, Article 15.

which outlawed unrestricted public access to a UBO register of trusts as contrary to the Declaration of the Rights of Man and the Citizen of 1789 (*Déclaration des Droits de l'Homme et du Citoyen*), has a bearing over Luxembourg law.

If as a result of this administrative procedure the decision by the director of the AED to make the information available to the applicant is upheld, an extract from the RFT is issued. The extract states the purposes for which the information is made available and the applicant is bound to use the information exclusively for those purposes. A fine of between €1,250 and €1.25m may be meted out in case of use of the information for purposes other than those specified in the extract.[44]

In one case the information in the RFT can be directly accessed by any member of the public without a legitimate interest test. If a trust holds a controlling interest in a company outside the European Union or the European Economic Area,[45] the information of its beneficial owners may be accessed simply by virtue of a written application to the director of the AED.[46]

To that effect, the registration procedure in the RFT includes a mention of whether a trust includes such a controlling interest in a company outside the European Union and the European Economic Area.[47]

This special treatment of trusts possessing a controlling interest in a company outside the European Union and the European Economic Area is consistent with Article 31(4)(d) of 5AMLD, which includes the same provision. Nevertheless, its rationale is not immediately clear, especially to the extent that the geographic reference to the European Union and the European Economic Area is not made explicitly but by a mention of Article 30(1) of the same AML directive (the obligation to create a UBO register of corporate entities). It may be opined that the background to this provision is the fact that all EU member states and the countries included in the European Economic Area must create UBO registers of their companies and other corporate entities, while third countries may not offer comparable levels of transparency. Nonetheless, since 1 January 2021 the United Kingdom is no longer a member state of the European Union and yet it is the Western country that pioneered the creation of a fully public UBO register of companies with its 'PSC Register' in 2016. If unrestricted public access to the UBO register of trusts is contrary to the right to privacy as established under the Declaration of the Rights of Man and the Citizen of 1789, it is not clear why the information of the beneficial owners of a trust with a controlling interest in a corporate entity outside of the European Union and the European Economic Area can be freely accessed without the requirement to demonstrate a legitimate interest as in all the other cases.

44 Law of 10 July 2020, Article 28.
45 The European Economic Area includes Iceland, Liechtenstein and Norway.
46 Law of 10 July 2020, Article 29.
47 Law of 10 July 2020, Article 14(1)(5).

3.4 How may beneficial owners restrict public access to their personal information?

Unlike the RBE, the RFT is not freely accessible to the general public. Apart from the case of trusts with a controlling interest in a company outside of the European Union and the European Economic Area, the information may be accessed only by virtue of a successful application where the applicant must demonstrate a legitimate interest in the context of the fight against money laundering and terrorist financing. Such an application cannot be to access the RFT generally but must aim at one particular trust. A decision by the AED to make such information available is first notified to the concerned beneficial owners, who may file an appeal and effectively 'freeze' the information for some time. This system provides an adequate protection of the fundamental rights of the beneficial owners of trusts and fiduciary contracts without undermining the existence and the functions of the RFT.

Nevertheless, a procedure similar to the one stipulated under Article 15 of the Law of 13 January 2019 in relation to the RBE also exists for the RFT. Article 31(1) of the Law of 10 July 2020 provides that in exceptional circumstances the beneficial owner of a trust may request a restriction to public access to his/her personal information if he/she would otherwise be exposed to a disproportionate risk of fraud, kidnapping, blackmail, extortion, harassment, violence or intimidation, or where the beneficial owner is a minor or otherwise legally incapable. In that case the information shall be made available only to the national authorities, banking and financial institutions, and bailiffs and notaries acting in their capacity as public officials.

A restriction to public access may be granted on a detailed assessment of the exceptional nature of the circumstances justifying it and for a maximum duration of three years, which may be renewed under a new application.[48] A complaint (*recours*) may be filed with the Luxembourg administrative court (*Tribunal Administratif*) within one month of the relevant decision.[49]

3.5 Entry into force

Article 17 of the Law of 10 July 2020 provides that the way to make electronic filings to the RFT shall be determined under a Grand Ducal Regulation.

Other aspects of the law shall be determined under a Grand Ducal Regulation, such as access by the national authorities to the RFT[50] and the duty payable by a member of the public to access the information in compliance with the required procedure.[51]

The procedure to make a filing with the AED in relation to a trust or a

48 Law of 10 July 2020, Article 31(3).
49 Law of 10 July 2020, Article 31(5).
50 Law of 10 July 2020, Article 25(2).
51 Law of 10 July 2020, Article 27(6).

fiduciary contract was published online on the website of the Luxembourg public administration.[52]

However, in the absence of a Grand Ducal Regulation as provided under the Law of 10 July 2020, it can be argued that the RFT is not yet in force at the time of writing.[53]

4. The case of a Luxembourg company controlled by a trust

No mention is made either in the Law of 13 January 2019 or in the Grand Ducal Regulation of 15 February 2019 of the case of a Luxembourg company controlled by a trust. The case was not contemplated in the additions to Article 1(7)(a) of the AML Law, which were inserted under the amending law of 25 March 2020.

The case of a company controlled by a trust was not covered by any of the FAQs or Circulars issued by the LBR in its capacity as authority in charge of the RBE to assist in the determination of the beneficial owners in a variety of cases.

As a result, three different views appear to be entertained by different Luxembourg professionals in this respect.

One approach suggests that all the persons listed in Article 1(7)(b) of the AML Law should be disclosed in the RBE in respect of a trust controlling a Luxembourg company.

This approach appears to be inconsistent with the letter and the spirit of 5AMLD and the Luxembourg AML Law. The beneficial owners for the purposes of the RBE are those mentioned in Article 1(7)(a) of the AML Law (ie, the individuals controlling more than 25% of a company or exercising ultimate control by other means). Article 1(7)(b) of the AML Law on the other hand lists the beneficial owners of trusts with no reference to their underlying companies. To the extent that the RBE grants unrestricted public access to its information, it would be a breach of the fundamental right to privacy of a number of individuals, ranging from settlors who are excluded from benefit to beneficiaries who are mere objects of the trustee's discretion, if their personal information were disclosed in the RBE. Of course, the personal details of all these individuals must be filed with the RFT in compliance with Article 1(7)(b) of the AML Law, but the RFT is not freely accessible to the general public.

Confusion in relation to this approach was generated by an incorrect construction of the Circular CSSF 19/732 of 20 December 2019, where the Financial Market Supervisory Authority (*Commission de Surveillance du Secteur Financier* – CSSF) indicated the criteria that financial intermediaries must follow to identify the beneficial owners of a variety of legal arrangements. Quite rightly, the CSSF followed Article 1(7)(b) of the AML Law and recommended that all the persons listed there must be identified by a financial intermediary

52 https://guichet.pulic.lu.
53 31 March 2021.

prior to entering into a business relationship with a trust. This is correct in the context of the customer due diligence which must be performed by financial intermediaries. It has nothing to do with the obligation of company directors to publish the information of the beneficial owners of their companies in the RBE, a matter which is outside the remit of the CSSF.

A second approach considers that in the context of most irrevocable and discretionary trusts, no individual can be identified who meets the statutory definition of a 'beneficial owner' under Article 1(7)(a) of the AML Law. As a result, the recommended approach is the default option that consists in listing all the directors of the concerned company as beneficial owners.

This approach is not as extreme as the previous one and does not involve a potential liability of company directors for breaching the fundamental right to privacy of a number of alleged 'beneficial owners' and for non-compliance with the GDPR. Nonetheless, in many circumstances it can be argued that some representatives of the trustee and perhaps of the protector can be described as 'individuals exercising ultimate control by other means' over the underlying company, and as such should be registered in the RBE.

For this reason, a third approach suggests applying the definition of Article 1(7)(a) of the AML Law to each individual case to identify whether they are exercising indirect control in excess of 25% or controlling influence by other means.

STEP Benelux issued a Position Paper to this effect in 2019, where the following three examples can be found.[54]

- **A revocable trust controlling a Luxembourg company:** In that case the settlor, who has retained the right to revoke the trust and take back the company shares, must be registered as a beneficial owner of the company; the representatives of the trustee may be disclosed as well based on their actual powers.
- **An interest in possession trust (or 'fixed trust') controlling a Luxembourg company:** If any beneficiaries have an interest in excess of 25% of the underlying company, they must be registered as beneficial owners of that company in the RBE; the representatives of the trustee and possibly of the protector may be disclosed as well based on their actual powers.
- **An irrevocable and discretionary trust controlling a Luxembourg company:** The representatives of the trustee and possibly the protector are the beneficial owners of the underlying company; such 'representatives' may be the managing directors or the beneficial owners of a corporate trustee and a corporate protector based on their actual ownership structure.

54 The Position Paper, in French, may be freely requested from STEP Benelux.

It goes without saying that all the persons having a relation to the trust listed in Article 1(7)(b) of the AML Law must be registered as beneficial owners of the relevant trust in the RFT.

As regards the RBE, the examples above show that only the persons who qualify as 'beneficial owners' for the purposes of Article 1(7)(a) of the AML Law must be disclosed in the publicly accessible RBE. Any company directors overstepping this rule may expose themselves to a personal liability for breach of the fundamental right to privacy of certain individuals, as well as for an infringement of the GDPR.

The harmonisation of these approaches, possibly in the form of an EU Regulation, would be a welcome development to remove a source of legal uncertainty.

Netherlands

John Graham
Graham Smith & Partners International Tax Counsel

1. Introduction

In the Netherlands, the legal entity ultimate beneficial owner register (the entity UBO register) has been implemented after significant delays resulting from a referral to the Council of State, which reviews proposed legislation. In particular, there were questions as to the impact on privacy and whether access to the public was proportional. Prior to that, Parliament had added a provision that persons registered in the register should be able to see how often their information has been accessed (other than by the authorities), and that the authorities should be able to see who has accessed information. There should also be a review of the legislation in light of the impact on the privacy of ultimate beneficial owners (UBOs) after one and four years.

The Act Implementing the Registration of Ultimate Beneficial Owners of Companies and Other Legal Entities (the Act) was finally passed on 23 June 2020 and took effect on 27 September 2020. Registration must be carried out by new entities within eight days of incorporation. Existing entities have 18 months from the effective date of the legislation to register. For legal entities, the directors are responsible for registration, while in other entities, those responsible for day-to-day management or the owners must register the UBOs.

The legislation is based on the Fourth and Fifth EU Anti-Money Laundering Directives (EU 2015/849 and EU 2018/843 – 4AMLD and 5AMLD) and consists of a single Implementing Act (*Implementatiewet registratie uiteindelijk belanghebbenden van vennootschappen en andere juridische entiteiten*), which changes a number of existing laws:

- the Trade Register Act (*Handelsregisterwet*);
- the Money Laundering and Terrorist Financing (Prevention) Act (*Wet ter voorkoming van witwassen en financieren van terrorisme*);
- Book 2 of the Civil Code (*Boek 2 van het Burgerlijk Wetboek*);
- Book 2 of the BES Civil Code, which applies to Bonaire, St Eustasius and Saba (*Boek 2 van het Burgerlijk Wetboek BES*); and
- the Economic Offences Act (*Wet op de economische delicten*).

The legislation provides for a register of ultimate beneficial owners, in which the ultimate beneficial owner is defined as a natural person who is the ultimate owner of, or has control over, a company or other legal entity. Certain entities are excluded and these are covered in more detail below.

A separate trust register will be introduced. Draft legislation has been published and a consultation period has been completed. This is dealt with in section 3 below.

The UBO register for entities also covers foundations and other legal entities which might otherwise have been expected to fall under the trust register.

An advocacy group called Privacy First requested the Dutch court to suspend the application of the legislation on the basis that it contravenes basic rights and/or to refer the matter to the Court of Justice of the European Union. The court decided not to suspend the legislation, as it would place the Netherlands in contravention of the EU directive. It also decided not to refer the matter to the Court of Justice of the European Union because a similar case had already been referred from Luxembourg. The Dutch court did not exclude the possibility that the Court of Justice of the European Union could decide that all or part of the directive should be declared invalid.

2. The legal entity UBO register

The UBO register is administered by the Chamber of Commerce, which is a non-government entity and will be part of the trade register covering companies and businesses. The Chamber of Commerce also maintains the register of foundations.

2.1 The UBO

A UBO must always be a natural person. For the definition the legislation refers to the Money Laundering and Terrorist Financing (Prevention) Act.

The definition of a UBO in the legislation is somewhat vague: a natural person who is the ultimate owner of or has control over a company or other legal entity. The implementing decree to the Act provides more guidance.

A UBO is any individual who:

- owns more than 25% of the shares of the entity;
- has more than 25% of the votes of the entity;
- has an economic interest in the entity in excess of 25%; or
- has actual control over the business of the entity.

An entity may have several UBOs if more than one individual falls within these definitions.

If an entity does not have a UBO falling under these definitions, it must register a pseudo-UBO – namely, its 'higher management personnel'. This is defined as all the managing directors ('*bestuurders*') but not supervisory directors ('*commissarissen*'), or, in the case of a partnership, all the partners with the exception of limited partners in a limited partnership. Such a UBO does not need to have any ownership interest or voting rights in the company. This can result in different registrations for a company with a two-tier board (separate boards of supervisory directors and managing directors) and a single tier board (ie, a board with executive and non-executive directors). In the latter case all would need to register even though the non-executive directors could be considered to have a similar function to the supervisory directors. This can be relevant in the case of an SE (European company), which can use either system.

In the Netherlands it is quite common for legal entities to be directors of companies or partners in partnerships. For pseudo-UBO purposes one would normally expect then to look at the board of directors of these entities rather than their own UBOs.

In determining the pseudo-UBO, one should register the management of the company itself and not the management of the entity at the top of the structure, although supervisory bodies have been known to take different views on this.

In the case of a real UBO, it will not always be easy to determine who has an interest in excess of 25%. For instance, in an entity with preference shares giving a right to a fixed dividend, it will depend on the profits of the year concerned as to whether their interest is sufficient to require registration. This is based on whether the shareholder concerned has received more than 25% of the profits available for distribution in the year concerned and can only be determined once the accounts for that year have been prepared. If the shares have been sold in the meantime, the person concerned will not need to be registered. One could imagine a situation where a company's accounts are delayed for some time, so that the period during which a person is registered is either very short or maybe non-existent.

The explanatory notes to the legislation (*Memorie van toelichting UBO-register*) indicate certain examples where actual control may exist – for instance, where a person has the right to appoint more than half of the managing directors or supervisory directors of an entity.

In certain cases one could imagine that a bank or other major financier might effectively have control. Major suppliers might also have effective control in certain cases. In a family business it is also conceivable that a member of the family (the '*pater familias*') might have control if everybody does as he/she asks.

The government has indicated, although not very clearly, that if an individual finances the purchase of shares with a profit-sharing loan, he/she is still considered the UBO rather than the person providing the loan.

Where individuals are married in community of property and the ownership is part of the community of property, the actual shareholder will be considered the UBO. The Chamber of Commerce will not take account of marital property rights.

Foundations, which have no owners, are also required to register a UBO. This even applies to charitable entities where each member of the board is considered a UBO even though normally the directors are expressly forbidden from receiving any benefit.

A foundation is required to register as a UBO anybody who has received at least 25% of the funds available for distribution in a year. This is stated to be based on the funds which were available for distribution during the previous year and is determined at the time the accounts are prepared. A person will then remain a UBO until he/she no longer receives such a distribution.

While there will be a separate trust register, trusts can also be relevant in the context of the entity UBO register. There may be a trust at the top of the structure. While the Act refers to the Money Laundering and Terrorist Financing (Prevention) Act for the definition of a UBO, one could take the view that the UBO of a trust for the purpose of having that trust as a client or for the purposes of the trust register is not the same as that under the entity UBO register for a trust owning an entity. In the case of a fixed trust one might consider the beneficiaries, but in the case of a discretionary trust this would quite likely not be appropriate. While it might seem logical to register a pseudo-UBO in such a case, this is not entirely clear.

Furthermore, the Money Laundering and Terrorist Financing (Prevention) Act treats foundations as trust-like entities, while they do not fall under the trust register, and this raises the question as to whether the founder and other parties must be registered even where they have no control or financial interest.

2.2 Entities covered

The following entities incorporated/set up under Dutch law and certain European entities are covered by the legislation:

- public companies (NVs), unless they are listed on a stock exchange recognised by the European Union or a stock exchange subject to similar international standards, in which case they are considered to provide sufficient documentation on significant shareholders, even though this may be less than would be required for the UBO register. All 100% subsidiaries of such companies are also excluded;
- private companies (BVs);
- european companies (SEs) and European cooperative societies (SCEs) with their registered offices in the Netherlands;
- church associations (religious entities but not necessarily Christian);
- associations;
- house owners' associations;
- mutual insurance companies;
- cooperatives;
- foundations;

- partnerships, including limited partnerships;
- shipping companies (*'rederijen'*); and
- european economic interest groupings (EEIGs), whether or not with a registered office in the Netherlands, provided they are set up under Dutch law.

Dutch charitable entities will normally take the form of a foundation and are therefore covered by the legislation.

The following entities are excluded:

- entities not incorporated/set up under Dutch law except as referred to above;
- companies listed on a stock exchange recognised by the European Union or subject to similar international standards, together with their 100% subsidiaries. Even if one share of a subsidiary is held by a party other than the listed entity it will not qualify for this exemption. Presumably an entity with a nominee shareholder will also not qualify;
- sole traders (it will generally be clear who the owner is from the existing registration); and
- public bodies (on the basis that they will only have a pseudo-UBO, although this logic has not been applied to charitable foundations).

Religious organisations were also excluded in the early proposals, since giving details of individuals in that case is an indication of their religious beliefs. It was finally decided that in individual cases a person could request exemption from being registered. Since the Dutch rules on exemption from registration basically only apply if police protection is granted, this would mean that somebody would remain registered until after his/her life had already become endangered.

Foreign entities are not required to register. This means that a non-Dutch company registered in the Netherlands or a foreign company with a branch in the Netherlands does not have to register a UBO. The justification is that foreign entities incorporated in other EU countries will have to register their UBOs in that country, but that obviously does not apply to non-EU entities.

For certain purposes, in particular corporate registration and accounts filing requirements, the Netherlands also has the concept of a formal foreign company, which is a foreign entity managed in the Netherlands and having its address there. Such entities are required to comply with most Dutch corporate requirements, but they do not fall under the UBO legislation.

In recent years it has become more common for Dutch companies to redomicile to other EU countries and to convert into a company incorporated under the legislation of that other country. Even though such an entity is no longer a Dutch company, the government still considers it to be incorporated under Dutch law, which means that it has to reregister in the Netherlands and file details of its UBOs. Although most likely the information will already be registered in another EU country, the difference in implementation may mean that different information has to be published in each country as to its UBOs and also different information may be available to the public. Furthermore, it will be necessary for somebody to ensure that the registration is kept up to date in the Netherlands even though nobody is located there. This also applies to the SE, the SCE and the EEIG. It seems remarkable that an entity should need to register in several jurisdictions even though under EU law it is only incorporated in one.

2.3 Information available

Part of the information provided will be available to the public, while part will be available only to certain government entities, including supervisory authorities such as the Dutch Central Bank, the Authority for the Financial Markets, the Financial Supervision Office, the tax authorities and the Financial Intelligence Unit. Other authorities entitled to access the information include the Fiscal Intelligence and Investigation Service, the Military Intelligence and Security Services, Royal Netherlands Marechaussee (a form of police responsible for border protection and security and which falls under the Ministry of Defence) and the National Police Internal Investigations Department (which investigates corruption in the civil service). The full information will not be available to other parties, even if they have a requirement to carry out anti-money laundering checks (eg, banks, lawyers, civil-law notaries, accountants and others).

The information available to the public is as follows:

- full name;
- month and year of birth;
- nationality;
- country of residence; and
- nature of interest and level of interest in bands. the exact level of the interest will not be given, but rather whether it is more than 25% but not more than 50%, more than 50% but not more than 75%, and more than 75%.

Where a UBO has an exemption from his/her name being provided, the band within which the interest falls must still be given, even though no name is given.

The additional information which must be registered with the Chamber of Commerce but which is only available to the authorities is as follows:

- tax identification number (Dutch number where applicable and foreign number where the individual has been granted a foreign number on the basis of residence elsewhere);

- day of birth;
- place and country of birth;
- address;
- copy of identity documents and other supporting documentation to verify the identity of the UBO; and
- copy of documentation to support the type of interest and level of interest.

Copies of the following types of document or relevant parts thereof should be filed to the extent that they indicate the type and level of the economic interest of the UBO:

- shareholders' register;
- articles of association;
- depositary receipt holders' register;
- deed of incorporation;
- other notarial deeds;
- members' register;
- incorporation contract;
- trade register registration;
- structure diagram; and
- other relevant documents.

It appears that where more than one document indicates the size of holding, they should all be filed.

A UBO will be entitled to see whether a significant number of requests have been made with respect to him/her, excluding requests by the authorities, but he/she will not be entitled to see who has actually made the request.

A request for access to the public part of the register is open to anybody on payment of a fee. The person searching should be required to identify him/herself on a sufficiently reliable basis and the Chamber of Commerce will register this and can register the citizen service number (which is also used for tax purposes). An access code can be obtained from the Chamber of Commerce, although it does not appear to require the citizen service number. The Financial Intelligence Unit and other authorities will have access to the details of who has accessed the register.

A search can only be carried out on the basis of a request relating to an entity, so it will not be possible to make a request on the basis of the UBO's name to determine what entities he/she is a UBO of. Searches by the authorities will not be restricted by this provision.

The registration is maintained for 10 years after deregistration of the company. There appears to be no limit to the period during which the information on a former UBO remains registered while the company still exists (this is somewhat different from the trust proposals). Whether this is in accordance with data protection legislation is open to question.

2.4 Exemption from name being public

The AML directives (Article 30(9)) provide for an exemption for UBOs where there is a risk of kidnapping, violence, blackmail or intimidation. In that case the information must still be provided to the authorities, but it is not available to the public. The Dutch restrictions do not go as far: the person concerned must be under police protection under Dutch law or similar laws in a different country. This means that somebody may be exempted from their name being made public elsewhere within the European Union, but would not be exempt in the Netherlands. Around 250 people are subject to police protection in the Netherlands.

The arrangement also means that a person can only be exempt from registration once their life is in danger, which would seem to be too late and does not cover many of the other situations such as fraud. An individual has to make an application to the police for such protection.

The government considers that the Chamber of Commerce does not have the expertise to deal with more nuanced legislation (although it appears that it has to be able to deal with nuanced legislation on registering trusts and trust-like entities).

Minors and those without legal capacity to act can also be exempt, but will have to file an application to this end: the exemption is not granted automatically.

An entity is required to maintain up-to-date information in respect of its UBOs, even if the UBO is exempt from the requirement to have his/her details made public.

If a request is granted, it will be valid for five years in the case of somebody under police protection or, in the case of minors and those without legal capacity to act, until they no longer qualify; in other words, when the minor reaches the age of 18 or the person without legal capacity to act regains it. However, the five-year period will be automatically extended for a further five years if the person under police protection still qualifies.

A request for exemption will mean that the UBO's name will not be published until the request has been decided on (including any appeals).

The requirement for a UBO's name to be public goes beyond the requirements of the directive and also beyond the requirements under Dutch law. For instance, charitable entities do not have to publish the names of their directors if there is a real danger to their personal safety or that of their families. Police protection is not required. This exemption will be rendered pointless by the limited exemption in the UBO register.

2.5 Advisers

Lawyers, accountants, civil-law notaries, banks and others are not permitted to rely on the register for their own compliance purposes. They are therefore required to obtain largely the same information. This can result in significant duplication of effort, since an entity will most likely have to provide information on its UBOs separately to its bank, accountant, lawyer, tax adviser and civil-law notary, in addition to registering it for the UBO register. Furthermore, the advisers and banks will be required to check the information in the UBO register, resulting in yet further duplication, and to report any discrepancy they may have found with the information at their disposal to the Chamber of Commerce. This will not apply if they have filed or intend to file a suspicious transactions report with the Financial Intelligence Unit.

As mentioned above, regulators do not always take the same view as to who should be considered a UBO so that discrepancies may be justified.

The authorities are also required to inform the Chamber of Commerce of a discrepancy, unless this would unnecessarily affect them in carrying out their legal obligations – for instance, if it might affect an ongoing investigation.

Where an adviser provides advice on how to avoid being registered as a UBO, this will be a disclosable matter under DAC6 Mandatory Disclosure Directive, even if the objective has nothing to do with tax.

2.6 Foundations

Foundations in the Netherlands fall under the UBO register and not the trust register. This means that the definition of a UBO for a foundation is different from that of a trust, even where they have similar activities. In most cases the parties registered as UBO of the foundation will in fact have no financial interest in it.

Foundations are also required to keep a register with the names and addresses of parties to whom a distribution has been made which does not exceed 25% of the amount available for distribution in a financial year. The amount and the date of distribution must also be recorded. This should be kept for seven years, the normal time for keeping bookkeeping records.

In the Netherlands it is not uncommon for a so-called administration foundation (*stichting administratiekantoor* or STAK) to hold shares in a company and for the foundation itself to issue depositary receipts to other parties. The objective of this is often to split the economic interest in a share from voting rights. The depositary receipt holder has the economic rights while the foundation has the voting rights. Such foundations will themselves be required to register a UBO (normally on the basis of the management since it will usually not itself have an individual beneficiary). The depositary receipt holder is not a beneficiary of the foundation (this has been confirmed by the government). However, a company whose shares are held by the STAK will need to register the depositary receipt holders as UBOs if they have a holding in excess of 25% and also the foundation (or, in fact, its management), since it will normally have the voting rights with respect to the shares concerned.

2.7 Administrative matters

The government has taken the view that the costs of complying with the legislation are negligible. There is a requirement for the UBO to provide information to the company and the estimate is that it will take the company an average of two hours to register the UBO, and that it can do this for €39 or if external advisers are used they would cost €60 per hour. These are significantly lower rates than the government pays when it obtains external advice.

The tax authorities are responsible for enforcing the legislation. There is a special department to deal with this: the Bureau of Economic Enforcement. While the tax authorities consider legislation enforceable, they have stated on the basis of a review that enforcement will be of only limited effect. They also will only take action if informed by the Chamber of Commerce. They consider that it will be difficult to determine whether the information is correct since it is not always possible to obtain information from other countries, especially where somebody has set up a non-transparent structure. They also consider it is quite likely that a person who does not want to be shown as a UBO will simply show incorrect information or may use other types of entity which do not fall under the legislation, although it is not clear what these might be other than foreign entities.

There are administrative and criminal sanctions. Criminal sanctions apply in particular to the failure to have adequate information, failure to register it and keep it up to date, failure as a beneficiary to provide the trustee with the necessary information, failure to report discrepancies, and failure to indicate the registration number on written documents of the trust. Where such failures are deliberate, the maximum penalty can be two years in prison, a fine of up to €21,750 or a community service penalty. In many cases an administrative penalty would apply.

3. Trust register

Draft legislation has been introduced for a trust register which will apply to trusts and trust-like entities. To a large extent the rules are similar to those in the UBO register for legal entities. However, there are some differences. The summary below is based on the draft legislation.

Once the legislation takes effect, new trusts will have one week to register after the requirement arises. Existing trusts will have three months to register. This is an extremely short transitional period. On the other hand, it may be difficult for trusts which need to register but are not registered to enter into a relationship with the bank or other professional without the unique registration number referred to below.

This register will be run by the Chamber of Commerce, but, unlike the legal entity register, it will not form part of the trade register, but rather will be separate.

3.1 Registration requirement

A trust is required to register if:

- the trustee is resident or established in the Netherlands; or
- the trustee is resident or established outside the European Union and acquires Dutch real estate or enters into a business relationship in the Netherlands. A 'business relationship' is defined in the Money Laundering and Terrorist Financing (Prevention) Act as a business, professional or commercial relationship with a party covered by that act, which relates to the professional activities of that party and which can be expected to last some time. This will therefore include dealings with a bank, accountant, lawyer, civil-law notary or tax adviser.

There is no requirement for registration if the trust is resident or established elsewhere in the European Union if the trust is already registered in another EU state.

The definition of a trust for purposes of the register follows the definition in Article 2 of the Convention on the Law Applicable to Trusts and on Their Recognition (the Hague Trust Convention):

the legal relationships created – inter vivos *or on death – by a person, the settlor, when assets have been placed under the control of a trustee for the benefit of a beneficiary or for a specified purpose.*

Trust-like entities are also required to register and will comprise entities with the following characteristics:

- they do not have legal personality and do not have a business (since these would be covered by the entity UBO register);
- assets are contributed by the participants;
- the assets are used for common account; and
- the assets are used for the benefit of the UBO(s).

This means that the entities covered will normally be involved in holding funds or assets, often for investment purposes. For Dutch purposes this will typically cover the fund for common account (*fonds voor gemene rekening*), a form of investment fund.

Member states are required to notify the European Union of entities which will be considered as trust-like entities and the Netherlands has notified the fund for common account.

It is conceivable that other structures commonly used in estate planning could also fall under the definition of a trust-like entity or even be considered a trust, including certain forms of usufruct and gifts subject to conditions.

It should be noted that unlike the case in the entity UBO register, foreign entities can also fall under the trust register legislation.

Foundations are required to register in the entity UBO register as they are legal entities and therefore do not fall under the trust register.

3.2 Trustee obligations

The requirement to register falls on the trustee of a trust or the person who is in a similar position in a trust-like entity. For a fund for common account the equivalent person is the manager of the fund. They have four main obligations:

- to obtain and keep sufficient, accurate and current information on the UBOs;
- to register the information in the register;
- to ensure that the information in the register is sufficient, accurate and current; and
- to inform a party with which the trustee enters into a transaction with an 'obliged entity' (under the directive these are parties such as accountants, tax advisers, civil-law notaries) that he/she is acting on behalf of a trust or similar entity.

It may not always be easy for a trustee to obtain information on UBOs. Unlike the situation with legal entities such as companies, a UBO may not even be aware that he/she is a UBO and the trustee may never have had contact with the person concerned; in particular, founders may have been dead for many years or a legal entity may no longer exist.

Trustees are required to file the required information and to inform the UBOs. In certain cases the trust deed may not allow the trustee to inform the UBOs. Since trusts will not be set up under Dutch law, the trustee may have to choose between compliance with Dutch law and compliance with the law of the jurisdiction of the trust.

On registering, the trust will receive a unique number which it must use on all written documentation prepared on behalf of the trust.

3.3 UBOs

A number of parties involved with a trust will always be considered a UBO, including:

- the founders;
- the trustees;
- the protectors, if applicable;
- the beneficiaries or, if separate beneficiaries cannot be determined, the

group of persons in whose interest the trust has mainly been set up or is active; and
- any other natural person who, through direct or indirect ownership, or by other means, has ultimate control over the trust.

It should be noted that this is not an exhaustive list, so other persons might also be considered as a UBO. It is not clear what other parties might be considered as such, which is important since sanctions apply if an entity fails to register a UBO. There can in particular be issues if there is a corporate trustee, which is not uncommon. Should the managers of the corporate trustee be considered the UBO or should one look to the UBOs of the corporate trustee? Or might the staff be considered the UBO? Furthermore, in many cases a corporate trustee may be a 100% subsidiary of a listed company such as a bank. The legislation and explanatory notes do not cover the situation where legal entities are a founder or trustee. Who should then be registered as UBO? There are various possibilities – for instance, the owner of the entity or the management of the entity.

In some cases it may be difficult to determine individual beneficiaries. In such cases the group of people can be considered the UBO. This is the case, for instance, where there is such a large group of beneficiaries that it is impossible to identify all the individual beneficiaries. Furthermore, in certain cases beneficiaries may not be certain because they will only be determined at some point in the future. Here it will be necessary to provide a description so that they can be determined in due course.

Unlike the UBO register, it is not necessary for a UBO to have an ownership interest or voting rights of more than 25%. In particular with funds for common account there could be thousands of UBOs and some of these might themselves be legal entities or other funds for common account. Furthermore, they can change on a daily basis. If the exact beneficiaries cannot be determined, for instance because it is uncertain as to who they are or it is such a large group, this can be described by category.

In the case of a discretionary trust it will not be clear what level the ownership interest is for a UBO, while in the case of a founder there may be no ownership or voting interest at all. Some beneficiaries may only be so if they meet certain conditions. Also here it is unclear whether they should be shown as a UBO.

The UBO of a trust for purposes of the trust UBO register may not necessarily be the same as the UBO of a company which is held by a trust. In theory, for a corporate structure one should look through the trust, but this will not be straightforward, in particular for a discretionary trust. In the case of a company held by a trust it may be concluded that no UBO can be determined and therefore the management of the company would be the UBO.

3.4 Information available

As with the main UBO register, part of the information will be public and part will only be available to authorised authorities.

The public information is as follows:

- name and type of trust;
- date and place of establishment;
- object;
- first name and family name of each UBO;
- month and year of birth;
- nationality;
- country of residence; and
- type and size of interest in bands.

The non-public information relating to the UBOs is as follows:

- Dutch or foreign tax number;
- day of birth;
- country and place of birth;
- address;
- copy of valid identity document;
- copy of documents showing why that person has the status of UBO and how the size of their economic interest is determined; and
- copy of documents showing the information in respect of the trust.

As is the case with the UBO register for legal entities, it is only possible for a person to obtain an exemption from the requirement for their information to be public if they are under police protection, or if they are a minor or other person who does not have legal capacity to act for themselves. Documentation must be sent and, where it is not in Dutch, a translation must be provided. The register will still show the type and size of the interest but without any information as to whom it belongs.

The access rules are basically similar to the entity UBO register. The public and non-public information will be available to the relevant authorities as for the entity register. Although the directive allows for the possibility, obliged entities will not be entitled to access the additional information for the purposes of their client risk assessments.

The public information will be available to anybody and this goes further than the provisions in the directive. Those who wish to have access will be required to register and pay a fee. Registration will require adequate proof of identity. It is not clear how this will operate for legal entities which are required to obtain information from the register (eg, banks or professionals). Will they need to register each individual person in the compliance department?

UBOs will be entitled to obtain information as to how often information on them has been obtained from the register. Financial institutions and civil-law notaries will have access to non-public information on UBOs who are exempt from public registration.

Information on UBOs will remain available in the register for 10 years after the requirement to register the UBO concerned has ceased to apply.

It is unclear whether this broad access is compliant with the right to privacy under the EU General Data Protection Regulation or under the European Convention on Human Rights. The government considers that data protection legislation will already have been taken into account in determining the directive itself and therefore does not need to be taken into further account. It is doubtful whether this logic automatically applies where the domestic legislation goes further than the directive, particularly with respect to access.

Beneficiaries are required to cooperate in providing the information required. Failure to do so can be a punishable offence. However, in certain cases it will not be clear where a beneficiary is to be found or the trustee may be specifically forbidden from informing the beneficiaries that they are such and therefore from asking them for information.

After registration, the Chamber of Commerce will notify the UBOs of the trust that they have been registered.

3.5 Administrative matters

Discrepancies must be notified to the Chamber of Commerce by the relevant authorities or obliged parties. The Chamber of Commerce will then notify UBOs and the Ministry of Finance. The trustee must subsequently determine whether the information needs to be changed or not. If the information does not need to be changed, the notification is withdrawn.

The trust will receive a unique number which will have to be shown on all of its documentation. It is unclear how this will work in the case of a trust which is not subject to Dutch law and only has to register because it has a qualifying business relationship with a Dutch party.

While those dealing with the trust can use this number to determine the fact that it is registered, the number will not be publicly available in the register, so it will not necessarily be possible to check whether one has the right trust.

Sanctions are similar to those for the entity UBO register.

Poland

Aldona Leszczyńska-Mikulska
Tomasz Piejak
GWW

1. Legal basis for introducing the Polish UBO Register

The requirement of ultimate beneficial owner (UBO) registration in the Central Register of Beneficial Owners (UBO Register) came into force on 13 October 2019 as a requirement of the Act of 1 March 2018 on counteracting money laundering and terrorist financing, known as the AML Act.[1] This act is a response to the obligation to implement into Polish legislation the provisions set forth in Directive (EU) 2015/849 of the European Parliament and of the Council of 20 May 2015 on the prevention of the use of the financial system for the purposes of money laundering or terrorist financing, amending Regulation (EU) No 648/2012 of the European Parliament and of the Council, and repealing Directive 2005/60/EC of the European Parliament and of the Council and Commission Directive 2006/70/EC, unofficially known as the Fourth Anti-Money Laundering Directive (4AMLD).

Apart from the Regulations of the Minister of Finance of 16 May 2018 respectively on reporting of information on beneficial owners and on requests for and making available information on beneficial owners, which define technical issues such as the manner of and the procedure for submitting a report to the UBO Register and downloading information thereof,[2] the AML Act is the exclusive legal basis regulating the functioning of the UBO Register.

On 8 April 2021 the President signed the Act of 30 March 2021 amending the AML Act which essentially constitutes the introduction of Directive (EU) 2018/843 of the European Parliament and of the Council of 30 May 2018 amending Directive (EU) 2015/849 on the prevention of the use of the financial system for the purposes of money laundering or terrorist financing, and amending Directives 2009/138/EC and 2013/36/EU, known as the Fifth Anti-Money Laundering Directive (5AMLD) into Polish legislation. On 30 April 2021 the Amendment Act was published in the Polish *Journal of Laws* and entered

1 In Polish: *ustawa z dnia 1 marca 2018 r o przeciwdziałaniu praniu pieniędzy oraz finansowaniu terroryzmu (t.j. Dz.U z 2020 r poz 971 ze zm.).*

2 In Polish: *rozporządzenie Ministra Finansów z dnia 16 maja 2018 r w sprawie zgłaszania informacji o beneficjentach rzeczywistych (Dz U z 2018 r poz 968)* and *rozporządzenie Ministra Finansów z dnia 16 maja 2018 r w sprawie wniosków o udostępnienie informacji o beneficjentach rzeczywistych oraz udostępniania tych informacji (Dz U z 2020 r poz 965).*

into force, with some exceptions, 14 days after its publication. Some of the amendments are to enter into force respectively three and six months after publication of the Amendment Act.

2. Who is affected? Understanding the term 'UBO' under the AML Act

2.1 Direct or indirect control; decisive influence

The term of 'ultimate beneficial owner' set forth in the AML Act in principle reflects the definition provided for within 4AMLD. A beneficial owner is a natural person or natural persons controlling directly or indirectly a given entity through his/her rights that arise from legal or factual circumstances and enable him/her to exert decisive influence over actions or activities undertaken by the latter. The Amendment Act to the AML Act, which has recently entered into force, makes clear that a beneficial owner is any natural person controlling an entity and exerting decisive influence over its actions or activities. The amendment is an attempt at more precise implementation of the definition set forth in 4AMLD; however, it only reaffirms that the AML Act does not and never has provided for the *numerus clausus* of natural persons that may be considered beneficial owners, and that entities ought to analyse the entire legal and factual circumstances in order to identify properly all natural persons who effectively control them. In other words, whenever an entity comes to a conclusion that a given natural person satisfies any premise whatsoever allowing for the assumption that the latter controls the said entity by exerting decisive influence, such a natural person should be considered a beneficial owner.

2.2 Specific examples pertaining to beneficial owners of legal persons (corporate entities)

The aforementioned premise of control (decisive influence) constitutes a general matrix in which the identification of beneficial owners should be carried out and hence must always be taken into account. Nevertheless, the AML Act, following 4AMLD, provides for the exemplary list of beneficial owners of legal persons (corporate entities) whose share capital is divided into shares allocated to shareholders, and consequently it is possible to determine a percentage that may be an indication of ownership or control.

(a) Right of ownership of more than 25% of shares or voting rights

In this respect, the AML Act is in principle no different from 4AMLD. Regardless of whether there are other natural persons controlling and exerting decisive influence over a given legal person, a natural person or natural persons having the right of ownership of more than 25% of the total number of shares in that legal person or more than 25% of voting rights in a decision-making body (also as a pledgee or user or on the basis of arrangements with other persons having voting rights) will always be considered beneficial owners of that legal person. The same applies to a natural person or natural persons who control a legal person or legal persons that jointly have the right of ownership of more than 25% of the total number of shares or more than 25% of voting rights in a legal person in question (ie, indirect ownership).

(b) ***Shares under the common property of spouses***

Under such circumstances that a given shareholder acquired the right of ownership of more than 25% of the total number of shares upon the conclusion of marriage and establishment of legal community property, such shares are included in the common property of the spouses. However, in general only the person reflected in a register of shares (ie, exercising corporate rights of shareholders) will be reported as a beneficial owner, unless the spouse of this shareholder is a person who, based on facts, actually exercises control over the company and can exert decisive influence over its activities or actions. In such case, the spouse of the shareholder should also be reported as a beneficial owner.

(c) ***Shareholders' agreements and other similar arrangements***

It might happen that no shareholder holds the right of ownership of more than 25% of the total number of shares in that legal person or more than 25% of voting rights in a decision-making body, but some of the shareholders may have concluded a shareholders' agreement or another similar arrangement based on which they undertook to exercise their voting rights jointly. If as a result of such an agreement the shareholders exercised jointly more than 25% of the rights to vote, they might be reported to the UBO Register even though none of them acting separately holds more than 25% of voting rights.

(d) ***Control through some of the rights referred to in the Accounting Act of 29 September 1994***

Furthermore, a natural person or natural persons authorised to manage independently financial and operational policy or to appoint and dismiss a majority of members of management, supervisory or administration bodies of a legal entity, who exercise the rights referred to in the Polish Accounting Act, are considered beneficial owners of that entity.

(e) ***Holding a senior managerial position***

Ultimately, in the absence of documentation which may cast doubt on the ability to determine the identity of possible beneficial owners and in cases where no suspicions of money laundering or terrorist financing have been identified, a natural person or natural persons holding a senior managerial position should be reported as beneficial owners. Generally, such persons are management board members or commercial proxies of a legal entity.

2.3 Beneficial owners of entities owned by the State Treasury or public sector entities

A reporting obligation also applies to entities owned, fully or in part, by the State Treasury or public sector entities. Such entities should identify their beneficial owner taking into account the general premise of control (decisive influence). In such cases, beneficial owners will be mainly competent ministers or relevant executive bodies regulated by law.

2.4 Beneficial owners of partnerships

The above-mentioned specific examples pertain to beneficial owners of legal persons (ie, considering the Polish legal system they are limited essentially to limited liability companies (in Polish: *spółka z ograniczoną odpowiedzialnością*) and joint-stock companies (in Polish: *spółka akcyjna*)). The AML Act, however, does not provide for any guidelines with respect to other entities that do not have legal personality and yet are obliged to report to the UBO Register. Herein lies the issue of partnerships whose main characteristic is that control over them does not result from holding a specific percentage of shares in the share capital or voting rights, but rather is vested indivisibly with all the partners who have the right to conduct a partnership's affairs and represent it.

Under Polish law there are various legal forms of partnership and each of them has its own characteristics. In the absence of specific guidelines, identification of beneficial owners must be conducted within the above-described general matrix – that is, taking into account who controls a given entity based on the entire legal and factual circumstances and hence exerts decisive influence over its actions.

The conclusion of the above is that, generally speaking, those partners who have the right to conduct a given partnership's affairs and to represent it should be considered beneficial owners thereof. If the conduct of a partnership's affairs has been entrusted to persons other than its partners, such persons can also be deemed as beneficial owners. It may also happen that those partners who are not vested with the right to conduct the partnership's affairs (so-called passive or limited partners) will be considered beneficial owners. This might be the case where, based on the entire legal and factual circumstances, such passive partners are equipped with effective legal tools to block actions which are key from the perspective of a partnership's operations. For example, a passive partner might be considered a beneficial owner where a deed of partnership requires the unanimous consent of all partners to conduct affairs related to the partnership's core business or where a partner can effectively object to conducting such affairs. However, the determination of beneficial owners of partnerships and ultimate conclusions in this respect may vary, depending on each specific case.

2.5 Beneficial owners of trusts

Although trusts are legal instruments unknown to Polish law, the AML Act provides for guidelines on who should be treated as a beneficial owner of such legal arrangements in the case that such arrangements appear in a given ownership structure subordinate to an entity obliged to identify its beneficial owners in accordance with the AML Act. According to the said act, as it now stands, a beneficial owner of a trust is a natural person being a settlor, a trustee, a protector (if any has been appointed), a beneficiary or any other person exercising control over the trust.

The amendment to the AML Act clarifies that a beneficial owner of a trust is any natural person meeting the above criteria and therefore makes it clear that it is not sufficient to identify one beneficial owner. In other words, it is necessary to identify and report all natural persons meeting the criteria for being beneficial owners. This amendment aims at the proper implementation of changes introduced by 5AMLD.

In addition, the Amendment Act introduced clarification that in cases where natural persons benefiting from a given trust are yet to be determined, the class of persons in whose main interest the trust has been established or operates should be reported to the UBO Register and be in the public domain. The clarification in question is actually the more accurate implementation of 4AMLD and not 5AMLD, which has not introduced any changes in this respect.

The AML Act does not refer to legal entities such as private foundations. Similarly, trusts and private foundations are legal entities unknown within the Polish legal system. The only foundations allowed to be incorporated under Polish law are those established to pursue socially or economically useful aims consistent with the fundamental interests of Poland and not for the private interests of particular individuals, in particular: healthcare; development of the economy and science; education and upbringing; culture and art; social care and assistance; environmental protection; and care of historical monuments.

According to 4AMLD, beneficial owners of private foundations are natural persons holding equivalent or similar positions to those pertaining to trusts. Given that there are no legal guidelines in this respect in the AML Act and taking into account the current practice in cases where there is a private foundation subordinate to an entity obliged to identify its beneficial owners in accordance with the AML Act, the latter should analyse the entire legal and factual circumstances and, based on such, indicate all natural persons controlling and exerting decisive influence over the foundation. Therefore, literal interpretation of the Polish AML provisions, including the amendments which have recently entered into force, leads to a conclusion that only those natural persons who actually exert decisive influence over a private foundation should be considered beneficial owners of the latter and not necessarily all persons holding equivalent or similar positions to those listed in the case of trusts (ie, a founder, foundation board members, protectors and beneficiaries).

3. UBO Register

3.1 Public domain; no legitimate interest required

The UBO Register in Poland is, and always has been, in the public domain available via the ICT system free of charge with no need to demonstrate a legitimate interest to have access to any information submitted to it. Since trusts are unknown to Polish law, there is no separate register for such legal arrangements, although the amendment to the AML Act, in response to obligations imposed by 5AMLD, extended the catalogue of entities obliged to report information on their beneficial owners and the scope of information itself to trusts whose trustees or persons holding equivalent positions have their place of residence in Poland or establish a business relationship or purchase real estate in Poland on behalf or on account of a trust. As a result, certain foreign trusts will be obliged to report to the Polish UBO Register. However, in such cases, information on these trusts will be reported to the very same UBO Register and, for the time being, there are no provisions of the AML Act limiting access to information on trusts by imposing an obligation to demonstrate a legitimate interest.

3.2 Information that should be reported to the UBO Register

Information that should be reported to the UBO Register is not complex and essentially encompasses the basic identification data of the entities obliged to report and their representatives. When it comes to information on beneficial owners themselves, it encompasses their first and last name, citizenship, country of residence, Polish identification number (PESEL) (or the date of birth in cases of persons without a PESEL number) and, finally, the description of size and nature of the participation or of the rights of a given beneficial owner in the reporting entity. The said description is limited to a concise indication of whether a given natural person exerts direct ownership rights (ie, if they are a shareholder or partner of a given entity, the value of their contribution to the entity, and if they are vested with special preferences where such preferences may concern in particular the voting right, the right to dividend or the participation in distribution of assets upon liquidation).

Where a given natural person exerts indirect ownership rights in a given entity, such indirect rights should be briefly described – for example, by indicating that a given person is the majority shareholder having the right of ownership to 75% of shares in company X that, in turn, is the sole shareholder having the right of ownership to 100% of shares in company Y being subject to reporting to the UBO Register (ie, the said natural person indirectly holds 75% of the shares of company Y and hence has a sufficient percentage to be considered beneficial owner of the latter). The system also allows for providing a brief description in the case that a given natural person is not, either directly nor indirectly, the shareholder or partner in a given entity, but that based on legal or factual circumstances exerts decisive influence over actions or activities undertaken by this entity and, as a result, should be reported as a beneficial owner thereof.

The amendment to the AML Act provided for some significant changes when it comes to the scope of information to be reported to the UBO Register. Until now, in the case of a beneficial owner having multiple citizenship, the system allowed for inserting only one citizenship and if one of them was Polish, then only this fact should have been reported. Upon the entry into force of the amendments to the AML Act, all the possessed citizenships are subject to reporting.

Another important change results from the inclusion of certain foreign trusts when it comes to the reporting obligations. Namely, it is now required to describe the class of persons in whose main interest the trust is established or operates in the case that the beneficiaries thereof are yet to be determined. Currently, the system technically does not allow for inserting information on a group or class of persons, but only on specified natural persons. Since, as opposed to the AML Directives, the AML Act does not contain clear provisions requiring the analogous application of the guidelines pertaining to trusts to entities such as private foundations, it is unclear whether it will be mandatory to report analogous information in the case of the latter. Given that under Polish law the provisions requiring the indication of the class of possible beneficiaries in the event of the specific beneficiaries not being determined refers only to trusts, it is justified to argue that there is no obligation to report the class of possible beneficiaries in the case of private foundations. What is more, there are grounds to argue that only those natural persons who actually control and exert decisive influence over a foundation will be reported as beneficial owners and not necessarily all natural persons irrespective of whether they are actually able to influence the foundation or not.

3.3 Statutory periods

Information should be reported to the UBO Register no later than seven days from the date on which an entity obliged to report has been entered into the National Court Register (known as the KRS and being the Polish equivalent of a register of companies and other entities) for the first time and, in the case of a change in the information provided, within seven days of that change. These periods do not include weekends and statutory public holidays. The amendment to the AML Act clarified the issue that previously had been raising doubts. Namely, in the case of a change of provided information, the seven-day period is regarded as starting from the date of its registration in the National

Court Register, if a given change becomes effective only upon registration with the National Court Register (eg, changes in articles of association), or from the date of carrying out a given juridical act, if its effectiveness does not depend on the registration with the National Court Register (eg, a sale of shares or appointment or dismissal of management board members). Due to the inclusion of certain foreign trusts in the UBO Register, the amendments additionally specified that in the case of such legal arrangements the seven-day period is regarded as starting from the date of establishment of a trust, the transfer of a registered office or place of residence of a trustee to Poland, or the establishment of a business relationship or the purchase of real estate in Poland.

It is worth noting that the UBO Register operates separately and independently from the National Court Register. Therefore, any changes, even though they may have nothing in common with the beneficial ownership in a given entity (eg, the change of a registered office), must be reported to the UBO Register, under threat of penalty, within the said seven-day period, as there is no automatic exchange of information between the National Court Register and the UBO Register.

4. Entities obliged to report

As of now, entities obliged to report information on their beneficial owners are companies with their registered offices in Poland. In other words, a reporting obligation has been imposed only on Polish companies, which is likely to change upon entry into force of the amendment bill, which also imposes such obligation on certain foreign trusts. The reporting obligation does not concern, for example, branch offices in Poland established by foreign companies.

As a general remark, a report to the UBO Register can be submitted only by a person authorised to represent an entity via means of electronic communication in accordance with the manner of representation set forth in the articles of association or deed of partnership. Such a report cannot be submitted by a person acting under a power of attorney except for a so-called commercial proxy, which is a specific power of attorney comprising the empowerment for judicial and extra-judicial acts connected with conducting the enterprise and should be filed with the National Court Register.

A report must be signed with a qualified electronic signature or a signature confirmed by an ePUAP-trusted profile, a Polish nationwide platform for communication of citizens with public administrative bodies. It is not possible to submit the report in paper format.

4.1 General partnerships

General partnerships (in Polish: *spółka jawna*) are entities without legal personality that may, in their own name, acquire rights and assume obligations in which each partner is liable for the obligations of the partnership without limitation, jointly and severally with the other partners and with the partnership, except that the partnership's creditors may claim upon the assets of the partners only if execution upon the assets of the partnership has proven ineffective.

Unless otherwise provided for in a deed of partnership, each partner has the right to represent the partnership and to conduct its affairs. Generally, therefore, each partner has the right to submit a report to the UBO Register on behalf of a general partnership.

4.2 Limited partnerships

Limited partnerships (in Polish: *spółka komandytowa*) are partnerships of at least one partner, called the general partner, who bears unlimited liability towards creditors for obligations of a partnership, and at least one partner (limited partner) who bears liability only up to the so-called limited liability amount specified in a deed of partnership.

Only general partners have the right to conduct a limited partnership's affairs and represent it. Unless otherwise set forth in a deed of limited partnership, each general partner is authorised to represent it independently and, hence, each general partner has the right to submit a report to the UBO Register on behalf of a general limited partnership. Limited partners are not allowed to conduct a limited partnership's affairs or represent it, except in situations where they act under a power of attorney granted by the general partner.

4.3 Limited joint-stock partnerships

Although limited joint-stock partnerships (in Polish: *spółka komandytowo-akcyjna*) are entities without legal personality, they combine characteristics of both limited partnerships and joint-stock companies. Persons who have the right to conduct the affairs of a limited joint-stock partnership and to represent it are general partners. As opposed to other partnerships, a limited joint-stock partnership has no limited partners, but shareholders who do not conduct the affairs of the partnership do not represent it either unless they are granted a power of attorney to do so. Shareholders are not liable for the obligations of the partnership, which makes it more similar to a joint-stock company.

In general, each general partner has the right to submit a report to the UBO Register on behalf of a limited joint-stock partnership.

4.4 Limited liability companies

Limited liability companies (in Polish: *spółka z ograniczoną odpowiedzialnością*) are legal persons whose share capital is divided into shares determining the right of ownership and actual influence over a company. In these companies, the sphere of ownership rights (the shareholding) is clearly separated from the conduct of the affairs of a company which is vested in members of a management board, although there are no obstacles for shareholders to be concurrent members of a management board. Generally, shareholders are not liable for obligations assumed by a limited liability company.

Since a limited liability company is represented and managed by members of a management board, a report to the UBO Register can be submitted by the members in accordance with the manner of representation set forth in the articles of association.

4.5 Joint-stock companies

Similar to limited liability companies, joint-stock companies (in Polish: *spółka akcyjna*) are legal persons in which the sphere of ownership rights is separated from the conduct of the affairs of a company, with the main difference between these types of company being that a joint-stock company allows for better capital fluctuation which facilitates the acquisition of new investors. In addition, shares in such companies can be listed on a regulated market (public limited companies).

It is worth mentioning that public limited companies are explicitly excluded from the obligation to report to the UBO Register. Regardless of this, according to the current practice of the Ministry of Finance, in the event of an entity obliged to report being owned by a public limited company (ie, where that entity is subordinate to a public limited company in an ownership structure), the obliged entity must identify beneficial owners of that public limited company even though the public limited company itself does not have to do so. This raises practical problems since a stockholding structure in public limited companies can be variable, which ultimately results in representatives of a reporting entity being obliged to frequently monitor its ownership structure and report appropriate changes in beneficial ownership within the short statutory reporting deadlines. This also clearly contradicts the wording of 4AMLD.

4.6 Extension of list of reporting entities

The amendment to the AML Act significantly extended the list of entities obliged to submit reports to the UBO Register. The amendment encompasses previously mentioned foreign trusts whose trustees or persons holding equivalent positions who have their place of residence in Poland as well as trusts whose trustees or persons holding equivalent positions establish business relationships or acquire real estate in Poland on behalf or on account of a trust. As a result of the review of legal solutions adopted in other member states, the list has been extended to include: professional partnerships (in Polish: *spółka partnerska*), European economic interest groupings, *Societas Europea*, cooperatives, *Societas Cooperativa Europaea*, associations subject to registration in the National Court Register, and foundations (meaning public foundations incorporated under Polish law to pursue socially or economically useful aims consistent with the fundamental interests of Poland and not being foreign private foundations).

5. Sanctions

5.1 Administrative penalties

Entities that have not complied with the obligation to report information on their beneficial owners in a timely manner are subject to a financial penalty of up to PLN1 million (approximately €250,000). The amendment to the AML Act made it clear that such penalty might be imposed not only for the failure to report, but also for submitting information that is inaccurate or inconsistent with the facts.

Given that the penalty is an administrative penalty, it should be expected that the minister of finance, although acting within the framework of administrative discretion, will be guided by the directives indicated in the Code of Administrative Procedure. Certainly, the amount of the penalty should be commensurate with the gravity and circumstances of the violation. One circumstance that should affect the amount of the penalty is whether the entity is a subsidiary in the international capital structure. In practice, persons representing such an entity are likely to face problems obtaining information about natural persons at the top of the structure and who exercise ultimate control over it. In such situations, one should rather expect the authority to impose a small penalty, provided, of course, that the entity proves that it has been unable to obtain information despite acting with due diligence. It cannot be ruled out that the authority will refrain from imposing a penalty if the entity notifies the minister of finance about the violation and that it is unable to rectify it within the prescribed period.

5.2 Criminal liability

Persons submitting a report to the UBO Register are obliged to give a statement on the accuracy of the information reported to the register and of being aware of criminal liability for making a false statement. If the information reported is proven false or inaccurate and concurrently the perpetrator has been proven to have known or been able to anticipate such falsity or inaccuracy, he/she may be subject to a term of imprisonment of between six months and eight years, depending on the gravity of the case. However, the court may mitigate, or even not apply, such penalty if the alleged perpetrator voluntarily corrects a false statement before the court case has been settled.

5.3 Civil liability

Although there are no explicit provisions allowing natural persons who believe themselves to have been wrongly or unduly reported to the UBO Register to apply for the removal or correction of their data, entity representatives who report information on beneficial owners and update such information are liable for damage caused by reporting false data and by failure to report and change data subject to entry into the register within the statutory period, unless the damage is a result of *force majeure* or is exclusively the fault of the aggrieved party or a third party for whom the person reporting and updating information on beneficial owners is not responsible. In such cases, an injured party may demand redress for the damage suffered on the basis of general principles set forth in the Civil Code. If reporting of false data results in personal interests being jeopardised, the injured party may also demand that the person who reported the false data remove it by updating information in the UBO Register.

The AML Act does not provide for any specific procedures allowing a natural person to request that information on him/her be withdrawn from public access or removed from the UBO Register. In cases where a person feels unjustifiably reported to the UBO Register, he/she may in our view apply to the minister of finance claiming that the data on him/her is incorrect or that he/she denies being a beneficial owner of a given entity at all. If the minister of finance finds the said notification justified, it is likely that the entity would be obliged by the Ministry of Finance to re-submit a correct report within three working days from the date of receipt of the respective request, under threat of the above-mentioned penalties. However, it remains uncertain whether the refusal to address the issue by the minister or his/her decision, which is unsatisfactory to any party, could possibly be appealed on to an administrative court. Similarly, there seem to be no specific legal tools allowing a person to request that information on him/her be withdrawn from public access (kept confidential) if the reported person is in fact a beneficial owner of a given entity.

Portugal

Nuno Cunha Barnabé
António Vidal
Abreu Advogados

1. Portuguese legislation

The Portuguese legislation regarding the public register of beneficial ownership originated in the EU Directive 2015/849, of the Council of 20 May 2015 (the Fourth European Directive on the prevention of the use of the financial system for the purposes of money laundering or terrorist financing – 4AMLD), which was transposed into Portuguese law by Law No 83/2017 of 18 August 2017 and Law No 89/2017 of 21 August 2017, subsequently regulated by Ordinance No 233/2018 of 21 August 2018 and Ordinance No 200/2019 of 28 June 2019.

Law No 89/2017 of 21 August 2017 created a central registry for beneficial owners (*Registo Central de Beneficiários Efectivos*, hereinafter CRBO), which consists of an online portal where the entities subject to the obligation of registration with the CRBO must comply with their reporting obligations, namely the identification of their beneficial owners.

The reporting is made by filing a declaration which includes relevant data to identify the ownership structure of the entity under registration, its shareholders and/or associates, and the members of its management bodies, as well as certain personal details regarding its beneficial owners.

It was only on 31 August 2020, after being requested to do so by the European Commission some six months prior, that Portugal transposed the Fifth European Directive on the prevention of the use of the financial system for the purposes of money laundering or terrorist financing (European Directive 2018/843 – 5AMLD), via Law No 58/2020.

As such, the beneficial owner legislation comprises the following:

- Law No 83/2017 of 18 August 2017, as amended by Law No 58/2020 of 31 August 2020, which lays down measures to combat money laundering and the financing of terrorism, and where the criteria for determining who is considered a beneficial owner are set;
- Law No 89/2017 of 21 August 2017, as amended by Law No 58/2020 of 31 August 2020, which creates the CRBO, thus determining which entities are subject to the obligatory registration, and what information must be provided; and
- Ordinance No 233/2018 of 21 August 2018, as amended by Ordinance

200/2019 of 28 June 2019, which regulates the functioning of the online portal utilised for the registry and consulting of the beneficial owner.

It should be noted that while Law No 58/2020 of 31 August 2020 came into force on 1 September 2020, most of its changes have not yet been implemented or included in the online CRBO portal. Therefore, further legislation and regulations may be needed to accommodate the changes introduced by this law. However, no substantial changes to the beneficial owner regime are expected since the changes brought by 5AMLD do not imply any substantial amendment to the CRBO.

2. Central Registry for the Beneficial Owner in Portugal

Pursuant to the establishment of the CRBO, all obligated entities must duly comply with the obligations set forth in the legislation referred to above on a timely basis.

Among these obligations, the most relevant is the submission of the initial declaration of beneficial owner, which holds all the legally required information in a single document and which should be executed either within 30 days of the entity in question being incorporated or within 30 days of any act that implies the applicability of any of the criteria set out below (see section 2.1).

After the valid submission of the initial declaration, any changes to the information submitted should be duly updated within the next 30 days, under penalty of an administrative fee being applied (although, to date, no fees have been applied for late compliance).

Finally, the information submitted must also be confirmed once per year, starting in 2021. The annual confirmation can be performed manually – also through the online CRBO portal – or automatically when submitting the annual accounts, for companies subject to that obligation.

All of the aforementioned obligations can be executed by the person(s) legally in charge of the management of the entity under registration, or else by any person or entity that holds equivalent functions in other legal entities that may not have a normal management structure. In addition, all of these obligations can be executed – and usually are – by lawyers, accountants, notaries and solicitors, whose delegated powers are presumed.

2.1 Obligated entities

As a general rule, the following entities are subject to the beneficial owner registration in Portugal:

- associations, cooperatives, foundations, civil and commercial companies, as well as any other collective entities subject to Portuguese law or to foreign law, insofar as they exercise activity or enter into any contract or practice any legal act in national territory that determines obtaining a tax identification number or TIN (*Número de Identificação de Pessoa Colectiva*, abbreviated to NIPC) in Portugal;[1]

- representations of international legal persons or those under foreign law who exercise any type of activity in Portugal;
- other entities which, pursuing their own objectives and activities differentiated from those of its members, are not given legal personality;
- the fiduciary management instruments registered with the Madeira Free Trade Zone (trusts); and
- the external financial branches registered in the Madeira Free Trade Zone.

Other than the above-mentioned entities, there is also a specific regime applicable to trusts and other legal entities without legal personality which hold a structure or functions similar to a trust.[2] These entities shall also be subject to the obligation of registering with the CRBO in Portugal in the following situations:

- if the trustee, the legal representative for the management, or the entity occupying a similar position is an obligated entity, according to the criteria set forth above;
- if the entity is required by tax law to obtain a Portuguese TIN;
- if the entity establishes business relations or carries out occasional transactions with obligated entities, according to the criteria set forth above; or
- if the respective trustee, the person legally in charge of the management, or the person or entity occupying a similar position, acting in any of these capacities, establishes business relations or carries out occasional transactions with obligated entities or, regardless of whether these situations occur, if the person or entity in question is established or resides in Portugal.

In addition, it should be noted that some entities are automatically excluded

---

1 It has been the position of Portuguese banks in general that a foreign collective entity which opens a bank account in Portugal is obliged to register with the CRBO, as the law imposes as a condition to holding a Portuguese bank account that the holder first obtains a Portuguese TIN. However, that interpretation may be considered illegal on the grounds that since the banks already possess such information, as a result of complying with their own duties of 'know your customer' (KYC) and due diligence under the legislation and regulations on the prevention of money laundering and terrorist financing, requiring the customer in addition to publicly disclose the account beneficial owners is beyond the scope of the law. Ultimately, the doubt can be raised as to whether the requirement that any foreign collective entity which practices an act or enters into a contract in Portugal must register with the CRBO, when no business is carried on in Portugal or with any Portuguese counterparts, complies with EU law on the grounds of proportionality.

2 Please note that for the purposes of being obliged to register the trust in the Portuguese CRBO, the law does not distinguish between business and charity trusts, both being subject to the register. In general, the type of trust (eg, revocable or irrevocable, discretionary or fixed) is not differentiated by the Portuguese CRBO.

from the beneficial ownership register obligation, such as diplomatic and consular missions, international organisations of a public nature, entities belonging to the central, regional or local administration of the Portuguese State, independent administrative entities, the Bank of Portugal, the regulatory entity for the media (ERCS), professional associations, companies with shares admitted to trading in regulated markets, consortiums, complementary groupings of companies, condominiums (although subject to conditions), insolvent estates and heritages.

2.2 Submitted information

For every legally obligated entity or natural person, Law No 89/2017 of 21 August 2017 determines the corporate or personal information that must be submitted before the CRBO.

As of the present date, the declaration for the beneficial owner regarding most legal entities (ie, excluding trusts and other special entities that follow a different regime) only requires the identification of the person submitting the declaration (the 'declarant'), the corporate information regarding the entity under registration, and the identification of the beneficial owners. This is most relevant, as up until 31 August 2020, the Portuguese legislation also required the full identification of every single shareholder and member of the board of directors.

In this regard, the entity under registration must be identified through the following details:

- Portuguese TIN (NIPC) or, in the case of a non-resident entity, the TIN or equivalent number issued by the competent authority of the jurisdiction of residence, if any;
- firm or name;
- legal nature;
- headquarters, including the jurisdiction of registration, in the case of foreign entities;
- economic activity code (*Código de Actividade Económica*, abbreviated to CAE);
- unique legal entity identifier, when applicable; and
- institutional email address.

As for any natural person being identified, the following personal information must be submitted to the CRBO:

- full name;
- date of birth;
- place of birth;
- nationality or nationalities;
- full address of permanent residence, including country;

- passport or other valid identification document;
- Portuguese TIN, when applicable, and, in the case of foreign nationals, the TIN issued by the competent authorities of the state of their nationality, or any applicable equivalent number; and
- email address, if existing.[3]

Pursuant to Law No 58/2020 of 31 August 2020, a vast amount of information that had been obligatory to disclose has now been revoked for most civil and commercial entities, and as such, these only have to provide the aforementioned data regarding the entity under registration and its beneficial owners, and not in respect also of their shareholders and directors (if natural persons).

However, due to the fact that this is recent legislation and, as of 30 April 2021, the CRBO online portal has not yet been completely updated, the previous information regarding the directors of the entity under registration is still being requested. Consequently, it is not yet possible to submit a declaration of beneficial owner for a commercial company without identifying and providing complete information on all the members of the board of directors, although it is no longer necessary to identify the shareholders.

2.3 Identifying the beneficial owner

For most of the entities under registry (civil or commercial companies), the method of assessing who their beneficial owners are, according to Law 83/2017 of 18 August 2017, is based on the following criteria:

a) the natural person or persons who ultimately own or control, directly or indirectly, a sufficient percentage of the shares or of the voting rights or participation in the capital of a legal person;

b) the natural person or persons exercising control by other means over that legal person;

c) the natural person or persons who hold the senior management, if, after exhausting all possible means and on condition that there are no grounds for suspicion:

(i) no person has been identified in accordance with the above paragraphs; or

(ii) doubts remain as to whether the person or persons identified are the beneficial owners.

Portuguese legislation clarifies that for the purposes of assessing the status of a beneficial owner, when it is a corporate entity, the holding by a natural person of participations representing more than 25% of the share capital of the entity should be considered as an indication of direct ownership.

---

3 Unlike obliged entities, the law does not specify which type of email address can be provided with respect to the beneficial owner.

Furthermore, the holding of a participation representing more than 25% of the share capital of the entity by a corporate entity that is under the control of one or more natural persons, several corporate entities that are under the control of the same person, or the same natural persons, or when any other control indicators and other circumstances are verified shall be considered as an indication of indirect ownership.

2.4 Beneficial Owner Register for Trusts

Apart from in the context of the Madeira Free Trade Zone regime, Portuguese law does not recognise the concept of a trust. Portugal is also not a signatory of the Hague Convention on Trusts Recognition. Consequently, the characterisation of a trust under Portuguese law and the regime that applies to trusts with respect to any Portuguese assets and counterparties cannot be determined in general and must be determined on a case-by-case basis.

Under Portuguese law, a trust is typically treated as a contract whereby the owner of property (ie, the settlor) transfers ownership to a trustee who holds the property according to the settlor's instructions and for the benefit of a designated person or persons. Considering this definition, we believe it is important to highlight three points under Portuguese law: (i) the trust lacks legal personality; (ii) the trust fund might have some autonomy as an aggregate of assets (without legal personality) that it is placed under the legal control of a trustee; and (iii) the trustee is regarded as the legal owner of the assets before third parties.[4]

In light of such a characterisation, as a rule, transactions involving a trust are deemed to be made with the trustees, as legal owners of the trust assets. However, it is important to assess the degree of control of the trustees as this may lead to a different conclusion and/or characterisation of the trust relationship.

More specifically on the applicability of the CRBO to trusts, as highlighted above, specific criteria apply to trusts and other centres of collective interest without legal personality and with a similar structure or functions.

For clarification on the criteria set out above, the 'obligated entities' as per Law No 83/2017 of August 18 2017 pertain to a broad list of financial entities, as well as other non-financial entities such as auditors and lawyers, among others. Nonetheless, and regardless of the verification of the criteria set forth in Law No 83/2017 of August 18 2017, the obligation of submitting to the beneficial owner registry may be applicable to a trust if it establishes a legal connection to Portugal which requires it to obtain a Portuguese TIN[5] (as discussed in section 2.1 above), which is an extremely broad criteria to apply.[6]

---

4 Portugal adopts the theory of undivided and absolute ownership of property adopted as per the Portuguese Civil Code.

5 For example, enter into a contract for the lease of a property in Portugal, open a bank account with a Portuguese bank, formalise a distribution of assets or addition before a Portuguese notary.

6 Please see footnote 1, in respect of the potential incompatibility of this criteria with EU law.

According to the specific criteria set for determining the beneficial owners of trusts, as per Law No 83/2017 of 18 August 2017, the following people should be identified as beneficial owners of a trust:

- the settlor;
- the trustee or trustees;
- the protector(s), if applicable;
- the beneficiaries or, if they have not yet been determined, the category of persons in whose interest the trust fund was established or exercises its activity; and
- any other natural person who has control over the trust through direct or indirect participation or through other means.

Other than the different set of criteria set forth for determining who shall be considered the beneficial owner of a trust, there is also a substantial difference in the information to be submitted before the CRBO.

Different from the information that is mandatory to submit for most entities, which is limited to the entity under registration and its beneficial owners, trusts currently have to provide vast information and on a much more complex level, including personal data regarding: the settlor; the trustees and substitutes (if any); the legal representatives of the trustees, when these are legal persons; the protectors, when applicable; all beneficiaries, when they are determined; and any other natural person who holds effective control over the trust.

In addition, for each of these individuals or legal entities, all the personal or corporate information identified in section 2.2 must be inserted, along with the following even more extensive list of information regarding the entity under registration:

- the Portuguese TIN or, in its absence, and provided that it is not compulsory to obtain it on national territory for the purposes of the exercise of activity, an equivalent functional number issued by the jurisdiction of residence, if any;
- name and identification;
- date of incorporation and duration, when determined, as well as the date and nature of the respective modifying and extinctive facts;
- object or type;
- governing law;
- assets constituting the trust fund or the collective interest centre without legal personality;
- name and registered office of the trustee, when not a natural person;
- rights and obligations of the trustees among themselves, in case of joint powers; and
- all elements provided for in the first two bullet points above relating to the management company, when applicable.

All of the above information is likewise applicable to trusts administered by trustees operating within the Madeira Free Trade Zone regime.

In light of the above, it is safe to say that the beneficial owner obligations that befall trusts constitute a heavy burden when compared to the much simpler version applicable to most civil and commercial entities.

However, it should be noted that Law No 58/2020 of 31 August 2020 has recently introduced the possibility of exemption from all beneficial owner obligations in Portugal for trusts and similar structures which are not resident in Portugal. This exemption requires evidence, which is achieved by presenting a certificate of registration or by direct consultation of the information from the public register of beneficial owners of the EU member state or third state/jurisdiction holding such information.

2.5 Private foundations

While there is no specific regime set forth for foundations governed by private law, the Portuguese legislation refers this matter to the criteria used for assessing the beneficial owners of trusts.

As such, Law No 83/2017 of 18 August 2017 states that in the case of non-corporate entities, such as foundations, or of legal arrangements of a nature similar to trusts, the beneficial owners considered should be the legal or natural persons with positions equivalent or similar to those mentioned above regarding trusts.

Considering that there is no specific regulation on private foundations, other than the referral to the regime applicable to trusts, these entities follow the exact same legal provisions, not only regarding the identification of the beneficial owners, but also concerning the applicable information to be submitted and all restrictions on its access by third parties.

2.6 Access to third parties and legitimate interest

According to Law No 89/2017 of 21 August 2017, some of the information submitted by obligated entities must be available online and accessible by third parties.

The publicly available information is quite restricted for most entities and only includes the Portuguese TIN, corporate name, legal nature, headquarters, economic activity code (CAE) and email address. In fact, most of this information is already accessible online, sometimes even on the entity's corporate website.

As for the information disclosed on the identified beneficial owners, third parties can freely access only the full name, month and year of birth, nationality, country of residence, and economic interest, which is to say the reason for being appointed as beneficial owner of the entity.

In order to access this information, it is necessary to hold a valid digital certificate and insert the Portuguese TIN of the entity in question. While the user is confronted with a text box destined to explain the motives behind accessing said information and therefore must provide justification, there is no specific regulation on the justification and this is not subject to the scrutiny of the entity managing the CRBO to a test of 'legitimate interest' for accessing the register. This means that the reasons identified by the third party are neither controlled nor verified.

Even though 5AMLD hinted towards the introduction of a more restrictive system for the access of information submitted by trusts, through the control and assessment of the legitimate interest of the third party accessing the information, such provisions were not included in the Portuguese legislation.

As such, there is currently no control or threshold over who is granted access to the basic information regarding an entity that has fulfilled its obligations regarding the CRBO, whether it is a commercial company or a trust, notwithstanding the fact that the difference in the mandatory information is significant.

2.7 Consequences for non-compliance

Not registering with the CRBO entails the following prohibitions:

- intervention as a party in any business having as its object the transfer of property, whether for a consideration or free of charge, or the constitution, acquisition or sale of any other fruition or guarantee-related rights over any immovable assets;
- distribution of the company's profits or advance dividends;[7]
- execution of supply agreements, public works contracts or acquisition of services and assets with the State, autonomous regions, public institutes, municipalities and specific private social solidarity organisations, as well as renewing such agreements;
- competing for the concession of public services;
- admittance to trading on a regulated stock exchange market any financial instruments representing its share capital or convertible on the said share capital;
- launching public offers of distribution of any financial instruments issued by the entity; and
- benefiting from the support of any European structural or investment funds, as well as from public funds.

Furthermore, the lack of compliance with the duty to maintain an updated

7 In addition, the beneficiary may not benefit from the Portuguese participation exemption regime, which provides, in general, for an exemption of withholding tax on dividends distributed in respect of a minimum shareholding of 10% of the capital and voting rights of the Portuguese subsidiary, provided that such shareholding has been maintained for a minimum one-year period before the distribution.

record of identification elements of the beneficial owner constitutes a punishable offence, sanctioned through a fine that can amount to between €1,000 and €50,000.

It should be noted that despite not having been enforced as of the present date, the submission of incorrect or invalid information can lead to a crime of 'false declarations', foreseen and punishable by Portuguese penal law.

3. Access restrictions

In very specific situations it is also possible to request a restriction of access to the information submitted regarding one or more beneficial owners.

However, this can only occur when: (i) the identified beneficial owner is legally invalid; (ii) the identified beneficial owner is a minor; or (iii) if the access to such information is susceptible of leading the beneficial owner to situations of fraud, threat, coercion, kidnapping, extortion, stalking or other types of violence or intimidation.

While this is a possibility that is seemingly available to every beneficial owner with a legitimate fear of the aforementioned situations occurring, the reality is much more complicated: the concrete situation must be assessed by the president of the entity managing the CRBO, the National Institute for Registries and Notaries, which only occurs after a thorough and lengthy assessment of the risk claimed by the beneficial owner.[8]

In practice, a beneficial owner can submit a request to restrict his/her personal information and only receive a valid decision on his/her request (either an approval or a dismissal) several months later, with very few cases having been fully enforced in the past two years. For this reason, this is a scarcely used resource in protecting the beneficial owner's personal information and has led many identified natural persons to consider that it simply is not worth committing the time and effort in order to protect their information.

Even so, and with full acknowledgement that this mechanism is currently flawed, it remains one of the only resources put in place to prevent third parties from easily gathering personal information on the appointed beneficial owners, and thus one can only hope that it is substantially strengthened in order to be of use to those who deem it necessary for their wellbeing.

Finally, in case the entity managing the CRBO refuses the request for restriction of access of the information, the applicant can log a hierarchy appeal against the CRBO president's decision or file a judicial claim before the administrative courts, which are competent to annul the CRBO's decision.

---

8 In our experience, such requests can take several months to be decided. However, until the decision is taken the register is suspended, meaning that the information inserted in the CRBO is not available to the public.

Slovenia

Tatjana Andoljšek
OPAM LAW, Odvetniška pisarna Andoljšek d.o.o.

1. EU framework and the Slovene legislation

The Fifth Anti-Money Laundering Directive (Directive (EU) 2018/843) (5AMLD) was implemented in Slovenia by the Prevention of Money Laundering and Terrorist Financing Act,[1] published in the *Official Gazette* of the Republic of Slovenia in 2016 and amended subsequently in 2019 and 2020. It was enacted on 19 November 2016.

The two regulations governing the establishment and management of the Register of Beneficial Owners (the BO Register) are the Rules on the establishment, maintenance and management of the Register of Beneficial Owners[2] enacted on 9 December 2017, and the Tariff for accessing data in the Register of Beneficial Owners,[3] enacted on 1 January 2018.

2. Definition of a beneficial owner

Slovene legislation has implemented the term 'beneficial owners' (in Slovene: '*Dejanski lastnik*') to identify the ultimate beneficial owner of shares or capital stakes. Rules are defined separately for corporate entities having share capital, Slovene entities without share capital and Slovene institutions, and foreign funds, institutions and similar foreign entities.

2.1 Beneficial owner of corporate entities having share capital

Article 35 of the Prevention of Money Laundering and Terrorist Financing Act defines the beneficial owner of a corporate entity as:

- any natural person who:
  - is directly or indirectly the holder of a sufficient capital stake, shares, voting or other rights on the basis of which it participates in the management of the economic entity;
  - directly or indirectly participates in the capital of the economic entity with a sufficient share; or

1 In Slovene: *Zakon o preprečevanju pranja denarja in financiranja terorizma* (ZPPDFT-1).
2 In Slovene: *Pravilnik o vzpostavitvi, vzdrževanju in upravljanju Registra dejanskih lastnikov.*
3 In Slovene: *Tarifa nadomestila stroškov za dostop do podatkov iz Registra dejanskih lastnikov.*

   - has a controlling position in the management of the economic entity's assets; or
- any natural person who indirectly arranges or provides resources to the economic entity due to which he/she has the ability to control, direct or otherwise substantially influence the decisions of the management of the economic entity on financing and operations.

The criteria used to determine the beneficial owner are the ownership of more than 25% of capital stake, voting rights or other management rights, or the ownership of 25% plus one share in the public limited company.

Conditions applied for preparation of the annual consolidated financial report under the Companies Act may be used to determine the controlling position of a natural person with respect to the asset management.

If no natural person can be identified as the beneficial owner using the aforementioned criteria and conditions, the management members of the corporate entity are registered as beneficial owners. Only persons duly registered as members of the management within the court register are registered as beneficial owners in the latter case.

2.2 Beneficial owners of entities without share capital and of Slovene institutions

Beneficial owners of entities without share capital (ie, societies, institutes, political parties, trade unions, religious communities) are considered to be the members of their respective management bodies.

Notwithstanding the basic rule described above, a beneficial owner shall be:

- the founder of the institution, if he/she exercises a controlling position under the statutes or internal rules;
- the custodian of the institution, as determined by the law governing institutions; or
- the representative of the institution, if the founder of the institution cannot be considered the beneficial owner.

Please note that trusts cannot be established under Slovene law.

2.3 Rules for determining beneficial owners of foreign funds, institutions and similar entities

Please note that these rules apply to both EU and non-EU entities.

Beneficial owners of foreign funds, institutions or a similar entity under foreign law, which accepts, manages or distributes financial assets for a specific purpose, shall be the following:

- any natural person who is:
   - the founder under the foreign law;
   - the custodian of the assets;

  - the recipient of benefits from the managed assets provided that future beneficiaries are determined or can be identified; or
  - the potential protector appointed to represent and protect the interests of the recipients of benefits from the assets;
- persons in whose interests the foreign entity was incorporated or is being managed if individuals who will be beneficiaries of such foreign entity have yet to be determined or identified; or
- any other natural person who exercises ultimate control over the foreign entity under foreign law, through direct or indirect ownership or by other means of control.

Please note that trusts cannot be established under Slovene law.

3. Obligation to determine the beneficial owner

Obligation to determine the beneficial owner lies with the entity in question. Slovene entities (both corporate with share capital and those without share capital) are obliged to determine their respective beneficial owners at all times for the purpose of their registration with the Slovene BO Register.

Foreign funds, institutions and similar entities are obliged to determine their beneficial owners for the purpose of their registration with the Slovene BO Register in the following cases:

- if the foreign entity's custodian has its registered office or residence in Slovenia;
- if the foreign entity's custodian concludes a business relationship[4] or acquires real estate in Slovenia on behalf of the said foreign entity; or
- if the foreign entity's custodian has its registered office or residence in several member states or he/she concludes a business relationship or acquires real estate in several member states but has not yet registered in any BO register in any of the other member states.

4. The Beneficial Owners Register

The BO Register was established in 2016 and the final deadline for registration expired on 19 January 2018.

The BO Register is managed by the Slovene Agency of the Republic of Slovenia for Public Legal Records and Related Services (*Agencija Republike Slovenije za javnopravne evidence in storitve* – AJPES) in electronic form.

The Slovene BO Register is registered with the central European platform established under the first paragraph of Article 22 of the Directive (EU)

---

4 The term 'business relationship' is defined under Article 3 of the ZPPDFT-1 as *"any business or other contractual relationship that a party enters into or establishes with an entity, which is obliged to report the UBO under this Act, and is related to the performance of such person's activities and is presumed to be permanent when establishing a contact, unless otherwise provided by this Act."*

2017/1132 of the European Parliament and of the Council of 14 June 2017 relating to certain aspects of company law, as amended.

All data on entities and beneficial owners is registered in a single BO register.

4.1 Obligation to register data

Individual registrations of the initial beneficial owner and all subsequent changes must be made within eight days of their registration or their change in the Slovene Business Register or the Slovene Tax Register.

Registrations for certain entities are made automatically by the Business Register (eg, individual entrepreneurs, natural persons performing business activities, and single shareholder limited liability companies).

4.2 Published data

The following data is registered with the BO Register:

- data on the business entity (name, address, registered office, registration and tax number, date of incorporation and dissolution);
- data on the beneficial owner (full name, permanent or temporary residence address, date of birth, tax number, citizenship, held percentage of ownership, and date of registration and deregistration from the BO Register); and
- for foreign funds, institutions and similar entities, data on persons for the benefit of which the fund or institution was established.

All data, including all changed data, is kept for five years after deregistration of the business entity from the business or tax register.

All data is entered through the application on the AJPES webpage.

4.3 Public access to published data

The following data is public and available for insight free of charge through the AJPES webpage[5] with the obligation of a prior user registration with the AJPES system:

- personal name;
- month and year of birth;
- country of permanent and temporary residence;
- nationality;
- amount of ownership or form of control of actual owners; and
- the date of entry and deletion of the beneficial owner from the register.

Public searches in the search engine are only possible using the name of the

5 www.ajpes.si/eRDL/Iskalnik/Javni.

entity/company and not the name of an individual. The general public does not have the option to search for all entries for a specific beneficial owner.

Persons or organisations showing a legitimate interest in money laundering, terrorist financing and related pre-trial offences also have the right to file an application with the Slovene Office for Money Laundering Prevention to access the data on the date of birth and nationality of the beneficial owners.

The current legislation does not allow a request to withhold data of a beneficial owner from being published. We are not aware of any past legal objections raised against publication of data.

5. Fines for non-compliance

5.1 Fines for business entities

A fine of between €6,000 and €60,000 may be imposed upon a legal person which does not determine or determines false data on its beneficial owner, does not implement or manage such data, or does not update or store such data, which fails to provide all data to qualified official bodies or courts, or which does not register data on its beneficial owner or registers false data within the set deadline.

A fine of between €400 and €2,000 may be imposed upon the responsible person of the legal person.

5.2 Fines for beneficial owners

A fine of between €400 and €2,000 may be enforced upon a natural person who is the beneficial owner of a business entity but does not provide it with all required information.

Spain

Alberto Perez Cedillo
Alberto Perez Cedillo Spanish Lawyers and Solicitors

1. Overview of legal framework

The Spanish legal framework with regard to the information duties imposed on ultimate beneficial owners is mainly included within the following:

- Law 10/2010 of 28 April 2010 on Prevention of money laundering and financing of terrorism (hereinafter Law 10/2010);[1] and
- Royal Decree 304/2014 of 5 May 2014 approving the regulation of Law 10/2010 (hereinafter Royal Decree 304/2014).

The above legal framework was recently modified by virtue of the following:

- Royal Decree-Law 11/2018 of 31 August 2018 in order to be adapted to the EU Directive 2015/849 of 20 May 2015 (the Fourth EU Anti-Money Laundering Directive – 4AMLD); and
- Order JUS/319/2018 of 21 March 2018 approving the new forms for filing the annual accounts of those parties required to publish them at the Commercial Registry, which came into force on 28 March 2018 and requires identification of the ultimate beneficial owner and the control structure.

2. Overview of legal persons

The main types of company in Spain are as follows:

- the private limited liability company (*Sociedades de Responsabilidad Limitada* – SL), which makes up 92% of legal persons in Spain and 96% of new incorporations; and
- the joint stock company (*Sociedades Anónimas* – SA), which makes up 7.5% of legal persons.

3. Overview of trusts

Spain is not a signatory to the 1985 Hague Convention, and generally trusts as legal arrangements (domestic or foreign) are not enforceable in Spanish courts.

1 Spanish translation: *Ley 10/2010, de 28 de abril, de prevención del blanqueo de capitales y de la financiación del terrorismo.*

Analysis of the operational risks of foreign trusts has demonstrated that the number of trusts is quite modest, and that they mainly appear as remitters of funds from abroad (thus not operating directly in Spain, nor having direct relationships with obliged entities[2] in Spain).

Anti-money laundering (AML) and combating the financing of terrorism (CFT) obligations apply to trustees, and Royal Decree 304/2014 (Article 6) requires obliged persons (including trustees) to identify and verify the identity of the settlor, the trustees, the protector, the beneficiaries, and any other natural person who exercises ultimate effective control over express trusts or similar arrangements, even through a chain of control or ownership.

The same Royal Decree obliges trustees of express trusts to report their status to obliged entities when they wish to establish business relationships or intervene in a transaction. Article 9.6 of Royal Decree 304/2014 allows obliged entities to access the notaries' Single Computerised Index[3] to verify beneficial ownership.

The Single Computerised Index allows notaries to carry out, electronically, periodic communications with the General Council of Notaries with regards to data contained in the documents notarised so that they can be processed and subsequently sent to each of the recipients according to the information obligations, both corporate and with the administrations. On the other hand, the Single Computerised Index facilitates the elaboration of statistics about notarial activity, which leads to important aspects of legal and economic life in Spain being made available by the notaries to the general public.

In recent years, law enforcement authorities have noted an increase in the use of individual companies or networks of companies (both domestic and foreign) in large-scale money laundering schemes. The SL is the type of legal person most commonly used in money laundering schemes, which is unsurprising considering that it dominates the Spanish corporate landscape.

Legal persons are used for money laundering in several ways, from simple self-laundering, through smurfing, and the use of front companies with or without legitimate business activities, to the use of complex, multi-layered and offshore corporate structures. One trend that has been noted in money laundering cases is a shift away from using newly created simple front companies with no legitimate business activities towards laundering money through established companies which also conduct other, legitimate business (eg, trading companies).

Spain is not an international centre for company formation and administration, nor is it a source country for legal arrangements, other than as described above.

---

2 Article 2 Law 10/2010, 28 April 2010, Prevention of money laundering and financing of terrorism.
3 Spanish translation: *El Índice Único Informatizado Notarial.*

4. Notarial databases – Single Computerised Index

In Spain, notaries and registrars[4] are public officials, and are also obliged entities under the AML/CFT law.

In all instances, notaries are required to collect information pertaining to all parties involved in an act or transaction (ie, not only the person who ultimately covers the expenses of the notary's activity).

Because notaries act under delegated authority from the Ministry of Justice in incorporating legal persons, the involvement of a notary is required at the company formation stage, as well as subsequently, in the case of SLs, to validate specific changes in ownership.

In addition to company services, notaries conduct some 300 different types of activity. When duly executed, notarial acts and deeds are presumed to be valid, self-authenticating and self-executing, as well as probative.

Since 1 January 2004, all the information collected by notaries is uploaded twice a month to a database: the Single Computerised Index, which is managed by the General Council of Notaries.[5]

In addition to the basic information collected, the database includes scanned copies of ID documents and notarial deeds. The required ID documents are the Tax Identification Number (NIF) for nationals and the Foreigner Identification Number (NIE) for foreigners. All financial transactions to be carried out in Spain require an NIF or an NIE depending on whether you are a national or a foreigner. The database contains information pertaining to more than 70 million notarial deeds, 96 million transactions, 140 million natural and legal persons and 49 million objects.

Before the Register of Beneficial Owners (UBO Register) was created at Companies House, Spain principally relied on the notary profession's Single Computerised Index for information on beneficial ownership of legal persons. This includes information obtained and recorded by notaries when incorporating entities or conducting certain other acts or transactions by persons and entities, and information on the transfer of shares of SLs. On the other hand, there are several weaknesses in the system relating to sanctions for breaches, and the lack of effective controls on the transfers of shares in public limited companies (SAs) that are not publicly listed.

The information contained in the Single Computerised Index is available to all competent authorities. For example, law enforcement agencies (National Police, Guardia Civil), specialised prosecutors (National Prosecutor's Offices against drugs and organised crime, corruption and other economic crimes),

---

4 Spanish translation: *Registradores Def Registrar* is the Spanish public official who works at the Land Registry Offices of Spain where real estate is identified by means of the name of the municipality, the Land Registry Office and Registry Section and the Land Registry Property Number. It is advised to also furnish, if available, the volume, book and sheet number where the property is registered.

5 Spanish translation: *Consejo General del Notariado.*

Customs, and the SEBPLAC[6] (Anti-Money Laundering Supervision Authority) have direct, online access via a token system, with results delivered in real-time. Other authorities (eg, the judiciary and the Secretariat of the Commission) may request access to specific information.

5. European directives and Spanish legislation

Royal Decree-Law of 31 August 2018, which incorporated, among others, 4AMLD, introduced a new single additional provision in the 2010 law, which specifically states that "legal persons must present a statement of those who are its beneficial owners" in the competent Commercial Registry because of their domicile (Sections 1 and 4). This implied that the UBO Register was no longer to be run by the notaries but by the commercial registrars at Companies House.

5.1 Notaries' position

Reluctant to give in, the notaries association declared at the time as follows:[7]

> *Order JUS/319/2018 supposes a very serious infringement of the fundamental right to privacy from the moment in which, without the existence of a previous law, it is obliged to deposit the information on the beneficial owner in the Mercantile Registry, the registrars attributing the power to decide who can or cannot access that information.*
>
> *The registrars intend by this procedure to unilaterally change the legislation applicable to the Commercial Registry.*
>
> *In Spain, the Government has already decided in the Regulation of the Laundering Prevention Law (art. 9.6) that it would be the Data Base of the Real Holder of the General Council of Notaries that would provide such information.*

5.2 Registrars' position

The registrars replied, arguing as follows:[8]

> *It cannot be said that it threatens the privacy of small and medium-sized entrepreneurs since it only collects what is already established today.*
>
> *The publicity of the beneficial ownership, which refers only to those cases in which 25% or more of the capital stock is held, is carried out after qualification by the registrar of the legitimate interest alleged by the applicant.*
>
> *Access can be modulated if it can expose the beneficial owner to a risk of fraud, kidnapping, blackmail, violence or intimidation.*
>
> *At the moment there is already a notarial database of real ownership (...), but as it is not a public registry, it cannot give a complete answer to the provisions of the Directive.*

---

6 Spanish translation: *Servicio Ejecutivo de la Comisión de Prevención del Blanqueo de Capitales e Infracciones Monetarias.*

7 Official statement of the CEPYME and General Council of the Spanish Notaries after appeal against Order 319/2018.

8 Reply of the Spanish Registrars to the CEPYME and General Council of the Spanish Notaries appeal.

Litigation between both professional groups of notaries and registrars ensued, threatening the effectiveness of the government's fight against criminal money laundering and tax fraud schemes.

The management of the UBO Register finally fell to the property and commercial registrars, who launched the new registry on 25 October 2018 with updated information on the individuals who directly or indirectly control the company.

6. The new UBO Register

6.1 The new form 'Declaration of beneficial ownership' pursuant to Ministerial Order JUS/319/2018 of 21 March 2018

The main novelty under Order JUS/319/2018 of 21 March 2018 giving effect to the new form for submission of statutory annual accounts to Companies House by reporting persons is the document named 'Declaration of beneficial owner identification'. Said document must include non-accounting information made mandatory by application of the provisions of 4AMLD.

Article 30.3 of 4AMLD, the transposition period of which ended 26 June 2017, sets out that:

> *Member States shall ensure that the information [...] is held in a central register in each Member State, for example, a commercial register, companies register [...], or a public register.*

Reporting persons and authorities may demand accurate information concerning the beneficial ownership of legal persons from the registers.

In consequence, all legal entities with a registered address in Spain that file accounts in Companies House are subject to identifying the ultimate beneficial owner, except: (i) the companies listed on a regulated market of the European Union or equivalent third countries (Article 4.2(b) of Law 10/2010); or (ii) their majority-owned subsidiaries as long as they are subject to providing information that ensures the adequate transparency of the beneficial owner (Article 9.4 Royal Decree 304/2014 of 5 May 2014 which develops Law 10/2010).

All separate accounts must include the duly completed official form concerning the beneficial owner. Failing that, the accounts will not be accepted and will be declared incomplete subject to remedy. Blank forms will not be accepted.

The new form is only for separate accounts and it is not mandatory for consolidated reporting persons. Therefore, the parent company submitting separate and consolidated financial statements must fill in said form together with any other documents that integrate or come with separate accounts. Subsidiaries must also incorporate the beneficial ownership declaration into their separate accounts. The fact that the parent company has reported said document does not excuse its subsidiaries from reporting their own.

Regardless of company size or the preparation of the abbreviated separate financial statement, the document is still compulsory.

Subject to the official template, the beneficial ownership document is to be completed (as mandatory) according to the official template – even if the submitting company or undertaking were allowed by law to lodge its financial statements without having regard to official templates for balances, profit and loss, and annual reports.[9]

6.2 Liability for completing the form

As provided for under Section 9.1 of Law 10/2010, companies' officers or other legal persons must obtain and maintain adequate, accurate and up-to-date information concerning the ownership thereof.

The declaration must be completed by those preparing and signing the annual accounts and submitted together with the annual accounts. Having regard to the terms of the legislation for the prevention of money laundering, the officers of the company or undertaking lodging separate financial statements are then the 'reporting persons' who identify the beneficial owner of said company or undertaking, pursuant to the provisions of Section 4 of Law 10/2010 of 28 April 2010 for the prevention of money laundering and terrorist financing and implementing regulations (Sections 8 and 9 of the Implementing Regulations approved by Royal Decree 304/2014 of 5 May 2014).

The new forms are applicable to separate accounts reporting for financial years commencing 1 January 2017. For any financial statements related to previous years (before 1 January 2017) the aforementioned template will not be necessary for separate accounts.

The declaration under the beneficial ownership form accompanying annual accounts refers to the situation that is current at the time of accounts year-end of the statements being lodged (following standard year-end dates, 31 December), unless otherwise arising from the document or stated otherwise in the document.

If after year-end and before filing a change of circumstances takes place, the officers aware of said change must submit a new beneficial ownership declaration form signed by them stating the relevant date when the change materialised.

Likewise, the officers of the company are responsible for amending any out-of-date register information whenever the corporate structure may have changed as a result of capital increase or capital reduction operations (eg, mergers, demergers, transformations etc) or arising out of any other company resolution leading to changes in the beneficial ownership status as then currently registered.

---

9 See Annex 1: Declaration of Beneficial Owner Identification (1).

In any event, a natural person ceasing to be the beneficial owner may ask the officers of the company to amend or update the registry data in the manner set out above through a new declaration stating the new relevant data.

The form is non-accounting in nature and thus it is not part of the financial statements but a mandatory attachment, in the same manner as other documents such as the submission request for environmental declaration. To monitor its submission, the filing of the accounts is not considered complete without it. New error tests have been devised, which alert the user that the obligation of declaration completion has not been complied with through the relevant computer application.

If auditors must verify the annual accounts, it is understood that the auditor extends the scope of its role to include verification that the form has been duly completed from the formal standpoint.

All legal persons domiciled in Spain that submit their accounts to Companies House in Spain are subject to the obligation of identifying their beneficial owner(s), except for those companies listed on a regulated market pursuant to Article 3.6(a)(i) of the directive and Section 9.4 of Law 10/2010. That is to say, listed public limited companies domiciled in Spain are exempt or free from said obligation, but not those with shares listed on the Alternative Investment Market[10] (AIM), which is a multilateral trading system under the terms provided by the equity market's legislation.

Branches of foreign companies located in Spain that file their accounts must also complete the aforementioned beneficial ownership declaration concerning the beneficial owner(s) of the relevant company.

The obligation of identifying the beneficial owner bears down on all legal persons domiciled in Spain.

7. The concept of 'beneficial owner'

The following persons will be deemed beneficial owners.

- A natural person or natural persons that ultimately possess or control an interest (whether directly or indirectly) of more than 25% of the capital or the voting rights of a legal person, or who through resolutions or articles of association provisions may otherwise exercise control (whether direct or indirect) over the legal person's management. This is under Section I of the template form under the heading 'Beneficial owner being a natural person holding more than 25%'.
- If there is no natural person in possession or control (whether directly or indirectly) of more than 25% of the capital or voting rights of the legal person, or who may otherwise exercise control (whether direct or indirect) over said legal person, it will be deemed that the officer or

10 Spanish translation: *Mercado Alternativo Bursátil (MAB).*

officers of the company exercise such control. Whenever the appointed officer is a legal person, the control will be deemed as exercised by the natural person appointed by the legal person's officer. This is under Section II of the template form under the heading 'Equivalent beneficial owner being a natural person'.

- A natural person or natural persons holding 25% or more of the property of the legal instrument or legal person administering or distributing funds; or, whenever the beneficiaries are yet to be appointed, the category of persons for the benefit of whom the legal instrument has been created or the legal person acts for. In the absence of a natural person holding or controlling (whether directly or indirectly) 25% or more of the aforementioned property, the natural person or natural persons ultimately responsible for the direction and management of the legal instrument or legal person will be deemed the beneficial owner(s), either through a company control structure or ownership.
- Natural persons who possess or control 25% or more of the voting rights of the board of directors of a foundation, or of the relevant representative body of an association, considering any resolutions or provisions in the articles of association that may impact on the establishment of the beneficial ownership.

If no natural person or persons fulfil the criteria set out above, beneficial owners will be the members of the board of directors of a foundation, or the relevant representative body or management board of an association.

In application of the above, when dealing with a state-owned or local authority-owned public undertaking, the natural person or persons in management positions at the relevant date of the declaration will be deemed the beneficial owner(s).

Legal persons cannot be beneficial owners. Beneficial owners are always natural persons (one or more). Sections I and II of the template form only allow for natural persons.

If the member is a legal person, such information must be reflected under Section III of the form, and the company control structure must be identified until it reaches the beneficial owners. If a member is a legal person and there are no beneficial owners for the member, then Section II of the form must be completed with the names of the officers of the single-member company as equivalent beneficial owners.

In companies where all members are natural persons, if every member holds more than 25% of the capital, the details of every one of them must be written under Section I with the corresponding percentage of direct interest held. If any of those members, being natural persons, holds more than 25% and others do not reach that percentage, Section I will only require the information concerning the members holding an interest of more than 25%.

Regarding the officers, all of them in principle should be included. This may incorporate the single officer, joint officers or joint and several officers, or the members of the board of directors. If one of the officers is a legal person, the natural person appointed as an officer for said legal person must be included in this case. (Section 8b Royal Decree 304/2014.)

In the case of other undertakings which are not corporations but also submit their accounts (eg, foundation trusts, associations, cooperatives etc), and whose management body structure is not similar to that of corporations, the members of any management body must be identified (eg, trustees, governing body members etc).

8. The concept of indirect beneficial ownership

As already explained, generally speaking a 'beneficial owner' is a natural person or natural persons that ultimately possess or control an interest (whether directly or indirectly) of more than 25% of the capital or the voting rights of a legal person, or who may otherwise exercise control (whether direct or indirect) over the legal person's management. There is indirect beneficial ownership whenever the natural person (or several persons jointly) who is the ultimate beneficiary holds an interest higher than 25% in the company reporting through intermediate companies – said person controls, ordinarily, through interest over 50%.

In the case of indirect beneficial ownership, the heading 'Breakdown of companies acting within the company control structure' under Section III of the form allows for the submission of the control scheme in normal detail, including the following:

- the beneficial owners themselves, being natural persons, may simultaneously hold direct and indirect interests in the reporting entity. To this effect, each case must be detailed as arising from the last column of Section I;
- the reporting entity itself may have beneficial owners who hold an indirect interest together with others who hold direct interests. In this case, only those holding indirect interest must complete Section III; and
- the reporting entity itself may have several beneficial owners with an indirect interest. In this case, all beneficial owners with indirect interest must complete Section III and provide their identification details by means of their Spanish NIF or equivalent code in the first column.

The concept of 'control' arises from the application of statute concerning consolidated financial statements as provided for under Article 42.1 of the Spanish Code of Commerce (*Código de Comercio*) and the Rules for the Preparation of Consolidated Financial Statements (and Sections 1 to 5 of the Directive 2013/34/EU of the European Parliament and the Council) whether the company prepares such accounts or not. In particular, the assumption of control is given whenever a company, a parent undertaking (controlling or dominant party), bears a relation to another company, a subsidiary undertaking (controlled or dependent) in any of the following scenarios:

- where it holds the majority of the voting rights;
- where it has the power to appoint or remove most of the members of the management body;
- where it is able to make free use of the majority of the voting rights, pursuant to arrangements concluded with third parties; or
- where it has appointed through its votes the majority of the members of the management body, who may act in the office at the time of the preparation of the consolidated financial statements and during the previous two years.

It is worth noting that the assumption of control is given when the majority of the members of the controlled undertaking's management body are members of the management body or senior directors of the controlling undertaking, or of another entity dominated by the controlling undertaking. In this case, if the company whose officers have been appointed is related to another as in the cases mentioned above, the consolidation requirement does not take effect.

9. Disclosure of public record data

The contents of the duly filed declaration, upon the Companies House registrar's authorisation for its entry into the official record of Companies House, will be held on the public record (for disclosure) in accordance with Article 30.3 of 4AMLD, subject to personal data protection rules. To this effect, any access to such information concerning beneficial ownership will be carried out under the Companies House rules for 'official disclosure'. Data is available to all competent authorities that have entered into an agreement with the registry.

Annex

Readers should note that the following forms are the author's translation of official forms available at the Spanish Companies House (*Registro Mercantil*).

Once this form has been created, you will then be able to complete an update of the declaration of beneficial owner identification.

DECLARATION OF BENEFICIAL OWNER IDENTIFICATION (1) **BO**

IDENTIFICATION OF BENEFICIAL OWNER

Information concerning natural persons in accordance with articles 3.6) and 30 of the Directive (EU) 2015/849 of the European Parliament and of the Council of 20 May 2015, on the prevention of the use of the financial system for the purposes of money laundering or terrorist financing, which amends Regulation (EU) 648/2012 of the European Parliament and of the Council and revokes Directive 2005/60/EC of the European Parliament and of the Council and Directive 2006/70/EC of the Commission; in accordance with sections 4.2 b) and c) of the Spanish Act 10/2010 of 28 April for the prevention of money laundering and terrorist financing, and with section 8 of the Implementing Regulations for Act 10/2010 of 28 April for the prevention of money laundering and terrorist financing; approved by Royal Decree 304/2014 of 5 May.

I. Beneficial owner being a natural person holding more than 25%

NAME(S) & SURNAME(S)	DNI/FOREIGN ID CODE	DOB (DD.MM.YYYY)	NATIONALITY/CODE (2)	COUNTRY OF RESIDENCE CODE (2)	% INTEREST DIRECT	% INTEREST INDIRECT (3)
1	2	3	4	5	6	7

II. Equivalent beneficial owner being a natural person

If there is no natural person who holds or controls more than 25% of the capital or the voting rights, do state the beneficial owners such as officers or those responsible for management, pursuant to the provisions of Section 8 of the Implementing Regulations for Act 10/2010 of 28 April.

NAME(S) & SURNAME(S)	DNI/FOREIGN ID CODE	DOB (DD.MM.YYYY)	NATIONALITY/CODE (2)	COUNTRY OF RESIDENCE CODE (2)
1	2	3	4	5

III. Breakdown of companies acting within the company control structure

If beneficial ownership is indirect, please break down the company control structure.

DNI/FOREIGN ID CODE	COMPANY CONTROL STRUCTURE TIER	CORPORATE NAME	NIF/FOREIGN ID CODE	NATIONALITY/CODE (2)	REGISTERED ADDRESS	REGISTRY DATA LEI (WHERE APPLICABLE)
1	2	3	4	5	6	7

INSTRUCTIONS FOR COMPLETION

By declaring the 'beneficial owner' of the company or entity that deposits individual - non-consolidated - accounts, the institutions subject to this obligation comply with the provisions of Directive (EU) 2015/849 of the European Parliament and of the Council of 20 May 2015 on the prevention of the use of the financial system for the purpose of money laundering or terrorist financing, and amending Regulation (EU) 648/2012 of the European Parliament and of the Council, and repealing Directive 2005/60/EC of the European Parliament and of the Council and Commission Directive 2006/70/EC, and in Sections 4.2.b) and c) of the Spanish Act 10/2010, of 28

continued on next page

April, on the prevention of money laundering and the financing of terrorism, implemented by Section 8 of the Implementing Regulations of Act 10/2010, of 28 April, on the prevention of money laundering and the financing of terrorism, approved by Royal Decree 304/2014, of 5 May.

All legal persons domiciled in Spain that deposit accounts are subject to the obligation of identifying the beneficial owner, except for companies listed on a regulated market: article 3 6.a).i) of Directive (EU) 2015/849 of the European Parliament and of the Council, of 20 May 2015, and Section 9.4 of the Spanish Act 10/2010, of 28 April.

The 'beneficial owner' is the natural person or taxable persons who meet the requirements provided for under the Directive and under Spanish legislation.
As regards the concept of 'control' and 'indirect control'. The following will be subject to the regulations on consolidated accounts: Article 42 of the Code of Commerce and Rules for the Preparation of Consolidated Annual Accounts, and Article 6.a).i) of Directive (EU) 2015/849 of the European Parliament and of the Council of 20 May 2015 (which refers to Article 22, paragraphs 1 to 5, of Directive 2013/34/EU of the European Parliament and of the Council).
The duly filed declaration, upon being cleared by the Registrar of the CH for entry into the register, will be available for official disclosure of public record in accordance with Article 30.3 of Directive (EU) 2015/849 of the European Parliament and of the Council of 20 May 2015. To this end, access to information on beneficial ownership shall be made in accordance with the rules on data protection and in accordance with the rules for holding information in public record for open disclosure to Companies House: Article 30.5 of Directive (EU) 2015/849 of the European Parliament and of the Council of 20 May 2015: Article 12 of the Code of Commerce, and Articles 77 *et sequentes* of the Companies House Procedure.

Beneficial owner

Concerning the reporting company or entity, a beneficial owner is understood as the natural person or persons who ultimately control, directly or indirectly, more than 25% of the capital or of the voting rights of the company or entity; or who otherwise may exercise the control, direct or indirect, of the legal entity's management. Concerning the concept of 'control' and the counting of the voting rights if control is indirect through controlled undertakings, please see Article 42.1 of the Code of Commerce.

Beneficial owners will be those who hold or control 25% or more of the voting rights in a board of trustees, in a foundation trust, or in a board of representation, in an association, having regard to their resolutions and articles of association that may affect the determining of said beneficial ownership.

Failing the above, the control will be deemed to be exercised by the officer or officers of the reporting entity. When the officer appointed is a legal person, the control will be deemed to be exercised by the natural person appointed by said legal person management.

Indirect beneficial owner

If dealing with indirect beneficial ownership, you must provide a breakdown of the company control structure through which the voting rights are held:

a) You must commence by identifying the controlling legal person with immediate interests in the company or reporting entity, until reaching the ultimate beneficial owner.

b) Each controlling legal entity in the company control structure will be identified by its corporate name, nationality code, registered address and registry data (and the LEI, where applicable).

Note: If necessary, use as many copies of this sheet as may be necessary.

(1) Companies listed on a European Union regulated market or on a regulated market of an equivalent third country are exempt.
(2) Country code as per ISO 3166-2 standard.
(3) Break down acting companies under Section III.

CREATE A NEW FORM

Now you may proceed to complete the submission request for the Companies House, by filling in the details of the entity filing the document, as well as the actual natural person submitting the request.

AT THE COMPANIES HOUSE OF MADRID
Provincial seat of the Companies House

DECLARATION OF BENEFICIAL OWNER IDENTIFICATION

IDENTIFICATION OF ENTITY SUBMITTING THE DOCUMENT

Company's name NIF: B88888888

Registry data:

Volume: Folio: Sheet number:

IDENTIFICATION OF DOCUMENT FOR WHICH REGISTRATION IS REQUESTED

Information update concerning the identification of the beneficial owners of the aforementioned entity

IDENTIFICATION OF THE PERSON SUBMITTING THE REQUEST

Date of request: (dd.mm.yyyy)

Name(s) & Surname(s) DNI

Address: Postcode:

Town/city: Province:

Telephone: Fax E-mail address:

The submitting party authorises the Companies House to send any notification by email in relation to this submission to the email address provided in accordance with Section 322 of the Spanish Mortgage Act *[Ley Hipotecaria]*.

SIGNATURE OF THE SUBMITTING PARTY: 2D Code

For the purposes of Regulation (EU) 2016/679 of the European Parliament and of the Council of 27 April 2016 on the protection of natural persons with regard to the processing of personal data and on the free movement of such data (RGPD), we hereby inform you: 1.- That with respect to the personal data expressed in this document, the Registrar is responsible for the processing, the purpose of which is to comply with the registry regulations, which is the legitimate basis for such processing. The information contained in them will only be communicated in the cases provided for by law, or with the aim of satisfying the requests for disclosure of official data that are formulated in accordance with registry legislation (sections 2, 4, 9 and 12 of the Preliminary Part of the Companies House Procedure [R.R.M.] and Instructions of 29 October 1996 and 17 February 1998). 2.- As soon as it is compatible with the specific regulations applicable to the CH, the interested parties are recognised as having the rights of access, rectification, suppression, opposition, limitation and portability established in the aforementioned RGPD, and may exercise them by writing to the address of the Register. Similarly, the user can go to the Spanish Data Protection Agency (AEPD www.agpd.es) and contact the CH's data protection representative at dpo@corpme.es. The period of conservation of the data will be determined in accordance with the criteria established in the legislation of the CH, resolutions of the General Executive of the Registries and the Notary's Office and association instructions. 3.- Obtaining and processing your data in the manner indicated is a necessary condition for the provision of these services.

[Bar code recorded]

CREATE A NEW FORM

Lastly, we complete the details for the person or persons issuing the certification for the updated information concerning the beneficial owners.

CERTIFICATION OF DIGITAL PRINT FOR THE UPDATE OF THE BENEFICIAL OWNERS SHEET **H**

COMPANY | NIF B88888888

REGISTERED ADDRESS:

TOWN/CITY: | PROVINCE: | DATE OF REQUEST:

NAME(S) & SURNAME(S) OF THE PERSON(S) ISSUING THE CERTIFICATION	DNI/FOREIGN ID CODE	POSITION HELD
First Officer		

SIGNATURES:

THE AFOREMENTIONED PERSON(S) CERTIFY/CERTIFIES THAT THE DECLARATION OF THE BENEFICIAL OWNERS SHEET GENERATES THE FOLLOWING DIGITAL PRINT

[Bar code recorded]

United Kingdom

Iskra Doukova
Edward Reed
Macfarlanes LLP

1. Introduction

By way of a short introduction on the historical context, the transparency initiatives that have come to fruition in the Persons with Significant Control (PSC) Register (for companies and LLPs) and the Trust Register (for trusts) have a common political origin in the revised standards of the Financial Action Task Force (FATF).[1] At the G8 Summit hosted by David Cameron's coalition government in Northern Ireland in 2013, against the backdrop of the financial crisis, transparency was adopted as the basis of "lasting growth and stability".[2]

In parallel with promoting automatic exchange of information, supporting the work of the Organisation for Economic Cooperation and Development (OECD) to help governments combat tax evasion and working with the OECD's Base Erosion and Profit Shifting project to combat tax avoidance, the G8 committed to bringing into the daylight:

> *information on who really owns and profits from companies and trusts, making it available to tax collection and law enforcement agencies, for example through central registries of company beneficial ownership.*[3]

The published papers of the G8 Summit include a general G8 action plan principles note as well as a discrete UK action plan "to prevent the misuse of companies and legal arrangements".

This G8 initiative ran in tandem with the European Union's anti-money laundering initiatives, starting also in 2013 with the planned implementation of the Fourth EU Anti-Money Laundering Directive (4AMLD) and (more recently, in 2020) its Fifth Anti-Money Laundering Directive (5AMLD). Because of the association with the FATF principles, the regime planned at the G8 Summit comes with 'dissuasive sanctions'. An edited version of the G8's first three principles repays reproduction here.

---

1 It is understood that the Council of the European Union, sitting as the Economic and Financial Affairs Council (ECOFIN), endorsed the Commission's Anti-Money Laundering Action Plan on 5 November 2020, which, among others, includes the creation of a single EU AML rulebook, as well as a pan-European AML supervisor. As AML underpins many transparency initiatives, it will be interesting to see if a harmonisation of the rules will impact the PSC and Trust Register regimes in the future.

2 www.gov.uk/government/collections/g8-communique-and-documents.

3 www.gov.uk/government/news/g8-summit-prime-ministers-remarks.

- *Companies should know who owns and controls them (and share that information).*
  In other words, ignorance is no longer bliss.
- *Beneficial ownership information on companies should be accessible onshore to law enforcement, tax administrations and other relevant authorities including, as appropriate, financial intelligence units. This could be achieved through central registries... some basic company information should be publicly accessible.*
  To put it differently, registers are here to stay.
- *Trustees of express trusts should know the beneficial ownership of the trust... this information should be accessible by law enforcement, tax administration and other relevant authorities including, as appropriate, financial intelligence units.*
  Finally, private structures are not immune to this new scrutiny.

Inherent in these early declarations is an early distinction in the accessibility of the information recorded as a result of implementing the initiatives: public vehicles are more transparent than private, but (as we will see) companies may bring trust ownership into the daylight.

If there was ever any question over the political imperative in the initiatives, the more detailed UK Action Plan[4] to prevent the misuse of companies and legal arrangements introduces a number of actions prefaced by the comment "this is a matter of good corporate governance as well as a means to tackle a wide range of illicit activity". The following are edited highlights, clearly inspired by the G8 principles.

- Ensure the Companies Act 2006 and UK Money Laundering Regulations oblige companies to know who owns and controls them, by requiring that companies obtain and hold adequate, accurate and current information on their beneficial ownership.
- Amend the Companies Act 2006 to require that this information is accurate and readily available to the authorities through a central registry of information, maintained by Companies House. Consult on whether information in the registry should be publicly accessible.
- Ensure that trustees of express trusts are obliged to obtain and hold adequate, accurate and current information on beneficial ownership regarding the trust.
- Put in place mechanisms to ensure that the relevant competent authorities have access to information on trusts and ensure effective mechanisms to share this information with other jurisdictions, in line with bilateral and multilateral agreements.

---

4 https://assets.publishing.service.gov.uk/government/uploads/system/uploads/attachment_data/file/207520/UK-Action-Plan.pdf.

The statement concludes:

implementation of the measures will be through, and at the same time as, transposition of the Fourth EU Money Laundering Directive and UK Money Laundering Regulations, changes to the Companies Act 2006, as well as through other relevant bilateral and multilateral agreements.[5]

Finally, the government committed to leaning on the Crown Dependencies and Overseas Territories to ensure the adoption there of equivalent measures.

As ever with modern regulation, there is considerable fine detail around the regimes. The UK Government's Department for Business, Energy & Industrial Strategy (BEIS) published a review of the implementation of the PSC regime in March 2019,[6] which records the impact of the regime (aimed at corporates and certain partnerships) on a variety of stakeholders, including law enforcement agencies and so-called civil society organisations. The research shows that two-thirds of businesses were already keeping records before the introduction of the regime. Surprisingly perhaps, the mean and median cost of compliance with the regime is thought to be extremely low. More interestingly, 22% of businesses had used the PSC regime to look up information about other businesses. Of those, nearly two-thirds were looking up information about clients and customers, and again nearly two-thirds found the information useful or very useful. All law enforcement agencies had used the PSC regime "to inform criminal investigations". In other words, whilst primarily designed as an intelligence tool for the authorities, these initiatives may have commercial ramifications.

Questions remain however over the quality of the data supplied, which is currently subject to little or no verification, as well as over the structure of the public register itself, which has to be searched by business name and cannot currently be searched by PSC. In other words, it is still comparatively difficult to determine whether a particular individual is the PSC of more than one business. It would be surprising if this element did not form part of a future evolution of the current regime.

Finally, it is worth noting that in keeping with the overall transparency logic and other initiatives to tax non-resident owners of UK residential real estate, BEIS has introduced into Parliament a draft Registration of Overseas Entities Bill[7] designed to create a beneficial ownership (aka OEBO) regime, originally due to come into effect at the beginning of 2021, for vehicles acquiring UK real estate or participating in a public tender in the United Kingdom. It is expected to create a new register, in which overseas companies will need to register details

5 https://assets.publishing.service.gov.uk/government/uploads/system/uploads/attachment_data/file/207520/UK-Action-Plan.pdf.

6 https://assets.publishing.service.gov.uk/government/uploads/system/uploads/attachment_data/file/822823/review-implementation-psc-register.pdf.

7 https://assets.publishing.service.gov.uk/government/uploads/system/uploads/attachment_data/file/727915/Draft_Registration_of_Overseas_Entities.pdf.

of their beneficial owners as a condition to acquiring or dealing with UK real estate or participating in a tender.

2. The 'Persons with Significant Control' (aka PSC) regime

2.1 What is the PSC regime?

The PSC regime requires certain entities to identify and record details of the persons who have 'significant control' over them. In a topic already rich with acronyms, these break down into:

- persons with significant control (PSCs); and
- relevant legal entities (RLEs).

To comply with the regime, an entity and its officers will need a good working knowledge of the following:

- general company law (eg, Section 168 Companies Act 2006, which permits the passage of an ordinary resolution to remove a director);
- the constitutional documents of the company, including any shareholders' agreement, trust or other arrangement (eg, the levels of voting rights which shareholders hold and the terms on which any investor has invested in a company);
- the intricate terms of the PSC regime; and
- any supervening fact pattern which may inform the analysis (eg, special short-term contractual arrangements, such as mortgages and nominee arrangements, and unwritten rules as to who exercises 'control').

As noted, the PSC regime emerged from the Government's drive towards transparency, as well as the United Kingdom's obligation to implement certain aspects of 4AMLD. It was implemented in April 2016, principally by amendments to the United Kingdom's central companies legislation – the Companies Act 2006 – and updated and expanded in June 2017 to implement remaining aspects of 4AMLD.

The regime is contained in various pieces of legislation/regulation, supplemented by multiple pieces of guidance:

- Acts of Parliament:
  - Part 21A and Schedules 1A and 1B, Companies Act 2006 (came into force on 6 April 2016);
- delegated legislation:
  - Register of People with Significant Control Regulations 2016 (as amended) (SI 2016/339) (PSC Regs 2016);
  - Limited Liability Partnerships (Application of Companies Act 2006) Regulations 2009 (SI 2009/1804) (as amended);

   - European Public Limited-Liability Company (Register of People with Significant Control) Regulations 2016 (SI 2016/375);
   - Unregistered Companies Regulations 2009 (SI 2009/2436) (as amended);
   - Scottish Partnerships (Register of People with Significant Control) Regulations 2017 (SI 2017/694);
- guidance published by BEIS:[8]
   - statutory guidance for companies on the meaning of 'significant influence or control'[9] (SIOC Guidance);
   - statutory guidance for LLPs on the meaning of 'significant influence or control';[10]
   - statutory guidance for eligible Scottish partnerships on the meaning of 'significant influence or control';[11]
   - non-statutory summary guidance for companies;
   - guidance for companies, SEs, LLPs and eligible Scottish partnerships;
   - guidance for PSCs of companies, SEs, LLPs and eligible Scottish partnerships;
- other guidance:
   - joint Law Society and City of London Law Society Q&A on the PSC Register (ed November 2019).[12] BEIS has signified that it does not disagree with any of the statements made in this Q&A.

2.2 To what entities does the PSC regime apply (ie, who has to keep a register)?

The PSC regime applies to the following:

- companies registered under the Companies Acts (ie, public limited companies, private companies limited by shares, private companies limited by guarantee and unlimited companies);
- limited liability partnerships (LLPs) incorporated in the United Kingdom;
- European companies (*societates europapaeae* or SEs) registered in the United Kingdom;[13]
- certain unregistered companies;

8 www.gov.uk/government/publications/guidance-to-the-people-with-significant-control-requirements-for-companies-and-limited-liability-partnerships.

9 https://assets.publishing.service.gov.uk/government/uploads/system/uploads/attachment_data/file/675104/psc-statutory-guidance-companies.pdf.

10 https://assets.publishing.service.gov.uk/government/uploads/system/uploads/attachment_data/file/675103/Statutory_guidance_LLPs.pdf.

11 https://assets.publishing.service.gov.uk/government/uploads/system/uploads/attachment_data/file/621569/170622_Eligible_Scot_P_GUI_June_2017.pdf.

12 www.lawsociety.org.uk/Topics/Business-management/Guides/Joint-Law-Society-and-CLLS-QA-on-the-PSC-Register.

13 Under EU Exit legislation, SEs registered in the United Kingdom automatically convert into a new form of legal entity – '*UK societates*' – with effect from IP completion day (broadly, the date on which EU law ceases to apply in the United Kingdom).

- Scottish limited partnerships;
- Scottish qualifying partnerships (ie, general Scottish partnerships where all partners are limited companies, or are unlimited companies all of whose own members are limited companies).

2.3 To which entities does the PSC regime not apply (ie, who does not have to keep a register)?

The PSC regime does not apply to entities with voting shares admitted to:

- an EEA regulated market[14] (which includes the London Stock Exchange Main Market);
- any market specified in Schedule 1 PSC Regs 2016 (a 'Schedule 1 market') (which includes NASDAQ and the New York Stock Exchange); and
- overseas entities (yet).

Note that since 26 June 2017, the PSC regime does apply to companies admitted to trading on a multilateral trading facility in the United Kingdom, such as AIM.

2.4 What must entities subject to the regime do?

Entities subject to the regime must:

- keep a PSC register;*
- take reasonable steps to identify their PSCs/RLEs;
- request of their registrable PSCs/RLEs confirmation of their details;
- record details of their registrable PSCs/RLEs in a PSC register;* and
- file details of their registrable PSCs/RLEs at Companies House.

*There is an exception for Scottish partnerships, which do not keep a PSC register but are required to make filings at Companies House.

2.5 Who is a PSC?

The term 'PSC' always refers to an individual (ie, a natural person).

An individual is a PSC if he/she satisfies one or more of five conditions. These are as follows, in ascending order of complexity, starting with more 'structural conditions' and ending with more of a 'substance over form' perspective.

- **Condition 1 (share ownership):** Holding – directly or indirectly – more than 25% of a company's shares (measured by the nominal value of shares actually in issue) or the right to participate in more than 25% of an LLP's assets on a winding-up.

---

14 Under EU Exit legislation, this will change to a 'UK regulated market or an EU regulated market' on IP completion day, although the substance of the exemption will remain the same.

Figure 1. PSC Register flowchart – overview

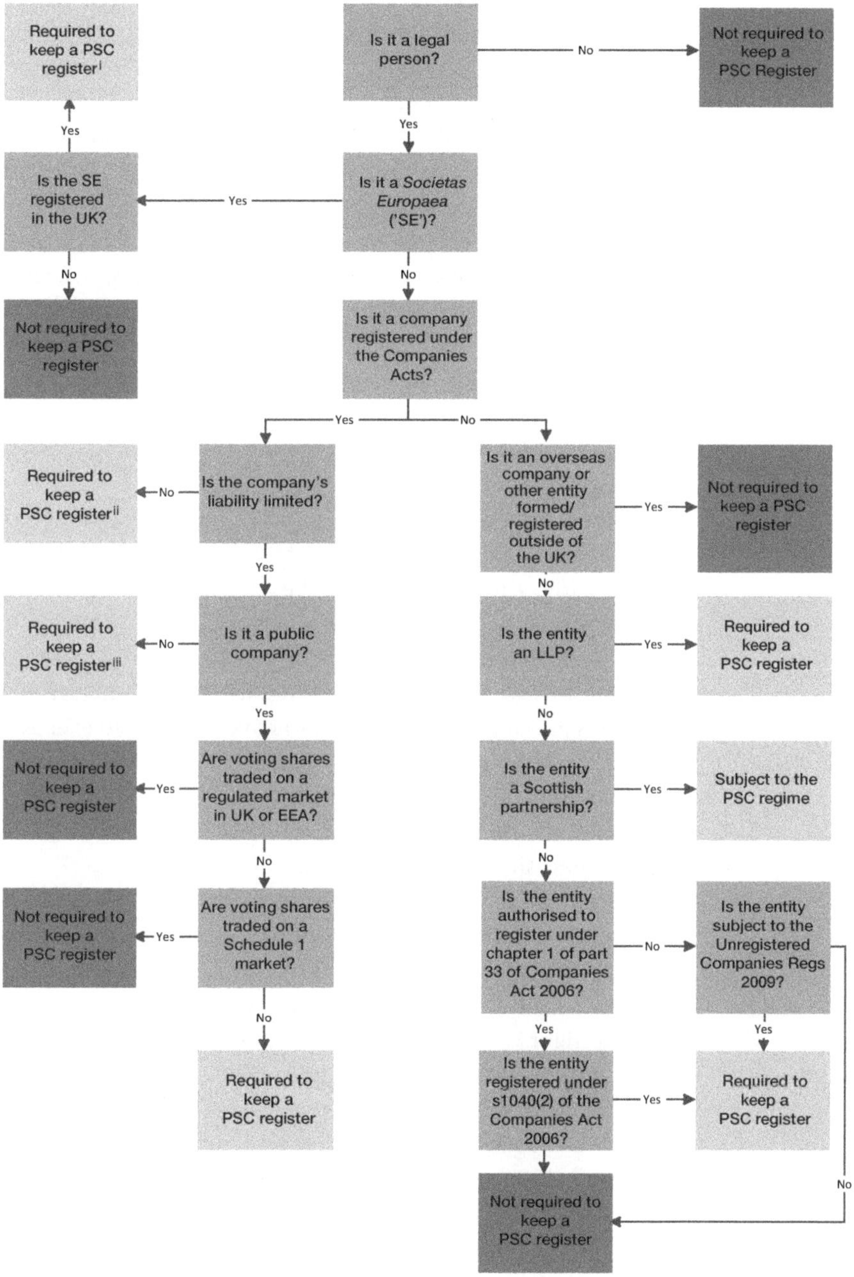

i An SE registered in the UK will not always automatically have to keep a PSC register, because the SE's voting shares could be admitted to trading on an EEA market or a Schedule 1 market.

ii In principle a company does not have to keep a PSC register simply because its liability is unlimited, this is because, in theory, certain stock exchanges might allow unlimited companies to admit their shares to trading.

iii In principle a company does not have to keep a PSC register simply because it is not a public company, this is because, in theory, certain stock exchanges might allow private companies to admit their shares to trading.

- **Condition 2 (voting rights):** Holding – directly or indirectly – more than 25% of a company's or LLP's voting rights.
- **Condition 3 (control of board seats):** Holding – directly or indirectly – the right to appoint or remove a majority of a company's board of directors (measured by number of board votes, not the number of directors) or a majority of an LLP's managing members (again, measured by number of votes). Note that this may be discernible only from the articles of association or a separate agreement, such as a shareholders' agreement or LLP agreement.[15]
- **Condition 4 (influence/control over a company):** Exercising, or having the right to exercise, significant influence or control (SIOC) over a company or LLP. Note:
  - this is a much broader condition which is based more on circumstances than structure;
  - statutory guidance exists for companies and LLPs;
  - key distinctions:
    - 'significant influence' and 'control' are two separate concepts that need to be analysed separately; and
    - similarly, the condition can be satisfied by having a right to exercise SIOC (even if SIOC is not actually exercised) or by actually exercising (even if there is no formal right to do so);
  - the statutory guidance contains various circumstances in which a person is presumed to exercise, or to have the right to exercise, SIOC, unless shown otherwise;
  - the statutory guidance also contains various 'safe harbours' where a person is presumed not to exercise, or to have the right to exercise, SIOC unless shown otherwise; and
  - companies and LLPs should take care – this condition will normally capture situations where a person really has control but does not satisfy any of the other conditions.
- **Condition 5 (influence/control over a trust or firm):** Exercising, or having the right to exercise, SIOC over the activities of a trust or firm with no legal personality that would itself satisfy one of the other conditions. This contains a two-stage test – both stages must be met.
  - Would the trustees of the trust or members of the firm, in that capacity, satisfy condition 1, condition 2, condition 3 and/or condition 4?
  - If so, does someone have the right to exercise, or actually exercise, SIOC over the activities of that trust or firm?

---

15 Note also that different views exist on whether merely holding more than 50% of a company's voting rights satisfies condition 3, but the general consensus now appears to be that it does. However, it always needs to be looked at on a case-by-case basis.

Various deeming provisions (see section 2.10 below) help to navigate less than 'plain vanilla' situations which would otherwise give rise to doubt over whether a condition applies or not (eg, where shares are jointly held).

Separate, but similar, conditions apply to eligible Scottish partnerships.

2.6 How to approach the PSC analysis

In simple terms, companies should:

- review the register of members to identify shareholdings;
- review the register of members and the constitutional documents (eg, articles of association) to identify levels of voting rights;
- review the constitutional documents (eg, articles of association) and any *ad hoc* investment-driven rights to identify rights to appoint to the board; and
- review arrangements in the round to identify possible examples of SIOC.

LLPs should:

- review the register of members;
- review the constitutional documents (ie, LLP agreement) to identify levels of voting rights, managing member appointment rights and entitlement to assets on a winding-up; and
- review arrangements in the round to identify possible examples of SIOC.

The following 'person by person' examples (Examples 1 to 5) introduce the concepts that will be relevant in the majority of straightforward cases. The analysis may however be complicated by deeming provisions (see section 2.10 below) designed to address more complex fact patterns, so that a 'condition by condition' analysis will be indicated in anything other than simple scenarios: the latter approach is adopted in Example 6.1 and following (below).

(a) Person-by-person analysis

Example 1: direct holdings (simple)

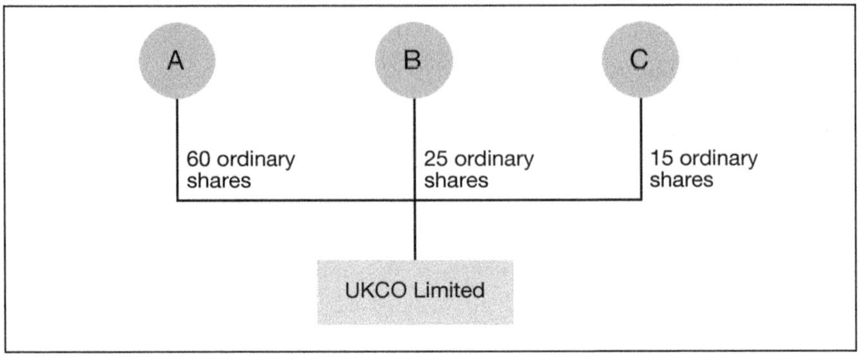

- A, B and C are all individuals.
- All shares are ordinary shares of £1.
- Each ordinary share carries one voting right.

Who is the company's PSC?

- A: holds more than 25% of shares and voting rights (condition 1 and condition 2) and, by virtue of those voting rights, the right to appoint and remove directors (condition 3).

Example 2.1: direct holdings (more sophisticated)

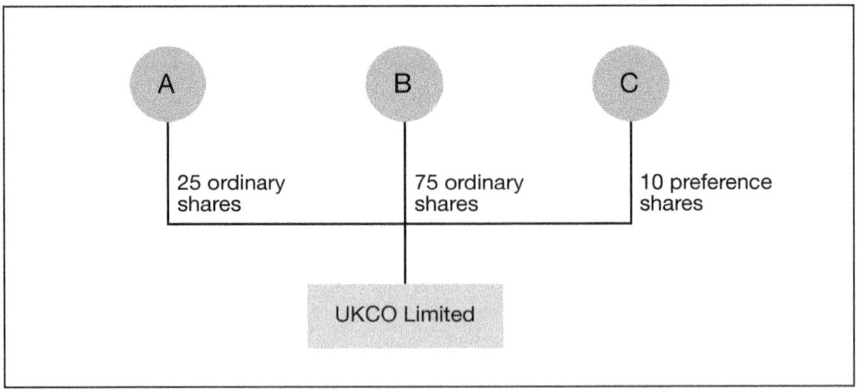

- A, B and C are all individuals.
- Ordinary shares of 1p and preference shares of £1.
- Each ordinary share carries one voting right; preference shares are non-voting.

Who is the company's PSC?

- B: holds more than 25% of voting rights (condition 2) and, by virtue of those voting rights, the right to appoint and remove directors (condition 3); and
- C: holds more than 25% of shares (by nominal value) (condition 1).

Example 2.2: direct holdings, condition 1 and condition 2 overlap

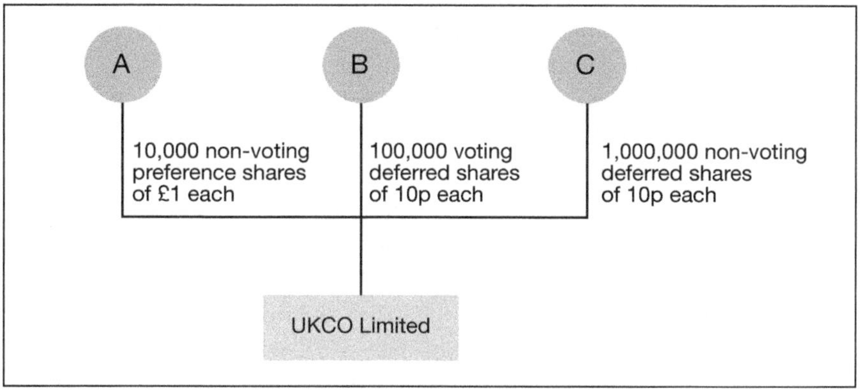

- A, B and C are all individuals.
- Ordinary shares of 10p, preference shares of £1 and deferred shares of 10p.
- Each ordinary share carries one voting right; preference shares and deferred shares are non-voting.

Who is the company's PSC?

- A: holds: (i) 8.33% of UKCO's shares (by nominal value); and (ii) no voting rights, and so does not satisfy condition 1 or 2.
- B: holds: (i) 8.33% of UKCO's shares (by nominal value); and (ii) 100% of its voting rights, and so satisfies condition 2 (and, by virtue of those voting rights, condition 3) but not 1.
- C: holds: (i) 83.33% of UKCO's shares (by nominal value); and (ii) no voting rights, and so satisfies condition 1 but not 2.

2.7 What is 'holding indirectly'?

The PSC regime is designed not simply to identify the individual named at face value on a register of members, but also those who may be economically interested at a greater distance, or who exercise governance-level influence or control.

Accordingly, conditions 1, 2 and 3 can also be satisfied by an individual who holds an indirect interest in the company or LLP. In headline terms, this happens where:

- X (an individual) holds a 'majority stake' in a legal entity; and
- that legal entity satisfies conditions 1, 2 or 3.

This analysis also applies where X is interested through not one but (potentially) a chain of legal entities, each of which holds a majority stake in the next one down. In either case, X satisfies conditions 1, 2 or 3 'indirectly'.

There are four ways to hold a majority stake:

- hold a majority of voting rights;
- be a member and have the right to appoint or remove the majority of the board of directors;
- be a member and control the majority of voting rights pursuant to an agreement; or
- exercise or have the right to exercise 'dominant influence or control'.

Note that the first limb of condition 5 can also be satisfied 'indirectly' (as it is directly referable to conditions 1, 2 and 3). The concept of 'holding indirectly' does not apply in the same way to condition 4 or the second limb of condition 5. However, it is generally understood that these conditions, which are more expansive and 'circumstance-based', will capture indirect forms of significant influence or control.

2.8 What is an RLE?

In some cases, the person who satisfies one or more conditions will not be an individual, but rather a legal entity. In some cases, a legal entity that satisfies one or more of the conditions may need to be registered in place of an individual. The PSC regime uses the term 'RLE' to refer to these kinds of legal entity. An RLE need not be a body corporate, but an entity with no separate legal personality (eg, an English trust or partnership) cannot be an RLE.

An RLE is a legal entity that:

- satisfies one of the conditions (and would be a PSC if it were an individual); and
- is subject to its own disclosure requirements.

The legal entity is subject to its own disclosure requirements if:

- it is subject to Part 21A, Companies Act 2006 (ie, the PSC regime) (which includes SEs, LLPs and unregistered companies);
- it is subject to the Scottish partnerships PSC regime;
- its voting shares are admitted to trading on an EEA regulated market;[16] or
- its voting shares are admitted to trading on a Schedule 1 market.

16 See previous footnote.

So, publicly traded foreign companies can (in the right circumstances) be RLEs, but 'unlisted' entities cannot be RLEs if they are established outside the United Kingdom.

Example 3: indirect holdings

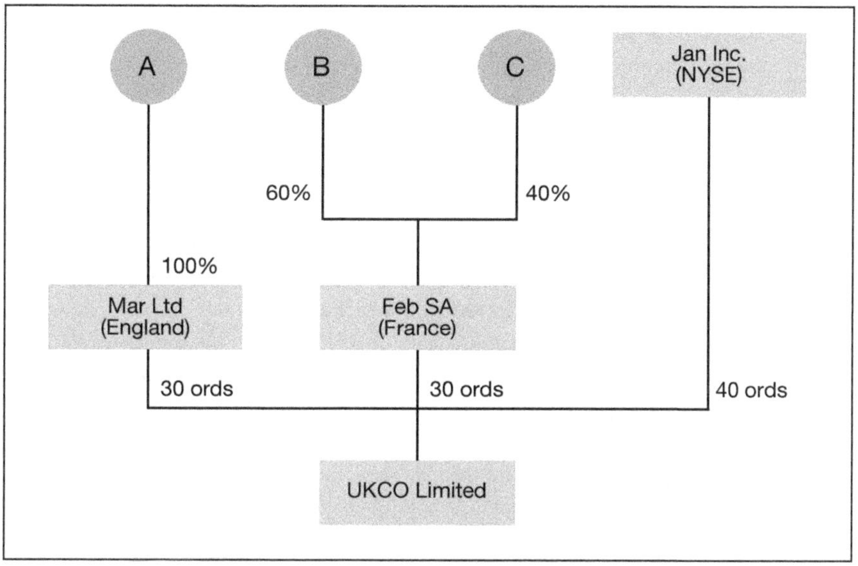

- All shares are ordinary shares of £1 with full voting rights.

Who are the PSCs and RLEs?

- A: holds majority stake in Mar, which holds more than 25% of shares and voting rights, and so satisfies conditions 1 and 2 indirectly.
- B: holds majority stake in Feb, which holds more than 25% of shares and voting rights, and so satisfies conditions 1 and 2 indirectly.
- Mar: holds more than 25% of shares and voting rights, so satisfies conditions 1 and 2, and is subject to Pt 21A, Companies Act 2006, and so is subject to its own disclosure requirements.
- Jan: holds more than 25% of shares and voting rights, so satisfies conditions 1 and 2, and is admitted to a Schedule 1 market, and so is subject to its own disclosure requirements.

Feb also satisfies conditions 1 and 2. However, it is not incorporated in the United Kingdom and its voting shares do not appear to be admitted to trading on any of the qualifying markets. It is therefore not subject to its own disclosure requirements and so cannot be an RLE. C does not satisfy any conditions because, although Feb satisfies conditions 1 and 2, C does not have a majority stake in Feb.

2.9 Who needs to be registered? Where? How many times?

With presumably a view to providing clarity on the true PSC and to capping the number of potentially registrable entities, not all ostensible PSCs and RLEs are to be recorded in a PSC register; only 'registrable persons' and 'registrable RLEs' are recorded.

A PSC or RLE is not registrable if he, she or it only holds an interest indirectly through:

- a legal entity which is an RLE; or
- a chain of legal entities, at least one of which is an RLE.

In other words, the PSC regime works 'up' the chain and requires registration in this scenario of the first RLE. Accordingly, if there is no RLE to register, you register the PSC instead. Where this rule comes into play, this will not always stop a PSC (who has been supplanted by an RLE) being registered in the PSC register of the affected RLE (see Example 4).

Where there may be more than one reason to register, you need to register under each condition that is satisfied, subject to one exception: a person is not registered under condition 4 if they also satisfy conditions 1, 2 and/or 3.

Example 4: direct/indirect (1)

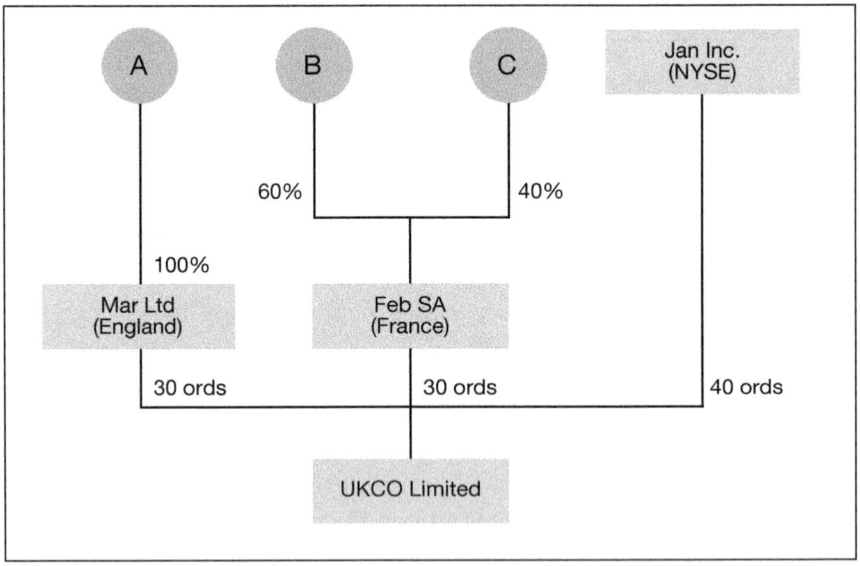

Whom should UKCO register?

- Mar is registrable – satisfies conditions 1 and 2 directly and is an RLE.
- A is not registrable – satisfies conditions 1 and 2 only indirectly through an RLE.*

- Feb is not registrable – satisfies conditions 1 and 2 but is not an RLE.
- B is registrable – satisfies conditions 1 and 2 indirectly, but not through an RLE.
- C is not registrable – does not hold a majority stake in Feb and so does not satisfy any conditions indirectly.
- Jan is registrable – satisfies conditions 1 and 2 directly and is an RLE.

  * Note that Mar will keep its own PSC register and A will be registrable in that register.

Example 5: direct/indirect (2)

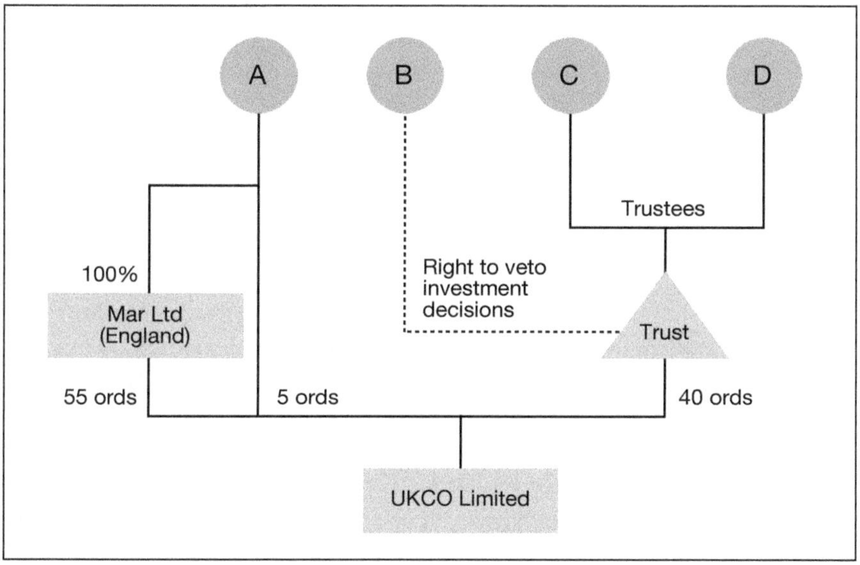

Whom should UKCO register?

- Mar is registrable – satisfies conditions 1 and 2 directly and is an RLE.
- A is registrable – satisfies conditions 1 and 2 indirectly through an RLE (Mar) but also directly (and so not only indirectly).
- Trust is not registrable – it is not a legal entity.
- C and D are registrable – satisfy conditions 1 and 2 directly because the shares will be held in their names as trustees (Trust is disregarded).
- B is registrable – appears to have SIOC over Trust, and C and D (in their capacity as trustees of Trust) satisfy conditions 1 and 2.

2.10 Deeming provisions

Schedule 1A Companies Act 2006 contains various 'deeming provisions' that alter the analysis:

- shares held jointly are all held by each joint holder (para 11);
- shares or rights subject to joint arrangement are all held by each party (para 12);
- voting rights attaching to treasury shares are disregarded for condition 2 (para 15), but not for condition 1;
- shares held by a nominee are deemed held instead by the beneficiary/principal (para 19);
- rights are treated as held by the person who controls them (para 20);
- rights exercisable only in certain circumstances are counted only when those circumstances exist (para 22(1));
- but rights temporarily incapable of exercise are still counted (para 22(4)); and
- rights attaching to shares held by way of security are generally regarded as held by the provider of security (and not the beneficiary) (para 25).

2.11 What is SIOC?

In simple terms, where the activities of a company can be directed positively or negatively (eg, by veto) this is *prima facie* indicative of control; where the involvement of a given individual falls short of that measure, but the company 'generally adopts' the suggestions of the person in question, that will be indicative of 'significant influence'. The guidance is careful to note that neither significant influence nor control needs to be supplemented by any feature of benefit (economic or otherwise) to the PSC in question (see Sections 2.7 to 2.11 of the SIOC Guidance and Section 3).

The extent to which this analysis must be approached critically and objectively is illustrated by the following (not uncommon) example: A and B settle a trust; the trust owns a company of which A and B are the directors and which is preponderantly debt-funded by A and B themselves. A and B clearly do not fulfil condition 1, condition 2 or condition 3 (unlike the independent trustee). The better argument on condition 4 is that they probably do satisfy condition 4 (depending always on the terms of the debt): whilst the status alone of a major creditor does not grant *de facto* 'control', it might amount – not being a third-party loan relationship covered by one of the rebuttable safe harbours – to the alternative of 'significant influence'.

(a) SIOC over a trust or firm

Condition 5 contains a two-stage test – both stages must be met.

- Does the trust or firm satisfy conditions 1, 2, 3 and/or 4?
- Does someone have SIOC over the trust or firm?

SIOC over a trust might commonly take one of the following, fairly conventional forms, which will be visible from the drafting of the trust deed itself:

- the right to:
  - appoint or remove any of the trustees or other fiduciaries;
  - direct distributions;
  - veto distributions;
  - direct investment decisions of the trust; or
  - veto investment disposals; or
- the power to:
  - amend the trust deed; or
  - revoke the trust.

However, whereas powers may have been expressly reserved to various power holders (settlors, tenants for life, key beneficiaries, protectors, enforcers, guardians etc), the condition may also bite where influence is exerted by someone exterior to the architecture of the trust and the genuine fiduciaries (eg, the trustees) not only consider, but perhaps invariably adopt, the proposals of this outsider. In other words, while fiduciaries are required in law on pain of personal liability to take a genuine independent decision on a matter, if a particular trustee is accustomed to consult and follow the wishes of, for example, a non-beneficiary settlor, spouse or other senior family member (perhaps expressed in a letter of wishes), the question remains open as to whether SIOC is being exercised. A similar question would arise in more complex scenarios (eg, a debt-funded trust). If a settlor largely funds a structure by debt and (even allowing for a non-recourse loan agreement) the trust fund might be described by a non-trust lawyer observer as 'mortgaged' to the settlor, could that settlor be described as having SIOC over the trust, irrespective of the beneficial situation or the rectitude of the trustees?

2.12 What is not SIOC?

Section 4 of the SIOC Guidance identifies roles, typically of a professional nature, which do not in ordinary plain vanilla scenarios entail SIOC *per se*: this would ordinarily except customers, suppliers, advisers, regulators, liquidators and receivers.

2.13 How to approach an analysis

It is tempting to approach the analysis 'person by person' as in the introduction to the concepts above. However, the analysis will be more reliable and leave less space for missing out potential PSCs or incorrectly registering a PSC if it proceeds 'condition by condition'. It may also reduce unnecessary analysis where a given person does not satisfy a condition. It is also much easier when trying to incorporate 'deeming provisions'.

Example 6.1 (condition 1): simple fund structure

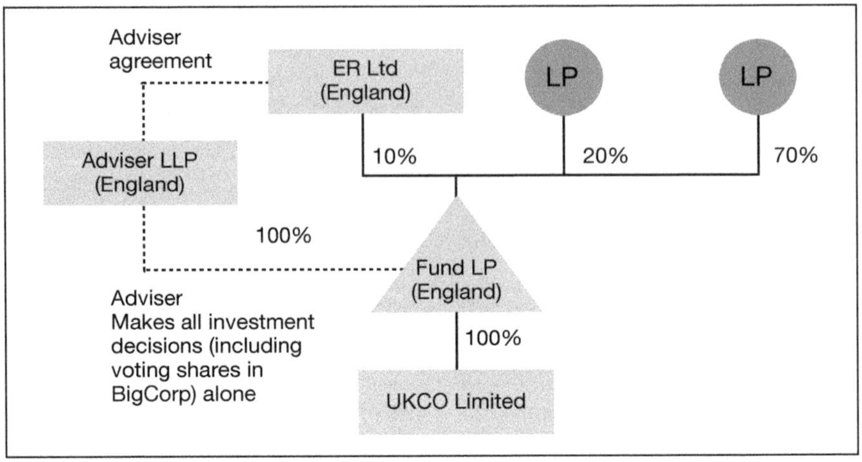

Whom should UKCO register?

- Condition 1.
  - Fund LP has no legal personality – it cannot be registered.
  - The person who holds legal title to shares in UKCO is ER (as the general partner).
  - Although ER (as the general partner) holds 10% of interests in LP, it holds all of UKCO's shares in its name.
  - ER is an RLE and so is registered under condition 1.
  - ER is not holding as nominee for LPs, as ER has its own interest in the shares.
  - LPs are disregarded (para 25(1)).

Example 6.2 (condition 2): simple fund structure

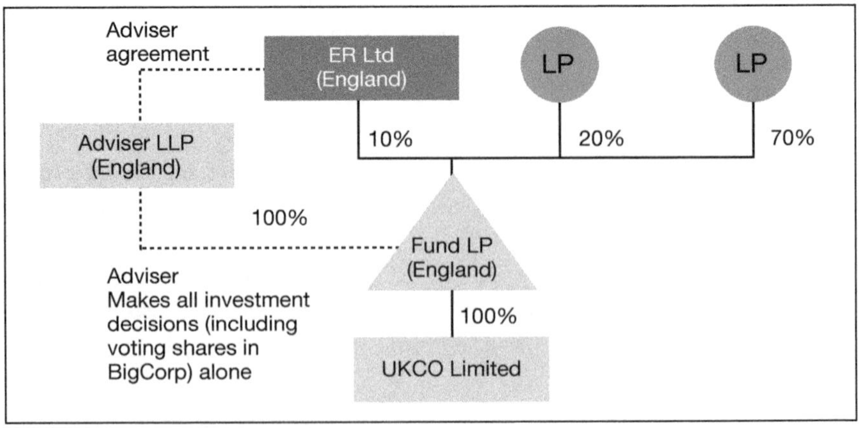

Whom should UKCO register?

- Condition 2.
  - As ER (as the general partner) holds all shares in UKCO, it also holds all voting rights.
  - However, under the adviser agreement, Adviser directs how voting rights are exercised.
  - Under para 20, Adviser is regarded as holding voting rights.
  - Adviser is an RLE and so is registered under condition 2.
  - But, does ER have residual discretion not to vote according to Adviser's directions?
  - If so, ER might also control voting rights and so be registered under condition 2.
  - LPs are disregarded (para 25(1)).

Example 6.3 (condition 3): simple fund structure

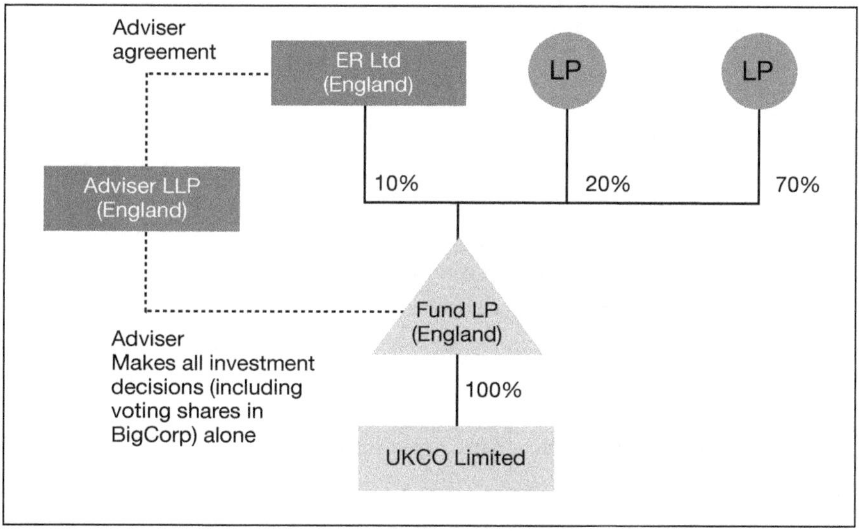

Whom should UKCO register?

- Condition 3.
  - Again, Fund LP has no legal personality – it cannot be registered.
  - The person who holds more than 50% of voting rights in UKCO will be able to appoint and remove directors at will.
  - Adviser therefore also registered under condition 3.
  - It therefore follows, if ER is registered under condition 2, ER is also registered under condition 3.
  - LPs are disregarded (para 25(1)).

Example 6.4 (condition 4): simple fund structure

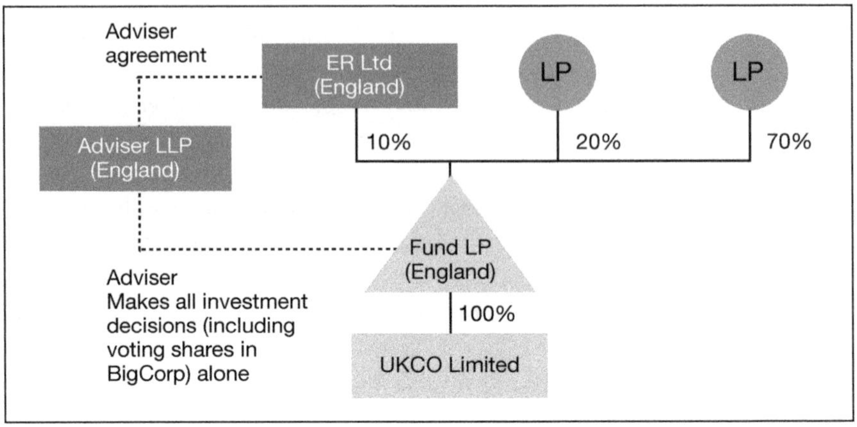

Whom should UKCO register?

- Condition 4.
  - Again, Fund LP has no legal personality – it cannot be registered.
  - LPs unlikely to exercise any control over UKCO owing to limited partnership law.
  - Adviser can most likely exercise SIOC over UKCO through 100% voting rights holding.
  - The same is possibly also true for ER.
  - However, ER and Adviser not registered under condition 4, as each is registered under conditions 1, 2 and/or 3.
  - The residual question is whether there is anyone else with SIOC over UKCO?

Example 6.5 (condition 5): simple fund structure

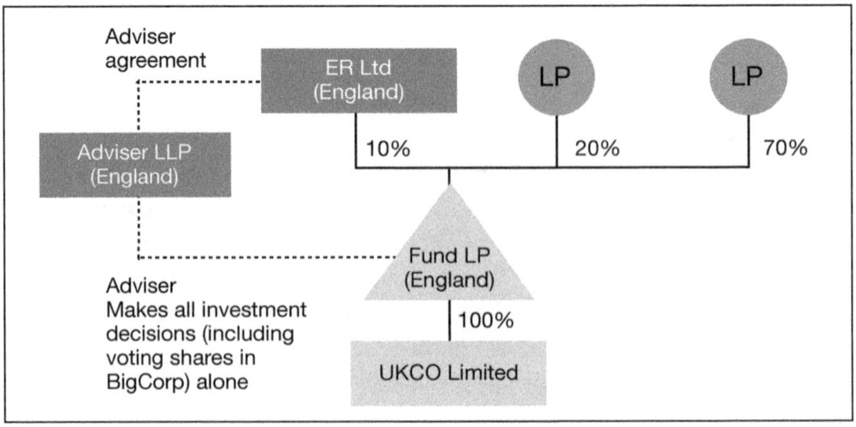

Whom should UKCO register?

- Condition 5.
  - Fund LP would satisfy conditions 1, 2 and 3 if it had legal personality.
  - So, does anyone have SIOC over Fund LP?
  - ER will normally have SIOC over a limited partnership (see statutory guidance).
  - Has ER devolved SIOC to Adviser?
  - Does ER (as the general partner) retain residual SIOC by virtue of right to remove and replace Adviser?
  - Definitely register Adviser under condition 5.
  - Probably safe to register ER under condition 5 as well.

Example 7: typical private trust company (PTC) structure

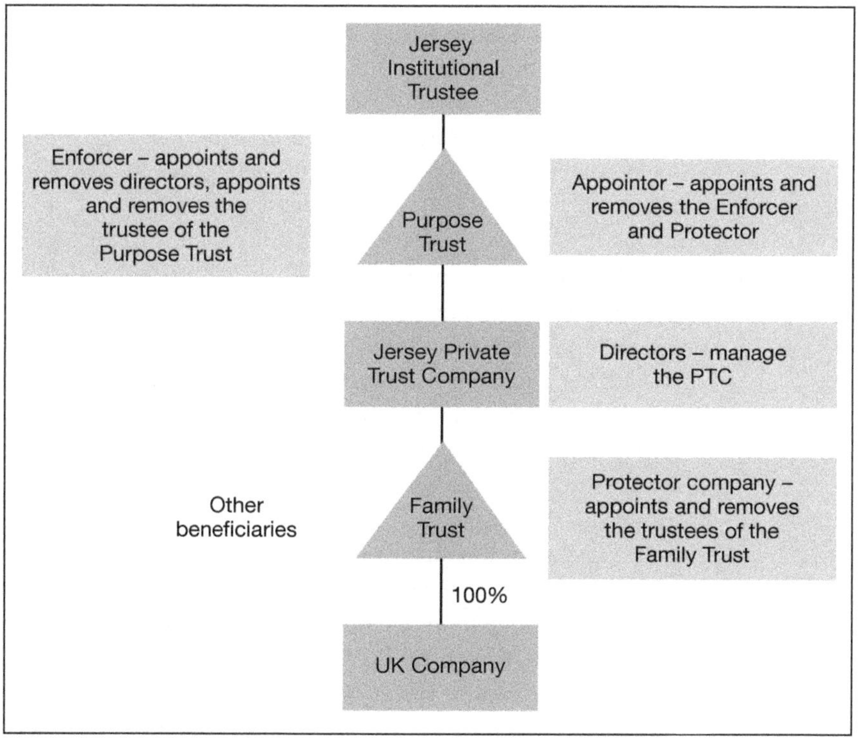

It is impossible without many illustrations to cater for all scenarios. However, the inclusion of a private trust company (PTC) structure adds some degree of complexity to a standard operating company holding structure, via the import of the PTC's own holding and governance architecture.

Typical PTC structure:

- a UK operating or holding company;
- owned by a family trust;
- the trustee of the Family Trust is a (non-UK incorporated) PTC – popular with clients who want to soften the impact of the loss of control inherent in settling assets on trust whilst involving themselves or family members and advisers via the board of the PTC;
- the PTC is owned by a purpose trust, to prevent succession issues arising – in brief, the purpose of the trust is to own the shares of the PTC; and
- the trustee of the Purpose Trust is an overseas institutional trust company.

There are other parties involved too:

- a protector vehicle, which may or may not have powers in relation to the Family Trust, such as the power to hire and fire the trustees;
- the directors of the PTC;
- an 'enforcer' of the Purpose Trust, which will have the power to hire and fire the trustees of the Purpose Trust; and
- an 'appointor', somebody with the ultimate power to hire and fire the enforcer.

How does the PSC regime apply?

- The Family Trust would meet conditions 1 to 3 were it an individual: it owns 100% of the UK Company. In discrete cases, a question may arise as to whether anyone has a 'majority stake' in the PTC. In this case, the majority stake is held by the Institutional Trustee, who (being incorporated overseas) will not be registrable. It will then, in turn, be necessary to see whether anyone holds a majority stake in the Institutional Trustee etc.
- It is also necessary to consider condition 5 (SIOC): does any individual have the right to exercise, or actually exercise, SIOC over the activities of the Family Trust (see section 2.11 above)? If they do, they will need to be included in the UK Company's PSC register.
- Note that the trustee of the Purpose Trust also satisfies conditions 1, 2 and 3 (indirectly) and so it will be necessary to check whether anyone has SIOC over the activities of the Purpose Trust too. If they do, they too will need to be included in the UK Company's PSC register.
- It is also important to consider whether any individual (akin to the concept of a 'shadow director' of a company) issues instructions that are generally followed. This could include the settlor, beneficiaries, protectors, enforcers and appointors, depending on the terms of the trust and the nature of the arrangements (eg, how they operate in practice).

- Protectors: although it is not clear from the SIOC Guidance, it is arguable that protector committees do not have to be registered if the members cannot individually exercise SIOC. For example, an individual member of a committee of protectors will typically need to obtain the majority or unanimous consent of the other protectors in order to exercise any rights that they may have. It is possible for a corporate protector itself to satisfy condition 4, and it may be necessary to register the protector if it is also subject to its own disclosure requirements.
- PTC directors: the SIOC Guidance refers to persons likely to exercise SIOC in the running of the trust, which in the context of a PTC would likely be the directors. However, there are certain 'safe harbour' roles and relationships which would not, in the normal course, result in a person being considered to be exercising SIOC over a company. For instance, if the directors of the PTC act individually without any director exerting influence over the other, it is likely that they will fall within the safe harbour as regards the PTC itself. Accordingly, the better argument may be that it is unlikely that the directors of the PTC would be regarded, purely by virtue of that office, as having SIOC over the family trust.
- Enforcer: if an enforcer has the right to appoint directors of the PTC, this is arguably in effect equivalent to a right to appoint and remove trustees. Consequently, depending on the facts, the enforcer may well be an individual who has the right to exercise SIOC over the trust. Of course, a more purist approach might be to maintain that the trustee of the family trust remains the same and that, although the enforcer can appoint and remove the trustee's board, the directors from time to time should still act independently.
- Appointor: the right to appoint the enforcer or protector (who then has the right to appoint directors of the PTC or trustees of the trust) is also arguably in substance the same as having the right to appoint and remove trustees. Therefore, they may also need to be disclosed on the PSC register, subject always to the purist approach described above.
- Institutional trustee: non-UK trustee companies will not be registrable entities for the purposes of the PSC regime, unless their voting shares are admitting to trading on one or more of the relevant securities exchanges.

2.14 Confirming PSCs/RLEs – administrative issues and enforcing the regime

The legislation (Companies Act 2006) is prescriptive about the lengths to which a company must go to populate its register accurately.

- Companies must take reasonable steps to identify registrable persons (Section 790D(1)).
- Companies must serve notice on anyone they suspect or know is registrable (Section 790D(2)).

- Companies may also serve notice on someone who may know of a registrable person (Section 790D(5)). This is technically optional, but in practice may be required to demonstrate that the company has taken reasonable steps.
- Companies must also serve notice on becoming aware of any change (Section 790E).
- If the recipient does not comply, the company can ultimately impose restrictions (Schedule 1B). Again, this is technically optional, but in practice may be required.
- Companies cannot enter PSC's/RLE's details in register until all details are known (Sections 790M(2), (5)).
- Companies cannot enter an individual's details until they are all 'confirmed' (Section 790M(2)), which means:
  - supplied by the individual (Section 790M(9)(a)); or
  - supplied by someone else with individual's knowledge (Section 790M(9)(b)).
- Registrable persons and RLEs are also under an independent duty to supply information (Sections 790G-790H).

2.15 Recording PSCs

- Companies must register prescribed particulars (Section 790K).
- This includes 'nature of control'.
- The wording for the nature of control is prescribed by PSC Regs 2016 (Schedule 2).
- For conditions 1 and 2 (and condition 5, where it is referable to condition 1 or 2), the company must record the relevant 'band'.
- Companies must never have an empty PSC register.
- If the company cannot record a PSC/RLE, it must include a 'holding statement' from PSC Regs 2016, taken from the following list:
  - no registrable person (Reg 10);
  - registrable person not yet identified (Reg 11);
  - registrable person identified but particulars not yet confirmed (Reg 12);
  - company not yet finished taking steps to identify registrable persons (Reg 13);
  - recipient has failed to comply with Section 790D(2) or 790E notice (Regs 14–16); or
  - company has imposed restrictions (Reg 17).

2.16 Filing at Companies House

- Companies must file details at Companies House within 14 days of updating register.

- There is a range of forms to choose from:
  - PSC01 – notice of PSC;
  - PSC02 – notice of RLE;
  - PSC03 – notice of other registrable person;
  - PSC04 – change of PSC's details;
  - PSC05 – change of RLE's details;
  - PSC06 – change of other registrable person's details;
  - PSC07 – person ceasing to be PSC, RLE or other registrable person;
  - PSC08 – notice of additional statement in PSC register; and
  - PSC09 – update to statements in PSC register.
- There are equivalent forms for LLPs and eligible Scottish partnerships.
- SEs use company forms.

2.17 Other things to be aware of

- Registration of other kinds of person (Section 790C(12));
- Prescribed contents of warning and restrictions notices (PSC Regs);
- Right to inspect PSC register (Sections 790N-790T); and
- Right to keep PSC register centrally at Companies House (Sections 790W-790ZE).

2.18 What is recorded?

- Required particulars – PSCs:
  - name;
  - service address;
  - country or state (or part of the United Kingdom) in which PSC ordinarily resident;
  - nationality;
  - date of birth;
  - usual residential address or 'URA';
  - date on which PSC became a registrable person;
  - nature of control over the company; and
  - if any restrictions on disclosure are in place, a statement to that effect.
- Required particulars – RLEs:
  - corporate or firm name;
  - registered or principal office;
  - legal form and governing law;
  - register of companies in which it is entered (including the state);
  - registered number;
  - date on which RLE became a registrable RLE; and
  - nature of control over the company.
- Recording the nature of control.

- The PSC register must contain one of the prescribed statements of control.
- In some cases, the company needs to record the extent of control.

2.19 Exemptions from publication – the protection regime

A limited basis exists for an individual who is or proposes to be or in appropriate circumstances who used to be a PSC of a company to apply to Companies House to restrict disclosure of:

- his/her usual residential address or 'URA' (Sections 243 and 790ZF Companies Act 2006); or alternatively
- all of the PSC information (Section 790ZG CA 2006) on the public register.

A non-exhaustive list of possible reasons is available on the government website.[17] The threshold is high: the applicant must reasonably believe that if the secured information is disclosed by the registrar, the activities of the company or one of the personal attributes of the applicant when associated with that company will put him/her at serious risk of being subjected to violence or intimidation.

The regime is broad-minded in its understanding of this principle: the guidance gives (amongst others) the example of possible religious sensitivities. The BEIS report from March 2019 quotes amongst various examples fears of intimidation or violence because the activities of the company involve conducting medical experiments on animals.

The URA, like the day of birth, does not appear publicly unless used as a service address, but normally remains available not only to specified public authorities but also to credit reference agencies (CRAs). A successful application can result in the URA being kept from CRAs. A successful full application to restrict all of the information results in an effectively 'blind' public record.

For example, the following statement may instead appear on Companies House: "The person with significant control's details are not shown because restrictions on using or disclosing any of the individual's particulars are in force under regulations under 790ZG in relation to this company."

2.20 How does the protection regime work?

If the 'specified circumstances' apply in relation to the secured information:

- Companies House must omit or remove the secured information from the public register;
- Companies House must not use or disclose secured information except for three permitted purposes:
  - communicating with the person to whom an application relates;

17 www.gov.uk/government/publications/restricting-the-disclosure-of-your-psc-information/restricting-the-disclosure-of-your-information.

- disclosure to a specified public authority; and
- disclosure to a credit institution or a financial institution.
- The company itself must not use or disclose secured information except for four permitted purposes:
  - communicating with that person;
  - complying with a statutory requirement to send particulars to the registrar;
  - where that person has given consent; and
  - complying with money laundering regulations.

2.21 What are 'specified circumstances'?

Specified circumstances exist where an application has been made in relation to information (which would ordinarily fall to be recorded in the PSC register) and that application:

- has not been determined by the registrar and has not been withdrawn under Regulation 40 PSC Regs;
- has been determined in favour of the applicant (unless the determination has ceased to have effect);
- was unsuccessful and a period of 42 days beginning with the date of the notice to that effect has not passed;
- was unsuccessful and an appeal in respect of the application has not been determined; or
- was unsuccessful and the applicant has successfully appealed.

2.22 Practical result of the protection regime being in force – PSC register

- The company is still obliged to keep a PSC register, but in the event that a member of the public requests to inspect the register, the register is treated as not containing the secured information. In other words, it becomes legitimate for the company to permit inspection of the register that does not contain the secured information.
- Two registers are kept on the company books: one with the information already redacted and one with the information but in a secured envelope.

3. The UK Trust Register or Trust Registration Service

The United Kingdom has implemented a separate beneficial ownership register for trusts, known as the UK Trust Register or Trust Registration Service (the Trust Register).

The Trust Register has been in existence since 2017. It was introduced by the Money Laundering, Terrorist Financing and Transfer of Funds (Information on the Payer) Regulations 2017[18] (the 2017 Regulations), which came into force from 26 June 2017 in connection with the transposition of 4AMLD.

---

18 Available at www.legislation.gov.uk/uksi/2017/692/contents/made.

The scope of the Trust Register was subsequently materially extended by the Money Laundering and Terrorist Financing (Amendment) (EU Exit) Regulations 2020[19] (the 2020 Regulations) as part of the United Kingdom's implementation of 5AMLD with effect from 6 October 2020.[20]

As of the date of writing (May 2021), some HM Revenue & Customs (HMRC) guidance on the new regime with effect from 6 October 2020 was published on 17 May 2021.[21] It is expected that HMRC will continue to update this throughout 2021 and in early 2022.

3.1 Background – the dual purpose of the Trust Register

The Trust Register was designed to serve two purposes. First, it fulfils the United Kingdom's obligation under 4AMLD and 5AMLD to maintain a central register of the beneficial ownership of certain trusts. Second, it is also the way in which trusts that are liable to UK tax must register with the UK tax authority, HMRC, to notify HMRC of a UK tax liability. In other words, it is intended to help HMRC track trusts with a UK tax liability and to digitise the self-assessment tax reporting process (by replacing the existing paper form 41G).

This dual purpose underpins much of the United Kingdom's approach to the Trust Register and explains many of the instances in which the United Kingdom has deviated from the provisions of 4AMLD and 5AMLD when implementing the Trust Register in the United Kingdom.

A pertinent example of this is the way in which the Trust Register applies to non-UK resident trusts. Article 31 of 4AMLD (both in its original form and as amended by 5AMLD) on the face of it applies only to trusts which have a threshold connection to the member state – the relevant connecting factor under 4AMLD was the governing law of the trust; 5AMLD subsequently changed this from the governing law to the place where the trust is administered/where the trustees are resident. However, in order to achieve the United Kingdom's intended dual purpose, the scope of the UK Trust Register goes beyond the directives – by capturing not only UK resident trusts but also non-UK resident trusts in certain instances even if they are not administered in the United Kingdom and may have no UK resident trustees.

3.2 What obligations do the 2017 Regulations and 2020 Regulations impose?

The regime imposes two separate obligations on trustees:

---

19 Available at www.gov.uk/eu-withdrawal-act-2018-statutory-instruments/the-money-laundering-and-terrorist-financing-amendment-eu-exit-regulations-2020.

20 Certain parts of the 2020 Regulations will not come into force until 6 April 2021 and 10 March 2022 – see Regulation 1. Part 4 of the 2020 Regulations (which provides for changes required with effect from the end of the Brexit transition period, namely in relation to references to the European Economic Area) also came into effect at the end of the transition period on 31 December 2020.

21 Trust Registration Service Manual, HMRC internal manual, www.gov.uk/hmrc-internal-manuals/trust-registration-service-manual.

- Regulation 44 (Record-keeping): First, an internal record-keeping obligation on the trustees of 'relevant trusts'[22] to maintain accurate and up-to-date written records relating to the trust's so-called 'beneficial ownership'. They must share this record on request with law enforcement authorities (including HMRC) and other bodies who have anti-money laundering client due diligence obligations (eg, law firms, financial institutions, accountants and trust and company service providers – referred to as 'obliged entities' within the meaning of 4MLD and 5MLD or 'relevant persons' within the meaning of the UK regulations) with which the trustees enter into a business relationship.[23] Records are to be kept for five years from the final distribution and (normally) deleted thereafter.
- Regulation 45 and 45ZA (Registration): Second, for a sub-group of those 'relevant trusts' (referred to as 'taxable relevant trusts', 'type A trusts', 'type B trusts' and 'type C trusts' in the 2020 Regulations), a further obligation to register that beneficial ownership information on a central register.

This chapter will focus primarily on the obligation for certain trusts to register on the UK Trust Register.

3.3 Which trusts have to register on the Trust Register?

The first iteration of the Trust Register introduced by the 2017 Regulations only required 'taxable relevant trusts' (broadly, UK resident express trusts and non-UK resident express trusts with a UK tax liability) to register. The scope of the Trust Register was, however, extended by the 2020 Regulations, which removed UK tax liability as the (only) trigger for registration and widened the population of trusts potentially 'captured' by the regime to include more trusts outside the United Kingdom. In particular:

---

22 A 'relevant trust' is defined in Regulation 42(2)(b) 2017 Regulations (as amended by the 2020 Regulations) as:

(i) a UK resident express trust (which by exclusion protects certain situations analysed under English law as involving trusts which arise by operation of law – see paragraph 3.2 below);

(ii) a non-UK resident express trust which receives UK source income or has assets in the UK, on which the trustees are liable to pay certain UK taxes (being income tax, capital gains tax, inheritance tax, SDLT, land and buildings transaction tax and SDRT; and

(iii) any other non-UK resident express trust which is not an excluded trust and whose trustees:

a. acquire an interest in UK land; or

b. enter into a business relationship with a relevant person in the UK, where at least one of the trustees is resident in the UK and the trust is not an 'EEA registered trust'.

23 Service providers (so-called UK relevant persons) are still required to collect their own client due diligence information in the normal way. In addition, under the 2020 Regulations (see Regulation 30A, 2017 Regulations (as amended)), from 10 March 2022 service providers will also need to: (i) obtain proof of a trust's registration on the Trust Register if the trust is required to register; and (ii) cross-check the client due diligence information gathered as part of taking on the client against the information on the Trust Register. Any material discrepancies must be reported to HMRC as soon as reasonably practicable after discovery. This relates only to new clients however and a report only needs to be made once. As of the date of writing, it is understood that service providers do not have to review the records of existing clients or make reports as part of refreshing existing client due diligence.

- all UK resident express trusts now have to register – whether or not they have a UK tax liability. These are referred to as:
  - 'taxable relevant trusts'[24] if they have a UK tax liability; and
  - 'type A trusts'[25] if they do not have a UK tax liability (and assuming they are not registered elsewhere in the European Economic Area (EEA));
- non-UK resident express trusts are required to register not only: (i) if they have a UK tax liability (and are therefore 'taxable relevant trusts');[26] but also (ii) if they:
  - enter into a business relationship with a UK relevant person and have at least one UK resident trustee (referred to as a 'type B trust');[27] or
  - acquire an interest in UK land, even if they have no UK resident trustees (referred to as a 'type C trust').[28]

(a) Determining where a trust is resident for these purposes

A trust is a UK resident trust for these purposes if:

- all the trustees are resident in the United Kingdom;[29] or
- at least one trustee is resident in the United Kingdom and the settlor was resident and domiciled in the United Kingdom when: (i) the trust was set up; or (ii) the settlor added funds to the trust.[30]

Non-UK resident trusts are defined by exception: a trust is a non-UK resident trust for these purposes if it is not a UK resident trust.[31]

It is worth noting that there is potential under this test (which is broadly in line with – but not identical to[32] – the normal residence test for trusts for UK income and capital gains tax purposes and is not wholly unique to the Trust Register regime) for non-UK resident trusts inadvertently to become UK resident and therefore find themselves within the scope of the Trust Register – even if they do not have a UK tax liability, a UK business relationship or an interest in

---

24 Regulation 45(14) 2017 Regulations.

25 Regulation 45ZA(1) and 45ZA(2)(a) 2017 Regulations (as amended by the 2020 Regulations).

26 Regulation 45(14) 2017 Regulations.

27 Regulation 45ZA(1) and 45ZA(2)(b) 2017 Regulations (as amended by the 2020 Regulations).

28 Regulation 45ZA(1) and 45ZA(2)(c) 2017 Regulations (as amended by the 2020 Regulations). A non-UK resident express trust which acquires an interest in UK land is registrable irrespective of whether it has any UK resident trustees. If it has one or more UK resident trustees, it falls within the definition of a type B trust; if it has no UK resident trustees, it is a type C trust only.

29 Regulation 42(2)(c)(i) 2017 Regulations.

30 Regulation 42(2)(c)(ii) and 42(2)(d) 2017 Regulations.

31 Regulation 42(2)(e) 2017 Regulations.

32 It is worth noting that the residence test for trusts under the Trust Register is not identical to the normal residence test for UK income and capital gains tax purposes. In particular, the Trust Register test requires the settlor to be UK resident *and* domiciled at the relevant time (whereas the residence test for tax purposes requires the settlor to be UK resident *or* domiciled). In addition, unlike the residence test for tax purposes, the Trust Register residence test does not cater for the possibility of the settlor being deemed domiciled in the UK for tax purposes at the relevant time. These discrepancies may complicate the application of the Trust Register in practice and may lead to illogical results in certain situations.

UK land. For example, in certain jurisdictions (eg, the United States) where trusts are often used for estate-planning purposes, it is common for the settlor to act as the sole or a co-trustee. In this scenario, if the settlor does not resign as trustee before becoming resident in the United Kingdom, the trust may inadvertently become a UK resident trust and therefore would automatically come within the scope of the Trust Register.

(b) *Definition of 'express' trust*

The starting point in relation to both UK resident and non-UK resident trusts is that only 'express' trusts are required to register.[33]

This is not defined in the 2017 Regulations or the 2020 Regulations, but (based on the FATF definition) it is understood to mean a trust 'clearly created'[34] by a settlor (ie, a trust established intentionally by the settlor). As a result, this will not include trusts which come into existence by operation of law or as a matter of equity rather than intent – for example, trusts arising on intestacy, implied, resulting or constructive trusts, and trusts created under a court order such as on divorce.

HMRC has also confirmed that authorised unit trusts are not express trusts.[35]

(c) *Excluded trusts*

In addition, certain trusts – which are express trusts but which are considered 'low risk' – are excluded from registration. The full list of excluded trusts is set out in Schedule 3A (Excluded Trusts), 2017 Regulations (as amended by the 2020 Regulations) and is beyond the scope of this chapter. However, by way of example, the following types of trust, which are particularly relevant in a private client context, are considered 'low risk' trusts for UK purposes:

---

33 See definitions of 'taxable relevant trust', 'type A trust', 'type B trust' and 'type C trust' referred to above.

34 See General Glossary, International Standards On Combating Money Laundering and the Financing of Terrorism & Proliferation: The FATF Recommendations, adopted by the FATF Plenary in February 2012 and updated June 2019 available at: www.fatf-gafi.org/recommendations.html.

35 HMRC, Trust Registration Service (TRS) – Frequently Asked Questions (FAQs) (22 November 2017), available at: www.step.org/system/files/media/files/2020-03/TRS_Guidance_FAQ_-_22_November_2017.pdf, 4. However, the same cannot be said for *unauthorised* unit trusts.

Type of trust	Comment
Trusts relating to jointly held property[36] (eg, land or bank accounts) where the legal and beneficial owners are the same.	There will however still be a requirement to register if there are beneficial owners who are not also legal owners. For example, if parents hold a property jointly for themselves and their children or one spouse holds a property for both spouses.
Charitable trusts which are: • registered as charities in Scotland, Northern Ireland or England and Wales;[37] or • which are exempt and excepted from registration by the relevant statute (eg, because their income is below the registration threshold).[38]	As of the date of writing (May 2021), it is unclear whether the following would be excluded trusts: • charities in Northern Ireland that are on the 'deemed list' (and waiting to be registered); • restricted funds (eg, endowment funds) held by a charity but not registered separately with the Charities Commission; • nominee or bare trust arrangements in respect of assets held for a charity; and • non-UK charities that are recognised by HMRC as a charity for UK tax purposes.
Trusts holding sums or assets of a pension scheme which is a registered pension scheme.[39]	

continued on next page

36 Schedule 3A(9).

37 It is expected that (in order to avoid unnecessary temporary registrations), charitable trusts pending approval of registration as charities will not be required to register in the interim, provided that the trustees have a genuine expectation that registration will be accepted.

38 Schedule 3A(5).

39 Schedule 3A(3). A registered pension scheme is a registered pension scheme for the purposes of Part 4 of the Finance Act 2004.

Type of trust	Comment
Trusts holding the benefit of life policies or retirement policies which only pay out on death, terminal or critical illness or permanent disability of the person assured.[40]	The trust will however have to register when the policy pays out, unless: • this is on death; and • the trust is wound up within two years of the death (see 'trusts arising on death' below). Following uncertainty and industry consultations, HMRC also recently confirmed that this includes trusts holding policies with a surrender value (this being in practice a scenario of increasingly historical interest). Trusts holding such policies would therefore be excluded from registration until such time as the policy is actually surrendered or it pays out (unless this is on death and the trust is wound up within two years as set out above).
Trusts which are required to meet statutory conditions in order to benefit from some beneficial status.[41]	For example, trusts for vulnerable beneficiaries or employee trusts.
Certain commercial trusts.[42]	For example, relating to bond issues or syndicated loans.

continued on next page

40 Schedule 3A(4).
41 Schedule 3A(16) – (22).
42 Schedule 3A(14).

Type of trust	Comment
Trusts arising on death under a person's will.[43]	A trust established under an individual's will which holds only property comprised in a person's estate need be registered only if it remains in existence for more than two years after the death of the individual or if it at any point accepts an addition of assets from outside the person's estate.
Pilot trusts.[44]	A trust which holds no more than £100 and which is in existence before 6 October 2020 will not be required to register (unless or until further assets are added to the trust). However, a trust which is established on or after 6 October 2020 will be required to register even if it holds less than £100 of assets. It is not clear what the policy imperative is behind this distinction. However, this will clearly impose an additional burden where pilot trusts are established in the future – for example, to receive death benefits under a pension policy or to receive assets under a will (the latter example in particular is common in certain jurisdictions (eg, the United States) for estate-planning purposes).

43 Schedule 3A(7) and (8).
44 Schedule 3A (6).

The underlying principles behind the list of excluded trusts set out in Schedule 3A are that either the information is already available, since the trusts are required to register in some other way (eg, pensions and charities), or that there is a low risk of the trusts being used for money laundering or terrorist financing purposes (eg, trusts involving co-ownership or those which are required to meet specified statutory conditions).

HMRC published some further guidance in relation to this list of excluded trusts on 17 May 2021 in the Trust Registration Service Manual, HMRC internal manual, see footnote 21 above; however, this does not (yet) address all the areas of uncertainty highlighted above. However, it should be noted that given the dual purpose of the Trust Register (see above), a trust that has UK tax liabilities will still have to register even if it falls within one of the exempt categories set out above.

(d) Nominees and bare trustees – not generally exempt

It had been hoped that nominee and bare trust arrangements would be included in the list of excluded trusts in Schedule 3A. However, there is no general exemption for such arrangements.

There are some interesting conceptual questions that arise in relation to nominee and bare trust arrangements in this context and which may be answered differently in different EU jurisdictions. For example:

- is a nominee arrangement an express trust (or equivalent to a trust) or is it just an agency arrangement?; and
- is there any difference between a nominee arrangement and a bare trust in this context – for example, because nominees have to follow instructions whereas bare trustees typically have at least some discretion in how they administer assets?

These questions are beyond the scope of this chapter. It is also worth noting that as of the date of writing this is still a much-discussed part of the Trust Register regime. For now, however, it is clear that bare trust and nominee arrangements will only be excluded from registration in certain specified situations (eg, in the context of certain commercial activities and the normal custody arrangements for portfolio investments). In other situations, nominees and bare trustees will be required to register.

This will include for example where real estate is held by a nominee or where assets are held by parents as bare trustees for their minor children or where four co-owners (the maximum registrable at the Land Registry) hold for five. In practice however (for the reasons set out in section 3.6(b) below), this will only be relevant if the nominee/bare trustee is UK resident or the asset held is UK real estate that is acquired after 6 October 2020.

3.4 Non-UK resident trusts

As explained in section 3.3 above, following the changes made by the 2020 Regulations, non-UK resident express trusts are required to register if they:

- have a UK tax liability (and therefore fall within the definition of 'taxable relevant trusts');[45]
- enter into a business relationship with a UK relevant person and have at least one UK resident trustee (referred to as a 'type B trust');[46] or
- acquire an interest in UK land (referred to as a 'type C trust').[47]

3.5 Non-UK resident trusts with a UK tax liability ('taxable relevant trusts': Regulation 45)

A non-UK resident express trust will be required to register on the Trust Register by virtue of being a taxable relevant trust in any year if:

- the trustees receive UK source income or hold assets in the United Kingdom – directly or through an underlying entity which is 'look through' for tax purposes (eg, a nominee or partnership); and
- the trustees have an actual liability to pay certain relevant taxes,[48] being:
  - income tax;
  - capital gains tax;
  - inheritance tax;
  - stamp duty land tax (SDLT);
  - stamp duty reserve tax (SDRT); or
  - land and buildings transaction tax (in Scotland) or land transaction tax (Wales).

A full summary of all the circumstances in which a non-UK resident trust may meet the above conditions is outside the scope of this chapter. However, some particular points of interest are set out below.

- Non-UK resident trusts can fall in and out of the Trust Register regime depending on when the relevant UK tax liability arises. For example, a non-UK trust which directly holds a non-income producing UK asset will only be a taxable relevant trust for a year in which an inheritance tax 10-year anniversary or exit charge arises.
- Unlike the PSC regime which only applies to UK-incorporated entities (which, by definition, will have a clear and conscious link to the United Kingdom), the Trust Register may capture non-UK resident trusts with minimal connections to the United Kingdom. Although the OEBO

45 Regulation 45(14) 2017 Regulations.
46 Regulation 45ZA(1) and 45ZA(2)(b) 2017 Regulations (as amended by the 2020 Regulations).
47 Regulation 45ZA(1) and 45ZA(2)(c) 2017 Regulations (as amended by the 2020 Regulations).
48 Regulation 45(14) 2017 Regulations.

regime (see above) will apply to non-UK entities acquiring UK real estate or participating in a public tender in the United Kingdom, this will still require a conscious presence in the United Kingdom.

For example, a non-UK trust with no other UK connections which has purchased UK shares directly or through a custodian would need to register, since SDRT is payable on the transaction (even though this is normally deducted automatically if settled through CREST). This is due to the wide scope of the 'relevant taxes' and is a function of the fact that the Trust Register is designed not only to comply with the United Kingdom's EU obligations, but also to track trusts with a UK tax liability, even where that tax liability may be deducted at source.

- However, an important limiting factor in this context is that the UK tax liability must fall on the trustees directly.

  In most cases (due to the way in which 'relevant trust' was defined in the 2017 Regulations) the trustees also need to hold assets situated in the United Kingdom or assets which give rise to UK source income directly (unless the assets are held through a look-through entity – for example, a nominee or partnership).

As a result, the following scenarios will not result in a non-UK trust being a taxable relevant trust for these purposes:

- where the UK tax liability is attributed to someone other than the trustees – for example, the settlor or a beneficiary (because the trustees have no UK tax liability for the year in relation to the directly held assets);
- a non-UK resident trust with no UK resident beneficiaries which receives, for example, UK source dividend income (because the trustees have no liability to pay any of the relevant taxes in those circumstances);
- a non-UK resident trust which is only liable to pay UK value-added tax, corporation tax or the annual tax on enveloped dwellings (because these taxes are not relevant taxes);
- where a relief applies to cancel out the UK tax liability or reduce it to zero (including under a double tax treaty). However, in practice, if the relief needs to be claimed and a Unique Taxpayer Reference (UTR) is required to do so, the trust may still need to register (potentially ticking the 'taxable' box) to obtain a UTR (this is an illogical result and it is hoped that this will be addressed in the future);
- by concession from HMRC, where the only UK tax liability is less than £100 on a bank or building society interest income; and
- where UK assets are held through a non-nominee company (because the liability falls on the company rather than the trustees). However, where the company is holding UK assets as nominee for the trustees, there is a

requirement to register (even though the trustees do not have direct legal ownership of the assets, the tax liability in relation to those assets still falls directly on the trustees).[49]

Similarly, a UK inheritance tax charge on UK residential property held through one or more non-UK companies in a trust structure would not trigger registration (although the liability is on the trustees rather than the company, the liability does not relate to a UK asset – since the mechanics of the charge are such that the charge is on the value of the non-UK shares held directly by the trustees and not on the underlying UK property).[50]

3.6 Non-UK resident trusts with no UK tax liabilities (Regulation 45ZA)

Where a non-UK resident trust is not a taxable relevant trust, from 6 October 2020 the next question to consider is whether the trust nevertheless needs to register because the trustees have:

- entered into a business relationship with a UK relevant person and there is at least one UK resident trustee (referred to as a 'type B trust');[51] or
- acquired an interest in UK land (referred to as a 'type C trust').[52]

(a) Type B trusts: non-UK resident trusts with no UK tax liabilities which engage UK relevant persons

A significant uncertainty surrounding the changes to the Trust Register required by 5AMLD was whether a non-UK resident trust which has no UK tax liabilities would be required to register simply because it engages a UK relevant person (including, eg, banks, investment managers, custodians, lawyers, accountants, tax advisers, trust and company service providers and property agents). This uncertainty was to a large extent due to:

- differing interpretations as to the requirements of 5AMLD. In particular, on the face of it Article 31 of 4AMLD (as amended by 5AMLD) seems to apply only to trusts which are administered in the relevant member state, such that a business relationship should only trigger registration in a member state if the trust is also administered or has trustees resident in that member state; and
- the dual purpose of the UK Trust Register. As explained in section 3.1 above, the UK had already gone beyond the requirements of 4AMLD in relation to non-UK resident trusts when it introduced the Trust Register

---

49 HMRC, Trust Registration Service (TRS) – Frequently Asked Questions (FAQs) (22 November 2017), available at: www.step.org/system/files/media/files/2020-03/TRS_Guidance_FAQ_-_22_November_2017.pdf, 10, 15.

50 It is understood that HMRC has confirmed this in correspondence with STEP (the Society of Trust and Estate Practitioners).

51 Regulation 45ZA(1) and 45ZA(2)(b) 2017 Regulations (as amended by the 2020 Regulations).

52 Regulation 45ZA(1) and 45ZA(2)(c) 2017 Regulations (as amended by the 2020 Regulations).

in 2017 in order to achieve the dual purpose of both complying with its EU obligations and using the Trust Register to track and deal with tax reporting for all trusts with a UK tax liability (including both UK resident and non-UK resident trusts). It was therefore possible that the United Kingdom would also adopt a broader approach in the way that it chose to implement the changes required by 5AMLD.

Following a consultation in early 2020,[53] the United Kingdom confirmed that it would take a 'measured approach' in relation to the implementation of 5AMLD. In particular, the 2020 Regulations confirm that a non-UK resident trust is only required to register on the Trust Register by virtue of entering into a business relationship with a UK relevant person if the trust has at least one UK resident trustee.[54]

In this context, timing and the definition of 'business relationship' take on considerable importance. In particular:

- a non-UK resident trust which has at least one UK resident trustee is required to register if it enters into a new business relationship with a UK relevant person after 6 October 2020. Existing business relationships which predate the 2020 Regulations therefore are not expected to trigger a requirement to register;
- 'business relationship' is defined in 4AMLD and in Regulation 4 of the 2017 Regulations. In particular, some 'element of duration'[55] is required. HMRC's view[56] in 2020 was that this would normally involve an ongoing relationship which at the outset is expected to last for more than 12 months. However, caution is required here as it is possible that the UK courts will interpret the definition of 'business relationship' more widely.[57] HMRC also recently published further guidance moving away from the earlier '12 months' threshold, as well as the idea of having a set threshold altogether. Instead one must look at the nature of the business relationship and "[a]s a general rule, a business relationship that goes

53 Fifth Money Laundering Directive and Trust Registration Service Technical consultation document Publication date: 24 January 2020, available at https://assets.publishing.service.gov.uk/government/uploads/system/uploads/attachment_data/file/860269/Technical_consultation_document_Fifth_Money_Laundering_Directive_and_Trust_Registration_Service.pdf and Fifth Money Laundering Directive and Trust Registration Service Summary of Responses 15 July 2020 available at https://assets.publishing.service.gov.uk/government/uploads/system/uploads/attachment_data/file/901008/Technical_consultation_Fifth_Money_Laundering_Directive_and_Trust_Registration_Service_-_Summary_of_Responses.pdf.

54 A trust which has a UK resident trustee will still be non-UK resident for these purposes if there is at least one non-UK resident trustee and the settlor was not resident and domiciled in the United Kingdom when funds were contributed to the trust.

55 Regulation 4(1) 2017 Regulations.

56 Fifth Money Laundering Directive and Trust Registration Service Summary of Responses 15 July 2020 available at https://assets.publishing.service.gov.uk/government/uploads/system/uploads/attachment_data/file/901008/Technical_consultation_Fifth_Money_Laundering_Directive_and_Trust_Registration_Service_-_Summary_of_Responses.pdf [Accessed on 30 September 2020], paragraph 2.14.

57 There is existing case law in support of this view: see *Online Tax Rebate v HMRC* (2019 – Upper Tribunal).

beyond a one-off, short lived transaction is likely to have the requisite 'element of duration'".[58]

The guidance also notes the following 'indicators' which may suggest that a new business relationship has the expected 'element of duration':

- *"where the nature of the relationship is such that an ongoing relationship would be assumed in the circumstances (for example an accountant preparing regular accounts on behalf of the trustees);*
- *where the trustees or the relevant person explicitly or implicitly state an intention to establish an ongoing business relationship;*
- *where the time reasonably required to complete the business activity necessitates the formation of an ongoing relationship, for example, the purchase of land or property, which may be expected to take many months to complete."*

- counter-intuitively, registration is only required if the trustees enter into the business relationship directly. For example, if the trustees own a company which enters into a business relationship, it is understood that this would not require the trust to register (unless there is some other reason for registration (eg, a UK tax liability)); and
- 'EEA registered trusts'[59] are excluded from registering on the basis of this limb. A trust which is registered elsewhere in the European Economic Area[60] is not required to be registered in the United Kingdom unless the trust has UK tax liabilities[61] or acquires UK real estate.[62]

(b) Type C trusts: Non-UK resident trusts with no UK tax liabilities which acquire UK real estate

Non-UK resident trusts with no UK tax liabilities also need to register if they acquire UK real estate.

Unlike in relation to non-UK trusts which engage a UK relevant person, there is no requirement that a non-UK resident trust which acquires UK real estate must have at least one UK trustee. Although this goes beyond the requirements of 5AMLD, a broader approach was adopted in this context, in part in order to correspond with the planned introduction of the OEBO regime. However, by way of concession, where there is no UK trustee, the 2020 Regulations provide that the information on the register will not be publicly available (see section 3.8 below).

---

58 Trust Registration Service Manual, HMRC internal manual, www.gov.uk/hmrc-internal-manuals/trust-registration-service-manual/trsm24030.

59 Regulation 42(4) 2017 Regulations (as amended by the 2020 Regulations).

60 Following the end of the Brexit transition period, this term includes all non-UK countries with a trust register regime with broadly equivalent effect to the UK regime. See Part 4 of the 2020 Regulations.

61 See definition of 'relevant trust' and 'taxable relevant trust': Regulation 42(2)(b) 2017 Regulations (as amended by the 2020 Regulations) and Regulation 45 (14) 2017 Regulations.

62 See definition of 'type C trust': Regulation 45ZA(1) and 45ZA(2)(c) 2017 Regulations (as amended by the 2020 Regulations).

As with non-UK resident trusts which engage a UK relevant person:

- registration is only required if the trustees acquire UK real estate directly (and not, eg, via a wholly owned company). In particular, the trustees must be registered at the HM Land Registry as the legal owners of the real estate.[63] There is no requirement to register if the legal title is held by a nominee for the trustees. However, in these circumstances, it is likely that the nominee will need to register (see above); and
- on the face of it and as of the date of writing, the registration requirement is understood to only apply to new acquisitions of UK real estate made on or after 6 October 2020.

It is also worth noting that:

- in practice, it is likely that trustees who acquire UK real estate will, at some point, be subject to UK tax and will therefore need to register under a different limb as 'taxable relevant trusts';
- the requirement to register on the Trust Register under this limb is separate and in addition to the planned introduction of the OEBO register for non-UK entities which acquire UK real estate. This may result in certain non-UK trusts with corporate trustees which acquire UK real estate having to register on multiple registers – both on the OEBO register and on the Trust Register. However, the information to be registered will not necessarily be the same: the OEBO register will generally require information about the beneficial ownership of the corporate trustee rather than about the beneficial ownership of the trust; and
- the EEA registered trust exception referred to above does not apply to type C trusts. In other words, a non-UK resident trust which is registered in the European Economic Area (or equivalent post-Brexit) will still need to register in the United Kingdom if the trustees acquire UK real estate.[64]

(c) Foundations and legal arrangements similar to trusts

Although 4AMLD also applies to "legal entities such as foundations and legal arrangements similar to trusts", neither the 2017 Regulations, the 2020 Regulations nor HMRC's guidance expressly deals with the application of the Trust Register to these types of entity/arrangement.

Regulation 6(3) of the 2017 Regulations confirms that the term:

'beneficial owner', in relation to a foundation or other legal arrangement similar to a trust, means those individuals who hold equivalent or similar positions to those set out in [Regulation 6(1)] in relation to trusts.

63 Regulation 42(5) 2017 Regulations (as amended by the 2020 Regulations).

64 See definition of 'type C trust': Regulation 45ZA(1) and 45ZA(2)(c) 2017 Regulations (as amended by the 2020 Regulations).

However, the definitions of 'relevant trust', 'taxable relevant trust', 'type A trust', 'type B trust' and 'type C trust' do not expressly refer to such entities/arrangements.

Nevertheless, the general consensus among commentators – which would arguably be in line with the European legislation from which the principles derive – is that (on a purposive interpretation of the 2017 Regulations and now the 2020 Regulations), foundations and legal arrangements similar to trusts should be treated in the same way as trusts for Trust Register purposes. In other words, non-UK resident foundations and legal arrangements similar to trusts will also arguably need to register on the Trust Register if they:

- have a UK tax liability;
- enter into a business relationship with a UK relevant person and have at least one UK resident trustee-equivalent; or
- acquire an interest in UK land.

This may result in inconsistencies in practice between different EU jurisdictions. For example, it is possible that a legal arrangement in one jurisdiction will not be considered similar to a trust in that jurisdiction – but the same legal arrangement may be considered similar to a trust in the United Kingdom and may therefore need to register on the UK Trust Register if it satisfies one of the triggers for registration. This point is not currently covered by HMRC's guidance and it is hoped that further guidance will be published in the future.

3.7 What information must go on the register?

The information that must go on the register depends in part on why the trust is required to register.

(a) All trusts that are required to register

All trusts that are required to register must disclose specified information in relation to their 'beneficial owners'.

The beneficial owners of a trust are defined[65] as:

- the settlor (the FATF definition being the natural or legal persons who transfer ownership of their assets to trustees by means of a trust deed or similar arrangement);[66]
- the trustees;
- the beneficiaries;
- where the individuals (or some of the individuals) benefiting from the

65 Regulation 6(1) 2017 Regulations.

66 See General Glossary, International Standards On Combating Money Laundering and the Financing of Terrorism & Proliferation: The FATF Recommendations, adopted by the FATF Plenary on February 2012 and updated June 2019 available at: www.fatf-gafi.org/recommendations.html.

trust have not been determined, the class of persons in whose main interest the trust is set up or operates; and
- any individual who has control over the trust.

'Control' for these purposes means individuals who hold certain powers[67] over the trust (whether exercisable alone, jointly with another person or with the consent of another person), including the power to amend the trust, make distributions or change the trustees. This category will therefore often (but not always) include a protector, guardian or enforcer of a trust.

There can be some fluidity over whether someone who ostensibly fits in one of the above categories in fact falls to be registered in that capacity: HMRC accepts that a contingent beneficiary does not have to be named on the Trust Register until the contingency is satisfied. In addition, members of a class of beneficiaries who are not specifically named do not have to be identified on the Trust Register unless they receive a benefit (financial or non-financial) from the trust.

Information also needs to be disclosed in relation to any other potential beneficiaries (including any individual referred to in a document from the settlor relating to the trust such as a letter of wishes).[68] HMRC has suggested that third-party reports of the settlor's wishes (eg, in a solicitor's attendance note) would not be considered as a 'document from the settlor' for these purposes.[69]

This aspect of the regime means that the disclosure obligations under the Trust Register are wider in scope than the disclosure obligations under other transparency and information exchange regimes such as the Common Reporting Standard.

The specified information to be disclosed includes various identifying details (eg, full name and date of birth) as well as (with effect from 6 October 2020 under the 2020 Regulations) the individual's country of residence and nationality, as well as the nature and extent of the individual's beneficial interest.[70]

Where the beneficial owner is a legal entity, identifying information must be provided in relation to the legal entity (including, eg, the legal entity's

---

67 Regulation 6(2) 2017 Regulations. The relevant powers for these purposes are the power to: (i) dispose of, advance, lend, invest, pay or apply trust property; (ii) vary or terminate the trust; (iii) add or remove a person as a beneficiary to or from a class of beneficiaries; (iv) appoint or remove trustees or give another individual control over the trust; (v) direct, withhold consent to or veto the exercise of a power mentioned above.

68 Regulation 44(5)(b), Regulation 45(1)(b), Regulation 45(10), Regulation 45ZA(1) and (3) 2017 Regulations (as amended by the 2020 Regulations).

69 HMRC, Trust Registration Service (TRS) – Frequently Asked Questions (FAQs) (22 November 2017), available at: www.step.org/sites/default/files/Policy/TRS_Guidance_FAQ_-_22_November_2017.pdf, 21.

70 The extent of the identifying details which need to be disclosed differs depending on whether the trust is a taxable relevant trust or a type A, type B or type C trust. The latter are generally required to report fewer identifying details. For taxable relevant trusts, see Regulation 45(6). For type A, type B and type C trusts, see Regulation 45ZA(3).

corporate or firm name, the registered or principal office of the legal entity and the nature of the entity's role in relation to the trust).[71]

Taxable relevant trusts,[72] type A trusts[73] and type B trusts[74] that are required to register and which hold a controlling interest (broadly, where the trustees hold more than 50% of the shares or voting rights in the entity or exercise significant influence or control over the entity)[75] in a third country entity must also disclose this fact on the register, together with the name, place of incorporation and registered office of the entity. This is because (as explained below) this has an impact on the circumstances in which third parties can access information on the Trust Register. Type C trusts (in broad terms, non-UK resident trusts with no UK tax liabilities which acquire UK land and which have no UK resident trustees) do not have to provide this information. This is because information about non-UK resident trusts which acquire UK land is only available to third parties if there is at least one UK resident trustee.[76]

(b) Trusts which have UK tax liabilities – much wider disclosure required[77]

Given the dual purpose of the Trust Register, taxable relevant trusts with UK tax liabilities are required to provide more information to go on the register than trusts required to register for other reasons.

In particular, the trustees of taxable relevant trusts must also provide specified information in relation to the trust[78] and its assets, including:

- the full name of the trust;
- the date on which the trust was set up;
- a statement of accounts for the trust describing directly held trust assets and identifying the value[79] of each category of the trust assets at the date on which the information is first provided to HMRC (including the address of any property held by the trust). This applies to all trust assets and not just UK assets;

---

71 The extent of the identifying details which need to be disclosed differs depending on whether the trust is a taxable relevant trust or a type A, type B or type C trust. The latter are generally required to report fewer identifying details. For taxable relevant trusts, see Regulation 45(7). For type A, type B and type C trusts, see Regulation 45ZA(3)(c).

72 Regulation 45(10) and (10G).

73 Regulation 45ZA(4).

74 Regulation 45ZA(4).

75 Regulation 42(6) 2017 Regulations (as amended by the 2020 Regulations). This is essentially the same test as that which applies for the purposes of the PSC register but with certain modifications – including, in particular, that references to 25% in that test should be read as references to 50%.

76 This is achieved by including non-UK resident trusts with no UK tax liabilities which acquire UK land in the definition of 'type B trust' when such trusts have at least one UK resident trustee.

77 A full list of information required to be submitted is provided at www.gov.uk/hmrc-internal-manuals/trust-registration-service-manual/trsm32080.

78 Regulation 45(2)(a) and Regulation 45(5).

79 The market value of the assets needs to be provided as at the date the assets were first contributed to the trust. HMRC's guidance however suggests that formal valuations are not required but merely a 'good estimate'. See HMRC, Trust Registration Service (TRS) – Frequently Asked Questions (FAQs) (22 November 2017), available at: www.step.org/sites/default/files/Policy/TRS_Guidance_FAQ_-_22_November_2017.pdf, 22.

- the country where the trust is considered tax resident;
- the place where the trust is administered;
- a contact address for the trustees; and
- the name of any advisers who are being paid to provide legal, financial, tax or other advice to the trustee in relation to the trust. However, HMRC guidance suggests that in practice only details of the agent acting on behalf of the trustees in relation to registering on the Trust Register will be required.[80]

By comparison, trusts which do not have UK tax liabilities and are required to register for other reasons only have to provide information about the beneficial owners of the trust and do not, for example, have to provide information about the trust or its assets.[81] However, it is unclear whether in practice some information about the trust may need to be disclosed for identification purposes. Recent HMRC guidance suggests that at least some general information about the trustees and the trust (including, eg, the trust name and the date it was created) will need to be provided in practice by all registering trusts despite the wording of the regulations.[82]

3.8 Who can access the information on the Trust Register: Regulation 45ZB?

The first iteration of the Trust Register (prior to the implementation of 5AMLD) was largely private – only certain law enforcement agencies in the United Kingdom and other EEA countries through the National Crime Agency had access to the information.

However, following the implementation of 5AMLD, third parties have access to the information on the Trust Register under the following provisions:

- Regulation 45ZB(1): if they have a 'legitimate interest' in accessing the information (but note this does not apply to all trusts on the register); or
- Regulation 45ZB(3): on 'written request' in relation to certain trusts – namely:
  - UK resident trusts (type A trusts);
  - non-UK trusts with a UK business relationship and at least one UK resident trustee (a type B trust); or
  - non-UK resident trusts with UK land and at least one UK resident trustee (a type B trust for these purposes),

if the trustees hold a controlling stake in a third country entity.

80 HMRC, Trust Registration Service (TRS) – Frequently Asked Questions (FAQs) (22 November 2017), available at: www.step.org/sites/default/files/Policy/TRS_Guidance_FAQ_-_22_November_2017.pdf, 23.

81 Regulation 45ZA(3) and (4).

82 Trust Registration Service Manual, HMRC internal manual, www.gov.uk/hmrc-internal-manuals/trust-registration-service-manual/trsm32020.

(a) Legitimate interest

The UK Government confirmed during the consultation process in early 2020 that it is conscious of the need to balance preventing money laundering and terrorist financing on the one hand with individuals' right to privacy on the other. For this reason, HMRC confirmed that each request under the 'legitimate interest' test:

> *will be reviewed on its own merits and access given only where there is evidence that it furthers work to counter money laundering or terrorist financing activity.*[83]

Pursuant to Regulation 45ZB(11), HMRC must take the following into account in determining whether someone has a legitimate interest in accessing the information on the register:

- Whether the person is involved in an investigation into money laundering or terrorist financing;
- Whether the request for information will further an investigation into a specified suspected instance of money laundering or terrorist financing;
- Whether the disclosure of the information to that person would be likely to prejudice criminal investigations or proceedings or other investigations by the authorities; and
- Whether, having regard to the information produced by the person making the request, it is reasonable for that person to suspect that the trust is being used for money laundering or terrorist financing.

In practice, this means that third parties will need to be able to identify a specific trust and provide detailed information as to why they suspect it is being used for money laundering or terrorist financing, as well as why access to the information on the Trust Register would assist in this context.

As mentioned above, third parties cannot access information about a non-UK resident trust under the 'legitimate interest' test if the only reason a non-UK resident trust is registered is because:

- it has acquired UK real estate and the trust has no UK resident trustees; or
- it has UK tax liabilities.[84]

---

83 Fifth Money Laundering Directive and Trust Registration Service Summary of Responses 15 July 2020 available at https://assets.publishing.service.gov.uk/government/uploads/system/uploads/attachment_data/file/901008/Technical_consultation_Fifth_Money_Laundering_Directive_and_Trust_Registration_Service_-_Summary_of_Responses.pdf, paragraph 2.46.

84 See the definition of 'accessible information' in Regulation 45ZB(8), which refers only to type A and type B trusts.

(b) ***Trusts with controlling interests in third country entities*[85] *– on 'written request'***

Where a trust has a controlling interest in a third country entity, third parties can in principle access the information on the Trust Register on 'written request' alone, without needing to show they have a legitimate interest in doing so.[86]

However, this access is not as unrestricted as it may appear. Based on the HMRC consultation materials,[87] it is understood that information will only be made available where the request is in line with the objectives of 4AMLD and 5AMLD. In other words, third parties need to be able to show that the request for information is connected with the detection or prevention of money laundering or terrorist financing. Third parties also need to be able to identify the specific third country entity in question and its relationship with the trust which holds the controlling interest.

As of the date of writing (30 September 2020), further guidance on how this process will operate is expected from HMRC. However, for now it seems clear that simple curiosity, a political agenda or a mere commercial competitive instinct will not be sufficient to gain access to the Trust Register.

As with the legitimate interest test above, third parties also cannot access information about a non-UK resident trust with a controlling stake in a third country entity if the only reason the trust is registered is because:

- it has acquired UK real estate and the trust has no UK resident trustees; or
- it has UK tax liabilities.[88]

In practice, this means that the only circumstances in which information about a non-UK trust will be available to third parties are where the trust: (i) has at least one UK resident trustee; and (ii) has either engaged a UK relevant person or has acquired UK real estate on or after 6 October 2020.

3.9 Safeguards and appeals in relation to data sharing

Pursuant to Regulation 45ZB(5), information on the Trust Register will not be made available if the individual in question:

- would be exposed to a disproportionate risk of fraud, kidnapping, blackmail, extortion, harassment, violence or intimidation; or
- is under the age of 18 or is incapacitated.

85 Following the end of the Brexit transition period, 'third country entity' is defined as a non-UK entity established in a territory which does not have an equivalent corporate beneficial ownership register: see 2017 Regulations reg 42, para (6)(b) (as amended by the 2020 Regulations).

86 The information which can be requested by third parties is listed at www.gov.uk/hmrc-internal-manuals/trust-registration-service-manual/trsm60050.

87 Fifth Money Laundering Directive and Trust Registration Service Technical consultation document Publication date: 24 January 2020, available at https://assets.publishing.service.gov.uk/government/uploads/system/uploads/attachment_data/file/860269/Technical_consultation_document_Fifth_Money_Laundering_Directive_and_Trust_Registration_Service.pdf, paragraph 4.15.

88 This is because Regulation 45ZB(3) only applies to type A and type B trusts.

If information is exempted from disclosure for one of the reasons set out above, HMRC will notify the person who requested the information and allow them to seek a review within a specified period.[89] However, as of the date of writing it is understood that the trustees of the trust and the individuals in relation to which information is sought will not be notified of a request to access the Trust Register and will not have a right to appeal a decision by HMRC to provide access to the information.

As at the date of writing, it is understood that HMRC is considering how best to identify which individuals may be incapacitated as at the date of an information request from a third party (and in light of the fact that HMRC may not notify trustees of a request to access the Trust Register). One option under consideration in HMRC's guidance as published on 17 May 2021 is to ask trustees to flag whether any registered individual lacks mental capacity at the time of registration.[90] However, this will obviously impose a burden on trustees and may create other issues in practice.

3.10 Deadlines – when does the information need to be provided?

Deadline	
By 31 January (after the tax year in which the trustees were first liable to pay any of the relevant UK taxes set out in section 3.5 above)	Trusts with a UK tax liability (ie, taxable relevant trusts) set up before 6 April 2021.[91]
10 March 2022 (however, HMRC recently announced an intention to extend this deadline until later in 2022. The precise date will be confirmed by HMRC later in 2021).[92]	Trusts with a UK tax liability (ie, taxable relevant trusts) set up after 5 April 2021 where the tax liability was incurred before 9 February 2022.[93]
	Trusts with no UK tax liability (ie, type A, type B and type C trusts) which fall within the regime before 9 February 2022.[94]

continued on next page

89 Regulation 45ZB(6) and (7).
90 www.gov.uk/hmrc-internal-manuals/trust-registration-service-manual/trsm32100 .
91 Regulation 45(3)(a) 2017 Regulations.
92 www.gov.uk/hmrc-internal-manuals/trust-registration-service-manual/trsm40010.
93 Regulation 45(3)(b) 2017 Regulations.
94 Regulation 45ZA(5)(a).

Deadline	
	Trusts registered under the first iteration of the Trust Register (ie, before 6 October 2020) and which incurred a relevant UK tax liability before 9 February 2022 must also register certain additional information in relation to their beneficial owners and potential beneficiaries[95] by this date, as well as information about any controlling stake they hold in a third country entity.[96]
Within 30 days	In any other case, trustees will generally have 30 days from the event triggering registration to register.[97] For example, this could be when the trust is set, when a UK tax liability arises, when a new business relationship is put in place or where UK real estate is acquired.
	Once a trust is registered on the Trust Register, trustees will also have 30 days from when they become aware of any changes to update the register.[98]

However, the upgraded trust registration system will not be available until later in 2021 (although HMRC is currently testing a beta portal), so trustees will not be able to register yet.

As of the date of writing, it is unclear whether a trust which exists now and falls within the regime before 9 February 2022 but is terminated before 10

95 This is the individual's country of residence and nationality, as well as the nature and extent of the individual's beneficial interest – see section 3.7(a) above.

96 Regulation 45(10A) 2017 Regulations as amended by Regulation 7(2)(d) 2020 Regulations.

97 For taxable relevant trusts, see Regulation 45(3)(c) 2017 Regulations, as amended by Regulation 7(2) of the 2020 Regulations. For type A, type B and type C trusts, see Regulation 45ZA(5)(b).

98 For taxable relevant trusts, see Regulation 45(10H). For type A, type B and type C trusts, see Regulation 45ZA(6).

March 2022 (or the new extended deadline to be announced by HMRC) would still need to register. In principle, the information to be registered should be the information which is current and up to date as of the date of registration. However, it is expected that a trust which is no longer in existence on 10 March 2022 would still need to register, and we are awaiting further guidance on this from HMRC. One of the reasons this question is important is because once on the register, the information will stay on the register for at least five years or at most 10 years.[99]

3.11 Penalties for non-compliance

HMRC has confirmed[100] that it intends to introduce the following penalties under the new regime introduced by the 2020 Regulations for trusts which fail to register or fail to update the register:

Administrative offence	Penalty
Failure to register/update details within time limit (first offence/inadvertent failure)	No financial penalty. At this stage, only a notification letter will be sent to the trustees notifying them of their error.
Failure to update details within the time limit (second and subsequent offences)	£100 per offence.
Deliberate failure to register or update details within the time limit	This may result in a 'financial' penalty. HMRC is still considering the likely amount of any such penalty and further guidance is expected.

Any trustee found to be involved in money laundering or terrorist financing might also be subject to a separate penalty regime.

It is understood that trustees will be able to appeal any penalty issued if they

99 Regulation 45(10J) 2017 Regulations (as amended by the 2020 Regulations).

100 Fifth Money Laundering Directive and Trust Registration Service Technical consultation document Publication date: 24 January 2020, available at https://assets.publishing.service.gov.uk/government/uploads/system/uploads/attachment_data/file/860269/Technical_consultation_document_Fifth_Money_Laundering_Directive_and_Trust_Registration_Service.pdf, paragraph 3.25 to 3.30 and Fifth Money Laundering Directive and Trust Registration Service Summary of Responses 15 July 2020 available at https://assets.publishing.service.gov.uk/government/uploads/system/uploads/attachment_data/file/901008/Technical_consultation_Fifth_Money_Laundering_Directive_and_Trust_Registration_Service_-_Summary_of_Responses.pdf , paragraph 2.34.

have a reasonable excuse for not complying with their obligations under the Trust Register regime.

3.12 Worked example

By way of example, how does the Trust Register apply to Example 7 (a typical private trust company structure) from the first half of this chapter (see above for a summary of the scenario)?

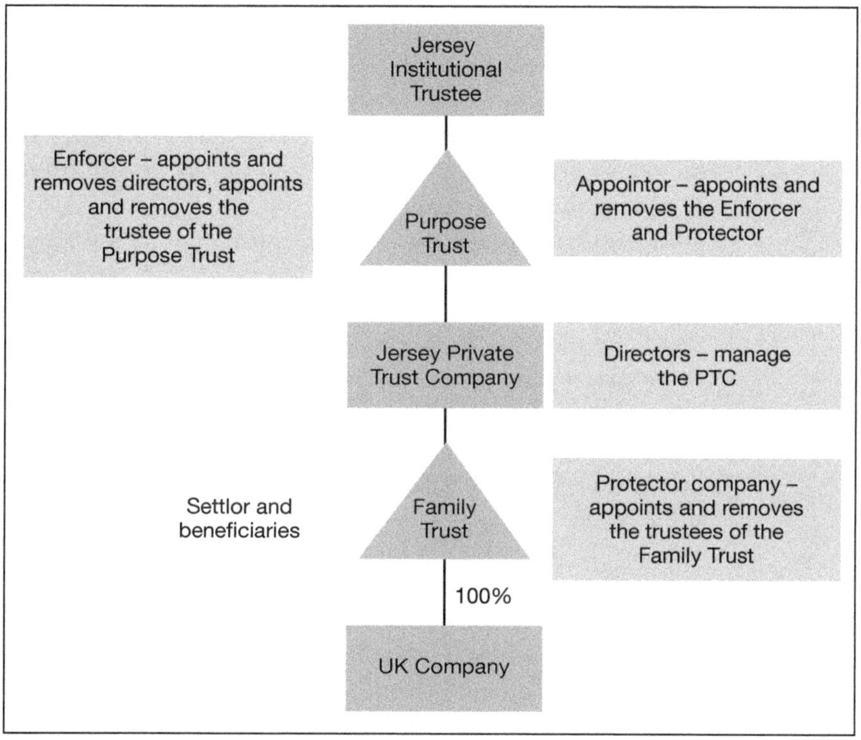

How does the Trust Register regime apply?

- It seems clear that both the Family Trust and the Purpose Trust are express trusts and unlikely to be excluded trusts.
- Both trusts are non-UK resident express trusts because the sole trustee is non-UK resident. As such, they will only need to register (in broad terms), if they:
  - have a UK tax liability;
  - enter into a business relationship with a UK relevant person and have at least one UK resident trustee; or
  - acquire an interest in UK land.

Tax liability:

- As the Family Trust holds a UK asset directly (the shares in the UK company), it will be a 'taxable relevant trust' in any year in which the trustees are liable for one of the relevant taxes listed above. For example, if the Family Trust trustee purchased the UK shares directly or through a custodian, the Family Trust would need to register, since SDRT is payable on the transaction (even though this is normally deducted automatically if settled through CREST). Alternatively, if this predated the Trust Register regime's introduction in 2017, there may be a UK tax liability in the future – for example, if income tax is payable on dividends from the UK company or on a 10-year anniversary charge or on an exit charge if the UK shares are distributed out of the trust. This will need to be monitored because (as discussed above) non-UK resident trusts can fall in and out of the regime on this basis.
- Once the trust is on the Trust Register, even if the Family Trust subsequently falls out of the regime (because it does not have a UK tax liability in a particular year), it is possible that the information will remain on the Trust Register until the trust is terminated. As of the date of writing, it is understood that it is not possible to 'de-register' a trust and it is unclear if this function will be introduced.[101]
- However, if the Family Trust has to register by virtue of having a UK tax liability in a particular year (and this is the only reason for registration), third parties will not have access to the information on the Trust Register.

Entering into a UK business relationship:

- Even if the trustees of the Family Trust or the Purpose Trust enter into a UK business relationship with a UK relevant person, this should not trigger registration while the trusts have no UK resident trustees.
- This underscores the importance of being clear at all times on the identity of all trustees and where they are resident.
- As discussed above, if the UK company enters into a UK business relationship, this will not trigger registration – registration is only required if the trustees enter into the business relationship directly.

Acquiring an interest in UK land:

- The Family Trust and the Purpose Trust do not appear to hold any UK land directly. However, this will obviously need to be monitored in future and the trustees should take advice on how best to structure any

101 There was a reference to allowing trusts to "close their record" in the January consultation – see paragraph 3.8 – but it is unclear if and when this will be implemented.

future acquisition as this could trigger registration (even if there are no UK resident trustees). However, if there are no UK resident trustees at the time of any such acquisition, the information on the Trust Register will not be available to third parties.

United States

Todd D Mayo
UBS

1. Introduction

In the United States, the Corporate Transparency Act[1] will establish a national, non-public registry of the beneficial owners of corporations, limited liability companies and most other types of entity. The US Treasury's Financial Crimes Enforcement Network (FinCEN) will maintain the registry. The registry will generally be accessible by law enforcement agencies for national security, intelligence, or law enforcement purposes, and it will be accessible by the US Internal Revenue Service (IRS) for tax administration purposes. Additionally, under certain conditions, it will be accessible by financial institutions conducting due diligence under anti-money laundering/ anti-terrorist financing (AML/ATF) laws and by their regulators. The registry will not include beneficial ownership information for trusts.

The creation of a beneficial ownership registry has been a long time coming. In 2008, Senators Carl Levin, Norm Coleman and Barack Obama first introduced a bill to require the disclosure of beneficial ownership information.[2] With some variation, the bill has been reintroduced every year since then.[3] Instead of creating a single national registry, these bills required each US state to maintain its own registry. For years, Delaware opposed the legislation.[4] In

1 Pub Law 116-283 (2020), Sections 6401 to 6403. For the purposes of this chapter, 'Pub Law' refers to a bill that has been enacted into law in the United States.

2 Incorporation Transparency and Law Enforcement Assistance Act, S 2956, 110th Congress (2008). For the purposes of this chapter, 'S' refers to a bill introduced in the US Senate.

3 See, for example, Incorporation Transparency and Law Enforcement Assistance Act, S 569, 111th Congress (2009); Incorporation Transparency and Law Enforcement Assistance Act, HR 6098, 111th Congress (2009); Incorporation Transparency and Law Enforcement Assistance Act, S 1483, 112th Congress (2011); Incorporation Transparency and Law Enforcement Assistance Act, HR 3416, 112th Congress (2011); Incorporation Transparency and Law Enforcement Assistance Act, S 1465, 113th Congress (2013); Incorporation Transparency and Law Enforcement Assistance Act, HR 3331, 113th Congress (2013); Incorporation Transparency and Law Enforcement Assistance Act, S 2489, 114th Congress (2015); Incorporation Transparency and Law Enforcement Assistance Act, HR 4450, 114th Congress (2015); Corporate Transparency Act of 2017, S 1717, 115th Congress (2017); Corporate Transparency Act of 2017, HR 3089, 115th Congress (2017); Corporate Transparency Act of 2019, S 1978, 116th Congress (2019); and Corporate Transparency Act of 2019, HR 2513, 116th Congress (2019). For the purposes of this chapter, 'HR' refers to a bill introduced in the US House of Representatives.

4 Suzanne Barlyn, "How Delaware Kept America Safe for Corporate Secrecy", Reuters, 24 August 2016, www.reuters.com/article/us-usa-delaware-bullock-specialreport-idUSKCN10Z1OH; Naomi Jagoda, "'Panama Papers' Could Boost Prospects for Corporate-Transparency Legislation", The Hill, 4 April 2016, https://thehill.com/policy/finance/275134-panama-papers-could-boost-prospects-for-corporate-transparency-legislation.

2019, members of the US Congress (Congress) agreed to amend the bill so that FinCEN, rather than the US states, would collect the beneficial ownership information. Delaware backed this new approach.[5] In October 2019, the US House of Representatives (House) passed the amended bill.[6] The US Senate (Senate) did not act on this bill, which (with modifications) was subsequently incorporated into the National Defense Authorization Act, a massive annual bill that sets US defence spending and defines aspects of US defence policy.[7] The defence bill also contains other provisions significantly strengthening AML/ATF laws.[8]

2. Overview

The Corporate Transparency Act requires reporting companies to disclose to FinCEN information about beneficial owners and applicants. Reporting companies generally are entities other than exempt entities, such as banks, financial institutions and certain companies having more than 20 full-time employees. Beneficial owners generally are individuals who own or control a reporting company. Applicants are individuals who form or register a reporting company. Subject to certain limitations and protocols – which generally aim to preserve the privacy of the information – FinCEN may disclose beneficial ownership information to law enforcement agencies for national security, intelligence, or law enforcement purposes; it may disclose the information to the IRS for tax administration purposes; and it may disclose the information to financial institutions and their regulators in connection with AML/ATF activities. This chapter explores these concepts in more depth.

The Corporate Transparency Act became effective upon its enactment, and the reporting obligations will become effective on a date that FinCEN will set by regulation.[9] FinCEN must adopt these regulations by 1 January 2022.[10] These

---

5 Letter from Jeffrey W Bullock to Maxine Waters and Patrick McHenry, 30 April 2019, https://maloney.house.gov/sites/maloney.house.gov/files/DE%20Sec%20of%20State.pdf. Mr Bullock was Delaware's secretary of state; Representative Waters was the chair of the House's Committee on Financial Services and the sponsor of the House's version of the Corporate Transparency Act; and Representative McHenry was the ranking member of the House's Committee on Financial Services.
In his letter, Mr Bullock endorsed the Corporate Transparency Act and expressed his support for having FinCEN rather than the US states collect the beneficial ownership information:

> *I support the framework contemplated in the legislation, which proposes the collection of beneficial ownership information at the federal level by the Financial Crimes Enforcement Network (FinCEN). I have long argued a piecemeal, state-based approach to the collection of beneficial ownership information would create loopholes vulnerable to exploitation by bad actors. I believe FinCEN possesses the expertise required to responsibly implement an effective and sustainable framework that safeguards privacy.*

6 Corporate Transparency Act of 2019, HR 2513, 116th Congress (2019).

7 William M (Mac) Thornberry National Defense Authorization Act for Fiscal Year 2021, Public Law 116-283 (2020).

8 Pub Law 116-283 (2020), Sections 6001 to 6511.

9 For any existing reporting company (ie, a reporting company formed or registered before the adoption of the regulations), the reporting obligations will be effective on a date set by the regulations. That date cannot be more than two years after the adoption of the regulations. 31 USC Section 5336(b)(1)(B).

10 31 USC Section 5336(b)(5). In April 2021, FinCEN issued an advance notice of proposed rulemaking, soliciting comments on the regulations implementing the beneficial ownership registry. See Beneficial Ownership Information Reporting Requirements, 86 Fed Reg 17,557 (1 April 2021) (ANPR). For the purposes of this chapter, 'Fed Reg' means the Federal Register.

regulations will also address issues such as the timing and manner of reporting by reporting companies.[11]

In areas where the act may be unclear or lack specificity, FinCEN's guidance in other areas may shed light on how it may interpret the act. For example, in 2016, FinCEN adopted regulations establishing the customer due diligence (CDD) rule, which generally requires financial institutions to verify the identity of beneficial owners of certain legal entities.[12] Under the CDD rule, financial institutions generally must collect the same beneficial ownership information that would have to be disclosed under the Corporate Transparency Act. The CDD rule thus potentially offers some insights into how FinCEN will interpret the act. Notably, the act requires FinCEN to modify the CDD rule so that it conforms to the act.[13]

In addition to adopting implementing regulations, FinCEN will inform the public of the new reporting obligations.[14] The IRS will help.[15] It may include information about these reporting obligations in its notices and forms.[16] US states may help too. A US state is eligible to receive federal funding if it notifies applicants and entities of these reporting obligations.[17] US states seeking those funds will generally provide a notice upon an entity's formation, will provide annual notices, and will include information about the reporting obligations on its website.[18]

3. Beneficial owners

The Corporate Transparency Act requires disclosure of the identity of each beneficial owner of a reporting company.[19] A 'beneficial owner' is an individual (ie, a natural person) who:

- exercises substantial control over the entity; or
- owns 25% or more of the entity's equity interests.[20]

An individual who meets either of these two tests is a beneficial owner, unless one of five exceptions applies.

---

11 *Ibid.*

12 Customer Due Diligence Requirements for Financial Institutions, 81 Fed Reg 29,398 (11 May 2016). The CDD rule became effective on 11 May 2018.

13 Public Law 116-283 (2020), Section 6403(d).

14 31 USC Section 5336(e)(1).

15 *Ibid.*

16 *Ibid.*

17 31 USC Section 5336(e)(2).

18 31 USC Section 5336(e)(2)(A). In the notices that they provide, the US states will state that they are providing the notices on behalf of the US Treasury for the purpose of "preventing money laundering, the financing of terrorism, proliferation financing, serious tax fraud, and other financial crime by requiring nonpublic registration of business entities formed or registered to do business in the United States". 31 USC Section 5336(e)(2)(B).

19 31 USC Section 5336(b)(1)(A) and (b)(2)(A).

20 31 USC Section 5336(a)(3). FinCEN requested comment on the degree to which the definition of 'beneficial owner' should harmonise with the existing definition of that term under the CDD rule or the existing definition of that term under federal regulations governing the reporting obligations of persons who own more than 5% of the publicly traded shares of a public company. ANPR Section IV(3)(a).

3.1 Substantial control test

An individual who exercises substantial control over an entity is a beneficial owner of that entity.[21] An individual may exercise control directly or indirectly.[22] An individual's control may arise through contract, arrangement, understanding, relationship, or otherwise.[23] In colloquial terms, this test asks: "Who pulls the strings?"

The Corporate Transparency Act does not define 'substantial control', but the CDD rule may offer some insights. Under the CDD rule, each executive officer of a corporation has substantial control over the corporation.[24] An executive officer includes the chief executive officer, chief financial officer, chief operating officer, president, vice president and treasurer.[25] Similarly, under the CDD rule, each senior manager and managing member of a limited liability company has substantial control over the company, and each general partner of a partnership has substantial control over the partnership.[26] Each other individual who regularly performs functions similar to those of an executive officer, senior manager or general partner also has substantial control over the entity.[27] Accordingly, a director of a corporation likely has substantial control over the corporation.

An individual can have substantial control without having an official role in the entity. For example, an individual would likely have substantial control over a limited liability company if, based on an understanding between the individual and the company's sole manager, the manager would act in accordance with the individual's directions.

3.2 Ownership test

An individual who owns 25% or more of an entity's ownership interests is a beneficial owner of the entity.[28] An individual may own those interests directly or indirectly.[29] An individual may own those interests through a contract, arrangement, understanding, relationship, or otherwise.[30] An individual thus is

---

21 31 USC Section 5336(a)(3)(A)(i). FinCEN requested comment on whether a reporting company can have more than one individual who has substantial control. ANPR Section IV(3)(c).

22 *Ibid.*

23 *Ibid.*

24 31 CFR Section 1010.230(d)(2). The standard that applies under the CDD rule differs slightly from the standard that applies under the Corporate Transparency Act. For the purposes of the CDD rule, a beneficial owner includes an individual who has 'significant responsibility to control, manage, or direct' an entity. 31 CFR Section 1010.230(d)(2). In contrast, for the purposes of the Corporate Transparency Act, a beneficial owner includes any individual who has 'substantial control' over an entity. 31 USC Section 5333(a)(3)(A)(i). Under the Corporate Transparency Act, FinCEN would have to conform the CDD rule to the act. Pub Law 116-283 (2020), Section 6403(d). Accordingly, FinCEN will potentially amend the CDD rule so that its definition of beneficial owner will apply the substantial control standard instead of the significant responsibility standard.

25 *Ibid.*

26 *Ibid.*

27 *Ibid.*

28 31 USC Section 5336(a)(3)(A)(ii).

29 *Ibid.*

30 *Ibid.*

the owner of any ownership interest held on the individual's behalf by an agent, by a nominee, or under a custodial arrangement. Under this test, there are at most four individuals who qualify as beneficial owners.

An individual trustee potentially is a beneficial owner of a trust-owned entity. A trustee of a trust is the legal owner of the trust property. Accordingly, if an individual is trustee of a trust that holds 25% or more of an entity's ownership interests, the individual likely would be a beneficial owner of the entity, because the individual trustee would own 25% or more of the entity's ownership interests. The CDD rule suggests that this conclusion is correct. Under that rule, a trustee of a trust is a beneficial owner of an entity in which the trust owns 25% or more of the ownership interests.[31]

In the United States, directed trusts and divided trusts are increasingly popular. In a directed trust, the terms of the trust vest a person – commonly called a 'trust adviser' or 'protector' – with the power to direct the trustee to exercise (or refrain from exercising) specific powers. For example, a trust adviser may have the power to direct the trustee concerning the investment of the trust property. In that case, the trustee typically cannot take any action with respect to the investment of the trust property, unless the action is in accordance with the trust adviser's directions. In a divided trust, the terms of the trust vest a person with some (but not all) trustee powers. For example, a trust adviser may have the power to invest the trust property. In that case, the trust adviser typically can directly take any action with respect to the investment of the trust property, because the trust adviser – not the trustee – is vested with the investment power.[32]

For the purposes of the Corporate Transparency Act, an individual trust adviser is unlikely to be a beneficial owner of a trust-owned entity under the ownership test, because a trust adviser is not the legal owner of trust property. For the same reason, an individual protector is unlikely to be a beneficial owner of a trust-owned entity under the ownership test. An individual trust adviser or individual protector potentially could be a beneficial owner under the substantial control test. This could be the case if, for example, an individual trust adviser is vested with the investment powers over the trust, the trust holds an interest in a limited liability company, and, through the company's operating agreement, the trust adviser has substantial control over the limited liability company.

3.3 Exceptions

There are five categories of individuals who are not beneficial owners. These

31 31 CFR Section 1010.230(d)(3).

32 For a more in-depth discussion of directed trusts and divided trusts, see Todd D Mayo, "Trust governance models", *International Family Office Journal*, June 2017, pp28–38.

individuals are not beneficial owners regardless of whether they satisfy the substantial control test or the ownership test. These exceptions are listed below.

- **Minors:** A minor is not a beneficial owner if the minor's parent or guardian is reported as the beneficial owner.[33] The laws of the US state in which the entity is formed determines whether an individual is a minor.[34] In most US states, a minor is an individual who has not attained 18 years of age. The Corporate Transparency Act does not specifically address what laws apply for the purposes of determining whether an individual is a minor if the entity is a non-US entity that registers in a US state.
- **Agents, custodians and nominees:** An individual acting as a nominee, intermediary, custodian or agent on behalf of another individual is not a beneficial owner.[35] Of course, an individual for whom a nominee, intermediary, custodian or agent is acting potentially is a beneficial owner if that individual has the requisite degree of indirect control or ownership.
- **Employees:** An employee of an entity is not a beneficial owner of the entity, so long as the individual is acting solely as an employee and the individual's control derives solely from the employee's employment status.[36]
- **Heirs:** An individual is not a beneficial owner of an entity if the individual's only interest in the entity is through a right of inheritance.[37] Thus, an individual who is a beneficiary of a decedent's estate would not be a beneficial owner of an entity in which the estate holds an ownership interest. This exception would seemingly block the attribution of the ownership interest held by the estate to the individual beneficiary, although the statute is unclear on this point. Assuming that it does block attribution, an individual who is a beneficiary of a decedent's estate and who directly owns an ownership interest in an entity would not be treated as indirectly owning any of the ownership interests held in the estate. This exception ceases to apply once an individual receives an ownership interest in satisfaction of the individual's inheritance right (eg, upon distribution of an ownership interest from a decedent's estate). This exception does not apply to an individual who is acting as the personal representative of the estate.
- **Creditors:** An entity's creditor generally is not a beneficial owner.[38] Its creditor, however, is a beneficial owner if the creditor exercises

33 31 USC Section 5336(a)(3)(B)(i).
34 *Ibid.*
35 31 USC Section 5336(a)(3)(B)(ii).
36 31 USC Section 5336(a)(3)(B)(iii).
37 31 USC Section 5336(a)(3)(B)(iv).
38 31 USC Section 5336(a)(3)(B)(v).

substantial control over the entity or owns 25% or more of the entity's ownership interests.[39]

4. Applicants

The Corporate Transparency Act requires disclosure of the identity of each applicant of a reporting company.[40] An 'applicant' is an individual who files an application to form an entity in a US state[41] or files an application to register a non-US entity to do business in a US state.[42]

5. Reporting companies

The Corporate Transparency Act requires each reporting company to disclose the identities of its applicants and beneficial owners.[43] A reporting company is any entity (other than an exempt entity) that:

- is formed by filing a document with the secretary of state (or similar official) of a US state;[44] or
- is formed under the laws of a country other than the United States and is registered to do business in a US state by filing a document with the secretary of state (or similar official) of that state.[45]

Reporting companies include corporations and limited liability companies, and they likely include limited partnerships, statutory trusts and civil law style foundations.[46] Reporting companies also likely include any general partnerships that file a formational document (or, if formed outside the United States, a registration document) with a secretary of state of a US state.

A trust presumably is not a reporting entity, because it is not formed by filing a document with the secretary of state of a US state.[47] Unlike an earlier version of

---

39 *Ibid.*

40 31 USC Section 5336(b)(1)(A) and (b)(2)(A).

41 31 USC Section 5336(a)(2)(A). FinCEN requested comment on whether this definition is sufficiently clear or whether it should expand the definition. ANPR Section IV(4). It also requested comment on whether a reporting company should have an obligation to report on an applicant in any report after its initial report. ANPR Section IV(25).

42 31 USC Section 5336(a)(2)(B). See also comments in note 47.

43 31 USC Section 5336(b)(1)(A) and (b)(2)(A).

44 31 USC Section 5336(a)(11)(A)(i). A reporting company also includes an entity that is formed by filing a document with an official of an Indian tribe.

45 31 USC Section 5336(a)(11)(A)(ii). A reporting company also includes a non-US entity that is registered to do business with an Indian tribe by filing a document with a tribal official.

46 Under the Corporate Transparency Act, a corporation, limited liability company or 'other similar entity' can qualify as a reporting company. FinCEN requested comment on how it should interpret 'other similar entity'. ANPR Section IV(1)(a) and (b). Notably, FinCEN specifically requested comment on whether a state-chartered trust company, a statutory trust, or a special purpose vehicle formed by filing with a secretary of state or similar office is a reporting company. ANPR Sections IV(1)(c) and IV(8).

47 This is certainly the case with an *inter vivos* trust, and it seems likely the case with a testamentary trust. Although a testamentary trust is formed by filing the decedent's will with the probate court, the probate court would not seem to be a 'similar office' for the purposes of the Corporate Transparency Act. Notably, in its ANPR, FinCEN does not expressly mention trusts (aside from statutory trusts). It does solicit comments on what types of entities qualify as reporting companies and it is possible that some commentators will express their opinions on whether FinCEN should interpret 'reporting company' to include a trust. See, eg, ANPR Sections IV(1) and (2).

the bill, however, the Corporate Transparency Act does not expressly exempt trusts from the disclosure requirements.[48] The act expressly classifies split-interest trusts (eg, charitable remainder trusts and charitable lead trusts) as exempt entities.[49]

6. Exempt entities

Exempt entities are not reporting companies. They thus are exempt from the beneficial owner disclosure requirements.[50] Exempt entities include:

- an entity that has a class of securities registered on a national securities exchange, such as the Nasdaq Global Market (Nasdaq) or the New York Stock Exchange (NYSE);[51]
- an entity that must file reports with the US Securities and Exchange Commission (SEC) because it has filed a registration statement for a public offering;[52]
- an entity that: (i) is formed by a US state, by a political subdivision of a US state, under an interstate compact between two or more US states, or under the laws of the United States; and (ii) exercises governmental authority on behalf of the United States, a US state, or a political subdivision of a US state;[53]
- a bank;[54]
- a credit union;[55]
- a bank holding company;[56]
- a registered money transmitting business;[57]
- a registered broker or dealer;[58]
- a securities exchange or clearing agency;[59]
- an entity that is registered with the SEC under the Securities Exchange Act;[60]
- a registered investment company (ie, a mutual fund);[61]
- a registered investment adviser;[62]

---

48 See 31 USC Section 5333(a)(1)(A) and (d)(4), as proposed by HR 6395, Section 6001.

49 31 USC Section 5336(a)(11)(B)(xix)(III).

50 31 USC Section 5336(a)(11)(B). FinCEN requested comment on whether each statutory definition of an exempt entity is sufficiently clear. ANPR Section IV(6). Notably, FinCEN also requested comment on whether an exempt entity should be subject to obligation to file an annual or other periodic report to support its qualification for the exemption. ANPR Section IV(9)(c).

51 31 USC Section 5336(a)(11)(B)(i)(I).

52 31 USC Section 5336(a)(11)(B)(i)(II).

53 31 USC Section 5336(a)(11)(B)(ii).

54 31 USC Section 5336(a)(11)(B)(iii).

55 31 USC Section 5336(a)(11)(B)(iv).

56 31 USC Section 5336(a)(11)(B)(v).

57 31 USC Section 5336(a)(11)(B)(vi).

58 31 USC Section 5336(a)(11)(B)(vii).

59 31 USC Section 5336(a)(11)(B)(viii).

60 31 USC Section 5336(a)(11)(B)(ix). This exemption does not cover entities that have a class of securities registered on a national securities exchange, entities that must file reports with the SEC because they have filed a registration statement for a public offering, any registered broker or dealer, or securities exchanges or clearing agencies. Those entities are covered by their own exemptions.

61 31 USC Section 5336(a)(11)(B)(x).

62 *Ibid.*

- a venture capital fund adviser;[63]
- an insurance company;[64]
- an insurance producer that has an operating presence at a physical location in the United States;[65]
- a registered entity (as defined under the Commodity Exchange Act), such as an exchange for commodities and option contracts, a swap execution facility, or a swap data repository;[66]
- a registered futures commission merchant, introducing broker, commodity pool operator, or commodity trading adviser;[67]
- a registered foreign exchange dealer;[68]
- a registered public accounting firm;[69]
- a public utility;[70]
- a designated financial market utility;[71]
- a pooled investment vehicle that is operated or advised by a bank, credit union, registered investment company, registered investment adviser, or venture capital fund adviser;[72]
- a 501(c) organisation, such as a tax-exempt charitable organisation, social welfare organisation, or tax-exempt business league;[73]
- a 527 organisation (a type of tax-exempt political organisation);[74]
- a 4947(a)(1) organisation (a type of charitable trust that is not tax-exempt);[75]
- a split-interest trust, such as a charitable remainder trust or charitable lead trust;[76]
- an entity that: (i) operates exclusively to provide financial assistance to or hold governance rights over a 501(c) organisation, a 527 organisation, a 4947(a)(1) organisation, or a split-interest trust; (ii) is a US person; (iii) is beneficially owned or controlled by one or more US persons who are

63 31 USC Section 5336(a)(11)(B)(xi).
64 31 USC Section 5336(a)(11)(B)(xii).
65 31 USC Section 5336(a)(11)(B)(xiii).
66 31 USC Section 5336(a)(11)(B)(xiv)(I).
67 31 USC Section 5336(a)(11)(B)(xiv)(II)(aa).
68 31 USC Section 5336(a)(11)(B)(xiv)(II)(bb).
69 31 USC Section 5336(a)(11)(B)(xv).
70 31 USC Section 5336(a)(11)(B)(xvi). To qualify for this exemption, the public utility must satisfy two requirements. First, it must provide telecommunications service, electrical power, natural gas, or water and sewer services. Second, it must provide these services within the United States.
71 31 USC Section 5336(a)(11)(B)(xvii).
72 31 USC Section 5336(a)(11)(B)(xviii). Pooled investment vehicles generally include registered investment companies and certain companies that would qualify as investment companies but are exempt from registration. 31 USC Section 5336(a)(10).
73 31 USC Section 5336(a)(11)(B)(xix)(I). A 501(c) organisation is an organisation described in Section 501(c) of the Internal Revenue Code of 1986 (Internal Revenue Code). If a 501(c) organisation loses its tax-exempt status, this exemption will continue to apply for 180 days after the loss of that status.
74 31 USC Section 5336(a)(11)(B)(xix)(II). A 527 organisation is an organisation described in Section 527 of the Internal Revenue Code.
75 31 USC Section 5336(a)(11)(B)(xix)(III). A 4947(a)(1) organisation is an organisation described in Section 4947(a)(1) of the Internal Revenue Code.
76 *Ibid.* A split-interest trust is a trust described in Section 4947(a)(2) of the Internal Revenue Code.

US citizens or are lawfully admitted for permanent residence; and (iv) derives a majority of its funding or revenue from one or more US persons who are US citizens or are lawfully admitted for permanent residence;[77]
- an entity that: (i) employs more than 20 employees on a full-time basis in the United States; (ii) in the previous year, filed a US income tax return showing more than $5 million of gross receipts or sales; and (iii) has an operating presence at a physical office in the United States;[78]
- an exempt subsidiary (ie, an entity that is owned or controlled (directly or indirectly) by one or more other exempt entities (subject to some exceptions));[79] and
- a grandfathered exempt entity (ie, an entity that: (i) has been in existence more than one year; (ii) is not engaged in active business; (iii) is not owned (directly or indirectly) by a non-US person; (iv) during the preceding 12 months has not experienced a change of ownership and has not sent or received more than $1,000 (including from any accounts in which the entity or any affiliate has an interest); and (v) does not hold any assets, including any ownership interest in another entity).[80]

With the written concurrence of the US attorney general and the US homeland security secretary, the US treasury secretary may exempt an entity or class of entities.[81] The US treasury secretary must conclude that requiring the beneficial ownership information from the entity or class of entities: (i) would not serve the public interest; and (ii) would not be highly useful in national security, intelligence, and law enforcement agency efforts to detect, prevent or prosecute money laundering, the financing of terrorism, proliferation finance, serious tax fraud or other crimes.[82] The US treasury secretary must adopt regulations to establish any such exemption.[83]

---

77 31 USC Section 5336(a)(11)(B)(xx). A US person is a United States person as defined in Section 7701(a)(30) of the Internal Revenue. 31 USC Section 5336(a)(14). A US person generally includes a US citizen, a US resident, a corporation or partnership formed in a US state, a US estate, and a US trust. IRC Section 7701(a)(30). The phrase 'lawfully admitted for permanent residence' is defined in Section 101(a) of the Immigration and Nationality Act. 31 USC Section 5336(a)(9).

78 31 USC Section 5336(a)(11)(B)(xxi). For the purposes of the gross receipts test, the entity may include the gross receipts of any entity that it owns and any entity through which it operates. 31 USC Section 5336(a)(11)(B)(xxi)(II).

79 31 USC Section 5336(a)(11)(B)(xxii). The exceptions are: (i) registered money transmitting businesses; (ii) pooled investment vehicles; (iii) exempt entities that operate exclusively to provide financial assistance to or hold governance rights over a 501(c) organisation, a 527 organisation, a 4947(a)(1) organisation, or a split-interest trust; (iv) exempt subsidiaries; and (v) grandfathered exempt entities.

80 31 USC Section 5336(a)(11)(B)(xxiii). The statute regrettably uses the term 'grandfathered' despite its racist origins. See Alan Greenblatt, "The Racial History of the 'Grandfather Clause'", NPR, 22 October 2013, www.npr.org/sections/codeswitch/2013/10/21/239081586/the-racial-history-of-the-grandfather-clause. A non-US person (or, in the language of the statute, 'foreign person') is a person who is not a United States person as defined in Section 7701(a)(30) of the Internal Revenue. 31 USC Section 5336(a)(7).

81 31 USC Section 5336(a)(11)(B)(xxiv). FinCEN solicited suggestions for any companies that it should exempt under this authority. ANPR Section IV(7).

82 *Ibid.*

83 *Ibid.*

7. Reporting by reporting companies

A reporting company must file with FinCEN a report identifying its applicants and beneficial owners. For each applicant and beneficial owner, the report must include the individual's:

- full legal name;
- date of birth;
- current residential or business street address; and
- FinCEN identifier or unique identifying number from an acceptable identification document.[84]

The reporting obligations will become effective on a date that FinCEN will set by regulation.[85] FinCEN must adopt these regulations by 1 January 2022.[86] Once the beneficial ownership disclosure requirements are effective, a reporting company must file a report upon its formation or registration,[87] and it must file a report after any change to the beneficial ownership information.[88] By regulation, FinCEN will establish the due dates for the reports.[89]

When reporting information about its applicants and beneficial owners, a reporting company generally is not required to provide any information about any exempt entity that has (directly or indirectly) an ownership interest in the reporting company.[90] Aside from reporting the exempt entity's name,[91] the reporting company does not have any obligation to report any information about the exempt entity, its applicants or its beneficial owners.[92]

The Corporate Transparency Act requires each existing reporting company to provide identifying information about its applicants.[93] This may pose a practical challenge. Given the passage of time since its formation or registration, a reporting company may be hard pressed to obtain that information. The act does not expressly address this issue. The regulations likely will. The act only penalises wilful failures

---

84 31 USC Section 5336(b)(2)(A). FinCEN requested comment on what steps a reporting company should be obligated to take for purposes of ensuring the accuracy and completeness of this information. ANPR Section IV(23). For purposes of ensuring that the registry contains information that is 'highly useful to authorised users', FinCEN requested comment on what additional information it should require each reporting company to provide about itself, its affiliates and its relationship to its beneficial owners. ANPR Sections IV(10), (11), (12) and (13).

85 For any existing reporting company (ie, a reporting company formed or registered before the adoption of the regulations), the reporting obligations will be effective on a date set by the regulations. That date cannot be more than two years after the adoption of the regulations. 31 USC Section 5336(b)(1)(B).

86 31 USC Section 5336(b)(5). In April 2021, FinCEN issued an advance notice of proposed rulemaking, soliciting comments on the regulations implementing the beneficial ownership registry. See Beneficial Ownership Information Reporting Requirements, 86 Fed Reg 17,557 (1 April 2021) (ANPR). For the purposes of this chapter, 'Fed Reg' means the Federal Register.

87 31 USC Section 5336(b)(1)(C).

88 31 USC Section 5336(b)(1)(D).

89 31 USC Section 5336(b)(1)(C) and (b)(1)(D). For a report of a change, the due date will be not more than one year after the change. 31 USC Section 5336(b)(1)(D).

90 31 USC Section 5336(b)(2)(B).

91 31 USC Section 5336(b)(2)(B)(i).

92 31 USC Section 5336(b)(2)(B)(ii).

93 31 USC Section 5336(b)(2).

to report,[94] so the regulations potentially will excuse an omission if the reporting company makes a reasonable or good-faith effort to obtain the information.

8. Reporting by non-US pooled investment vehicles

A pooled investment vehicle that is an exempt entity and is formed under the laws of a non-US country must file a written certification with FinCEN.[95] In the certification, the pooled investment vehicle must provide the identification information of an individual who exercises substantial control over the pooled investment vehicle.[96]

9. Reporting by exempt subsidiaries

An exempt subsidiary generally is an entity that is owned or controlled (directly or indirectly) by one or more other exempt entities.[97] When an entity ceases to qualify as an exempt subsidiary, it must file a report with FinCEN.[98] In the report, the entity must provide the identification information for each of its applicants and beneficial owners.[99]

10. Reporting by exempt grandfathered entities

An exempt grandfathered entity is an entity that: (i) has been in existence more than one year; (ii) is not engaged in active business; (iii) is not owned (directly or indirectly) by a non-US person; (iv) during the preceding 12 months has not experienced a change of ownership and has not sent or received more than $1,000 (including from any accounts in which the entity or any affiliate has an interest); and (v) does not hold any assets, including any ownership interest in another entity.[100] When an entity ceases to qualify as an exempt grandfathered entity, it must file a report with FinCEN.[101] In the report, the entity must provide the identification information for each of its applicants and beneficial owners.[102]

11. FinCEN identifiers

FinCEN will issue a FinCEN identifier to each individual or entity who requests one.[103] A FinCEN identifier is a unique identifying number assigned by FinCEN to an individual or entity.[104] FinCEN will issue only one FinCEN identifier to each individual or entity (including any successor entity).[105]

---

94 31 USC Section 5336(h)(1)(B).
95 31 USC Section 5336(b)(2)(C).
96 *Ibid.*
97 31 USC Section 5336(a)(11)(B)(xxii).
98 31 USC Section 5336(b)(2)(D).
99 *Ibid.*
100 31 USC Section 5336(a)(11)(B)(xxiii). For a discussion of these requirements, see footnote 82.
101 31 USC Section 5336(b)(2)(E).
102 *Ibid.*
103 31 USC Section 5336(b)(3)(A)(i).
104 31 USC Section 5336(a)(6).
105 31 USC Section 5336(b)(3)(A)(iii).

When requesting a FinCEN identifier, an individual must provide the individual's:

- full legal name;
- date of birth;
- current residential or business street address; and
- a unique identifying number from an acceptable identification document.[106]

An entity may request a FinCEN identifier after it reports its beneficial ownership information in accordance with the Corporate Transparency Act.[107] After receiving a FinCEN identifier, an individual or entity must report any changes concerning the individual's or entity's information.[108]

When reporting its beneficial ownership information, a reporting company may use an individual's or entity's FinCEN identifier *in lieu* of providing other information about the individual or entity.[109]

12. Acceptable identification documents

For the purposes of reporting beneficial ownership or obtaining a FinCEN identifier, an individual needs an acceptable identification document. An acceptable identification document is:

- a non-expired US passport;[110]
- a non-expired identification card issued by a US state or local government to the individual for the purpose of identification of the individual;[111]
- a non-expired driver's licence issued by a US state;[112] or
- if the individual does not have another form of acceptable identification document, a non-expired non-US passport.[113]

13. Prohibition against bearer shares

The Corporate Transparency Act prohibits bearer shares. Specifically, the act prohibits an entity from issuing a certificate in bearer form evidencing an interest in the entity.[114]

14. Access to beneficial ownership information

Under the Corporate Transparency Act, FinCEN must safeguard the beneficial

---

106 31 USC Section 5336(b)(3)(A)(i).
107 *Ibid.*
108 31 USC Section 5336(b)(3)(A)(ii).
109 31 USC Section 5336(b)(3)(B) and (b)(3)(C).
110 31 USC Section 5336(a)(1)(A).
111 31 USC Section 5336(a)(1)(B).
112 31 USC Section 5336(a)(1)(C).
113 31 USC Section 5336(a)(1)(D).
114 31 USC Section 5336(f).

ownership information and disclosure of the information is limited. The US Supreme Court has long recognised a right to informational privacy,[115] and these safeguards and limitations aim to ensure that the act comports with this right.

Under the act, FinCEN may disclose beneficial ownership information to the following:

- a US law enforcement agency engaged in national security, intelligence, or law enforcement activity for use in furtherance of that activity;[116]
- a law enforcement agency of a US state, local or tribal government if a court authorises the agency to seek the information in connection with a criminal or civil investigation;[117]
- a US agency on behalf of a law enforcement agency, prosecutor or judge of another country under: (i) an international treaty, agreement or convention; or (ii) if no treaty, agreement or convention is available and the other country is a trusted country, an official request by law enforcement, judicial or prosecutorial authorities of that country;[118]
- a financial institution conducting customer due diligence under AML/ATF laws, so long as the reporting company consents to the disclosure;[119]
- a US regulatory agency that supervises financial institutions for use in its supervisory and investigatory activities;[120] or
- the US Treasury Department (which includes the IRS) for tax administration purposes.[121]

Unlike some registries outside the United States, the beneficial ownership information that FinCEN collects is not accessible by the public or the media.[122] The registry is non-public.[123]

For beneficial ownership information that FinCEN provides to another agency, FinCEN and the agency must adhere to appropriate protocols.[124] FinCEN will establish these protocols. They will generally include:

- protecting the security and confidentiality of the beneficial ownership information that FinCEN provides;
- requiring the head of each requesting agency (on a non-delegable basis)

115 *Whalen v Roe*, 429 US 589 (1977).
116 31 USC Section 5336(c)(2)(B)(i)(I).
117 31 USC Section 5336(c)(2)(B)(i)(II).
118 31 USC Section 5336(c)(2)(B)(ii). This provision is not a model of clarity, but it generally seems to allow disclosure only for purposes of assisting in an investigation or prosecution (including national security and intelligence activities) and it generally seems to limit the further disclosure of the information.
119 31 USC Section 5336(c)(2)(B)(iii).
120 31 USC Section 5336(c)(2)(B)(iv).
121 31 USC Section 5336(c)(5)(B).
122 31 USC Section 5336(c)(2)(A) (generally prohibiting disclosure of beneficial ownership information).
123 See Pub Law 116-283, Section 6401(7)(A) (expressing Congress's intent to create a 'nonpublic database').
124 31 USC Section 5336(c)(2)(A) and (c)(3).

to: (i) approve the standards and procedures that the agency uses; and (ii) on a semi-annual basis, certify that those standards and procedures comply with FinCEN's requirements;

- requiring each requesting agency to establish and maintain a secure system for storing the beneficial ownership information that it receives from FinCEN;
- requiring each requesting agency to report on its procedures for ensuring the beneficial ownership information that it receives from FinCEN;
- for each investigation or other activity for which it requests beneficial ownership information, requiring the head of the requesting agency (or the head's designee) to provide a written certification that: (i) states that it has met the applicable requirements for obtaining the information; and (ii) sets forth the specific reasons why the beneficial ownership information is relevant to the investigation or other activity;
- requiring each requesting agency to limit, to the greatest extent practicable, the scope of the beneficial ownership information that it requests;
- within a requesting agency that has received beneficial ownership information from FinCEN, restricting the access to individuals: (i) who are directly engaged in the investigation or activity; (ii) whose duties require access to the information; (iii) who have undergone appropriate training (or who access the information through staff who have undergone appropriate training); (iv) who use appropriate identity verification mechanisms to obtain access to the information; and (v) who are authorised by FinCEN to access the information;
- requiring each requesting agency to establish and maintain a permanent, auditable system of standardised records of its requests for beneficial ownership information, including the reason for the request, the name of the individual who made the request, the date of the request, any disclosure of beneficial ownership information made by or to the agency, and any other information that FinCEN determines is appropriate;
- requiring each requesting agency that receives beneficial ownership information from FinCEN to conduct an annual audit to verify that the information has been accessed and used appropriately; and
- requiring FinCEN to conduct an annual audit of each agency that receives beneficial ownership information for purposes of verifying that the agency has accessed and used the information appropriately.[125]

By regulation, FinCEN may also establish other safeguards that it determines

125 31 USC Section 5336(c)(3).

to be necessary or appropriate to protect the confidentiality of the beneficial ownership information.[126]

FinCEN may reject a request for beneficial ownership information. There are four grounds for rejecting a request. First, FinCEN may reject a request if the request is not made in the form and manner that it establishes for requesting beneficial ownership information.[127] Second, it may reject a request if the requesting agency fails to meet any of the requirements for obtaining the information or protecting the security and confidentiality of the information.[128] Third, it may reject a request if the information is being requested for an unlawful purpose.[129] Fourth, it may reject a request if there is good cause to deny the request.[130] The Corporate Transparency Act does not elaborate on what good cause might be.

FinCEN may suspend or terminate a requesting agency's access to beneficial ownership information. The grounds for suspending or terminating a requesting agency's access generally are the same grounds as those for rejecting a request for beneficial ownership information.[131] Those grounds include repeated or serious violations of the protocols.[132]

Any officer or employee of a requesting agency who violates the protocols may be subject to civil and criminal penalties.[133]

15. Retention of beneficial ownership information

FinCEN must retain a reporting company's beneficial ownership information for at least five years after the entity's dissolution.[134]

16. Penalties

The Corporate Transparency Act imposes civil and criminal penalties on persons who provide false information to FinCEN or fail to provide information to FinCEN. The act also imposes criminal penalties on persons who misuse or improperly disclose beneficial ownership information.

16.1 Reporting violations

The act imposes penalties on certain reporting violations. Specifically, the act imposes civil and criminal penalties on any person who wilfully provides (or attempts to provide) false or fraudulent beneficial ownership information to FinCEN.[135] False or fraudulent information includes a false or fraudulent

---

126 31 USC Section 5336(c)(3)(K).
127 31 USC Section 5336(c)(6)(A).
128 31 USC Section 5336(c)(6)(B)(i).
129 31 USC Section 5336(c)(6)(B)(ii).
130 31 USC Section 5336(c)(6)(B)(iii).
131 31 USC Section 5336(c)(7).
132 *Ibid.*
133 31 USC Section 5336(c)(4).
134 31 USC Section 5336(c)(1).
135 31 USC Section 5336(h)(1)(A).

identifying photograph or document.[136] In addition, the act imposes civil and criminal penalties on any person who wilfully fails to provide complete or updated beneficial ownership information to FinCEN.[137] For the purposes of these provisions, an act is wilful only if it involves the voluntary, intentional violation of a known legal duty.[138]

Under a safe harbour provision (which likely will have limited utility), a person potentially is not subject to any civil or criminal penalties if the person promptly corrects an inaccurate report.[139] At the time of filing, the person must not be acting for a purpose of evading the beneficial ownership reporting requirements[140] and must not have actual knowledge that the report contains inaccurate information.[141] The person subsequently must promptly and voluntarily file a report containing the corrected information.[142] Crucially, the person must file the corrected report within 90 days after the filing of the report that contained inaccurate information.[143]

A person who commits a reporting violation is subject to a civil penalty of up to $500 for each day that the violation continues or has not been remedied.[144] The person is also subject to a fine of up to $10,000 and imprisonment for up to two years.[145]

16.2 Unauthorised use or disclosure of beneficial ownership information

The Corporate Transparency Act imposes civil and criminal penalties on any person who knowingly uses or knowingly discloses beneficial ownership information, unless the use or disclosure is authorised under the act.[146] The person must have obtained the beneficial ownership information from a report filed with FinCEN or from an authorised disclosure by FinCEN to a requesting agency.[147] For example, a FinCEN employee who, without authorisation, discloses to the media a report filed by a reporting company would have committed a violation under this provision.

A person who violates this prohibition against unauthorised use or disclosure is subject to a civil penalty of up to $500 for each day that the violation continues or has not been remedied.[148] The person is also subject to a fine of up to $250,000 and imprisonment for up to five years.[149] If the violation

136 *Ibid.*
137 31 USC Section 5336(h)(1)(B).
138 31 USC Section 5336(h)(6).
139 31 USC Section 5336(h)(3)(C)(i).
140 31 USC Section 5336(h)(3)(C)(i)(II)(aa).
141 31 USC Section 5336(h)(3)(C)(i)(II)(bb).
142 31 USC Section 5336(h)(3)(C)(i)(I)(bb).
143 31 USC Section 5336(h)(3)(C)(i).
144 31 USC Section 5336(h)(3)(A)(i).
145 31 USC Section 5336(h)(3)(A)(ii).
146 31 USC Section 5336(h)(2).
147 *Ibid.*
148 31 USC Section 5336(h)(3)(B)(i).
149 31 USC Section 5336(h)(3)(B)(ii)(I).

occurs while the person is violating another US law or is part of a pattern of any illegal activity involving more than $100,000 during a 12-month period, then the person is subject to a fine of up to $500,000 and imprisonment for up to 10 years.[150]

17. Conclusion

With the enactment of the Corporate Transparency Act, the United States is on the path towards establishing a national beneficial ownership registry. In its precatory statement, Congress declared that this act is vital for protecting national security interests, thwarting illicit activities, and bringing the United States in line with international AML/ATF standards.[151] Importantly, the act achieves those laudable goals while respecting the equally worthy right to privacy.

150 31 USC Section 5336(h)(3)(B)(ii)(II).
151 Pub Law 116-283 (2020), Section 6402(5).

About the authors

Tatjana Andoljšek
Partner, OPAM LAW, Odvetniška pisarna Andoljšek d.o.o.
tatjana.andoljsek@opam-law.com

Tatjana Andoljšek is the founding partner of OPAM LAW in Slovenia and Luxembourg, and a member of the Slovenia and Luxembourg Bar. She holds a Cambridge Master's in Law and an international MBA degree.

Tatjana gained broad international legal knowledge working on commercial and IP projects for the pharmaceutical industry, including patent litigations, research, development, manufacture and sales projects, as well as various international corporate and contractual business transactions.

Her position as a general counsel of a large international corporation comprised management of an extensive variety of litigation, corporate, international business commercial law, contractual, intellectual property, pharmaceutical law, regulatory consulting, compliance and EU law.

As a business attorney of choice, she focuses on legal business strategic planning, legal structuring, counselling and legal execution of business international operations of her international corporate clients and privately owned entities active in the international context. She is fluent in seven languages, including English, Italian, German and French.

Stéphanie Auféril
Partner, Arkwood
stephanie.auferil@arkwood.fr

Stéphanie Auféril advises families on all their wealth management tax matters, notably cross-border. Her expertise is particularly recognised in the following areas: French–US strategies: she assists numerous US persons with their relocation to France or investments in France, as well as French individuals relocating or investing in the United States; wealth planning via trusts for foreign families, notably US persons having French connections; and assistance to families and family businesses in their structuring, development and estate planning in a domestic and international context. Stéphanie is a member of STEP (Society of Trusts and Estate Practitioners). She is an active member of the IACF Wealth Management Commission (*Institut des Avocats Conseils Fiscaux*) and TIAETL (the International Academy of Estate and Trust Law). She is a regular lecturer at UNIL (Lausanne University) in the context of the master of advanced studies in international taxation (MASIT). Stéphanie is a founding partner of Arkwood SCP. She was previously principal at Baker & McKenzie in Paris, in charge of the wealth management practice.

Nuno Cunha Barnabé
Partner, Abreu Advogados
nuno.c.barnabe@abreuadvogados.com

Nuno Cunha Barnabé is a graduate of the law faculty of the University of Lisbon (1996), where he lectured in tax, public finances and economics law (1996–1999). He was a senior tax consultant formerly at Arthur Andersen Portugal (1996–2000). He is a founding judge of the Portuguese tax arbitration court (2011). Before joining Abreu in 2019, he was head of the tax practice at PLMJ and coordinator of the firm's private clients (2000–2019). Nuno is currently a senior partner at Abreu, where he co-heads the firm's tax practice being responsible for private clients. He has over 20 years' experience in tax law and specialises in wealth taxation advising high-net-worth individuals, family offices, private banking and asset manager businesses in Portugal and Portuguese-speaking countries. Nuno is a member of STEP (Society of Trust and Estate Practitioners) (Central London branch, 2017) and of TIAETL (The International Academy of Estate and Trust Law) (2017). He is recognised by *Chambers Europe, Legal 500, Who's Who* and *Best Lawyers* directories as a Tier 1/leading lawyer in tax and private clients.

Jérôme Barré
Managing partner, Barré & Associés
jbarre@barreassocies.com

After working in the legal and financial department of the Axa Group and in the tax departments of the Fédération Nationale du Crédit Agricole and the Confédération Nationale du Crédit Mutuel, Jérôme Barré joined Rothschild & Cie Banque as legal and tax director in 1992.

From 1997, he created and managed the wealth and family businesses department of several international law firms, such as Arthur Andersen International and Ernst & Young.

His experience in the banking and insurance sectors, as well as in public offerings, gives him a very pragmatic legal and tax background. He is also involved in tax litigation and in the management of tax audits.

Within the framework of his activities, he follows and accompanies individuals – and more particularly family groups – in a national and international environment. He is frequently involved in the transfer and restructuring of assets, for individuals or family businesses.

Jérôme is a lecturer in Master II at the University of Paris IX Dauphine, the University of Paris Descartes and the Ecole Supérieure de Commerce de Paris. He regularly writes articles for newspapers (*Le Figaro, Les Echos* etc) and specialised magazines (*Gestion de Fortune, Agefi, Actifs* etc). He also speaks on BFM TV (Integrale Placement) and Boursorama (Ecorama).

Luigi Belluzzo
Equity partner, Belluzzo International Partners
luigi.belluzzo@belluzzo.net

Luigi Belluzzo is a founding partner of Belluzzo International Partners, equity partner in the London firm, where he leads the Italian Desk, and chair of the board of the Swiss firm and the Italian firm, named Belluzzo Mercanti after the merger on 1 January 2021.

His expertise includes planning for high-net-worth individuals, trusts and family offices, with a strong emphasis on both domestic and international planning, governance and inheritance issues. Corporate taxation and reorganisation, tax litigation, structured finance and M&A complete his background as a TEP (Trust and Estate Practitioner), OECDC and ICAEW, with experience and competence particularly focused on cross-border issues across Europe.

Luigi teaches at SDA Bocconi University in Milan and is a regular speaker at major conferences in Italy, the UK and internationally. He has published a significant number of works, including the *Italian Guide on Estate Planning* for Il Sole 24 Ore and articles for Il Sole 24 Ore and *Trusts & Trustees* (Oxford University Press).

He is vice chair of STEP Europe and a member of the International Fiscal Association and ANCP.

Alberto Perez Cedillo
Founding partner, Alberto Perez Cedillo Spanish Lawyers and Solicitors
apcedillo@apcedillo.com

Alberto Perez Cedillo is founding partner of Alberto Perez Cedillo Spanish Lawyers and Solicitors, president of the Spanish Chapter of the Society of Trust and Estate Practitioners (STEP) and a member of the Private Client Advisory Committee of the Law Society of England and Wales.

As a dually qualified Spanish *abogado* and English solicitor, for 20 years Alberto has been closely involved with private international law/the conflicts of law, and with a variety of international matters advising clients on international succession, cross-border inheritance and estate planning issues. He has expertise in multi-jurisdiction litigation, including forum disputes, international enforcement, international treaties and analysis of Spanish law and practice in the context of international litigation.

Alberto has often appeared as an expert in European and Spanish law before the High Court of England and Wales and regularly lectures to the various professional associations to which he belongs.

Angeliki Chimona
Senior associate, Phi Lambda Law Firm
a.chimona@phi-lambda.com

Angeliki Chimona is a member of the Athens Bar Association. She has been a senior associate in Phi Lambda Law Firm's private client, tax and corporate department for over four years. She holds degrees in commercial law and Greek taxation.

Angeliki primarily focuses on corporate, commercial and civil law projects, while frequently participating in tax and commercial law seminars and conferences in order to deepen her legal skills. In addition, she has been involved in a number of wealth management projects, as well as other sophisticated tax and estate projects in both Greece and Europe.

Iskra Doukova
Senior solicitor, Macfarlanes LLP
iskra.doukova@macfarlanes.com

Iskra Doukova is a senior solicitor in Macfarlanes' Private Client department. She has considerable experience of advising on a broad range of private client issues, including tax, asset structuring, estate and succession planning, wills, trusts and developing transparency initiatives, including the Common Reporting Standard automatic information exchange regime and the UK Trust Register.

Much of her work has an international dimension. She acts for high-net-worth individuals and internationally mobile families (a number of whom have no significant UK connections), as well as their advisers, family offices, charities and trustees.

Iskra is a member of the Society of Trust and Estate Practitioners (STEP) and holds the STEP Advanced Certificate in UK Tax for International Clients. She is also a member of Macfarlanes' environmental, social and governance and sustainability working group.

George Economides

Partner, E&G Economides LLC
george.economides@economideslegal.com

George Economides is a partner at E&G Economides LLC, a full service law firm based in Limassol, Cyprus. He is also the vice-chairman of Totalserve Management Limited, an award-winning corporate, trust and tax services provider headquartered in Cyprus.

George obtained his Bachelor of Laws from the University of Westminster and subsequently gained extensive experience in accounting, auditing and tax with a leading Cyprus accountancy firm. His area of focus is tax, M&A, real estate, immigration and technology with IP & GDPR, and he is also involved in the firm's business development, marketing and operational activities.

George is a member of the Cyprus Bar Association, a member of the Individual Tax and Private Client Committee of the International Bar Association, a member of the International Tax Planning Association (ITPA) and a member of the Society of Trust and Estate Practitioners (STEP).

He has been recognised by the *Legal500* and has authored various publications on consecutive occasions as regards to M&A, tax, lending and finance, and technology/digital business.

Christiane Edelhauser

Senior tax manager, KPMG Austria
cedelhauser@kpmg.at

Christiane Edelhauser is senior tax manager at KPMG Vienna, Austria. She holds a law degree, is a certified compliance officer and used to hear civil and commercial law cases as a judge earlier in her career.

She also worked in compliance for an international banking group, specialising in regulatory compliance programs such as FATCA, QI and CRS. In particular, she held the position of group FATCA and QI responsible officer and led international project teams for the implementation of the OECD Common Reporting Standard.

At KPMG she engages in the design, implementation and training of regulatory compliance systems, supports regulatory certification procedures including risk management and internal control systems, and reviews systems and processes for regulatory due diligence and reporting obligations, at present focusing particularly on AML/KYC – and UBO registration requirements in Austria and the European Economic Area.

As a member of an expert panel she supported the rewrite of the Austrian UBO Directive and a new UBO Guidance published by the Ministry of Finance in 2020. As a legal and compliance subject matter expert, Christiane regularly lectures at seminars and publishes specialist articles in tax magazines and legal journals.

Petros-Fotios Chr. Fatouros

Managing partner, Phi Lambda Law Firm
p.fatouros@phi-lambda.com

Petros-Fotios Chr. Fatouros is a member of the Athens Bar Association, the Society of Trust and Estate Practitioners (STEP) (UK) and various other societies and associations. He holds an LLM from Boston University School of Law in banking and financial law.

He is managing partner and head of private clients in the tax and high-net-worth individuals department of Phi Lambda Law Firm in Athens, as well as head of Phi Lambda's multi-family office in Greece.

Petros-Fotios holds degrees in law and corporate accounting and has worked in a number of STEP derived projects and other wealth management-financed projects. In addition, he is a firm supporter and facilitator of legal *pro bono* work to those in need.

He leads Phi Lambda Law Firm's team supporting sophisticated high-net-worth and ultra high-net-worth families in connection with complicated structures, demanding audits and applicable regulatory compliance.

He often publishes articles in the *STEP Journal*, the *Legal500 Comparative Guide in Private Client*, the *Greek Law Digest* and other journals; he is also an elected member to STEP's elected steering committee of Business Families Special Interest Group.

John Graham
Partner, Graham Smith & Partners International Tax Counsel
graham@grahamsmith.com

John Graham is a partner at Graham Smith & Partners in Amsterdam. He holds degrees in commerce and fiscal economics and is a UK Chartered Accountant, registered accountant in the Netherlands and member of the Dutch Association of Tax Advisers.

Areas of particular expertise include international structuring for family businesses, the tax treatment of trusts, and advising individuals moving from one country to another.

He taught international tax law and EU tax policy at the School of International Studies at Avans University of Applied Sciences in Breda. He has edited, authored and co-authored books and contributed to a number of books and looseleaf services. He has written articles on a wide range of subjects, including trusts, international social security, the EU Parent Subsidiary Directive and tax abuse by international organisations. He speaks frequently at conferences on international tax.

Štěpán Holub
Partner, Holubová advokáti s.r.o.
stepan.holub@holubova.cz

Štěpán Holub is a specialist in multi-generational planning in the Czech Republic. He has successfully advised on many international legal transactions, involving several jurisdictions. He has also successfully represented his clients in front of different courts, including senators of the Parliament of the Czech Republic in front of the Constitutional Court.

Štěpán is a registered lawyer with the Czech Bar Association. He is also qualified as a mediator for business and civil disputes by the Czech Bar Association and the Brussels Bar Association. He is one of few members of the Society of Trust and Estate Practitioners (STEP) from the Czech Republic with the trust and estate practitioner's (TEP) qualification.

Based on multiple recommendations, he has been included in the publications *Chambers* and *Who's Who Legal* as a leading expert in the Czech Republic for the field of private clients. He speaks Czech, English, German and Swedish.

Aileen Keogan
Aileen Keogan Solicitor & Tax Consultant
ak@aileenkeogan.ie

Aileen Keogan is the principal of the firm Aileen Keogan Solicitor & Tax Consultant, a solicitor, chartered tax adviser and Society of Trust and Estate Practitioners (STEP) member. The firm is a boutique private client law firm in Ireland.

Aileen has specialised in private client matters for over 25 years. Her law and tax practice focuses on succession planning for individuals and businesses both international and domestic. She also provides consultancy to professionals on estate and tax planning, trusts and capital tax issues, and acts as expert witness in complex trust and tax cases.

Aileen has published widely on estate and trust planning, including *The Law & Taxation of Trusts* (Keogan, Mee and Wylie, Tottel 2007) and *Law of Capital Acquisitions Tax, Stamp Duty and Local Property Tax* (ITI annual publication). She is an elected council member of the Irish Tax Institute, a member of the Law Society of Ireland's Probate, Administration and Trusts Committee, their representative at TALC (a liaison committee between Irish Revenue and professional bodies), and a member of STEP Ireland committee, its representative in STEP Europe and the STEP EU Public Policy Committee.

Aldona Leszczyńska-Mikulska
Partner, GWW
aldona.leszczynska-mikulska@gww.pl

Before joining GWW, from 2004 until 2016 Aldona Leszczyńska-Mikulska worked for Wardynski & Partners law firm as one of the co-founders and head of its private client practice. Previously she worked for the tax departments of EY (international tax planning) and PwC (M&A). She is mainly involved in advising high-net-worth individuals in Poland, as well as family and closely held businesses. She often works closely with family offices of clients. She advises private clients and wealthy families on all matters concerning international capital structuring, and domestic and international tax planning. She has assisted clients in setting up trusts and private family foundations, as well as in resolving disputes regarding assets under the umbrella of trusts and foundations. She has taken part in many estate-planning projects and represented clients in estate, marital and family disputes. Her professional experience includes drafting and negotiating pre-nuptial and post-nuptial agreements. She is ranked as a tier one private client lawyer in Poland by *Chambers HNWI* and *Legal 500*, has a native knowledge of Polish and is fluent in English and German.

Saskia Lust
Partner, Loyens & Loeff
saskia.lust@loyensloeff.com

Saskia Lust co-heads the Family Owned Business & Private Wealth team in the Brussels office of Loyens & Loeff. Saskia advises on wealth optimisation techniques, both domestically and internationally. She specialises in international wealth and inheritance planning and focuses both on civil and fiscal law aspects. She advises on immigration and emigration, and specifically on (re)structuring of private wealth in an international context. She is an expert in international asset structuring through holdings, foundations and trusts.

Saskia is recognised as a 'Leading Individual in Private Wealth Law in Belgium' (band 2) by *Chambers*. She is also recognised as a 'Trust and Estate Practitioner' (TEP), is a member of the STEP Benelux Committee, and is listed as a thought leader in 'Private Client: Lawyers' by *Who's Who Legal* (2020). She has published articles and is a speaker at conferences on estate planning. She won the Lexology Content Marketing Awards 2019 in the category 'Legal Influencer for Private client – Europe'.

Paul Matthams
Partner, Stonehage Fleming; Advocate (non-practising) of the Royal Court of Jersey
paul.matthams@stonehagefleming.com

Paul Matthams is a partner in the family office division of financial services firm Stonehage Fleming. He joined the business in July 2018 after almost 19 years with the law firm Carey Olsen, where he was head of the trusts and the private wealth practice group of their Jersey office between 2005 and 2016. Paul is a graduate of Cambridge University and was called to the Bar of England and Wales in 1981. He qualified as an

English solicitor in 1988 and a notary public and Jersey advocate in 2001. He is a long-standing member of the Society of Trust and Estate Practitioners.

Todd D Mayo
Executive director, senior wealth strategist, UBS
todd.mayo@ubs.com

Todd D Mayo is an executive director, senior wealth strategist at UBS. He works with ultra-high-net-worth families, helping them to design and implement wealth strategies that reflect their values and goals. He helps them to create multi-generational structures for managing their wealth, fulfilling their philanthropic visions and optimising tax effects. He is the consulting editor of *Private Trust Companies: A Handbook for Advisers* (Globe Law and Business, 2020) and a contributing author to *Advising the Wealthy Client: A Handbook for Working with the Ultra Wealthy* (Globe Law and Business, 2020). He was a principal author of the New Hampshire Family Trust Company Act (which governs private trust companies) and the New Hampshire Foundation Act (which was the first act recognising civil law-type foundations in the United States).

Johanna Niegel
Head of Russia & CIS Desk and senior client adviser, Allgemeines Treuunternehmen (ATU)
office.frick@atu.li

Dr Johanna Niegel joined Allgemeines Treuunternehmen (ATU) after having worked with international law firms in Moscow, New York, Budapest and Vienna. She has specialised in international private foundations and trusts, as well as international tax.

Johanna took a doctorate in law at the University of Vienna Law School, Austria, and graduated with a master's degree from Columbia University School of Law, New York, having obtained a Fulbright scholarship. She was named a Harlan Fiske Stone Scholar for Superior Academic Achievement and holds the Parker School Recognition of Achievement with Honors in International and Foreign Law. More recently, she obtained an LLM in international taxation at the University of Liechtenstein. She is also a lecturer on its master's programme in corporate, foundation and trust law. Johanna is the editor of Trusts & Trustees' *Private Foundations: A World Review* and also an editor of the book *Private Foundations World Survey.*

Johanna is the chairman of the Vaduz Centre of Verein STEP, as well as the Verein's current deputy chairman, and serves on the Alpine Conference Organising Committee of the Swiss & Liechtenstein STEP Federation. She was awarded the STEP Founder's Award in 2017.

Paolo Panico
Paolo Panico's Law Chambers; Private Trustees SA
paolo.panico@privatetrustees.net
paolo.panico@barreau.lu

Paolo Panico is an *Avocat à la Cour* in Luxembourg and a Scottish solicitor. He is also a director of Private Trustees SA, an independent trust company in Luxembourg. He has an academic interest in the law of trusts and foundations and teaches courses at the University of Luxembourg and the University of Liechtenstein. He has published, amongst other works, *Private Foundations, Law and Practice* (Oxford University Press, 2014) and *International Trust Laws* (2nd edition, Oxford University Press, 2017). Paolo is a council member and chairman of the Europe Region of STEP, deputy chairman of the International Tax Planning Association (ITPA), a member of the executive committee of the Italian Trust Society (*Il Trust in Italia*) and an academician of TIAETL.

Michael Petritz
Tax partner, KPMG Austria
mpetritz@kpmg.at

Michael Petritz is a tax partner at KPMG and tax head of Smartstart Austria (the StartUp program of KPMG Austria). He specialises in international tax law, venture capital, M&A and high-net-worth individuals. He is a member of the tax committee of the Austrian Chamber of Public Accountants and Tax Advisers, president of STEP Austria (Society of Trust and Estate Practitioners) and lecturer and author of (international) tax publications.

Tomasz Piejak
Attorney trainee, GWW
tomasz.piejak@gww.pl

Before joining GWW in 2016, Tomasz Piejak worked for Wardynski & Partners law firm in Poland. He works with law and taxes within the framework of the practice consulting individual clients. He consults on Polish and international tax law, property protection, succession planning and inheritance. He has experience in coordinating structures and transactions extending to multiple jurisdictions, and in legal and tax advice with reference to personal and business financial standing. He has a native knowledge of Polish, and works on cases in English, French and Italian.

Edward Reed
Partner, Macfarlanes LLP
edward.reed@macfarlanes.com

Edward Reed is an English solicitor; he advises internationally mobile families on their asset structuring, personal tax and succession planning, wills and trusts. Having been educated both in the United Kingdom and France, he has developed an affinity for civil law issues generally and their interaction with common law. He is a bilingual French speaker and fluent in Italian.

With over 20 years' experience in the field, he advises on UK immigration and nationality law. He has administrative oversight of the firm's trust company, Embleton Trust Corporation Limited.

Edward is a contributor to or a member of the editorial board of various professional publications. He is also a member of the Law Society's Capital Taxes Sub-Committee and a former chairman of the steering committee of the Cross-Border Estates Group of STEP, as well as a trustee of a number of charitable trusts. Edward is ranked in the UK and Global editions of the independent *Chambers* guide and is recognised for his foreign expertise in relation to France. He is recognised in the "Hall of Fame" for his personal tax, trusts and probate expertise in the UK *Legal 500* guide.

John Riches
Founding partner, RMW Law LLP; Consultant, Withers LLP
john@rmwlaw.co.uk

John Riches works with prominent international family offices on a cross-border basis and deals with structuring for UK residents and resident non-domiciled families. He creates structures for active entrepreneurs to hold business interests and frequently advises on issues relating to the interaction of family and business governance. He is frequently listed in many publications as a leading private client adviser to international families. John has a deep interest in tax and regulatory policy and enters into regular dialogue with national and supranational bodies to represent the profession.

He has received numerous accolades over many years, including 'Trusted Adviser of the Year' at the 2011 STEP Private Client awards and the Spears Tax and Trust Lawyer of the Year Award 2017. He is regularly ranked in the top tier of private client lawyers globally in international directories, and is widely regarded by his peers.

Eleanor Riches-Lenaghan
Associate, RMW Law LLP
eleanor@rmwlaw.co.uk

Eleanor Riches-Lenaghan qualified as a private client solicitor in October 2020 and is an associate in boutique private client law firm RMW Law LLP. Prior to this, Eleanor undertook her training contract at Winckworth Sherwood LLP, gaining knowledge and experience in data protection and regulation, commercial real estate and licensing, property litigation and private client. Eleanor has a particular interest in cross-border policy, writing dissertations on beneficial ownership registers and deemed domicile for her Master of Laws. Since qualification, Eleanor has undertaken significant research into international tax policy issues. She has also co-authored a chapter on "Fiscal nomads: the impact of relocation on CRS and DAC6" in *Global Mobility of Ultra-High-Net-Worth Individuals* (Globe Law and Business, 2021). Eleanor is in the process of obtaining her STEP Diploma in Trusts and Estates.

Susanne Stauder
Salaried partner, Heuking Kühn Lüer Wojtek
s.stauder@heuking.de

Dr Susanne Stauder is a salaried partner in the white collar and criminal compliance department of Heuking Kühn Lüer Wojtek in Düsseldorf, Germany. She holds a degree in law and completed her doctoral thesis at Bucerius Law School, Hamburg on the topic of economic criminal law.

One focus of her work is advising large and medium-sized companies in the field of money laundering prevention. Most recently, she has been entrusted with the development of the regulatory money laundering requirements under the German Geldwäschegesetz on several occasions for financial companies and dealers in goods, and has advised Swiss banks on the implementation of and compliance with the legal regulations in connection with the prevention of money laundering within the scope of their cross-border activities. In addition, Susanne regularly advises companies in connection with their reporting obligations to the transparency register and also represents them in administrative fine proceedings before the Federal Administrative Office (*Bundesverwaltungsamt*). Furthermore, Susanne regularly defends executives in white-collar crime cases and conducts internal investigations into criminal offences relevant to commercial law.

She frequently publishes articles and book contributions, especially on topics and issues in the field of money laundering prevention.

Stephanie van Gils
Associate, Loyens & Loeff
stephanie.van.gils@loyensloeff.com

Stephanie van Gils is a member of the Family Owned Business & Private Wealth team in the Brussels office of Loyens & Loeff.

Stephanie advises on wealth and inheritance planning and focuses both on civil and tax law aspects. She advises clients on the tax consequences of immigration and emigration. She also assists clients in handling tax audits and tax disputes.

Stephanie regularly publishes newsletters and articles. She also frequently gives presentations, including on the Belgian UBO register.

António Vidal
Associate lawyer, Abreu Advogados
antonio.vidal@abreuadvogados.com

António Vidal has a degree in law from the University of Lisbon's Faculty of Law (2016). He has also completed his master's degree in business law at the Portuguese Catholic University, Faculty of Law (2018).

António started his professional career as a trainee at Abreu Advogados, mostly dealing with matters related to corporate, M&A and private client law, and is currently an associate at the firm, practising mostly in corporate and M&A law since 2019, while also accompanying and practising in matters related to private clients.

He has been particularly involved in matters related to procedures for incorporating and implementing companies in Portugal, providing advice on day-to-day matters in the life of companies, mergers, acquisitions and demergers of companies, and in the interpretation and application of the ultimate beneficiary owner legislation in Portugal.

António is currently completing his LLM in international business law at the School of Law of the Portuguese Catholic University.